Good Second Class
(But not even C.3)

Good Second Class
(But not even C.3)

Memories of a Generalist Overseas Administrator

by

TREVOR CLARK

The Memoir Club

BY THE SAME AUTHOR

A Right Honourable Gentleman
(Abubakar From the Black Rock)
(London, UK, Edward Arnold, division of Hodder & Stoughton, 1991)
[ISBN 0-340-56189-0 hb; ISBN 0-340-56275-7 pbk]
[Also published with alternative sub-title:
(The Life and Times of Sir Abubakar Tafawa Balewa)
(Zaria, Nigeria, Hudahuda Publishing Company, 1991)]

Was It Only Yesterday?
(The Last Generation of Nigeria's *Turawa*)
(Bristol, UK, BECM Press, British Empire & Commonwealth Museum, 2002)
[ISBN 0-9530174-7-8 hb; ISBN 0-9530174-8-6 pbk]

First published in 2004 by
The Memoir Club
Stanhope Old Hall
Stanhope
Weardale
County Durham

All rights reserved.
Unauthorised duplication
contravenes existing laws.

British Library Cataloguing in
Publication Data.
A catalogue record for this book
is available from the
British Library.

ISBN: 1 84104 085 1

Typeset by George Wishart & Associates, Whitley Bay.
Printed by CPI Bath.

Dedication

For My Dear Hilary,
who has shared nearly half of the
olla podrida mixed herein.

Contents

List of Illustrations ix

Foreword xi

Prologue xiii

Chapter 1   Patient Experience 1

Chapter 2   Natural Pleasure of a Learning Curve 26

Chapter 3   A Rude and Licentious Dislocation 56

Chapter 4   A Soldier's Life is Terrible Hard 94

Chapter 5   Baptism of Colonial Fire in 'The North' 115

Chapter 6   Confirmed in an Imperialist Faith 141

Chapter 7   Stranger in Paradise 160

Chapter 8   Pearls Around the Neck – Stones Upon the Heart 186

Chapter 9   Is it so Small a Thing to Have Enjoyed the Sun? 208

Chapter 10   The Sun Eclipsed 246

Chapter 11   The Lowest Political Rung (and a Philosophical Distraction) .. 259

Chapter 12   Images Move, into – Not Such a Dusty Life? 276

Chapter 13   Venturing into Print 292

List of Illustrations

I *hated* my party suit 2

Everyone paraded Princes Street on Saturday mornings 33

Kinross Platoon dressed to kill 40

Much work but some play: punting up the Cherwell 46

42 Gambian officers at Masrul: 2 would be killed, 1 to die of blackwater, 8 wounded (1 thrice), the CO would be replaced, the 2i/c medically boarded (as was the man in the very middle) 73

Map 80

The senior of two orderlies by tradition wore his commanding officer's home regimental cap badge; nobody had heard of skin cancers in 1946 (*cf* Chap. 1) 111

On leave, with the Laird of Glen Buchat 117

Governor Sharwood-Smith installs Adamu Jumba as First Class Chief of Bauchi (with his former DO, a visiting guest, mid rear) 147

It was backs to the wall for the flag in Okene 155

Showing the flag with staff to tenants during The Troubles 175

Formerly invisible bureaucrats were taught to give public interviews 177

Slicing into new life 194

In the Highlands as well, on leave 196

Chief Scout Governor Trench and Vice-President DSW inspect Scouts (Baden-Powell now plays baseball) 202

Lord Louis, with his minder, meets old soldiers (Princess Anne talks to war hero Jacob Vouza) 221

A visitor to greet was Michael Somare from Papua New Guinea (Solomon Mamaloni glowers) 231

One dog and his man 236

An Officer administering a Government 248

The front of a canvassing leaflet – did it garner votes? 263

Hilary looks up at me talking down to Lord (Dickie) Attenborough at a
    Filmhouse opening 278

HM reopening Scottish United Services Museum with Director's son
    (note Hilary's hat behind the boy) 282

Secretary of State for Scotland Ian Lang and Scottish Museums Council
    chairman at opening of Royal College of Surgeons museum 284

Looking back at the beginning (Edinburgh's Dynamic Earth exhibition). . . 302

Foreword

For the past half century, colonialism, the process of decolonization, neo-colonialism, and the long record of imperialism in general, has had a very bad press, and not just from those who stand among the eternally politically-correct. Swimming around in the shallow and conventional wisdom of hindsight, most contemporary historians have demanded to know how political administrators, backed by military might, and following hard on the heels of traders and the men and women of the cloth, dared expatriate themselves, and try to rule, subjugate, or otherwise pillage, countries and territories that were not their own.

According to these arguments, the blessings given to us in the great lottery of life by being British, or in the case of the author of this book, Scottish, never equipped us, nor justified our wish to rule over peoples less fortunate, less civilized, than ourselves. As the last great empires have withered away, the soviet one probably being the last – unless one defines the current *Pax Americana* as neo-colonialist – those historians who have generally damned the records of our imperial jurisdictions, usually discovering plenty of additional calumny to throw on top of the grave, now need to be challenged, particularly by those who were actually there, and took part in the admittedly sometimes rather clumsy, but normally skilled and benign, governance of the British Empire.

This is particularly true when one looks at what has come in place of these administrations, in much of Africa, Asia, and elsewhere. How often have these free states enjoyed better standards of education, health, nutrition, and other marks of human prosperity? Do they enjoy better governments? Whatever the answer, they are of course free: free to choose, to prosper or, frequently, to destroy themselves. Thus all too much of sub-Saharan African today.

As someone who researched and wrote his doctorate on economic development in West Africa in the late nineteen-sixties, and looked forward to a great future for that dark continent in revolt against its colonial masters, events have forced me substantially to revise my opinions and expectations. Elsewhere around the globe too, and Trevor Clark writes with humour, wisdom and sensitivity about the many lands he has visited or helped administer, the aftermath of colonialism has been a dire and wicked disappointment.

But this book is not just set in some hot and sticky, palm-fringed, colonial time-warp. Any story has a beginning long before its beginnings, and an ending that runs long after it ends. His childhood years, his climb into adulthood, his wartime, are all there to be read about and enjoyed. Then again later, after he left the Colonial Service, Trevor Clark led a very distinguished life, contributing greatly to civic governance in his home in Edinburgh, particularly through his great love and interest in that splendid city's performing arts, Galleries and Museums, but also in a host of other ways.

This book is about a man of distinction and his times, both at home and abroad, times that should not be forgotten. He writes about the need to 'keep the truth of our lives in the decolonizing years fresh and on record, against some future time when our imperial story might be treated with honesty and dispassion.' Trevor Clark does just that, bringing his past and his experience to life, with a subtle and enjoyable touch. *Good Second Class* is a first class read.

Dr Michael Shea CVO DL
Author, former diplomat and Press Secretary to Her Majesty The Queen

Prologue

So well does the serious mind of a Scotch education fit Scotsmen to the habits of industry, attention, and frugality, that they rarely abandon them at any time of life, and I may say never while they are young.
[Sir Joseph Banks, naturalist and explorer, 1814]

Autobiography is now as common as adultery, and hardly less reprehensible.
[John Grigg, *The Sunday Times*, 28 February 1962]

'I'M SURPRISED you're still here,' my doctor said, 'public medicine has done you no harm. You should write your record up.' To enlighten doctors of what their client felt at the receiving end of Æsculapius's wand, I wrote Chapter 1.

Some background had given all the Caring a context: it was hinted that I should go the whole hog. Encouragement by a comrade in arms to pen wartime memories, a few of which had already crept into Chapter 1, led to a version of Chapters 3 & 4. Remembrances of dim pasts in old boys' journals and college records spawned invitations to fill editors' yawning spaces. Obediently, Chapter 2 emerged. A colleague in far-flung places asked me to write what it had been to be a newcomer in a claustrophobic society. Chapters 7 & 8 followed, with inevitable consequences in 9 & 10. Writing elsewhere about a Nigerian statesman, and gathering colleagues' recollections of decolonization for an anthology, delayed the spatchcocking of 5 & 6. The tail of retiring afterthoughts trailed behind. Here we are at last. The squeamish should skip Chapter 1, yet what follows may be no more uplifting.

Readers may wonder that the first rule in a lifetime of official writing was to keep the First Personal Pronoun Singular to the barest minimum. When senior enough to have juniors, I would condense their drafts mercilessly, but never learnt to sub-edit my own ramblings. Yet this is all Me (*sc* Ego), through a succession of differing reflective spectacles. My other half joined me half way through.

Lyon generously sent greetings to all and sundry a while ago, that they should know that ensigns armorial had been devised: *Azure, on a fess Argent between a pearl proper* [for Hong Kong] *accompanied by two frigate birds volant proper* [for Solomon Islands] *in chief, and a Nigerian Northern Knot Argent in base, four oak leaves, two bendwise and two bendwise sinister Gules* [symbolic of the colonial service] ... *for Crest a hurt charged with the façade of a Greek temple Argent* [symbolic of museums]. This explains the dust cover. For those without the classics. the motto mocks my stature and status: *I walk tall.*

We do not know whether it was Sellars in *1066 and All That* who said, 'History is not what you thought', and Yeatman who added, 'It is what you remember', or *vice versa*, but to those who dispute my opinions of what happened during the war, in Nigeria, Hong Kong and the Pacific, or in other matters, I (as politicians jabber) 'would just say this.' I recall what I was part of at the time. Do you, perhaps, only remember what you believe you may have read about? Yes, my memory may be faulty or selective, and you may reinforce your view by returning to some printed source, but was that writer actually there too?

Many autobiographies of unknown folk with a mixture of variegated tales to tell have made it into print. If my life has fallen short of those whose memories are truly worth sharing, I can't really complain of utter failure. Many must envy me much, even if I think too well of myself. I acknowledge that Ambrose Bierce defined **Self-Esteem**, *n.* as 'An erroneous appraisement', which should always be posted beside the invitations for 'counselling' on the walls of present day common rooms and clinics. I pay tribute to Sheila Seacroft who, presented with an overfilled scuttle, threw out dross and ashes, reducing the residue to the present manageable nuggets of, not minerals of value, but combustible coke. The many missing fossils from the original mine are safely archived, unbowdlerized.

11 Ramsay Garden **Trevor Clark**
Edinburgh, 2003

CHAPTER 1

Patient Experience

If you mean to keep as well as possible, the less you think about your health the better.

[Oliver Wendell Holmes, Sr, *Over the Teacups* (1891)]

IN MY EIGHTIETH YEAR I was in bed with my spouse of thirty-six years standing. The telephone rang to announce that a book I had been editing of other unknown people's lives was accepted for publication. 'Very good' I quavered. 'I may now have time to stitch together all the patches of my own unimportant story.' This chapter is the downside of that quilt.

1928
I have been put to bed. I have spots. My skin itches. It is red. I am hot and miserable. Daddy is a doctor. He is always taking my temperature with a thermometer. I get soup in a special cup. It has a spout so I won't spill any. Mummy says I have Measles *and* Scarlet Fever. She taught me how to spell. She took me to Smith's bookshop in Glasgow. She looked for a book called *The Cat Sat on the Mat*, but they didn't have it. We got another and soon I could read it. We lived in Hyndland then. I used to push Daddy's dumb-bells round the lines on the carpet and pretend they were trams. Now we live in Giffnock. A French boy and girl live over the road, Louis et Paulette. I say, *'Bonjour'* to them and they say, 'Good morning' in a funny way. Their daddy is a consul. I wonder what that is. I am glad I am in bed, as I do not have to go to school …

Because now I am five, I am a new boy. At Giffnock Academy, round the corner. I like drawing and singing, and I could read already. We learn Do-Re-Mi with cardboard piano keys. They make no noise. Last week the boys laughed at me. Mummy bought me a kilt to wear. It was a tweed sports kilt, not a proper tartan. Mummy came from England, so she didn't know I needed a sporran. All the boys said it was a skirt and laughed, so I ran home. Now she thinks I don't want a kilt and got me velvet shorts for parties – but if I can't have a real kilt like all the other boys, I'd like a sailor suit …

I didn't have a hanky in bed once, so I put the bogies on the wall behind the mattress. Now that I am up again and playing downstairs with my Kliptiko and reading *Chick's Own* and *Fairyland Tales*, they have found them. They were so angry. I think they'd spank me, but I'm only just getting better. We are going to

I hated my party suit.

move again soon. One day some people came to the door when Mummy was shopping. They asked me how much the house was. I thought it must be an awful lot, so I said, 'I think it's a hundred pounds,' and they said if so they would take it. I told Daddy and he laughed …

1929

After we moved back to Glasgow, near the Botanics, I started at Glasgow Academy. I walk every day and walk home for lunch. Others get lunch at school. Mummy and Daddy keep telling people I'm not very strong. I know I'm not very good at fighting Beefy Steel. He frightens lots of the boys. He is the class bully. I like my class teacher, Miss Reid. She makes me read aloud a lot. One boy told me a real secret. Her name is Winnie. Beaky Carr teaches writing. One day I pushed past Mrs Leathem, the old lady teacher who helps him. I wanted to reach the blackboard as it was my turn to write something. He said I was a rude boy and made me bend over and gave me the strap on the B.T.M. I didn't tell Mummy and Daddy, but when we went to Hilton Park Golf Club on Sunday a boy in my class had told on me. His father is the Professional and now everybody knew. Mummy was ashamed and told me off but Daddy laughed. I go round with them and look for cigarette cards in the packets thrown away in the tee boxes. I sometimes hit a ball with a mashie or a putter. Daddy plays lots of golf. He was the first Captain of Hilton Park Golf Club. Mummy was the second Lady Captain. Daddy loves to go fishing. He says fresh air is good for me.

One day in school I kept going forward to see what was on the blackboard. The Master told me to tell my mother to get me glasses, but I didn't. But another day she took me to the pictures to see Charlie Chaplin and Felix the Kat and I did the same. I got out of my seat and went near the screen to read the words the people in the picture were supposed to be saying. Mummy made a fuss and took me home fast. Daddy took me to Dr Kerr Love, an Oculist. I have Short Sight and must wear spectacles. They say it's because I had Measles and Scarlet Fever at the same time. They say I had German Measles too, but I don't remember that. As I can't see the ball properly I needn't go for rugby practice any more. If I wear special specs with celluloid inside I can play cricket. As I'm no good anyway I bat last, and when I'm not Long Stop I stay at the Other End. It saves time changing over.

Whenever it is winter there's fog in Glasgow and I get Bronchitis. The folk in Clydebank, at the far end of the Byres Road, call it the Brown Kitties. It means I get off school so that I don't cough over everyone. Then I can read Arthur Mee's *Children's Newspaper* or a William book. Sometimes I keep being sick and get Bisodol because it's Acidosis. They took me once to a Nursing Home where I was put on a wooden table in the Consulting Room, and when I woke up I sat up and was sick everywhere and there was blood and it hurt.

That was to have my Tonsils and Adenoids Out. I don't know why they had to come out of my throat. Lots of other boys and girls get it too, but they gave me ice cream afterwards so it wasn't too bad. Now they say I have a weak heart and must go to hospital. I don't really know what a weak heart means, but I suppose I'm not very strong …

1930-31
I was taken to Mearnskirk Hospital in a taxi, and I said, 'Bother!' all the way. It is full of children. All the others have T.B. and are in big wards with big verandahs. When it is not raining they are pushed out in their beds on to the verandahs even if there is snow. They are always visited by men in black called Priests who give them wafers. They mustn't touch them with their teeth. I'm not allowed to see the wafers, but the nurses say they are not like ice cream wafers. I have three favourite nurses. They come from Denmark, Nurse Sommer and Nurse Winter (that's funny) and specially Nurse Kjargaard (she taught me how to spell it, it sounds like Care-Go). Nurse Kjargaard is the nicest, though they are all nice. Mummy says the other children all come from the Slums. Daddy is the kind of doctor who looks at slums. The Medical Super is Dr Dale, a nice big man who sees me every day when he comes round. So does Matron. When she comes everyone tidies everything up first. I am in a little room at the end of the ward because Daddy knows Dr Dale. I think Daddy comes above Dr Dale. The children keep coming to see me and ask what is wrong with me and I have to say I don't know, which gives them a laugh. They call me Sonny. They all have scars or bandages on their necks to show. They have all had Operations. I can hear them screaming when they have their Dressings done.

The Doctors shake me up and down and listen to my heart with a stethoscope and go away, then a Nurse puffs my pillow and straightens the sheets. A tall lady with yellow hair comes twice a week and rubs my chest and back and arms and legs very hard with cod liver oil. It is smelly. She is called a Masseuse. She flies an aeroplane every weekend. Daddy and Mummy brought me a Meccano Aeroplane Constructor Outfit and a Simplex Children's Typewriter so I could write letters home in bed. I'd rather read books than write letters. I now read *Adventure*. It comes out every Monday. I built an Armstrong-Whitworth *Argosy* Airliner with three engines after Daddy bought me the Accessory Set. The Masseuse said it did look quite like an *Argosy*. I would like to fly with her …

One day the Doctor came and looked at my Dignity, and then Daddy looked at it too. We have an aluminium hot water bottle which I said looked like my Dignity, and Daddy laughed but said I mustn't talk about it and Mummy scolded me but I heard her say, 'But it does!' Anyway they said I must have an Operation to take the end off. I don't know why. They wheeled me away to a Theatre. I have been to the Theatre at Christmas when Tommy Lorne was in Pantomime. He was got the sack by the Manager and went to the Workhouse, but it was all right at the end, we were able to laugh again and clap. There was no pantomime at this Theatre, it was quite different, but I was told I'd go to sleep and when I woke up my Dignity was bandaged and very sore, and I didn't dare have a Wee Ah-Ah. There was no ice cream. When they took the bandage off I knew I was having my Dressing done, so I knew to scream. Then other children came in and said they had heard and wanted to see Sonny's dressing. I wouldn't so they called me bad names. We had parties in the ward and played Harry Lauder on the gramophone and a man who sang Daddy's favourite song, 'Sea Fever'. Then after six months I was let home. I felt the same and didn't know what had been wrong with me. I suppose my heart is still weak ...

1932
This winter my cousin Helen and I were playing in her house. Uncle Hugh is a Mining Engineer. Helen locked herself in their bathroom and wouldn't come out. I banged on the door but she wouldn't. So I pushed on the frosted glass window on the door and it Broke. My left hand was cut and bleeding and there was a big fuss about whose fault it was. Daddy took me to the Western General Hospital where a doctor stitched my little and second fingers. I now know Daddy is Senior Deputy Medical Officer of Health for Glasgow, and the only doctor above him is Dr Macgregor. That is why every doctor helps him so much whenever anything is wrong with us. They poured so much iodine on my hand that when they took the bandage off to cut the stitches my hand was hard and dark brown, just like the Lean Streaky Ayrshire Bacon Mummy sometimes sends me to the Maypole Dairy in Byres Road to buy on Saturday morning. When it began to peel off, a little bit at a time, I ate some and it was all right. We are reading *The Wind in the Willows* at school and as I was off I could finish it on my own. Daddy has vaccinated me with a sort of dagger. He burnt it first in a Meths flame. He says now I shan't get Smallpox. It's left a big mark on my arm with sort of holes in it ...

Daddy sometimes takes me to see things because of his work. He took me to see slums he had condemned in the Gorbals. It was very dirty and the people showed us their cooking grates and their WCs which were nasty. I best remember Daddy turning a picture round on the wall and showing me all the bugs at the back. They said everyone would be moved to nice new houses. Another time he took me to the Gareloch on a tugboat, and we climbed up ladders on to some ships which were tied up because there was no work for them. It was the same at Clydebank where the shipyards were not building new ships. Daddy had Sanitary Inspectors with him who told me they were Port Health and were looking for rats and to see if the crews were well. One ship gave us lunch and we were helped by Lascars. They were dark brown and I thought it meant Rascals. One asked me if I'd like 'ice' but when it came it was 'rice' so I was disappointed ...

1933
There was an epidemic of diphtheria in Glasgow, so Daddy had to spend a lot of time finding where all the people taken into the Fever Hospitals had picked up the infection, and who they had been with. Then he got diphtheria himself and we were worried. Mummy told me he had to have something stuck in his throat so he could breathe, and I was sent for a holiday with my cousin. After he got better I got chickenpox, and of course more bronchitis. I just stayed in bed until I was getting better. It's always the same. I can get on with my Wonder Books, though, and I can borrow super G.A.Henty and Percy F. Westerman stories from the school library ...

1934-35
Because Daddy is important on the Clyde we got places to see the biggest ship in the world being launched at John Brown's yard. My Dinky Toy of her has '534' stamped underneath, because the real name was to be a secret. We heard her being named the *Queen Mary* by the Queen. We all thought Cunarders had to end in –ia. It was a beezer day with everyone shouting and such a splash on the river when it went in. They are now talking about a 535 and that the Slump is over. Mummy and Daddy are talking about moving to Edinburgh. I am making more friends at school and there isn't so much bullying, though I have had the strap again for talking in class. I don't want to change, though I do like Edinburgh when now we have a Morris Ten Six number CS 260 we sometimes go through on Saturday afternoons to the Zoo and Mummy brings back Crawford's Citron Stenna cakes for Sunday tea if we don't go to Hilton Park. They say the climate might be better for my chest and some of our seaside holiday friends from Blackwaterfoot in Arran live in Edinburgh. I hear them talking about how Dr Macgregor is not much older than Daddy and that it will be an awful long wait and no certainty that he'll get Dr Macgregor's job then, so that's why Edinburgh would be better.

So one day Daddy came home and said he had been to Edinburgh and they had said if he went there as Senior Deputy MOH., although the salary was less, they thought that when Dr Guy retired two or three years later Daddy would Get His Job. Then everyone in Glasgow wanted him to stay and he said he would and Mummy and Daddy had a terrible row. So we went to Edinburgh after all. I had always got class prizes, and Mummy said it was a wonder when I was off school so much. I became very nervous about a new school, but we stayed the summer holidays in North Berwick to break with Glasgow. They sent for me to see me at Edinburgh Academy and asked me to translate from their Latin book. It was more difficult than our Glasgow one.

1935
Mummy made another big mistake. Edinburgh Academy wore royal blue uniforms, so she bought me the blazer and shorts but said I could wear out the navy blue Glasgow Academy stockings with the stripes round the tops. I only wore them to my new school once, and refused to be laughed at again, so she had to buy the plain royal blue ones after all, but she got them from George Heriot's stockist, the same colour but cheaper. Actually Edinburgh Academy isn't so rough as Glasgow Academy, except for two things. Unpopular or bumptious boys are debagged during lunchtime, and there are great merry shouts if they're not wearing bumbags. Tougher boys play cockfighting which means trying to rip each other's fly buttons open. They leave me alone, maybe because I'm a 'Specky' and specs are dangerous if you break them. Anyway for my first winter I haven't had bronchitis, maybe because we keep going back to North Berwick for the beach and open-air swimming pool. But I won't go in if the temperature chalked on the blackboard goes below 45. But I got mumps instead and missed more lessons.

1937
Well, I seem to be OK now, I haven't had much wrong for a long time, except to have my eyes tested every year, and sometimes get stronger glasses. And of course the dentist. Fillings don't bother me much. They now say that it was getting measles and scarlet fever together that made me grow tall too; I have passed six feet, but so are three other school friends aged 14, and an English boy says we should get long trousers like him, but we don't want to be different. Lots of Watson's and Heriot's boys don't get longs till they've left school. I suppose they know what they're saying about measles and scarlet fever, I'd like to know why if so. Just two things have bothered me. Because I was so often sniffing or sneezing without actually having a cold, Daddy took me to one of the other doctors (he hasn't been a real doctor since he was in the navy during the Great War, which is why he only ever takes my temperature). The new man said I should have my nose cauterized. He soaked my nostrils with something on cotton wool like meths and then shoved an electric wire up and burnt one or two lines in them. There was smoke and a smell like roast pork, then more cotton wool and ointment. He said it would make my nostrils narrower so that the hairs would catch more of the bugs you breathe in and allergies would be less trouble. Anyway I think it has worked, I don't snivel much.

One night Daddy looked at me down there after my bath and said he wanted another doctor to look. He says I'm supposed to have two things, not just one, there in that scraggy bit between my legs. It's just made me realize what other boys mean when they talk about 'balls'. The doctor said to wait and see, and a month or two later down slowly came number two, so that was all right. Back in Glasgow when I had very secret conversations with someone about where babies came from I was told things about down there, but it was too silly, all about eggs cracking and cream coming out, which you rubbed on the mother. I couldn't believe any of it. Now that they think this is important enough to go to a doctor, I suppose some of it must be true.

1940

The first summer holidays since the war saw a large school party going to Tomich in the Highlands to do forestry. I had been having nose-bleeds, but after one night they stopped in the highland air. The fun was spoilt for me when using sickles to cut the bracken between the rows of young conifer saplings; George Mathewson swept his sickle to the left beside me when I was stretching mine out to the right, and his went right through my leather glove and cut my right thumb to the bone. Blood everywhere, gosh, 'here's a how-de-do' (we're all mad about G&S). Our English master, Eddie Mullens, bandaged it up fast and drove me into Beauly to a local GP. Eddie said afterwards the GP was drunk, taking ages to bring the two sides of the wound together with a sort of spring clip (Meccano Part No. 35). When two days later Eddie undid the bandage he found that one point of the clip was in the middle of the cut, and instead of pulling that part of the skin towards the other side, it kept it away. Sensibly he didn't go back to the GP but took the clip off and let it heal. There is a knob in the middle of the scar, for the rest of my life, I suppose. It balances the scar on the left hand.

1941

My call-up papers came during the Michaelmas vac, after my first term at Magdalen. They were deferred to finish my year, so long as I carried on military training in the University Senior Training Corps and took Certificate 'B', but I had to go for the medical at the Assembly Rooms in Edinburgh. I dropped my bags and coughed; then I filled the glass, in a corner of what used to be the Enlightenment's Music Hall. As I found I couldn't read any of the letters on the eye test, I supposed I would be C.3, and didn't look forward to the Pioneer Corps. At the end I was told I was 'Grade 4'. 'What's that?' I asked. 'Unfit for any form of military service.' I never expected that. Schoolfriends commiserated, my mother was pleased.

Our dentist has decided that my wisdom teeth have impacted, coming up squint under the molars in front. Father got me referred to the Dental School, where the Dean took them out, with League of Nations students staring down my throat. It was a brutal business, bloody and wrenching, with repeat jabs of the 'local'. The first took an hour and a quarter. He sent me home by tram, to recover and wait a week for the second. 'The next one should be easier.' It took an hour and twenty minutes. The young colonials peering in seemed more impressed than I.

1942

I went back to Oxford, Euripides, Plato and Homer (with enjoyable Tacitus) in the Hilary Term, and stayed in the STC while I made up my mind. I didn't want anyone saying I had changed to medicine to stay out of the army. Though the army had rejected me, they'd still say it. Being no good at sports had given me something of an inferiority complex, on top of being thought a 'Swot'. I could go for a medical again, so I went to the Oxford joint recruiting board. I looked over the changing cubicle wall and learnt off the first three letters. I thought that would *just* get me in, but that I'd better not learn off too many as I would be found out. Screwing my eyes up, I read the top letter and remembered the next two. I was passed A.1. My father was surprised, and my mother was furious and didn't understand how I could have done it. No future army MO ever queried my spectacles, or asked about their lens strength …

1943

On my embarkation leave 'specially selected for service with native troops in a tropical climate', my father took me to the Usher Institute in Edinburgh. I received a box of ampoules containing Bacteriophage, for dysentery. I also absorbed advice about avoiding sunstroke, alcohol and prostitutes, and never failing to take my quinine, but none about how to carry glass ampoules safely round the world. At London District Assembly Centre (the Hotel Great Central Marylebone) we were taken to Millbank, to be inoculated against cholera and yellow fever, have vaccinations checked and boosts given to the TAB & TT we'd had on enlistment – nobody yet learnt to fear side-effects of medicines. Half the drafts were given mosquito nets, but not mosquito boots, the other half boots but no nets. I got boots. We asked the stores corporal what the difference meant. He said it was a military secret, but (in hushed tones) nets went to East Africa (King's African Rifles, white settlers and glamour), and boots to West Africa; 'The Coast' (Waffs and the White Man's Grave). When my lot arrived in Lagos and had our first sleep ashore without mosquito nets (quartermasters not supplying them in the small hours), it was unsurprising how many went down with malaria not long after. At this stage I was one of the lucky ones. Did the East African drafts got mosquito boots at Mombasa? ...

I had remained fit but, six months after the YF inoculation, I began to feel weak, sweaty and dreadful on a field exercise in the Bombay Ghats. I was sick into my African Colonial Forces slouch hat. Malaria at last, I supposed, although the first diagnosis was 'small fever, or common mild chill.' Then they looked at my yellow eyeballs in the Field Dressing Station and called it Catarrhal Jaundice, or 'Infective Hepatitis' as inscribed on the chitty to our MO. 'Did you have a YF jab six months ago? ... I thought so, a common side effect. *(With a leer)* Don't drink for six months.' In bed in Deolali (home of the renowned Doolally Tap) I replaced my bevomited African hat with a Gurkha hat, thicker felt and with a pagri: much smarter (less smelly). ...

1944

Perspiring our way up and down mountainous valleysides across the Chittagong Hill Tracts and the Kaladan Valley, was a trial of strengths. Everything and everybody went on foot, except some jeeps and an occasional 15cwt carrying mail and minor supplies – all rations and ammunition were dropped from the air, just like Wingate's famous, better reported, Chindits. My father had said in a letter that he had mentioned my 'A1' cheat to an RAMC major. I was summoned to 6 (WA) Field Ambulance, to hear that the War Office had asked for a report on my present condition. With basic facilities in jungle, they reported that I 'was underweight for height, had survived a very strenuous march of 120 miles, and had eyesight that gave satisfactory vision with glasses; there was no equipment for a thorough examination, so [they] could recommend no action' themselves. More bluntly they told me that eyes had nothing to do with it; if I were constitutionally fit and could see with glasses then I was grade A. Whether they thought I'd written letters home, trying to swing the lead, or whether I was now hoping to have it swung for me I never knew; but none of this was very settling.

In one rush to get out of trouble we lost some minor baggage, including the haversack containing my spare boots and spectacles. The prescription was radioed out and in 17 days down from the heavens (an RAF or USAAF Dakota) came a new pair of army specs with the granny metal frames and flat arms for gas masks. Size 13 boots were less easy, and two pairs of size 12 PT shoes disintegrated; so I cut the toecaps out of a pair of size 12 Boots, African Other Ranks, For the Use of, with soles 4" wide, to avoid blisters (the troops called these boots 'cownose' – doubtless someone had gone round Africa with a tape measure, checking on the average of feet that were customarily bare, and had added a bit for socks and luck). Then I got fever ('clinical malaria' or PUO – Pyrexia of Unknown Origin, solved by double Mepacrine), and have never been tended so gently and sweetly as by the Sierra Leonean stretcher-bearers of 6 Field Ambulance, who took me to the Main Dressing Station for ten days, just like the wounded.

Now came a renewed embarrassment. Although my mother's wordily emotional reaction to my self-censored description of our first real action had steered me off writing the whole truth home on anything ever again, I had mentioned the lost glasses and the fever in one weekly rationed airgraph. Later my father wrote to say that he had now met a RAMC brigadier, and had commented that I was in Burma although originally graded unfit, and that he was worried about spectacles steaming up in jungles. This was nonsense. Glasses only steam if you go into hot and humid places from the cold, though sweat can blur them. We had no cold to come out of. Anyway, when I had a fever yet again the RMO Jake Weir said he had just had a confidential letter asking for me to have a full medical examination. I told him what my father had written. 'You do have a fever,' he said with some uncertainty, 'but I don't think it's just that. I'd better arrange for you to be evacuated with the next column of casualties.' I didn't see myself as a casualty. I didn't want my platoon or others to think I'd been pulled out because my father knew some WO brigadier. Jake said that orders were orders, and left it at that. The field ambulance CO told me that the letter required me to have a medical by a physician of lt-col rank and a specialist ophthalmic surgeon. We avoided each others' eyes. If wires hadn't been pulled, whose legs were?

At Chittagong I had cursory inspections from a medical specialist and an oculist, and learnt that although high myopia was refused on recruitment, once in, there was diffidence, unless the man's CO certified him as inefficient (= useless). The oculist recommended 'C' if my CO so certified me. A lt-col reported that my 'physical aspect [was] essentially negative'. An ordinary looking MO looked at whatever they and our RMO had written and questioned me about my childhood and the campaign. After 20 minutes, in which I mentioned the spare specs loss, he announced that he was a psychiatrist and would explain me to myself. I had been closely nurtured, I had been worried about my boots and spectacles, and I had a Mild Anxiety State. He was recommending 'B (Permanent)' for base or LofC duties only, and was that all right? Did that mean it was my decision, I have since wondered. I was still whacked and bemused; was I an idiot to have cheated the Oxford eye tests, or a coward not to insist that if myopia with spectacles was now officially OK for active service, I should go back to my unit? The medical board decided on 'B', subject to the CO's proviso. Our new CO didn't know me, but I heard no more from 1GambR ...

While anonyms were wondering where to post me, I was put into the Administrative Commandant's office at Dacca in Bengal as a supernumerary SSO (assistant Station Staff Officer). A soldier in 14th Army came up to the

All-India Radio studios to record a message to his sick mother back home, but the only station powerful enough to relay it far enough west to be relayed on to UK was Bombay. Some spare messenger had to ferry the acetate record in its straw and 3-ply packing. Who was most spare? Ask a silly question. A hitch to Dum Dum, Calcutta, on a USAAF DC3 was my very first flight ('Compassionate phonograph? No kidding! Sure, buddy.'), and I looked out with alarm at the wings flexing and buckling from my hard aluminum (Yank spelling) seat. Getting on board a RAF Transport Command *Dakota* (same plane, seats spelt *aluminium*) on to Bombay took much more arguing ('A gramophone record? You kidding? Show me your Movement Order! Looks pretty flimsy. Homemade?'). Nagpur, the fuel stop, seemed the hottest place in my life. When we re-embarked, the bucket-seat opposite was still occupied by Vera Lynn, the Sweetheart of the Forces who had been entertaining boys in 14th Army, some of whom had given her a leopard-skin coatee. The plane suddenly seemed freezing after Nagpur and I began to shiver and shake. The lady looked concerned, and saying, 'O, the poor boy, he must have malaria. Here, have this,' draped her leopard-skin round my shoulders. I repaid her kindness by being sick at her feet just as we bumped on to land, but was able to return the coatee stainless, with mumbled thanks. Sahiblike I talked my way on to a truck, found AIR Bombay, then straight to the British Military Hospital at Colaba. They confirmed Miss Lynn's diagnosis.

I spent my 21st birthday in hospital, listening to radio news of reinforcements to the Normandy landings, and reading Scott, Trollope and green Penguins. I never heard whether the record helped the soldier's mum, but Miss Lynn wrote to my mother with reassurance that she remembered the incident well. …

1945
In Ranchi I had another go of malaria. I also came up (or down) with something more original, Dengue Fever, carried by sandflies. It was over quicker than malarial bouts had been, but worse; every movement ached, the whole body turned to look sideways rather than bend the neck. I wasn't too clear what they gave me for it in the Indian Military Hospital; probably aspirin. The RMO, Jack Ratcliffe, liked to welcome me, once I was adjutant, to sit in on sick parades; he reckoned it was the best way to learn how to 'understand Africans.' He treated most like his own sons; the few cheeky or malingerers had an unnatural offence administered to chasten them – they had their temperatures taken up their bottoms by Nursing Orderly Corporal Samson. Apart from routine dentistry with foot pedal drills in Ranchi and replaced stoppings in Rangoon, I was never to need army medicine again.

1948
After being accepted for the Colonial Administrative Service, I had to go for a medical inspection at the Colonial Office in London's Victoria Street, by the Secretary of State's Chief Medical Adviser in person, Dr R (not yet Sir Richard) Brunel Hawes CMG. He waved away my sorry military history and demanded, 'Do you ever get backache?' – 'No.' – You will.' – 'Thank you, Sir, very much.' – 'No, tell you what, you're too tall, Africans like that, but if you find yourself in an office job for more than three months at a time, get yourself a desk and chair a foot higher than anyone else's – if you don't, don't come back to me in ten years' time and say you've got backache, I won't listen to you. *(Pause)* Got a monocle?' – 'No!!' – Get one.' – 'But I'm myopic, I need to see through both eyes at once.' – 'You haven't got the idea, have you? Look, you're going to Africa, you'll be going on safari or tour or bushwhacking, whatever they'll call it, you'll be on a horse or a bike, you'll be bashing through forest or bush, lianas or creepers or branches'll whip out and tear your glasses off. You'll be blind, you'll be lost. If you have a monocle round your neck, you can look for your glasses, if you haven't, you may never find them. Get yourself a monocle.' (He proved to be right about the back.) Shortly before leaving my mother insisted on having a mole with a hair growing through it removed from my right temple, for cosmetic reasons: I thought the procedure absurd, and regretted it even more when the ship's doctor on the way out charged me for removing the stitches.

1951
Malaria attacked again in my second tour in northern Nigeria, where the Bauchi provincial medical officer, Bach-loving Dr Frischmann from Mittel-Europa said, taking time off from a major epidemic of cerebro-spinal meningitis, 'Yaz, you haf it,' and sent me to bed with the new pills Quinacrine and Pamaquin. In that area it was probably MT (Malign Tertian). It wasn't worth sending blood samples off to Jos, 80 miles away, to make sure. One would be better long before any reply came, *deo volente*.

1954
At the end of my third tour, worn out with sacking corrupt chiefs and getting democratic elections organized at sundry levels, I was not feeling too good, so the latest MO referred me to the London Hospital for Tropical Diseases. They found Amœbic Dysentery and I chose to have that in Edinburgh's Eastern General, which dealt with tropical ailments. They told me to adopt the Muhammadan position of prayer, stuck up a dirty great polished steel sigmoidoscope, and pumped me with Emetine; they also found Giardiasis in my waste products, another amœbic infection, which surprisingly was curable by our old friend Mepacrine. My father, by now retired, went into his old

office library and came out with gloom about liver damage. I cheered up, although I never remember ever not feeling weary and willing to sleep, all my life. But for that, I might have achieved something, I suppose.

1957

Kaduna Nursing Home, the Senior Service hospital, found me back with a recurrence of Amœbiasis, and another of MT (Neither has given any sign of recurrence since then, so I must be hoaching with some varieties of antibodies). I began to complain of indigestion, which somehow instinct connected with what had been for years the standard daily anti-malarial, Paludrin, so I was switched to Daraprim twice a week. My father, deciding to go home in the middle of the film of *The King and I* because he was feeling groggy, collapsed inside his front door and died there of a coronary thrombosis, shortly before his 70th birthday. My mother called on his former senior depute and successor as Edinburgh's MOH, Henry Seiler, who couldn't have done more for her till I got home.

1959

A fresh surprise awaited in Okene, down near the Niger, when I had to have a major medical to prove that I was fit to face a transfer to the challenges of Hong Kong. In that middle belt of Nigeria it was routine to take a skin-snip to check on the ravages of the well-named *simulium damnosum* blackfly. This vile little insect secretes itself in riverain parts, and its bites pass on the tiny worm that burrows under the skin and, when it crosses the eyeballs, can create River Blindness. I was unknowingly infected with Onchocerciasis, though my eyes seemed all right. After two courses of Sulphathiazole tablets, lots of lively nasties still remained. Out with the blunderbuss: a subcutaneous injection of the drug did the trick. All the little worms died at once, or so it seemed, because my whole skin itched abominably as never before (or since). I was supervising the local constituency in the general election to Nigeria's first independent parliament, which I did in scratching misery to the puzzlement of all observers. Perhaps that's why the declaration was not universally popular.

1960-63

Hong Kong was not only the expected cultural shock. After years of starting work (including touring and walking about to see what was happening) around daybreak, going home for breakfast, and having a zizz after a very late lunch before tea and 'recreation' (or more usually overtime with the files when in station), now it was nothing but solid office work, dreary urban 9 to 1 and 2 to 5. I would fall asleep over lunchtime Cantonese lessons, or during afternoon routine meetings. I still had feelings of indigestion despite not having to take anti-malarials, and put it down to canteen 'club sandwiches'. But after a month or two of wishing I had stayed in Nigeria, I had a monstrous bloody flux in the secretariat lavatory and was whisked to Queen Mary Hospital. I had a duodenal ulcer, they poured barium in and took X-rays to confirm it, and thereafter Professor Alec McFadzean was my physician (and possibly distant relation through my Ayrshire great-grandmother). I had two recurrences and readmissions, and the Prof began to speak of surgery. Another X-ray showed a Hiatus Hernia, apparently accounting for occasional acidic regurgitations, so I began to sleep on a triangular foam cushion to prop me up.

Before leave Prof Mac suggested giving up my 15-25 cigarettes a day. *The Times* on the plane home said that the Chancellor was putting them up from 3s 3d to 4s 3d a packet; a shilling a day would pay for another long-playing record a month; and as I would be spending the leave swotting for my Bar Finals, likely to up the 25 to 40, I bought no duty-free on the plane and stopped smoking, cold turkey, on 16 March 1963. Another hæmorrhage hit me on holiday in Madrid where I was avoiding UK Income Tax, whither my widowed mother had refused to let me out of her sight, which added to strains. The hotel consulted the British Embassy, who kindly referred me to a nursing home before flying me to Heathrow. There I was forklifted into an ambulance en route to Charing Cross Hospital. The Spanish doctor had taken a lot of persuading that my stools had been jet black, but then kept injecting me with iron. At Charing Cross I eavesdropped on the consultation at the foot of the bed. 'Iron injections in this century? Treatment straight out of the Ark.'

1964

Back in the colony, after a lesser recurrence the Prof reluctantly advised the knife. I agreed. The question was, where to do it. Alec McFadzean had had the knife himself for the same reason, and had referred himself home to Glasgow because he had known his fellow professor of surgery only too well; but now there was a Singapore-born colleague, Mr G B Ong, who had held the world-esteemed Hunterian Lectureship, and whom he would trust with any part of his own anatomy. This man of distinction opened me up, took out two-thirds of my stomach in a Subtotal Gastrectomy to reduce acid squirting into the duodenum, cut the vagus nerve in a Vagotomy to reduce over-reaction to whatever stimulated acid-production, and repaired the Hiatus Hernia while he was at it. The curious thing during the slow return from anæsthesia to full consciousness, with tubes sticking out everywhere, was my dreamy impression of being faced with the most fundamental but intractable problem in the world – and solving it. Unhappily for the world, once quite awake I had forgotten it. Hence reports of patients who believe they have passed over to the other side, experienced strange things there, and then by God's grace been allowed to return to earth, ring bells with me. I lost a lot of weight (and have remained thin, apart from a progressively less modest pot, ever since). Nice to be off all pills again. Now I can get married, a bit late.

1967
I solved the sleepy afternoon syndrome. At one o'clock I would lock my office door, do the Royal Canadian Air Force 5BX exercises from a Penguin book at the 21-25 year level, follow that with 5 minutes of isotonics, have a cheese sandwich and Thermos soup lunch with fruit, and spend till 2 o'clock asleep flat on the floor. I knew it made sense. It couldn't last. Piles. Back to Queen Mary for nice Mr Richard Yu to perform. They took the routine blood pressure and asked if I had walked uphill to the hospital, then if I was very worried about the op. Since No to both, the conclusion was that I had Hypertension. After the Hæmorrhoidectomy, a series of blood tests ended in an assortment of prescriptions. Lifelong pills again, subject to periodic checks. What a bore. If no piles, I'd never have known. But everything's stable now. Could 5BX and isotonics have set it off?

1972
My wife, dear Hilary, senior tutor at Hong Kong's School of Physiotherapy, has had specifically ladies' surgery, my mother has passed on at 77 of renal failure postponed by hypertension pills and sleeping tablets, and I have to have another medical to prove that I am fit to face the challenges of the Solomon Islands. There is an uninteresting sort of reddish blistery thing on my left temple which none of my university medical friends can identify; and an X-ray disclosed Diverticulitis in the colon of which yet again I'd had no inkling. In good blunt Chinese way, Dr Rosie Young said it could lead to cancer, but I should eat roughage, keep regular, and think no more about it. Fit enough for the laid back Pacific anyway.

1974
The emergent nation of the Solomon Islands can afford two Consultants, a Physician Specialist and a Surgical Specialist. Bert Wilkins has just replaced Tony Cross as the latter; Tony had spent most of his time here researching the Poliomyelitis epidemic which devastated the islands in 1951-52, when many died or were paralysed, and devising procedures to straighten the limb-joints of over 150 Melanesian youngsters whose parents had refused them treatment (a sad product of the non-co-operating *Marching Rule* movement), now adult 'crawlers'. Hilary has been acting as locum for the solitary Physio, an American nun now on furlough, and exercises them in their post-operative splints, then

training them to walk on crutches. At last, they say, they feel like men, their 'calico' remains clean and they can eat their *kaikai* (food) with clean hands. But back in their village life, if they reject the bright lights of Honiara, they throw the prosthetics away and revert to what they've become used to; their strong arms paddle their canoes better than their friends who have had nether limbs bitten off by crocodiles or sharks. Bert has snipped out an irritating Nasal Polyp which has been flapping about in my nose.

1976
Bert has been at work again, this time repairing a Double Hernia which had emerged. He had noticed an uninteresting reddish blistery thing on my forehead while I was under, which he recognised as a skin cancer but didn't feel free to snip out without my waking consent. Permission duly given, he cut out a second found on a hand. In learned discussion of Actinic Ulcers and Solar Keratoses, I told him that in the far eastern war the soldiery had been advised to strip to the waist as protection against prickly heat, which had worked; so sunbathing seemed sensible. 'Ah well,' he said, 'Science is always inventing something new'.

1977
On the Copra ship coming home, somewhere on the 19-day Pacific crossing between Stevenson's grave in Samoa and Panama City, during the evening walk in flip-flops I stubbed my left big toe on a bollard. It hurt like hell, and I assumed I had cracked it. The whole leg swelled as far as the knee, became hard, shiny and angry red, and I took to my bunk, paracetamol and whisky. As we were the only passengers and the crew was under one score in complement, the second mate answered for medical care out of a first-aid book and a basic manual of *materia medica*. Hilary, full of forebodings about amputations, asked him what he could do. The good news was that one could radio to WHO in Rome, describe symptoms and follow instructions about where to apply the saw, like a passenger being talked down in a plane whose pilot had collapsed; the other news was that at that point half-way across the south Pacific we were out of radio contact. Happily the leg began to go down after two or three days supported on pillows, with music cassettes and half the books there had been no time to read in Melanesia.

1979
Politics are dangerous, particularly for the amateur. I was distributing leaflets for the general election at the gentrified Lady Stair's Close in Edinburgh's Royal Mile. Stepping carefully but to no avail over the algae-clad paving stones,

up went my feet in the air (not very dignified in a kilt) and down I came slap upon the point of my left elbow. I went home, where Hilary felt the sore bit and found it wobbling. She drove me straight to the Royal Infirmary Casualty Admissions. A registrar said the Olecranon Process was detached. They would screw it back at once. Clerked into the ward, they inquired about medications, and hearing about the hypertension cocktail said they would have to take a blood sample. Wheeling me into the theatre, they announced that as the Medical Laboratory Scientific Officers (= lab techs) were on strike there could be no lab report. They could not operate under a general anæsthetic.

A local would require a Byer's Block, a tourniquet round the upper arm to keep the potion (and my blood) from circulating; the local was injected and left for about 20 minutes, then I was jabbed and asked whether I could feel that. I could. Wait five more minutes and poke again. Yes, I still feel that. Give you a booster and wait a bit longer. Feel that? Yes. Well, that's the maximum dose, we'll wait a little and go ahead. Arm sandbagged into place, a screen was hung on a rail in front of my face; it covered my mouth and nose so that I had to keep blowing it away to stop breathing it in. Although there was no actual pain, I was fully aware of the scalpel cutting through, and when the Black & Decker drill started to buzz and whine I heard all about it. When finished I was sweating like a pig. Wheeled into a recovery room, I broke into minutes of uncontrollable shaking, the worst rigor I've ever had.

A fortnight later I returned for the stitches and a check X-ray. The screw was out. Out to the Princess Margaret Rose Hospital, designed for Edinburgh's TB children in the 30s, next to where my parents had built their home. Proper general anæsthetic, stainless steel pins and wiring inserted instead of loose screws, so that I would always set the anti-terrorist bells ringing at airports, and with minimum physio the arm was soon as it had ever been.

1982
The right foot and leg have swollen up again but this time the big toe had never been stubbed. Dr Ronald Seiler at the University Health Centre has pronounced 'Gout,' which is demoralizing when port and claret have never been standard tipples. Yet more pills, alas.

1983
Complaints about the number of pills being taken (couldn't chemists pound them all in a mortar and make one big one?) led back to the Royal Infirmary. Two nurses counting both wrist pulses at the same time disclosed a Cardiac Arrhythmia. Science having progressed, Dr Robertson prescribed a new selection of pills, so with the gout-repellers continuing, the request to reduce the number ended by increasing them.

Ronnie Seiler excised a grey scabby superficial growth near an ankle, and another blistery outbreak on a shoulder. That got me on to the Royal's Skin Clinic list, after which every six months a visit to the Professor of Dermatology, John Hunter, usually presenting several more to be burnt off by freezing with a liquid oxygen spray, or on a few occasions something which had to be removed by the duty plastic surgeon for a biopsy. So far all have been benign.

1988

Tripping (don't pick my feet up so much) over setts on the street on way to a Lothian Health Board meeting, the left knee was sprained and trouser leg split. I got to the meeting, limped home to lie up, watched the knee swell vastly, invited Dr Seiler to come and see, and was amazed when he took a syringe and aspirated enough blood from the haematoma to fertilize six verandah flower pots.

Driving about my City Council Ward at night, in search of complaining constituents or the Community Council meeting-place, began to add dazzling headlights to ocular doubts. Reference to the Princess Alexandra Eye Pavilion and Consultant Dr Hector Chawla uncovered one cataract advancing, one imminent. I had already half decided not to stand for election again. This determined me. By the time the first eye was done and settled it might be OK for the second.

The left eye was done, 'private' to avoid 18 months' 'waiting', at Murrayfield Hospital within a week of booking, under a general anaesthetic, and worth every penny. Myopia being so strong, no implant was needed, which simplified things, except for short sight having become long. When the bandage came off, what hit at once was the vivid blue of the nurse's tunic. However long the cataracts had been developing unknown, it had been enough for me to forget what true colours, particularly bright blue, had been like.

The haemorrhoids had reformed. Shorter waiting list for them. My first experience of a spinal epidural anaesthetic, followed by another normal injection to put me out. 'Very impressive,' said Mr Macwhatsit afterwards, who had ectomized them, 'Your piles were enormous,' while a kindly nurse explained how she remembered the days when a couple of smoking red hot pokers would be brought into the ward to cauterize such ambitious blood vessels.

A pre-op X-ray had indicated another fashionable symptom: like Ronald Reagan, there were Colonic Polyps to be seen, so a while later, two or three of them were burnt out by a little electric wire lasso. That put me on to another list, the PIU (Programmed Investigation Unit), an annual return to seek out any new ones.

By then the waiting list had matured sufficiently for a cancelled appointment to let my right eye back into Princess Alexandra's care, where senior registrar Dr Dhillon from Singapore talked me into having the second cataract done under a local, against all my instincts. Sedated, injected two ways into the head, and sandbagged into immobility (wedged, not concussed), it was painless, but a strange experience of changing lights, flashes and ill-heard theatre small-talk. It was quite another experience to be sitting up having lunch, totally unwoozy, only an hour later. But this time the follow-ups at the Eye Pavilion were less comfortable than to Dr Chawla's nice West End consulting rooms: queues, chaos and never the same doctor twice. Twice I had to return between appointments for repeat drops because Conjunctivitis had developed. The second time they had lost my papers and I wasn't on the list: 'Do you mind seeing Dr Dhillon, he's got a few minutes spare?' It took him a few seconds to observe what colleagues had missed, two minute stitches which should have fallen out naturally were *in situ*. As quickly, he nicked them out while I sat preternaturally still, and my eyes have never troubled me since.

1990
Checks for skin cancers and colonic polyps (latter confirming diverticulitis) having become routine, attention turned to some unsteadiness of the feet and clumsiness of the fingers. An appointment concluded that possibly neurology was involved. The registrar manipulated electrodes and cathode ray screens and could detect no electricity in my ankles and feet at all. Many weeks later again, a more senior registrar confirmed that there was some polyneuropathological defect around the feet and that electricity was indeed barely detectable. Silence followed, and eventually a telephone call to a secretary discovered that the Specialist saw no need to see me again. It would have been interesting to know what causes it and why nothing can be done.

1991
Suspecting that the left ear was glued up, and finding conversation at noisy occasions awkward, I betook myself to a hearing aid agency and invested in a small pink thing. It helps the higher frequencies, not least rustling paper and clacks of knives on plates, and can be useful at the theatre and parties, but I still duck like a giraffe to the level of those addressing me. The most recent chronic complaint has been a real pain in the neck. My mother had the same trouble. Physio and exercises make both the neck-ache, and the reluctance to twist the neck when reversing the car, worse. More X-rays proved positive Osteo-Arthritis and Reverse Spondylitis, all in the neck, something else to put up with, like the arthritic right pinkie which snaps like a trigger and is ruining my handwriting.

1996
Lack of stamina *etc* suggested a consultation – haemoglobin count down – why? Try the colon first: discovery, something like a white pigeon's egg up at the very top end round both corners, visible on the screen whence the Olympus

electronic periscope can go no further. 48 hours of wondering, then dear Dr Bob Heading confirms it is nothing sinister, merely a mucusoid deformity. But better go back on the ferrous sulphate pills and up the haemoglobin again.

The year ends with a bang, mid-November. Walking with Bill Fulton, late Professor of Medicine, Kenyatta National Hospital, Nairobi, to Scottish Opera's *Il Trovatore*, watching a car coming in across my front from the right, I was aware of a dunt and myself flat, looking at the setts under my face. An over-confident driver, had swept round on the wrong side from the left into the very minor road which I had begun to cross, and just missed my companion who had looked left just in time. I managed to get up, slightly shaken and probably bruised, told the apologetic and contrite young man (who had had good brakes) that he bloody well ought indeed to be sorry but I didn't need to be taken to hospital, and we went on to the Festival Theatre.

After Act One I was uncomfortable and aware that my right leg was twice the size of the left: Bill took one look and pronounced that we were getting a taxi straight to the Royal's A&E. The receptionist thought getting the details more important than finding somewhere for me to sit, but a tired-looking Dutch registrar admitted me. X-ray confirmed no broken bones. Sequences, dates and times over the next 32 days were lost in a succession of wards, with different groups of carers homing in from their various warrens in asynchronous routines for conflicting purposes. The leg looked revolting, big purple bubbles and lesser serous-yellow bubblets. There must be a Compartmental Pressure Syndrome; the squashed soft tissues had burst wildly out in protest against the aggressive invasion of their territories – nerves, muscles, cartilages, veins and arteries, probably also the Chinese meridians the acupuncturists prick. In theatre some meter was stitched into the leg to measure atmospheric pressure inside the CPS; this, wired to a recording monitor screen by the bed, trotted along between an unalarming zero and 15 or so. I concluded that they hoped it would settle down naturally. When I indulged in major movement in the effort to achieve the first 'motion' for three days, either I upset something or the meter started to register properly: the graph on the screen shot up to 80. After a hasty consultation I was invited to sign a consent to a Fasciotomy.

Mr Quaba performed the donation of a 7" x 3½" graft from the thigh to cover the gaping hole on the inside of the calf left by the loss of dead skin cut out. The outer slice was stitched up conventionally with clips and supposedly self-absorbent sutures (several had to be plucked out manually long afterwards). Early one morning I felt a violent stitch, and wondered whether in the fall I might have cracked a right rib.

A day later a procession surrounded me; after discussion of the stitch, evident when I breathed in deep or sharply, I was sent for scanning, front of queue, where the radiographer said that he had detected a Pulmonary

Embolism in my right lung, which was 'quite serious'. A clot from the leg injury had made its way up and settled. I was hooked to a pump which injected a controlled amount of Heparin into my bloodstream, requiring regular samples to be taken, so as to keep some level stable by adjusting the pump. Both lower arms became black with bruising from the needles. My third consultant now joined the team: I already had an orthopod and a plastics, seen by their registrars. Now as 'an elderly person' I had to have a geriatrician. He drew a picture of the lung's blood supply, and what it would look like when the clot was dissolved and the parts behind the damage resumed their business. Once the levels had stabilized, I would come off the pump and start on Warfarin in place of Heparin for an indefinite period. I was promised an abdominal endoscopy, which nobody ever arranged.

A young male nurse decided that the donor graft site showed sufficient signs of healing to expose to air and dry naturally. I inquired about the wire cages that used to keep bedclothes off limbs, but they went out with the ark: now a metal gallows sits under the mattress and projects a rod over the top. It only keeps the sheets off the part close under the gibbet. A few days later the whole site was furiously red and weepy; a swab demonstrated a staphylococcic infection, later boosted by an anaerobe. This proved stubborn: an antibiotic might slowly kill the *staphyloccus aurei*, doubtless a MRSA native of the ward, but the antidote to the anaerobe would quarrel with the Warfarin, so another delay was inevitable.

Even after 32 nights I was sent home a couple of days before those looking at staphylococci had recommended. Beds were needed for the expected Festive Season influx of self-inflicted wounds. Being in time for Christmas burdened my long-suffering Hilary. District Nurses dressed the leg beyond Twelfth Night, and by late January I had been discharged by the orthopods, been put on a three month call-back by the plastics, who might suggest tidying up after the gouge had settled down, and presumably been forgotten by the geriatrics; all I needed to know was the future of the Warfarin régime. Meanwhile I await the endoscopy of the stomach, inconveniently arranged for a readmission, involving stopping the Warfarin and repeat of the pumped Heparin for a few days: all of which might have been done while I was already in the ward.

1997

The endoscopy revealed two lesions, relics of the gastrectomy, and a recursion of a slight hiatus hernia; nothing to worry about. After a couple of months Dr Heading agreed that the Warfarin could stop after 3-6 months. This good news coincided with a return of the infection that spread itchy rashes all round and over the wound and graft sites. That indicated a second course of antibiotic, which made matters worse, with rashes on hands, stomach, back and limbs – a penicillin allergy. A final visit to the plastic surgeon allowed Mr Quaba to pronounce that the graft was fine as far as his discipline was concerned. A visit to Dermatology recommended a cream on the affected areas, and an alternative antibiotic seemed to start the final (repeat) process of healing satisfactorily. But the rashes went on, with itches and warts appearing where the angriness was worst. Back at home, Prof John Hunter tut-tutted: this was Eczema, with little doubt. So daily treks to Dermatology out-patients. Tripping over a cracked pavement I pulled the *Latissima dorsi* muscle round my back, and was crippled for weeks. Οιμοι, *eheu, hélas, ohime, o weh!* Alternatively, any four letters. But by autumn 1998 eczema had vanished. *Laus Deo.*

1999

Lightning never strikes twice? Tripping over a pavement on the way to dermatology OPD, balance was not regained and I crashed. Two kind ladies rushed to my aid, got me up and brought out a stool from the adjacent boutique, gently holding me on it while ringing 999. We were 100 yards from the Royal Infirmary of Edinburgh, so it wasn't *quite* half-an-hour before an ambulance crew arrived to deliver me to A&E, during which my angels missed two of their buses. After a couple of hours on a trolley, an X-ray confirmed a broken hip at the top of the femur. 'Admit and inform NOK'.

This was a Wednesday, but because I had to come off blood-thinning Warfarin and on to Heparin before slicing the thigh open, it was not till the Sunday that Mr Oliver let his senior registrar go in to screw a plate over the break and pin all together. My anaesthetist was the schoolboy son of the solicitor-general of the Solomon Islands in the late 70s. A friend brought in some ready-canned gin-and-tonics – not my usual tipple, but it seemed a shame not to use a nightcap. A fierce nurse caught me and solemnly instructed me in her experience of old ladies who always had a 'small' sherry at bed-time and displayed terrible withdrawal systems when admitted.

My principal memory is of the incredible patience of the nursing staff with patients who were self-centred, abusive, drugged, self-righteous and demanding, threatening and aggressive. On my second night, a man resisted every attempt to offer treatment: shouting for the manager, then the police, because any medication given against his will was going to get them ten years in jail. It went on from about 1 *a.m.* to 3 *a.m.* Then the next bed started to throw things at the nurses, bellowing for the doctor in charge and insisting on the presence of various named but unknowable individuals. Another spent most days, and part of the nights, demanding the toilet for Number One or Number Two. Then there was the sad old gent with a monotonously piercing voice in unintelligible dialect who reverted to babyhood whenever the nurses tried to move him, weeping and wailing like an infant, but with ten times the volume **'Ah've a sair leg!'**.

Curiously when taken off *all* my anti-hypertension, antacid and potassium pills, my blood pressure remained stubbornly normal. Some days after the op physios began moving my leg, and on to the Zimmer. I began to master stairs with sticks. I should have been out earlier but for a barium x-ray. This is unpleasant, hanging on to a platform that goes up, down and round like a big dipper to allow the stuff to follow gravity through one's inner tubes (the process observed on a screen), while trying to refrain from involuntary expulsion of the invasive stuff. The comforting radiologist said I had diverticular disease, 'which we already knew', and possibly new polyps. 26 days from admission, I was allowed home. Roll on Christmas (again).

All went well until Edinburgh's 2000AD festival, when (obeying my physios' injunctions to stop leaning forward, which reduced my awareness of where I was placing my feet) I tripped on the Lawnmarket's setts and had a Colles fracture. After attempts to reposition by traction, the RIE equipped me with an external fixator, a sort of Forth Road Bridge screwed through the flesh into the separated parts of the wrist to hold them tight. A repeat stay in Ward 5 led to severe constipation, which led to a colonoscopy 'to make sure', which wasn't helped by an infection of one of the screw wounds. I ended up with a wrist that was nearly as good as before, and leg problems not much further degenerated than they had begun to be already. The media are in arms about cross-infections under the NHS, and I am with them. Bring back the dragons, the nursing caps that control the hair, the daily starched white coats that cover the tweed outerwear, and the persons who scrub the floors every day on their knees!

2002
Is that all the novelty in an 80th year? No. In a 108 *mph* gale I was blown off my feet in Edinburgh's Lawnmarket. I fortunately broke nothing, but soft tissues suffered, and I was on a walker and sticks for six weeks before returning to my weak-limbed normality. Meantime geriatrician consultant Dr Cantley had commented on slowly rising urea and creatinine, whatever that may be, in my kidneys' waste products, and said not to worry, although my physical balance was troublesome. Once I had recovered from that and was back to 'normal' (for a creakily unsteady person), I tripped over the telephone stool while hurriedly answering a call I did not wish to take, split my head open to the skull on our long case clock, and scraped my thin-skinned shins on the stool. A taxi to A&E led to stitches and steri-strips and an overnight stay that protocol demands for 'head injuries'. The scrapes did not heal for months. But like the ITMA character Sophie Tuckshop, 'I'm all right now'. The zig-zag on my forehead makes me either an exceedingly mature Harry Potter or a Gorbachev *doppelgänger*. (I scraped my skull again at a Magdalen Gaudy, forgetting where a sixteenth century archway reduced headroom in an entry.)

Future?
So! Weary, doubtful about the globe beneath the navel, clumsy fingers, slight tunnel vision, weak muscles disliking upward slopes, varicosed ankles threatening ulcers, dribbles, fading memory, boring and repetitive thoughts, ptyalism (liability to expel crumbs on to a companion's tie or pendant during mealtime chatter), periodic leg cramps in bed or trains, flatulence both ways, pain in the neck, occasional mildly acidic nocturnal regurgitations, piles back, diverticular disease and a very prominent ileo-caecal valve, I just hope that any looks at my carapace, down my throat or up my bottom will still be benign, and the mind clear and modestly creative. Natheless I have joined those who ask, 'Why did I decide to come in here?' and 'While I'm down here relacing my shoes, what else could I be doing?' All that's left is resort to evening primrose oil, glucosamine and chondroite, all of which simply pass out again surplus to nature's requirements, and life-enhancing Glen Dronach to spark up the liver. As Ronnie Seiler said before retirement, state health has done me not badly, and it's quite a wonder that, like Mr Major once was, I'm still here. So, Gott sie danke, is the almost always superpatient Hilary, sometimes unhappy herself.

There is a Hypochondriack's broken thread, running through, not so much a quilt, as life's rusting hawser. Time to trace another, less fragmentary, wire or two which may twist the reality closer to the perception. If I have readers, those who have not skipped this chapter must now regret any thirst for the Whole Story as perverse. It was the kick-start, to have enjoyed ill-health.

Chapter 2

Natural Pleasure of a Learning Curve

I believe Education is about what happens to you and not what qualifications you get when you're 16.

[The Rt Hon Anthony Wedgwood Benn
(formerly Lord Stansgate), *The Sunday Telegraph* (1993)]

How different a world if mothers ensured that progenies could read before going to school. Books, magazines, papers, print would be natural from the start, school texts (or 'worksheets') would arrive without terror, literacy would provoke no lifelong subliminal associations with bells, corridors, and rules. My first year at Giffnock Academy leaves few memories. The three Rs had begun in the home, and the rest was colourful decoration. There must have been other things taught besides *Nymphs and Shepherds, O How Now Gossip Joan* (what she gossiped about, we never thought to ask), and *Dashing Away with the Smoothing Iron*; there is a misty recollection of Twelve Times Table, easy when learnt by rote, but also revision from pre-school homework. Clearer is the memory of being made to stand up in the drawing-room in front of visitors, to recite by heart Bernard & Elinor Darwin's forgotten masterpiece with its Hiroshige-like illustrations, which should be a modern cult classic – *The Tale of Captain Tootle-oo and the Cockyolly Birds,* and its sequel *Tootle-oo-Two.* These were nice coloured children's books from the Nonesuch Press that never quite made it into the set of Pooh, Tiggywinkle and Mole. It took several decades for rhetorical performances in public to lack acute embarrassment and the earnest wish to be somewhere far away (now I'm told I revel in a captive audience).

My father's old school, Hillhead High, was quite near our next home: no one told us it was not quite up to Glasgow Academy, they just wore different uniforms, and we had friends there whose fathers were our fathers' friends. There might be hints that they were 'rougher'; but they also knew that success came from hard work, and failure from expecting things to come as of right. One of the prizes my 12-year-old father had won there in 1900 was an atlas, 'For Map Drawing and General Excellence', on the flyleaf in copperplate by his Rector's hand. I came upon some of his maps, indeed neat and carefully watercoloured. I scrawled $^{10}/_{10}$ ★★ (two stars) all over them in blue or red pencils, as Miss Reid was wont to mark our classwork. I assumed that my father had drawn them from memory, and as I couldn't see how one could ever draw a whole map to accurate scale from memory, I should never be as clever as he. The naughtiness was that I vandalized them despite knowing not to vandalize my own school books.

I never got my hands on my mother's water-colours. Her father had been a Broadlands watercolourist of East Anglian distinction, Charles Harmony Harrison. My paternal grandfather William had been son of a farm servant Hugh, who had married a lass called Jean McFadzean (the farmer's daughter?) at Kirkoswald, Tam o' Shanter's parish; grandfather was a mining and civil engineer who had worked on the building of the West Highland Line of the Caledonian Railway, and on Queen's Park Football Club's first great stadium at Hampden Park, for which the directors voted him their personal thanks. My father, after qualifying at Glasgow as a contemporary and friend of O H Mavor ('James Bridie', the playwright), had like many young doctors gone to see the world as a ship's surgeon, and had joined the Royal Navy (not the RNVR, his stripes were not wavy) as a Surgeon Lieutenant two days before 4 August 1914. While posted ashore at Pompey he had met my mother, who had joined the Wrens and was a coding officer. A close friend of his was a regular officer, James Blackburn, 'Blackers'; she and her close friend Hilda Stanford, as customary, called each other by their surnames, so Stanford became 'Stanny' and Gladys Harrison became 'Harry'. George Clark remained George. Blackers and Stanny became Lieut & Mrs Blackburn, and in the Second World War Capt Blackburn came out of the RN Reserve to command *Jervis Bay*, an armed merchant cruiser, a POW after her sinking. They were parents of Lt Cmdr John Blackburn who died commanding the submarine HMS *Affray* when it was stranded with its crew of naval cadets in training. They lost their second son in a post-war army accident in the near east. They were my godparents, in practice if not by solemn undertaking at the font. Their grandson became a vice-admiral and Master of The Queen's Household.

Sensibly, George and Gladys had not married until 1921, long after they were demobbed and he, after his Cambridge DPH, became assistant MOH of Govan. The wedding was at St Columba's in London, after which she became to her Great Yarmouth family their Scotch sister. So much for my genes. I never heard a whisper of unfriendly words about my father. He taught me not to kick someone else in a dispute, and always asked me if I had had my 'palmies' when I came home from school, being himself child of a historic and global world where a sore hand or bottom was an ephemeral reminder of the social need to be good-mannered, attentive and honest, and was felt as improvement, not abuse.

As six or seven year-olds at Glasgow Academy we saw our Rector daily at prayers, where some miscreant had to pump the organ to accompany the *Church Hymnal*, and the lower middle classes sang the Treble Descant in the last verse (our sole Jewish classmate was excused Prayers). A white-haired patriarch, Dr Edwin Temple tried to teach every class once a week so that no child might be a stranger. When we were about eight our last period of the week under him was a multiplication of two eight-digit figures, or a long division of three or four digits into about ten or twelve – until you got it right you couldn't go home (never did we need the crutch of pocket calculators; they hadn't been invented). I wrote an essay protesting against homework: Dr Temple was shown it, and sent for me. I was terrified, but when I mumbled feebly that I hadn't really meant it, it was just to find something to write about, he patted me on the head and sent me on my way. He probably only wanted to get to know another very small boy among his hundreds. After my interrupted year at Mearnskirk hospital, which meant going back a class, I hardly remember him until Frank Royden Richards succeeded him: Richards was a good Rector, but I never adored him as Temple.

An unforgettable dominie was the gym master, 'Coalbags': retired Captain Colman-Smith drilled us in the traditional physical jerks but with a military air, later to exercise wartime wireless listeners. We couldn't forget Frank Coningsby, who taught music: mostly singing, but with records too, using *William Tell* to interpret pictorial music of thunder and hail, the succeeding calm, and the final gallop. He organized parties to hear Mr John Barbirolli explain, and guide the Scottish Orchestra through, more stormy weather inside *Fingal's Cave* at the City Hall; but Coningsby once belted one of the 'tough' boys on the calves till he cried. *Latin For To-Day Book One* was fun, under Captain Frank Batchelor ('Batchy'), who gave us Latin names in class; 'clerk' made me '*Scriba*', which occasioned embarrassingly ponderous explanations of how a feminine ending was a respectable irregular usage for a male. History was mostly about Scotland before 1603, although overwritten in the memory banks (incidentally, many boys wore a kilt to school between the wars). Geography meant cajoling Mummies into wheedling Empire Marketing Board ephemera out of shopkeeepers to decorate classroom walls, giving the master the chance to tell us about where things came from, and why they wouldn't grow here. None of us had to be told that milk came from cows, not bottles; we all spent holidays in the country or at the seaside near farms – the Clarks went regularly to Drumadoon farm at Blackwaterfoot on Arran. *Geographia* wooden jig-saws cut in the shapes of islands, counties and countries were much valued visual-aids to complement our teaching – one still remembers the problem for the jig-saw-maker over cutting Dunbartonshire, even more so Clackmannan with its 'Part of'.

Holidays: I remember when small a stay in Clovelly with its sandy beach and climb back up to the village; when bigger, one stay with my mother's in-laws in Great Yarmouth; Belgium, getting a steamer from Harwich (disappointing me because it was not the *Mauretania),* with the battlefields, fireworks in Bruxelles (as I spelt it, an early pedantry) and the Antwerp

Exhibition to follow; I still vividly remember the revetted trenches, the pillboxes and barbed wire preserved for the visitors from a war ended little more than a decade before. West Kilbride and Arran, several times, just mentioned; camping holidays, once we had acquired the Morris Ten Six, taking a tent as far as Oban and Brora, to Bamburgh where I collected tiger caterpillars on the beach, and once to Blackpool (a surprise so that I could see my wireless hero Reginald Dixon at the Tower, playing *I Do Like to be Beside the Seaside* on the Wurlitzer, and get his autograph) – on the last of those safaris out of Glasgow I drove the Morris round a field, to my parents' consternation: but I'd been watching my father at it, and so knew I knew how to shift gears and pedals. The BBC's Glasgow branch of the Scottish Children's Hour held a fancy dress party, where we saw in the flesh our Auntie Kathleen (Garscadden, formerly Auntie Cyclone), and Longfellow (Andrew Stewart) who read the *Incredible Adventures of Professor Brainstawm*. My mother made an aeroplane costume from silver material, and everyone said (she said) I should have won the prize, but the winner (everyone said, she said) was a Violet Elizabeth Bott related to the judges. Who can tell?

When ten my parents thought I should join the Wolf Cubs. The First Glasgow Pack was the junior branch of the First Glasgow Boy Scout Troop, the second to be set up after Baden Powell's original formal troop down south. Akela was a man (lady cub mistresses were unthinkable), and after the knot-tying, good deeding and drill he would sing (clean) music hall songs to a banjo, the best being one about *The Body in the Bag*. Once awarded my second star on my cap (the cub's second eye metaphorically opened) I could start qualifying for my Woodwork and Collector's Badges. We went to Auchengillan for a weekend camp under canvas. This was a mixture of fun and games (coupled with bashfulness and rudery, centred on the colours of pyjama stripes when going to bed in the tents, and who wore what under their kilt), and with a treasure hunt to be rewarded with Gold – which turned out to be golden Creamola crystals to make a fizzy drink. There was a church parade, which our Sixer missed, so as the Second (one yellow stripe round my arm) I marched in front of our Six and shouted out, 'Left Wheel' into the churchyard: shy-making, my first Command.

We had no piano, but at 11 I started lessons, and went to a tolerant second cousin's to practise. I had joined the Academy choir the year before; when it came to the performance of Coleridge Taylor's *Hiawatha's Wedding Feast* in the dining hall, we were joined by a fat old tenor (probably near his 40s) to sing, *Onaway! Awake, Beloved,* surprising us because we hadn't heard it in any practices. He reduced us to giggles when singing the line about strawberries. Next year it was to be *Trial by Jury,* from which a boy called Main frightened me into resigning, by saying there were lots of solos and I'd have to do one. It had been bad enough being made to sing part of the treble line of *Hiawatha* alone to my mother in the kitchen, *a cappella* and very *alla rustica* too. Like Flanders & Swann's warthog partner, I was shy. Passion for Gilbert & Sullivan had yet to be kindled. But one rootlet was watered: after the crystal set which my father and his cousin Frank Price had assembled had been abandoned, we acquired a Philips wireless set and I became a regular listener to Christopher Stone's 'New Records' (and also to Henry Hall), where one record stuck in memory for decades. At the time I thought the downward roulades of a throbbing low mezzo funny; but when as a post-war collector I identified it as Conchita Supervia's *Non più mesta* from Rossini's *Cenerentola* it was a double Ἀναγνώρισις. Forgive the conceit.

My favourite toy was Meccano, though I did also have a Hornby *Flying Scotsman* locomotive which only had little 4-wheeled coal and Sir Robert MacAlpine wagons to pull. Meccano brought out Modelled Miniatures, which were 'super', because they looked like the real things made small; my first was a green sports car, but my favourite was the cream streamlined Chrysler *Airflow*. It broke my heart when my father couldn't buy the real thing. I didn't mind that it was an American car, although I did think Meccano was much better than the American imitation, Erector. But it was a bitter blow when Modelled Miniatures were renamed Dinky Toys: it was such a childish name (but then, Meccano had begun life as *Mechanics Made Easy*).

My best friend, never met again after 1937, was Winky Williams, who went on to be an architect. In summer we walked two-and-a-half miles out on the Great Western Road to Anniesland and back together, for cricket practice. There was another boy, Kenneth Mackenzie Anderson, but although we met again at Oxford, it was a connexion that would not be tightened for years to come. My father's best friend at school had been a Bryce-Buchanan, who was now boss man at Albion motor works: his son David was also in the class, so it was assumed that we should also be good friends, but it didn't work out. We were all pleased that his father showed us over the factory, as Paton's father showed us over the Paisley cotton-spinnery and McColl's over McVitie & Price's biscuit bakery, where we were given samples in nice tins. The coæval I saw most of was my cousin Helen, most often on Sunday afternoons when the Hugh and George Clarks would each take their wife and child to visit Grannie, unless going to Hilton Park to golf. I collected a few class prizes at session ends, hating the walk and climb up to the stage of the City Hall and back.

I was happy in the end to go to Edinburgh. We arrived in time to wave at the King & Queen for their Silver Jubilee visit. There was one permanent blow: it took over three years for my parents to decide where to live. Despite my father's increasing desperation, my mother could never agree to live in any houses we looked at while flitting from one furnished accommodation to another. In the end they had to build (the arguments with the architects were another story, teaching how determined my mother was to get her own way and how easily she wrote people off). From mid-1935 till the end of 1938 we never settled long enough to carry on piano lessons, to join a local scout troop or any other 'social group' (the OTC was an alternative), to get my Meccano out of store, or to make friends with a schoolmate living near: of all that, it is the music lessons that I most regret. We shuttled back and forth between a bungalow in North Berwick, a flat in Dundas Street, a flat in North Berwick, a hotel in Great King Street, a flat in Abercromby Place, a house in Albert Terrace, a bungalow in Greenbank, and holidays, without having our own things around us. All that was brought out of store was, eventually, my Meccano. At last we had our newbuilt home, comfortably modern with half an acre. A few months later the war broke out, with black-outs and family confinement to the small 'study' to save curtaining-off and heating the 'public rooms'. All this was a psychological gap in development, and created a subliminal desire to have a home all of which was mine, which a wandering life was to postpone.

Meanwhile Upper IIA under 'Sweaty', never Tony to us, Munro proved a stress-free introduction to Edinburgh Academy: he was a patient teacher of French and Latin, and died at 92 at the time of first processing these words. Another new boy was son of the Rector of Dollar Academy who had come to rule over Daniel Stewart's College; we used to walk home together, braving Stinky Lane (Silvermills, now much changed) where rude keelie girls would ask us if they could look for eggs under our corps kilts. Archie became Town Clerk of Perth and Chief Executive of Tayside Regional Council. One old boy was to become boss of *The Famous Grouse*; another a maltster in undoubted support. The whole school did 10 minutes of open-air PT, lined up in our 'divisions' in the school yards under 'The Bud', the gym master, every day at mid-morning break, unless it rained hard; the ephors (= prefects), and boys in the Sevenths (our VII was everyone else's VI form) sauntering among us to quell slacking. The pot-stand and round ruler made in Woodwork were in use until very recently; the water-colours produced under 'Doddy', the one-handed Drawing Master, have fortunately not been conserved.

The Rector was Lionel Smith. He had been tutor to the Prince of Wales while a don at Magdalen (hence his MVO), had been director of education in Mesopotamia after the Great War where he had been a soldier, had Blues, wore a filthy pink Leander rowing scarf and could beat anyone at squash. He had turned down the headship of Eton. His 'Agh! Agh!' with concomitant gestures of not quite snapping fingers over his shoulder were easy to mimic. Like Temple, he contrived to take a class irregularly in every form, whether Scripture, reading, or some off-the-cuff subject. He was much loved. The

Jannie was a redoubtably stolid, stentorian and sternly tolerant Serjeant-Major, with a tailcoat, bright buttons and a top hat, who rang the bells, kept order in the yards, and must have done much we never knew.

1936, the point where the sheep and goats were divided into Classics, Modern and Stinks, saw a jump to IVth Classical. Bagwash, or 'The Bag', more rarely 'Atty', Atkinson, was form master, a redoubtable cricketer and general sportsman without despising the unathletic, and although a terror with the tawse (Edinburgh Academy did not speak of 'The Belt'), and a caustic tongue, was recognized as not really meaning it. Latin involved little blue books of Caesar and Virgil, whose illustrations of naked statues were best folded over in case of sniggers. Scripture meant alternate weeks learning a passage or a psalm on Sunday nights, for written repetition in first class on Monday morning, or reading a chapter of a gospel and facing oral questions. The Bag took a mark off me for spelling Nathaniel Nathanael, but never restored it when I produced my bible with my version as printed evidence. O, *so* unfair. French meant Captain Scott, 'Scabby', who overcame even the most inbred British inability to pronounce the French 'u' by giving a stinging palm to all who did not audibly *try* not to say 'oo'. I began to be friendly with another six-footer, despite his intimidating prowess at the more manly matters of boyhood; to be very aware of the only boy in long trousers (another did sport plus-fours) who would stand on a bench at breaks to deliver cod lectures about bogus subjects; and to be jealous of another swot who sometimes got better marks. George became a distinguished headmaster of a boarding prep school, Basil a curator of the portrait gallery and head of extra-mural studies in Edinburgh; John lost faith in trendy Anglicanism and ended as an Orthodox Archimandrite. We thought we knew all about Mussolini and Abyssinia, but didn't understand why Franco had started a civil war. We heard what our parents had to say about King Edward and 'Cutie', as the American (*foreign*) Mrs Simpson seemed to be known, before the Bishop of Bradford blew the gaff: foreign newspapers were not as unknown to the literate as the self-censoring home press pretended. Even to have seen George V once, a few yards away, quite apart from his Christmas wireless broadcasts, made it easy for any youngster to feel let down by a Prince of Wales believed to have had noble attitudes. It was no surprise one evening to see a ready-prepared supplement to the newsreel in the St Andrew Square Cinema (now a bus station) head-titled, 'Long Live King Albert & Queen Elizabeth.' (The Duke of York did not decide to be George VI until after the abdication was signed).

1937 brought intimations of adolescence. First ever long trousers in the winter term (George, Archie, two others and I had all been six-footers in shorts, and thought it perfectly normal); full uniform in the OTC First Year (one might be bolder on Fridays, as it was not done to tawse The King's khaki), and years to come of blanco and brasso on Thursday nights to face

Everyone paraded Princes Street on Saturday mornings.

inspection on parade after classes (anything dirty had to be shown cleaned at the Corps Office on Monday morning); not least, a creepy awareness of new words that must not be used aloud in public, despite uncertainty of what they meant. The form master was Billy Peel, gassed in the war, proven by his brave concealment of the misery of wheezing. He would end the week with an impromptu quiz: correct answers would move you above those with the wrong ones, so that your desk in class next week would depend on prowess in general knowledge at Friday's end. He would throw odd queries to disconcert his class, with the promise of a 'bun' for the successful answerer – the bun being a penny for the tuckshop, where it could buy a Milky Way with a picture card inside to celebrate the Coronation (these, rarely purchased with a 'bun', added to the cigarette card collection which had been growing ever since my father had been nagged into smoking Kensitas for the silk flags, later woven flowers, that had captivated me in Glasgow). The walls of his classroom were covered with aged prints of classical subjects, none of which were ever explained; double doors into the school hall gave us a minute or two's advantage over others at not being late for prayers (when living at North Berwick the train arrived at Waverley just in time to let me be permanently excused for lateness).

We sat School Certificate, the 'Oxford & Cambridge'. Credits ('Distinctions' had yet to be invented) in English, French, Latin, Greek, History, Mathematics

& *Additional* Mathematics reflected broad teaching in a practical school; but it was never clear that, while recognizing that the shape of questions on differential calculus made the formula towards the right answer easy to detect, I had any understanding of what this business of small differences was about. My strange success in statics, dynamics and the descendants of Napier's bones was to the credit of 'Beanie' Read, who had been shell-shocked; he gave worse than shell-shock to any boy who, banging a desk lid or dropping a book, made his nerves twitch. The history credit was due to Eddie Mullens, who would tend to my sliced thumb at Tomich. Eddie was one of the best of a superb variety of dominies: this year he took us through the French Revolution in a way that brought the tennis court and the flight from Versailles to vivid life, as convincingly as any Dickens or Orczy. That he always took particular interest in one boy a year was not at the cost of what he gave to all. I know several of those boys, and none came to any psychological or other harm, indeed all reached distinction in life. None of those he taught had anything but love and regard for him.

Second year Greek in Vth Classical lifted me above *Adventure* and *The Modern Boy* for leisure, but I remained sufficiently Meccano-indoctrinated to seek practical solace in the *Meccano Magazine* itself, in the cut-away diagrams and science fiction of *Modern Wonder* and in the realities of *Weekly Illustrated*, a precursor of *Picture Post*. I felt I was keeping my mind broad and grown-up with *Armchair Science*, a pocket monthly which left pocket money short (that encouraged walking home to save the tram fare after we came back from North Berwick to Churchhill). By this time my warmest friendship had focused on the middle son of a surgeon living at the opposite side of the town. David was to be wounded in minesweepers and rather later a professor of neurology and dean at Newcastle; his younger brother Geoffrey won a Fulbright, was ordained a Presbyterian minister who went to live among the poor of the Gorbals, and became Labour's first convenor of Strathclyde Regional Council. Others I had amiable relations with were Malcolm (son of Scotland's Chief Medical Officer), one day to adorn the Cabinet Office as an expert on Eastern Europe, and Jim (son of an eminent professor of history) who would be a mandarin in the Department of Employment. A smaller boy lived along the road whose father Ben (Ebenezer) was City Architect and a dear sparring partner of my father – mine wanted to pull the Royal Mile down as a revolting unhealthy slum, his wanted to restore it as a historical relic of vernacular architecture. I started a diary at this time, but when my mother seized it and read a description of her heated exchange with my father over something ending with a march out of the house, I vowed ever afterwards to rely on memory. Not a good basis for memoirs.

In a class essay I concocted an imaginative tale about finding family records in a trunk. This seemed to impress the master who marked it and I was told to rewrite it for the school *Chronicle*. Some goblin hexed me into giving some of the characters involved the names of classmates, with characteristics into the bargain. I was bidden to rewrite it 'without personal references', but without any implication beyond that: it was published without acclaim. There had been ructions behind the scenes of which I remained ignorant until the term report arrived with the Rector's comment that I showed 'signs of a perverted sense of humour.' It fizzled out, although I had little doubt that, when it came to appointing or nominating for election as school ephors, it was not only my uselessness at Games that left my name off the list. My father (I hope) realized that one thing he unquestionably and irremediably bequeathed to me was a tendency to pull legs, and to regard the great with less than total respect.

1938 meant VIth Classical under 'Cod' Rowe. It also meant Munich. Cod was a fine scholar, fierce because inherently shy, but keen to share his passion for Greek temples with not always receptive adolescents. As the hormones began to buzz through the bloodstreams in front of him, there would be communal fits of giggles at classical *doubles entendres*. These were not always assuaged by his comment that, 'laughter is a form of fear.' His greatest praise was, 'Not at all too half bad.' He introduced us to the practice of 'quoting' precedents, or similar constructions or references, as a means of sharpening memory and understanding, a technique which exposed my weakness in remembering in detail what I had not got by heart. I could remember the broad sweep; yet if I could not make all the connexions, I had at the time a partial photographic memory of a passage on the page, sometimes based on shape, which could be valuable in examinations of fact rather than thought.

The school had its first air raid rehearsals, down into the cellars. I passed my Certificate A in the OTC, without which no promotion would come. It brought a red star for my mother to sew on my upper right tunic sleeve. I also earned my first class shot's badge (for the lower sleeve) with the ·22 rifles in the range under the gym; for the first time the corps parade on Armistice Day outside the gym (our war memorial) seemed to have some meaning. It was Scottish Leaving Certificate year, an exam taken only two terms after the School Certificate (so I answered the Shakespeare questions from what I remembered from Mullens's *Dream* the year before rather than from the current set book *Lear* which Mr Quick had expounded to us in his high-pitched English drawl). Five Highers was a decent score. I began to play squash, always with boys not noticeable for their prowess at games, and now and then won a game or two.

The shades were closing. Abyssinia might be forgotten, but Nanking, Sudetenland, Bohemia & Moravia, Albania, successive quittings from the ineffective League of Nations, left little doubt what we were in for. My father went, on what would now be called a freebie swan, with councillors and officials to look at housing in another historic city, Prague, just after the Nazi take-over;

he and Ebenezer MacRae almost precipitated a fresh crisis by responding to one outstretched arm's greeting of 'Heil Hitler!' with a left-handed 'Heil McGonagall!' The foresight did not dissuade my parents from a holiday, their first overseas since Belgium a decade before, to St Brieuc in Brittany. This involved my first visit to London, an adventure few Scots boys enjoyed before the war, Tower of London, British Museum and all, material for an essay illustrated with cigarette cards as the 'holiday task'. France was memorable because I had my first beer, because as well as the Eiffel Tower we saw an amazing Gaumont newsreel which expanded to the size of a VistaVision screen of the undreamt future, and because the skimpiness of the messieurs' swimming briefs on the Breton beach was unbelievable. More memorable still was my father's realization from reading the papers that if we did not cut the holiday short we might not get home at all. The train to Paris was packed tighter than any troop train I was ever to share, with a refugee from central Europe arguing fiercely with an elderly-seeming *poilu* about the chances of negotiating a settlement. We arrived home on 1 September. Two days later I was in my father's Public Health Chambers, listening to a cheerless Chamberlain telling us that we were at war.

The first year in VIIth Classical saw a shrunken school: boys were whisked away to places less likely to be bombed, and the younger masters began to join the forces. Food rationing began; petrol rationing meant my father could not use his duty allocation to drop me at school; the tuckshop had little more to offer than buns; I began to take school lunches instead of sandwiches (they might enlarge Minister of Food Woolton's approved diet); clothes rationing began to bite, so shorts grew shorter as boys grew taller, annual replacement having become impossible (leading, like RAF tropical uniform styles, to long-term effects on fashion); the rite of passage to longs was further postponed (until the 1960s fetish for American blue jeans almost abolished shorts); an ignorant English official classed kilts with trousers at eight coupons, not knowing how many more yards they required (next year they went up to a still modest 16). Part of the playing fields at New Field was dug up, and boys excused games planted, weeded and scrabbled up potatoes with graips, under Cod's watchful eye. In winter the trek home by bike or tram was ill-lit under black-out. The remaining masters never gave up. The Rector took us in Homer, a helter-skelter race through the *Odyssey*, translating on the hoof without pausing over dreary German editors' cruces. The JTC (schools' officer training corps were now only junior training corps) was admitted unto the Local Defence Volunteers soon after Churchill invented them, to support home defence when invasion seemed likely, but only boys aged 16 or upwards, with parents' permission. I joined the LDV, which simply had a khaki armband bearing those letters worn on the JTC tunic sleeve; by chance our part of Edinburgh's perimeter was a drystane farm wall a few yards south of our home, so my mother provided wartime refreshments to the contingent whenever we were exercised.

Eddie founded a Play-Reading Society. Members took turns to choose a play, organize borrowing from public libraries, and cast among themselves. They met at a master's house or at a member's (whose mamma would eke out refreshments). J S Browne, a jollily unpompous English teacher with hair-raising tales of the psychological sophistication of Westminster schoolboys compared with ourselves, presided over some play-reading and gramophone evenings before joining the army. He had most of the Savoy operas on shellac; we got to know *Ruddigore* and *Princess Ida* despite the D'Oyly Carte having dropped them from their wartime repertoire. The school choir at last gained a recruit in this writer, having been guaranteed that this time *Trial by Jury* would not demand his solitary contribution. The performance would not be staged; there was a war on. War had not stopped the Carl Rosa from touring gallantly. A fellow's hint that Rossini's *Barber of Seville* was as good as a Savoy Opera led me to the King's Theatre, where I also saw from the gods *Butterfly* (an hour of tonal hints that *One Fine Day* was about to come, then it came, then half-an-hour of wanting it back), *Bohème* (Joan Hammond large in life, and Norman Allin as Colline jumping up on the iron bedstead, only to have it collapse under him), Gwen Catley in a sack in *Rigoletto*, and *Faust* (with the elderly wartime soldiers' chorus of ten tottering round the stage). The Christmas season at the Royal Lyceum was *Blossom Time*, with Richard Tauber as Schubert; the great trouper had a streaming cold but did not cancel, and sitting in the front row of the stalls I looked straight up at his very red nose and into his tonsils, in wonder that a world star was here in Edinburgh. I have endowed a seat in his memory.

Clever youngsters were not held back at the Academy in those days – it was practicable for a clever fifteen- or sixteen-year-old to get a bursary to St Andrews and still be young enough, after a first degree there, to be eligible for, and with the advantage of premature sophistication to win, a scholarship to Oxbridge. The 1939-40 boys in the third year of Classical VIIth were an outstanding lot: Michael was small of stature but great of heart, an all-rounder seldom met outside early Wodehouse – certain to be dux and win a scholarship, captain of rugby as electric scrum-half, vice-captain of cricket, head ephor, CSM of the OTC, tolerant and popular, ready to turn a hand to anything, and a rock for the Rector to lean on, doomed to die in Normandy in the Recce Corps; Harry was almost as clever, his equal at 'quoting' though less athletic, pointed in humour under a mask of retiring dourness – destined to become a Scots Guardsman and ultimately a Lord of Appeal in Ordinary, conspicuous in the Judicial Committee of the Privy Council; Colin was less bright intellectually, but brighter socially and in commentary on the passing show – doomed to die in the next chapter. The second year included Ian, known in and out of his family as 'Piglet' (from Pooh), whose fate was to be London City Editor of the *Birmingham Post*; and Jim, in many ways my closest friend in the VIIths, who would be a gunner up through Italy, then back to an unpeaceful and non-classical Greece, but achieve the strange feat of being a Scottish professor of French at a university in French-Canadian Montréal. On the Stinks side was Charles, a brilliant future professor and president of Edinburgh's Royal Society.

Most of these came on a school visit organized by Eddie to Stratford to see *Measure for Measure* and *The Merry Wives*. The modern theatre astonished us, and some of the small parts were taken by names that would one day mean something. We visited pubs discreetly for half-pints, took a train to Henley-in-Arden to walk 14 miles back through woods, and paddled skiffs and canoes on the Avon. Billy (one day to manage Cleghorn's up-market sports shop and be taken over by Lillywhite's) jumped into my canoe and turned us over, but we failed to drown.

The same boys were in the larger group, led by Eddie, which set up a first month-long forestry camp at Tomich village school, by Glen Affric. There, mentioned in the previous chapter, we assisted the war effort by cutting pit props and scything or burning carcinogenic bracken in the fir nurseries, while the Battle of Britain stoked up down south. My local Edinburgh policeman was on holiday at Cannich; he invited me to tea and took me and my father's rod out for an unsuccessful few casts into the local burn. Our one-armed art master helped the camp out, using up all the hot water and eating all the biscuits. This camp strengthened bonds with contemporaries in the un-classical branches of the VIIths: Jimmie, whose brother was already a POW after St Valéry, was himself to be wounded in the Western Desert in the Black Watch but survive to achieve secretaryship of the United Africa Company, directorship of Unilever, membership of the Monopolies & Mergers Commission, and heaven knows what else; Ian, London Scottish intelligence officer in Burma where we met again in Rangoon, and subsequently poet and head of English at Ampleforth; David, G&S tenor, naval officer, meteorologist and scientist, Strathclyde professor in management of technological innovation, and keeper of the flame of Scotland's and the Academy's greatest son, James Clerk Maxwell; Graham, a puzzle at the time, but in retrospect guaranteed to be a great character actor; Arthur, who was to leave early for the Indian Army and go into tea-planting in the East Indies; I must stop dropping given names.

Having been given a lance-corporal's stripe that year, I began the next as a serjeant, which surprised others even more than myself. I supposed that Mullens, who ran the corps, felt sorry that I had no distinctions apart from academic prizes. I joined the new air section of the corps, a precursor of the ATC, reinforcing the schoolboy craze for aircraft-spotting (identifying a rare Westland *Whirlwind*, said to fly at 360 *mph* 'on the level', was thrilling). This got us out to RAF Turnhouse where 603 Squadron had shot down one of the first planes of the war near the Forth Bridge. Whenever the sinking of a naval or merchant ship was announced, I drew a picture of it with coloured pencils in an exercise book (long disappeared): the Ministry of Information soon stopped helping the enemy by naming vessels lost.

Looking forward, and to my wish to be a doctor, misconstrued as 'supposing that I would have to do what my father did', I did an hour's Extra Science twice a week. To prepare for Oxford scholarship exams I was given texts to read on my own during free periods, but never given guidance on what I should get from them, and never tested at all. When the time came, Alfie suggested I try for a demyship at Magdalen, his old college, and at the *viva* I found myself speechless to explain why I preferred Horace to Virgil: I had never justified anything like that in oral discussion, and had no confidence in my capacity for public argument. I knew how to learn and how to feel, even how to direct, but not to take charge of group thought.

It was no surprise that the college wrote to say that my standard was not high enough to admit me as a commoner. The Rector pulled old rank and they agreed to let me take a face-saving token re-examination. My parents meanwhile decided it was time for me to be confirmed: but in which denomination? My Presbyterian father had been refused communion before a Great War naval action by a CofE padre, so when my mother went to early communion once a month he sat outside in the car reading the Sunday papers; I might sit beside her but not go up to the rails. Otherwise we went sporadically and alternately to the Presby and to the Pisky churches. The final choice of church for life was left to me. I concluded that the dour but righteous kirk services tended to depress me, but those with the set prayers which annoyed my father cheered me up, apart from imprinting words and ideas more clearly. I was instructed by a young priest at S Cuthbert's, a tiny satellite church in Fairmilehead, the Rev Penny, and confirmed as an Episcopalian by Bishop Warner.

There was a satisfying counterweight to the shame of the Oxford entry. I was promoted CQMS in the corps, but on the official inspection after the summer field day and exercises, the Kinross platoon which I commanded won the competition. The silver cup presented for this achievement was locked away in safety for the duration, so I was deprived of the pride of collecting it at the session's closing ceremony: instead, the agony of having to stand in a bran new cheviot suit with the dux medal round my neck while the chairman, the City Treasurer, representative of the Edinburgh Corporation which had bailed the school out with grant-in-aid while the war's deprivations made it insolvent, harangued me at excruciating Morningside length about having my name written in letters of gold. Fifty years on to the day I wore the same suit to give the Guest's address at the middle school prize-giving, which says something for endurance of pre-war quality.

Kinross Platoon dressed to kill.

We were off to camp again next day, three weeks' mostly torrential forestry at Tomich, where we were promoted to cutting trees down (adolescent cries of 'Timber!'), snedding them and clearing up the forest floor. I had a modest talent for the Savoy patter songs, delivered in a grotesque caricature of the D'Oyly Carte's wartime Graham Clifford; the school choir had given a concert performance of *Iolanthe* that summer (I had shied off trying for the Sentry's rôle when soloist Arthur left school early for the Indian Army, thus allowing George to become Head Ephor) – but as Lord Chancellor Ian was the only principal not to attend the camp and repeat the big numbers for a village concert, I at last sang in public, débuting in an appropriate Nightmare Song, accompanied by Jim on the school harmonium (despairing of my late entries).

Three weeks' much more boring harvesting followed at Balnagown at Kildary in Easter Ross, to which I cycled 50 miles on my very first Rudge-Whitworth (with its paper wrappings still protecting the paintwork), and where Cecil kept playing his clarinet (a good start for his future as head of BBC light entertainment). We slept in the top of an itchy granary formerly occupied by birds, with ropes for a hasty getaway should fire break out. Breakfast 6·45, work (mainly stooking, or tying hand-cut oats or unbound sheaves that the binder's knotting device had failed to tie) 7·30-11·30, dinner noon, work 1-6 with a piece and drink mid-afternoon, last meal 6·45, six days a week: if very wet overnight, start 9·30, end 7. The few volunteers for excitement of driving a tractor or tending the binder had longer hours for the same pay. One evening off was spent in Tain, where half a dozen hungry boys found nothing to eat on sale: yet a customer asked them to her home and fed strangers a high tea with meat and salad. Highland hospitality was not rationed (nor was another tradition: when they collected their bicycles, chained together, they found everything loose gone – tools, capes, lamps, books, tuck, even a pot of paste). There was one day off, when Jim took me to a gentleman farmer friend's home for tea, and schooldays were finally over.

Wartime Oxford was a shadow of what I had read in library efforts to learn about growing up. My father paid for my fees and keep. The college Vice-President, someone called C S Lewis, sent sage advice about not giving sons excessive allowances – not more than £300, agreeing that I ought to manage on £275. We Academicals travelled by overnight train, sending bicycle and box by 'Luggage in Advance'. Thereafter we usually went by overnight bus to save money. I was given rooms (study and bedroom tended by a morose but wise scout with a pinched long face, Mobey) 90 steps up in the attics of Magdalen's 18th century New Buildings, overlooking the deer park (if one climbed out to the roof to overlook the parapet). One saw much of another scout, Perkins, and the 'Boots' boy who cleaned shoes left in the corridor (in the black-out, he could not always see the mud to brush off). Most of the undergraduates along the corridor were medical students, 'reserved' from war service. I brought a potted plant to water, but had no wireless – the newspapers in the JCR kept the real war remote.

It is hard to describe how callow I felt among some of the English public schoolboys I met at table, tutorials and lectures. I had read some Aldous Huxley and failed to understand Eliot, but they seemed to have read them all with enlightened pleasure; I knew G&S, but they not only had their own gramophones but played Eileen Joyce's Shostakovitch; I drank rare halves of bitter in hall, but they knew all about audit ale and perry; I might have seen Tauber, whom they despised, but they talked of Pachmann and Solomon with apparent familiarity; they had developed their own dress taste, while I had never had anything beyond school outfits and Sunday best, chosen for me maternally; above all, they seemed possessed of superior wit in conversation and total assurance in tutorials. My two *bêtes noires* were an Etonian and a Rugbeian. 50 years later I smugly noted at gaudies that they had risen no higher on their ladders than I had on mine. I had yet to learn dissemblance, which their upbringing had taught them. Of course I soon found a circle of lifelong friends. Magdalen seemed by comparison with other colleges to have few narrow cliques, and fewer barriers between first year undergraduates and older years. Everyone was on speaking terms, until I knew about 90 of the 120 who were up by name. What now seems so unreal about both the modest provincials and the would-be Oscars and aristos was the extraordinary innocence of practically all: adulthood was still a pretence, and puberty a dangerous nuisance, best ignored because embarrassing, however much imagination might tinge day dreams.

I was reading Classical Honour Moderations in the school of Litterae Humaniores, a straight carry-on from school VIIths. Hardie and the other classical dons were away on war work, and our college tutor was a German refugee, Karl Otto Brink (after the war becoming Professor Carl Oscar Brink). The one-to-one tradition was impossible, and we gathered in threes or fours. His English was good but imperfect, and although Lewis & Short's standard Latin Dictionary's reviser, his ability to enthuse me in the deeper poetry, wisdom and vision clothed in the dead languages was limited. I had never been spoonfed into appreciating that there was more there than the crossword satisfaction of getting the grammars right and the metres and quantities correct. There lay my wartime deprivation in education: my parents approved of the classical tradition but could not assist me with it, and when the pedagogic leadership might have filled the gap, it was swamped or absent, pre-occupied with more important affairs.

I saw the President Gordon once, at my first 'Collections', the 'Don Rag' where tutors described us in terms that might now lead to suits of harassment. My work was, 'Good, but uninspiring and dull.' Gordon's successor was almost invisible, Sir Henry Tizard, away chairing an atomic bomb committee. I perversely joined the Liberal Club because its college rep was the only political canvasser who did not come round to recruit me. I went to one Liberal meeting, where Leslie Banks the actor addressed us; I asked him why the ending of the film *Cottage to Let* had been changed from the stage version. He did not know, and that was my last political act for nearly forty years. I joined the Ballet Club and the Film Society and discovered the pleasure of French films, which seemed to have been taken in real crumbling and smelly buildings instead of against squeaky clean Elstree or Hollywood sets; and also the attraction of actresses like Arletty playing sleazy ladies of indeterminate age. I tried to learn fencing, but the club had no foils or masks to lend.

The Dean of Divinity, Canon Adam Fox, sent me to a second year man who enlisted me as one of the servers at communion services. So began a lifetime's devotion to the Anglican collegiate and choral traditions; liturgical music always seemed a supreme way of expressing worship and belief, and dearly as I love to hear it on record, or in the concert hall with all orchestral and vocal batteries blazing, discomfort is present when treated like opera for agnostics or musicologists. In my years at Oxford, I must have attended more than 300 choral evensongs.

We were bound to join the Senior Training Corps if call-up were to be deferred until the end of the year in which we reached our 18th birthdays; as from school's Junior Training Corps, it was no longer a guaranteed path to a commission. An 'A' grade certificate B went straight to Octu, a 'B' had 6 weeks' pre-octu basic training first; a 'C' went into the ranks, to be called to fill any remaining vacancies after all As and Bs were taken; and a 'D' had no hope. Parades seemed endless, two or three a week; PT at 9 o'clock, others from 2 to 4·30, and occasional all-days 9·30-4·30. Battle-dress with leather gaiters was an uncomfortable change from the school kilt, but there were no buttons to polish or webbing to blanco. Exercises on sand tables or on Boar's Hill did not teach more of tactics and strategy than what had been instilled in the JTC, although grenades were something new; but reminded of what the papers now told us – the entry of Japan, occupation of Hong Kong and sinking of the *Prince of Wales* and *Repulse*, did not yet mark the end of the beginning. We paraded in Christ Church Meadows, and conspicuous figures became well enough known to the little bewhiskered and red-faced RSM for him to reward some nonconformist movement in drill by the field-gun bark, 'Round that tree, Mr X, AT THE DOUBLE!' X was often 'Mr Whalley!', one day to rejoin me in Bauchi, once 'Mr Wilson!', who would one day help to introduce me to the Hong Kong administration, and once or twice even 'Mr Clark!' I nevertheless qualified for Certificate B, grade 'A', though economy meant no yellow star to sew on our sleeve; as well, with no Mummies' needles and thread.

All were on fire-fighting and fire-watching rosters (quite distinct), four successive nights at a time from 11 *p.m.* to 7 *a.m.* We learnt at nights to sleep in the cold and draughts of Founder's Tower, and where to clamber over all the college roofs and other towers. During the long hot summer of 1942, lying on the lawn or on the roof sunbathing with our texts, we watched the RAF overhead. The diet was 'healthy', as war reminiscences remind us. We carried our meagre packages of butter, sugar and jam to breakfast, which tended to be pre-sweetened and burnt porridge (cornflakes on Sundays), followed by beans and fried bread, or bacon once a week. An occasional boiled egg replaced egg-powder concoctions. Lunch in college was thick soup with blobs of meat, to which mashed potatoes might be added; on Sundays a plain salad, boiled potatoes and two biscuits with national cheese. There was unlimited powdered milk in tins. Dinners are mainly memorable now for regular fusing of the table lamps.

All good things come to an end. I spent my last night up in Corpus, guest of Jim Whitelaw, Arthur Jacobs (musicologist in the making), Barry Evans (a gifted scholar who did no work and got a third) and others. It taught me not to mix drinks; after beer, cider, claret and possibly gin (the mixtures I remember) it would have been as physical an impossibility to climb back into Magdalen, as it has been a mental impossibility to forget how horrible was the illness of us all. Come daylight, we all went down, leaving instructions to the college porter to wire our results. Mine came when I had been in permanent uniform for a fortnight, a 'good second'. Not such a depressing description: the division into 'two-ones' and 'Desmonds' had yet to be introduced.

Four years after my alcoholic departure from Oxford, repatriating Africans from Rangoon, the college applied for my early release on the remarkable grounds of 'national interest and reconstruction', so that I might conclude my interrupted education. The Post Office franking marks of the time tell much – BRITAIN CAN MAKE IT EXHIBITION 1946; STAGGERED WORKDAYS FOR COMFORT; SAVE FOR THE SILVER LINING; SAVE YOUR WASTE PAPER FOR SALVAGE. Oxford in the autumn of 1946 was still not its traditional self – different from the reduced war years, yet not restored to gleaming spires, screaming choirs and steaming satires. Returned warriors who had been majors or greater, accustomed to saying, 'Come!' (and he blooming well cometh, *ek dum*) could not be treated *in statu pupillari* (which led to the frustrations of dons *in loco parentium* when managing schoolboys who had avoided the maturation of national service). To balance that, the returned possessors of campaign stars knew that if they did not work they would not get their degree, and most had learned to enjoy leisure responsibly and economically. Dons hinted that they were a pleasure to teach, not least those great Fellows who had used their brains and intellect in Whitehall or more esoteric back rooms. Our grants were a King's reward for having risked life and limb for Him and country, not (we thought) a bail-out for our fathers' successors' duty to see their progeny into the world intellectually equipped. We would qualify in a non-vocational subject, then decide what calling beckoned, and then begin to learn about that in the great world outside, and so make way for successors, except for the very few who might be admitted to the bocage and tenure of Ἀκαδημεια. Vocational training was limited to law and medicine.

That first winter was as cold as low-lying Oxford, squatting in a watery landscape, knew how to be. I had rooms in New Buildings again, over the poor deer freezing in their park, with a chilling trip down the stairs to almost underground ablutions (as ex-servicemen still knew them). To let in a good draught there was a fireplace, which had seen no coal for years and harboured a bird's nest. Each room had a double bar electric fire for warmth and toasting, but scout Ing had strict instructions to allow one dim bar to be switched on.

There would be no fires at all from 5 May till September. A stone hot water pig kept the bed warm (there was no electric plug in the bedroom). Those fresh from tropical service were grateful for the woollen long-johns they were allowed to retain from their military clothing. To-day's leisure and student fashions would not have had a hope. Officers' Van Heusen khaki poplin shirts abounded. The most common trousers were ex-battledress dyed chocolate, the only colour that subsumed khaki or airforce blue. For most of my two years I wore my Cameron Highlander kilt; at least a dozen 'young gentlemen' scattered around the colleges regularly wore the kilt in Oxford then without embarrassment, including the Ken Anderson from Glasgow. The old chef was back, and food was better cooked but no better in quality or quantity than during the war, still cold meat and grassy salad for Sunday lunch; but memories of ever living off the fat were hazy, although those returned from Africa or Asia had had ample novel diets.

The big question was, what should I read? I had chickened out of Greats. I had also, with sadness, concluded that it would take seven years to do medicine, and the thought of not being qualified or independent until 30 was unacceptable. Permanent mature studentship was not yet invented. What, I asked W J M (Bill) Mackenzie, the tutor who interviewed me, should I read that would be helpful in most directions once I could make up my mind what I ought to pursue in search of my daily bread? Nowadays I would have been asking for a 'soft option': he advised PPE (Philosophy, Politics & Economics). So the die was cast.

Mackenzie later professed Government at Manchester and Glasgow, as well as being involved in colonial constitution-making, and is one of my greater men (and an Edinburgh Accie). He tutored me in Political Institutions. For Philosophy I was allocated to T D W (Harry) Weldon, like Mackenzie fresh from Whitehall wearing airforce blue, a philosopher of world repute. My Economics mentor was G D N (David) Worswick, younger and more diffident in manner than those two, whose views would be influential in the days of national planning; and Burchardt oversaw my Economic Principles. The college, indeed most of the university, was returning to individual tutorials: one of the wonders of Oxbridge, apart from what exuded from ancient stones and habits, was that ordinary youngsters spent hours in the company, as well as under the tutelage, of great people. Since more came to mean worse, most of that has been lost.

One oddity was that although during the war one had hankered for the chiming of the bells, silenced except to warn of invasion, now they proved a quarter-hourly distraction, not least when finishing an essay or text at two in the morning. I had decided to build on my tropical experience and to take Colonial Government and Colonial Economics as optional subjects. The first brought me into the orbit of Margery Perham, the redoubtable lady who had

Much work but some play: punting up the Cherwell.

sparred with Elspeth Huxley about Kenya's settler politics and who knew everything about Lord Lugard (with whom gossip said she had been in love, a rival to Flora Shaw, Lady Lugard, the *Times* colonial correspondent who had coined the name of Nigeria). The second led me later to write essays for Peter Ady, a charming half-Burmese lady don who came into tutorials at the Institute of Economic Studies in riding breeches, still slapping her switch against her thighs, and to seminars with S Herbert Frankel.

This began to seem more part of my real world than Corn Laws or the constitution of the London County Council, Kant and backward-sloping demand curves. My mind recognized an affinity with Africa beyond fond memories of African Other Ranks in the RWAFF, some of whom were writing me letters that gave nary a hint of cadging. I sat at one series of lectures next to a Sierra Leonean called Luke, who spoke of administration as his work and colonial officers as his colleagues. After having a long talk with Colonel Drummond, the supervisor of the Oxford Colonial Service (Devonshire) Course, I applied for the Colonial Administrative Service, and had a hard time from my mother ever thereafter (having been away for over three-and-a-half years, I owed the rest of my life to her; otherwise, my parents would feel that they had never had a son at all, not that my father ever spoke in such terms, thinking as he did of fledglings and nests).

Clubs and societies did not have the appeal of 1941, and whereas the terror of public speaking had kept me from the Union then, now it was the callowness of amateur politicians that put me off. There were ample rewards in study, incompetent barefoot squash (gym shoes being unobtainable), cycling around the county (I was on two interminable waiting lists for a Sturmey-Archer 3-speed gear, and a lighting dynamo), the University Gramophone Library and social exchanges (usually tea and toast, alcohol being expensive). A teenager (a neologism not yet invented) called Peter Brook asked me to tea once. Having spent a small fortune on a windy-windy portable gramophone, I was going through a phase of record-borrowing and happened to say that I could listen to Chopin all day and all night. The future guru of world theatre thought that mightn't be good for me, and although I have never met him since, I haven't felt the same about Chopin again. Other acquaintanceships were warmer and lasting: John, who would head schools for children with problems; Reg, who would be an English don at Liverpool; Michael, who would abandon diplomacy to end as Provost of Sheffield Cathedral; Andrew, who would escape the Treasury and stiffen the Scottish Office; Dai, destined to become poet and Master of Emmanuel College (Cambridge needs Oxford blood from time to time, like C S Lewis). One of Magdalen's curiosities was that the historian A J P Taylor had a tame poet living in his gardener's shed; he turned out later to be called Dylan Thomas. We saw a little more of our new President, T S R Boase, than of Tizard; he was a gentle art historian and wasn't needed for extra-collegiate activities of state.

To insure against accidents, I took a 'section' (a paper on Political History, to qualify after four terms for an unclassified 'war degree', thus wearing a BA gown made from wartime blackout material and frustrating the proctors). My parents could not attend the 'graduation', and took it out on me by sending a 'stunned' letter of disapproval on hearing that I had been summoned for interview in London at the Colonial Office. This was the occasion of my second letter of exculpation (excusing my medical cheat was the first), the arguments of which follow.

I thanked them for the advice. They had upset me, it not being nice to go for interviews knowing that of the people you loved best one was discouraging and the other opposing you. These were only preliminary assessments. It was better to know one way or the other. It was my future that was uncertain. There was no surety that they would take me.

I was fit enough: I could compare myself with others under far greater stress in the army than I was likely to undergo again. I had nothing to fear. It was a job I believed could give pride and satisfaction. This was not a temporary enthusiasm: I had been thinking it over for a year now; I might have dabbled in 'hobbies' in the past – now there was something my interest could remain alive in, permanently. I would not commit myself until finally accepted or not. If accepted, they would almost certainly offer me the 15 month university course – if I said, 'yes', I could take a shortened honours degree, which would mean solid hard work throughout the summer vac. If I got as far as the final board, I would get advice on the value of degrees: if it were a temporary job, one would have to consider maximum paper qualifications (all they were) for a permanent billet; but that was not it. It was a job that required personal qualities, not paper backing. None of this explained why I wanted the job.

That was the hardest, because it was something they had not experienced, and if I got sympathy without understanding I should do well. I had been thinking, if the Colonial Service would not have me, of finding a job in the anthropological line: I could take a diploma after the PPE degree. I was interested in people (one day I would become leery of that corny protestation!), particularly people different from our own; partly why I eventually liked the Waff so much, and wanted to work with Africans. I had no crazy notions about devoted black men kow-towing, but I did want to deal with reality and vital people. They needed guides with sympathy, or when they left us, they would do it just as disgruntled Indians were departing now. If that sounded idealist, I wanted it to sound practical. I wanted to do something active at first: time to get stick-in-the-mud, chairborne and static when I was older (which would certainly come). If this made no sense, they should admit that I was *not* hysterical or bull-headed; but soberly believed that everything pointed in this direction. This feeling that they no longer had a son was my one real worry, and had been since I came home. I could not safely go on worrying much longer. I left it at that, and wondered for the first time for long enough about Anxiety States.

I record this at length, since it got it off the chest and out of the way, but its resonances rang quietly behind scenes yet to come. So I went through two sets of interview: the first was a couple of face-to-faces with serving officers. Number one was an ex-Indian Education service major, claiming to know nothing about west Africa, the old trick to find out what I thought I knew about it, discussing 'post-war Oxford', the African in the army, and my old Rector Smith whom he had known in Mespot after the first war. After queuing at Lyons for a lunch, the second quizzer was one Vickers, the epitome of the confident and competent Civil Servant, everything at finger-tips. He was human, neither over-powering nor unprepared to listen to another side. He said that about one in ten of those going to the final board were being taken; recruitment had been fast, and next year what with fewer vacancies and more ex-service applicants, the chances would be more like one in twenty. They had virtually stopped sending people out without doing the Devonshire course. Postponed application or acceptance of an offer would mean starting the whole process from scratch. His advice was to avoid smaller future chances of success (and loss of seniority), since a paper qualification, shortened or not, was only of value in getting a first job; the knowledge, academic or theoretical, that one might acquire was in any case less valuable than the training to think and to criticize; and one would get that through further residence and work, irrespective of degrees. Promotion would depend on what one had subsequently done. If ever looking for something else, one's qualification would then be x years' colonial administration, not the class or length of one's degree before those x years. After chat about army experience and medical categories, and more about the Post-War Undergraduate, and what did I do with myself and why did I want to join anyway, I had a go at him.

I said that the only people who showed any enthusiasm about the service were those who were actually connected with it. I was tired of the suggestion that it was something nobody worthwhile went into, and although I was satisfied that it was worthwhile, I should be pleased to hear his impartial opinion on whether it was a dead-end, and full of nonentities or people of licence, brawn and no ability. He admitted that he had begun as a colonial cadet, but was now an in-between, a Temporary Principal in the CO, uncertain of his own future. He would never advise anyone to enter who was looking forward to a comfortable life settled in one place, with a large salary and big pension guaranteed at the end of it. It was no job for someone keen on security, but for someone with ideas and initiative, a desire to do something practical and with an aim, in other words building up a country to a level where it could look after itself, and all the things which sounded priggish and airily idealistic, but were genuine, it offered a great deal and, at the least, reasonable prospects. He reinforced my prejudices rather than told me anything new. There followed a high-pressure personal grilling by Ralph Furse, the Director of Recruitment ('Aucuparius') in this same dreary and dirty building in London's Victoria Street, of which surprisingly I remember very little.

The board itself was, despite Vickers's forecast of nine in ten failures at that level, subsequently said to be a formality, since what Furse said, went. One was taken before a full table of distinguished-looking but anonymous gentry in Whitehall's Dover House. The individual interviews had covered everything I embrace in conducting such exchanges myself. I emerged from the final board drained but hoping to have seemed adequate. They had asked me the stereotyped things – did I have any views about serving under native superiors? 'I don't suppose they would have put one above me, if they didn't think he was fit and proper to be in charge.' – 'Ah! But suppose *you* didn't think he was?' – 'Well, I would have signed on, wouldn't I? I would have to get on with it.' – 'How would you feel if posted somewhere with no other white people around you?' – 'I have spent long periods with nobody else but my African platoon around me, and been very comfortable; I have shared a slit-trench with my orderly under fire more than once.' They seemed satisfied, although they didn't say so, I went round to see Dr Hawes as already told, and a few weeks later I received an offer of appointment. In the light of Vickers's advice (and still thinking that one day a degree might be invaluable) I asked specifically to be sent on the Devonshire Colonial Cadet Training Course at Oxford, which would allow me to carry on with a (shortened) proper Honours degree course. This was granted.

It meant pressure. Interrupting studies, Trinity term offered cycle trips to Blenheim with Michael (walking home with flat tyres), and to Burford with John. A last minute standing-up by a female guest (of whom I have not the smallest recollection) meant that I could concentrate on being just a committee member of Magdalen's Commemoration Ball, the first such lavish post-war event 'while the country starved'. In the long vacation there was a walk with friends up the Wye valley to Brecnoc. I stayed up an extra four weeks in college for extra economics tutoring with Miss Ady, having enjoyed a late spring and summer with the fritillaries in Addison's Walk and the gorgeous scent of the wistaria coating the façade of New Buildings. In Michaelmas Term 1947 I began the Devonshire course, which included full-time lectures every morning, while also concentrating on the lectures, tutorials, thrice-weekly seminars and studies necessary to prepare for Final Schools. The choice of Colonial Politics and Economics as special subjects lubricated the friction, but it was tough. Schools took place in the seventh week of term, not after the eighth as I had hoped, looking for extra time. A rather perfunctory *viva* followed at the beginning of the year.

So I was far from ashamed to receive a hand-written letter later in the vacation from David Worswick to say that I had earned a Second, 'a very creditable result, considering how little time you have had.' I was disappointed that Margery Perham had given me a $\beta+$ for Colonial Government, which I had felt (over-)confident about, but amazed and delighted that Herbert Frankel gave me an $\alpha =$ for Colonial Economics.

Seven years since matriculation, ten pounds and a capping *in nomine patris et filii et spiritus sancti* on 29 April (which the parents attended) earned the right to wear the MA gown, not made from blackout material. The rest of that year was relaxed, going to colonial lectures and what is now called socializing with my new group of friends on the Devonshire, many assigned to other colleges, as well as with my old Mods and PPE acquaintance. It is curious to think now of the co-ævals who became university celebrities at the time, nearly all in Union politics, Boyle, Benn, and others of whom chance or different interests briefly threw me in the way. I was still uncertain in the company of the unashamedly thrusting or omniscient. While remaining unenvious, I thought that my abilities, arising as they did from Meccano, from curiosity about how nature, rather than 'society,' worked, from the very practical demands made by enforced leadership in a war overseas among strange cultures, and from a middle class Scottish upbringing among professional people, must suit me better for the career that lay before me than for the lives in home civil, foreign, academic or teaching services that so many of my fellows sought. They also perhaps accounted for my knowledge of arts and culture, despite Homer and Euripides, Horace and Tacitus, and indeed maternal genes, being still superficial outside recorded music.

This made little difference to enjoyment of lectures at Rhodes House, and experience of Schools stood me in good stead compared with ex-service colleagues who had not been to university. Having three major Devonshire exams out of the way (in October I was told I had had the top equal marks), I could concentrate on the law at which I was now aiming as a back-up subject for the future. Professor Ida Ward tested the prospective West Coasters in their capacity to master tonal languages (some were deliberately incompetent in case they ended up in Igboland). At my final President's Collections Bill Mackenzie said that Mr Clark had entered the Colonial Service, for which he thought me well suited: and even from those friendly lips it still sounded as though I was not top drawer.

I went down with regret that Oxford years were over: the civilizing influence of ancient buildings, high intelligence and devotion among dons, and indefinable traditions, are more influential in giving one roots and moulding a balanced view of life, than the featureless hostels, superior portakabins, and shaky moorings of many post-redbrick institutions, which students who see university as some kind of vocational training imagine as giving them a classless vision of a better world. My last packet of cake, sugar and oranges from home was given to my old scout Mobey, for his wife and two small boys. We had had a momentary introduction to life elsewhere during the Hilary term of 1948, when three days were spent looking at the Metropolitan Police and Bow Street Magistrates' Court, followed by two weeks in London's County Council offices. During the summer vacation we were sent all over the country to study local government in action, so I found myself attached for four weeks to Midlothian County Council, and also to Edinburgh Corporation, where my father being MOH opened a few more doors to my colleagues than officialdom had prepared. We viewed everything, from a sanitary inspector proving the efficiency of a septic tank in the country by drinking the water that flowed out of it, to a station police serjeant demonstrating the tiny size of the birch kept for juvenile delinquents.

The most vivid memory is of the education committee interviewing several distinguished dominies for the rectorship of the Royal High School. We went down a mine and were shown the gleaming new pithead baths, where the manager, conscious of our presumed middle class susceptibilities and shyness if faced with native worth and virtue, assured us that the miners wrapped a modest towel round their middles when they went from tub or shower to the clothes lockers.

The final term of the course was spent between the London School of Economics and the School of Oriental & African Studies, specializing in regional work, the geography, anthropology, language and economic history of the territory to which we had now been assigned. Trades unions, co-operatives and penal systems loomed large and liberally. I had stated my preference for the Nigeria I only just knew, and the North thereof of whose *lingua franca* Hausa I had learnt the basics from a Yoruba army schoolmaster in Rangoon (Margery Perham was disappointed – she still thought of the North as feudal, backward, and no place for a man with progressive ideas). I was granted my choice and invited my SOAS 'mallam' (a future emir of Yawuri, Tukur) to listen to my 78s of rude Hausa army songs which the military welfare folk had recorded at Dum Dum at the end of the war. I stayed at a Colonial Office students' hostel, sharing a room with a British Guianan lawyer-to-be.

Most of the course was restive and wanted to get away to start the great work: much time was given to a lengthy petition proving that the allowances from the Colonial Office were insufficient to live on (those already married pointed out how they could not afford scrag-end in their meat ration). Star lecturers also appeared, including the TUC's general secretary, George Woodcock, the Chief Scout of the Empire, Lord Rowallan, and Nigeria's Chief Secretary, Hugh Mackintosh Foot, who demonstrated on a blackboard how one co-ordinated the administration of bodies of differing sizes and importance with a series of overlapping balloons: he was not wholly convincing.

London University seemed second-rate to Oxford eyes, not only because the city was noisy, crowded and filthy, and the buildings nondescript where not ugly: in what seemed a slide backwards to school days, we had to sign lists showing attendance at lectures (Oxford did not care if one never attended any). This snobbery led me to wonder whether I might not sign up after all for an external London diploma in anthropology. The idea was, of course, to have another paper to wave if the colonial service and I should part company. Instead the already incipient idea grew of reading for the (English) bar, which so many colonial subjects seemed to take in prolonged strides; Part I could be taken in five papers, one at a time. In naïve ignorance I imagined that there would be much lonely spare time during long Nigerian nights beside the hissing Tilley lamp, making it pleasant to polish little grey cells which must otherwise tarnish for lack of intellectual stimulation in Primitive Bush among Simple People. Brash novices think like that. I put down £100 and became a student of the

Middle Temple, confident that what I had already learnt at Oxford of Criminal Law and Evidence would speed me on my way.

A reunion of 81 West African Division proved how nice it was to find old army friends to be just as good mates in civvy street: we had as guest of honour Field Marshal Bill Slim. London in 1948 was not yet much brighter than in the dreary, rationed wartime years: pubs were shabby, pockets were far from full, tubes and buses crowded and dirty; there was every incentive to want to be out of it all. My main recollection of a treat was climbing to the stone seated gods at Covent Garden to see my first 'Ring' Wagner, *Siegfried*, with Set Svanholm and Astrid Varnay. It was a relief to order my kit, have it despatched to the Elder Dempster mailboat *Accra* at Liverpool, and with difficulty to disentangle my emotions from my mother's so as to get away to Nigeria. I thanked the Almighty that my father finally and fully understood. Colonial life will be for other chapters.

There is no need to detail the study of Nigerian laws, and the Hausa language to higher standard, or sparetime swotting of Roman Law, Criminal Law, Evidence, Contract & Tort *etc*, that helped confirmation in my colonial appointment, and completing Parts I of the bar, in Lagos or on leave when eating dinners; nor the stumbling block when English Law of Real Property defeated my comprehension and rote memory alike. A 1963 leave in rooms on Chelsea Embankment, travelling by London's famous convoys of No 11 buses to Gibson & Weldon's tutorial 'inn' in Chancery Lane, half way between Fleet Street and Carey Street, with reading breaks to Paris, Madrid and Dublin (to avoid six months of the year within the UK causing liability to Inland Revenue), did the trick. The crammers were brutally frank: if we did what we were told, we would pass; if we had a feel for the law, we might get a 'second'; only those favoured by heaven got 'firsts' (we knew that anyway). Doing what we were told meant copying in longhand all the notes dictated by the lecturers (one of whom had been a crown counsel in Kaduna, whom I took to *Götterdämmerung* at the Garden to hear Birgit Nilsson): what we had written ourselves would imprint itself on our memories. When they proved right by my passing the Real Property absurdity, there was little time left to concentrate on the entire Part II, all to be taken at once. When the results were published, I looked for my name in the innumerable list of third classes and saw it not. This was no surprise, in what was a part-time hobby rather than serious study, but the thought of the Hong Kong establishment having reason to sneer was not happy. I glanced upwards in curiosity to see how many firsts had been awarded – none. O well, it had been a tough year then. There was a small handful of 2·1s, and amazement struck: in the larger but still select group of 2·2s my name appeared. I sought dispensation from the few dinners I was still due to eat, and was called to the utter bar *in absentia* in November.

Education all this had been, but it was the great university of life that instructed me for many years until I went during a 1966 leave to Ashridge Management College. There the Advanced Course brought me together with the Director-General of the Automobile Association, the Managing Director of an ICI complex in Sunderland, a private copper miner from Northern Rhodesia, and other leaders in the real world. We were overwhelmed with insight into 'teaching machines', chart-flows, discussions of Power and of Leadership, critical paths, Objectives and Purposes, and all the early manifestations of MBA-itis and American know-how that was to swamp British commercial thinking and public service management; and also into Pretentiousness – possibly to compensate for those who had avoided Oxbridge, there were formal dinners, and chapel services at which we were encouraged to read the lesson. It was enjoyable, although there was no time to write the learned theses which we were assured many predecessors had indited while in residence.

What gave me a boost was that although only a despised and impractical bureaucrat, and a colonial one to boot, when the final candle-lit dinner was held my colleagues asked me to make the requisite valedictory speech to the assembled staff. Apart from in-service days on various new fads from time to time in Hong Kong, that was almost the end of any formal training in my life.

There was, much later, a couple of years of self-instruction. In 1996 the Museums Association had a major re-think of professional recognition. For decades its Diploma had been awarded to curators, conservators and allied skilled workers, for having proven their years of known service and passed written and practical examinations, with the right to subscribe themselves as Associate Member (AMA). Fellowship (FMA) might follow through competitive peer nomination and election. Two threats had been emerging to the MA's status – employees of national institutions were recruited on civil service terms and needed not to trouble themselves to acquire the diploma if they remained under the government's aegis; and besides the growth of a Museum Training Institute, new universities were desperate to increase their student numbers (in search of more government funding), by introducing degrees or postgraduate courses in various Museum Studies. The economic and financial future of the MA's education programme could not be assured. New routes to the grant of

'AMA' status were thrown open, widening the trawl to all who work in museums.

Having had nearly a score of years in lay museum administration, I registered under a route open to trustees and volunteer guides. This required proof to satisfy distinguished FMAs in a face-to-face review that I had undergone two years of at least 70 hours of Continuing Professional Development with a Mentor, in which I was successful in 1998 (My log actually amounted to over 700 hours). It separately required assessment and verification by professionals appointed by the Museum Training Institute that I had 'contributed to the development of the museums, galleries and heritage sector', through a portfolio of material evidence supporting a highly bureaucratic set of 'tick-off' and 'self-assessment' forms. Finding professionals conveniently placed and willing to assess and verify was difficult. The attainment by a graduate, barrister and experienced member of museum governing bodies at all levels (and enthusiastic guide and expositor of a national collection) of 'Scottish Vocational Qualification Level 4 Unit G.3' proved awkward, but successful. President's Collections 56 years before were expunged when a vice-president of the MA called my tour of the Royal Museum 'inspired and inspirational.' Magdalen's present President Anthony Smith stuck my tour *Blissful Ignorance* to the end. I must have been a slow developer.

I still learn something new every day, and scored Quiz Quotient 144 in the BBC's national *Test the Nation*. The trouble is, at 80, I forget far more. (What was I going to write next?)

CHAPTER 3

A Rude & Licentious Dislocation

Every man thinks meanly of himself for not having been a soldier, or not having been at sea.
   [Dr Samuel Johnson; *Boswell's Life of Johnson, vol iii* (10 April 1778)]

Get Ready!

IT TAKES some chicken to have the neck to write this chapter. History has ended. Politicians have decided that 'defence' is an embarrassing diversion of social resources, unless to interfere in other peoples' affairs which are no concern of ours. National service is too much to ask of a citizenry conscious of its rights and indifferent to duty. What may we learn from the Swiss, whose able-bodied men keep their equipment under the bed, and can be mobilized in 24 hours? Blimpery comes ill from one who was never brave, never sought danger, and let things take their course without doing much to take charge of events. Playing at soldiers featured in the last chapter; some of the least distinguished moments in wartime endeavour came in the medical history that ludicrously opened these pages. But for playing at soldiers I should have become a doctor. Here is sere memory holding open the door of what led me to be a wicked fascist imperialist beast of a piggish colonial administrator instead – my upbringing or environment would never have given me such a thought, had I not been a temporary gentleman in command of African soldiers.

That came about in this meandering way. The call came ten days after going down from Oxford, to catch the train from Waverley to Dunbar and to report to 165 Officer Cadet Training Unit. I was introduced on the platform to a fellow student, Frank Farrant, son of a Kirk of Scotland missionary; whose path was to keep crossing my own for many years.

Dunbar was by repute a Tough OCTU. Most of the intake was university youths who had been briefly 'deferred' to complete their first academic year (STC service counted towards our socially desirable initial period 'in the ranks'). Billeted in seaside houses and drilled on the high school playground, routemarched through the Lammermuirs and abseiling up and down the sand cliffs, lectured at and made to deliver instant ten minute lecturettes, much of it seemed just a carry-on from the school and university corps – except that we had white bands round our shoulder straps and caps FS, and proper blancoed gaiters BD in place of Oxford's crummy leather ones. There was a lack of reality (what did any yet truly accept we were being prepared for, except minor parts in a Ministry of Information film?), increased for me by the ease of acquiring a day pass on Sundays to go home and reassure my mother that I wasn't away at the wars.

The Officer Cadets' main instructor was a golden-haired demigod from the Camerons. He had been wounded at Dunkirk, but enjoyed a revealing tug-of-war as kilted anchorman to 'give the girls a thrill' (many activities had an enthralled female audience). A seaside town seemed more deserted than other places in wartime; despite young farmers being in a reserved occupation, its little shops and pubs were desolate. We should undergo three to four weeks of 'pre-OCTU' to rinse the civviness out of our systems, and then begin real training. Reveille was at 6 *a.m.*, PT consisted mainly of running, very quick marching, and throwing damned great logs around. We mounted night guards to repulse any Nazis presuming to land on Lothian beaches. There was a cross-country map race and an endurance run. Softy Englishmen complained of the cold in mid-summer. Going for a dental check, I discovered by accident from the necessary Army Form that I had an Army Number – 6107381, and should subscribe myself 'O.C.'

After the 'pre-OCTU' month came news that 165 was to be turned into a fast track six weeks' course, to transform experienced WOs and senior NCOs into instant temporary gentlemen, for the build-up of the new armies to clear north Africa and invade Europe. But we of D Company were to be sent to complete our drawn out, immature, process at 166, Douglas IOM, where RAF Regiment officers were trained to defend airfields. There was grief at home when we were not awarded embarkation leave before entraining for the troopship – the ferry from Fleetwood where Fisherman's Friends came from. The train arrived at Dunbar late, and continued so, criss-cross, to Carlisle where we changed for Preston where we overnighted in nissen huts, changed again at Poulton-le Fylde *(where?)* and eventually climbed aboard the *Snaefell*.

At Douglas we found ourselves billeted in 'Seaview' on the front, just along from a shore naval establishment full of Wrens (my Hilary being one, whom I was yet to meet). Within a day we saw the advantages of overseas service. Mr & Mrs Cringle, who ran the boarding-house, fed us well, but were doing well themselves out of the war; lack of rationing was appreciated by Manxmen as much as by the forces. Yet we were always hungry, and the extra real eggs and chips at the YMCA and Catholic canteens, when pay permitted, were ambrosia: ex-NCO cadets had more money, comparative plutocrats. Goodies might not be exported to the mainland (residents were permitted to take a dozen eggs when they went over). Our rapidly bonded Dunbar platoons were redistributed and made to take in 20 disgruntled London Scottish strangers, among others who believed they had been selected for Indian Army or Recce Corps. As these had done no pre-OCTU, we would all be treated as novices, to start all over again. At that age even a fortnight, affecting seniority against mates elsewhere, seemed too significant an eternity to bear. Here we mounted no guards against invaders. Against this, the hours were longer, with no half-day off.

An experienced Clydeside comrade instructed us in why soldiers never wore pyjamas. In an emergency, the extra seconds used to take them off before donning full service marching order might mean loss of life; consequential itch from bare blankets would toughen us up. He had been a sugar-planter in British Guiana. He taught us to soak our feet with meths and pot permang, kippering them hard and black, preventing blisters. My room mate was more interested in the availability in hardship-free Douglas of Vaseline Hair Tonic, a gold dust guarantee against baldness; he bought himself an officer's quality khaki gaberdine FS cap, the better to protect his coiffure – vaseline stains soon spoilt it.

Social life was as much as one might hope for. Snooker at the Y cost 1d a half-hour. A short Welshman, Tom Bibey, took me to hear mass for the first time at an RC church; standing at the back and not having a missal with the Latin, I had no idea what was going on, except for the perfunctory sermon. We rowed a boat out to the Tower of Refuge on St Mary's Rock the same afternoon, and exchanged cards for years after the war, until he died as Cardiff's Head Librarian. A dear lady, Miss Mona Cannell, entertained select numbers of cadets on Sunday evenings with tea, cakes and music, largely provided by a soprano Norah Moore (principal in Sadler's Wells after the war). One night a visiting Professor Reginald Paul, over to examine Manx schools, played for us, infinitely better than our in-house cadet pianist, Charlie Quirk (could he have become Professor Lord [Francis Charles] Quirk FBA CBE, master English linguist? He seemed at home, and *Who's Who* says His Lordship was at school in IOM). The Memorial Public Baths provided a weekly hot soak (Manx boarding houses did not expect holidaymakers to stay long enough, or want, to have baths), and even a swim: the sea was cold and dangerous – one of us, a Liverpudlian who thought well of his prowess in the waves, drowned on the front before our eyes, despite desperate attempts to save him.

There was regular cinema, mostly American. There was the Pulrose municipal golf course. My clubs were sent over from Edinburgh. No player dared risk losing irreplaceable balls, which prolonged every round. I made up a social golf trio with a charming Scottish baronet, Sir David Moncreiffe, who was to burn himself to death many years later, and a rather older Englishman, who oiled up to him and had been a lecturer in Japan before the war. One bright Sunday an army bicycle (no Sturmey-Archers) carried me out to Laxey, with its Great Wheel squatting drab and neglected. It was still delightful, despite the hills to sweat up and the terrifying descents down again, to arrive where French-speaking aliens lived in semi-internment. Apart from the invigorating scenery and quiet away from Khakiville, the countryside was alive with ripe, juicy brambles, and nobody but me caring to pick and enjoy the next best thing to the king of all fruits, the raspberry. Then the heavens opened, and I pedalled and paddled home.

Four and a half months of increasingly demanding infantry training included little recalled in detail. Having learnt at Dunbar to manage a motorcycle, here we honed that skill on the TT circuit, and drove 15 cwt trucks and $2^1/_2$ ton lorries round fields, learning to double-declutch with crash gears, and to fault-find when anything mechanical refused to function. 'Man management' featured in the classroom acquisition of officerlike qualities, seeming to be a matter of washed and mended socks, and getting them their food before one's own ('Dear John' letters and rivalry from GIs were not yet problems in 1942; but all my letters home enclosed socks for washing and darning, and our fortnightly clothing exchange never found issue socks long enough for me).

I got a rollocking when platoon serjeant for the week (with chevrons on a right arm-band), in command of a march. I knew not how to get the squad to march less briskly; starting not far off the light infantry 140 to the minute, the beggars wouldn't come down to the standard 120, let alone the highland 110-115, which suited my length of leg better anyway. In a week's weapon training we made fleeting acquaintanceship with the puny Boyes Anti-Tank Rifle, but also with strange and secret war-winning new small arms like *P*rojectile *I*nfantry *A*nti-*T*ank 'mortars' and sticky grenades for unravelling tanks' caterpillar tracks. All words, little of it visualized – I never saw or heard a PIAT or sticky bomb go off. We were also *told* about the Sten gun. We never saw one, allegedly made by blacksmiths in patriotic garages, and cheaper than Tommy guns: its illustrations looked like it. Before our week's leave came up, the rumour mill had it that 2nd lieutenants would only serve six instead of 18 months to earn their second pip (and a little more silver *per diem*); this was said to be a sop to the *Daily Mirror* which had been taking up the cudgels on behalf of Our Young Officers who Took All the Risks. There would also be a £10 rise in our clothing allowance on commissioning, with 225 clothing coupons (on which mothers, sweethearts and wives would batten). More to the point, from 1 October we ourselves would get another 6d a day.

Leave was busy. The ageing D'Oyly Carte were in Edinburgh, and I went to *Iolanthe* with my godparents' son John Blackburn RN (the DSC and Instructor CO who would go down in *Affray*). The railway was worse than before, but on the way back a Fleetwood canteen girl, impressed by white tabs, sold me two bars of Cadbury's Dairy Milk with Fruit & Nuts, unseen for two whole years. I prided myself on being a good sailor, in my father's tradition, but the Irish Sea was at its worst. A Wren near me was sick. Suddenly so was I, and a bar and a half was gone. The other half I had given to the Edinburgh friend I had first met at Waverley station. His state was worse. Forever I have remembered the brief poem: *Sail / Gale / Pale / Rail*. Douglas's OCTU was in the throes of a minor epidemic of impetigo, blamed on lack of greens.

To underline the change of use of 166 OCTU from aerodrome defence to infantry, at the halfway leave point had come a new CO – Lt Col Niven, brother of a film star, and possessor of quite the smartest and shiniest Sam Browne belt ever. We rarely saw him outside OCTU HQ in the Villiers Hotel, however. We started weekly 'night ops'. This included digging weapon slits (later known as slit trenches, never 'foxholes' to Britons), while blind in the pitch black; a patrol supposed to attack us blundered into the wrong platoon, casting Mk V thunderflashes wildly around (these were reclothed Brocks *Giant Cannon* for Guy Fawkes and Hallowe'en). We built bridges across rivers: these were great floating bags stuffed with kapok, which supported duckboards and transoms. All was now geared towards the grand finale, 'battle week', when all we had learnt (and would quickly forget) would be put to the test. The senior company was alleged to have been unacceptably shagged by their battle week, so we were made to redouble our PT, in bare feet and with yet more logs. A dentist attended to a stopping that my mother's home-made toffee had attacked, and I was fitted with two pairs of army granny steel-framed spectacles with the flat arms that, with luck, wouldn't let gas into masks. A few super-confident cadets began to purchase their Sam Browne belts and to spend hours on polishing them to look like David Niven's brother's, in anticipation of making an impression on their first adjutants; I was not yet certain that I might not be RTU'd (returned to unit, failed) and thought that my first batman might shine mine up with greater despatch if I wasn't.

'A' Coy passed out, and as they marched off to the boat we became senior company. We were required to name regiments of choice, three in due order. My mother insisted that I apply for the Black Watch (I suspected she would have said the Guards, but we didn't know anyone who would have 'spoken for' me, nor had I any desire to use my six feet and five-and-a-half inches to be a guardsman); she knew that some respectable young men joined that regiment. My father, being naval, had no thoughts on the matter. (Edinburgh was suffering from a smallpox epidemic, and he had to concentrate on stopping it.) My own information was that the Black Watch had even more Englishmen officers than the Argylls, and dutifully but reluctantly I only put the Camerons down as my second preference – and not because the tartan shops said Clark was a sept of that clan.

So came that final challenge. 8 *a.m.* found us in trucks trundling with most of our worldly possessions upon us, on our way to Spanish Head. From there it was nonstop 'fighting', marching, assaulting and cross-countrying to Ramsey. The first 'battle' ended facing the Calf of Man around Cragneash, then we marched behind Port Erin up South Barrule mountain to bivouac under groundsheet capes. A march to Beary mountain brought us to an alfresco demonstration of air, machine-gun, mortar and tank attacks, followed by a forced march across the hills, *via* part of the Snaefell rack-railway, to Glen Mona behind Ramsey. We were soaked the whole way. Another bivouacked night, then a morning of hurling live grenades around, firing an Anti-Tank rifle, followed by some other muddled 'battle', and south again into a tented camp in the middle of the island. Lights-out chatter centred on how to react to the unlikely but abominable possibility of an invert's fumbling approach; one of us had once experienced a grope in a tent, and the other seven expressed convincing horror that such things might be. Mail arrived, enclosing several packets of cigarette cards ordered from a dealer months before, an embarrassment to tuck away dry in a web haversack. Big assault next day on something somewhere, testing our stylized battle drill, and a further test – of individual mess-tin cooking. Then another 'battle' on the way back up to Laxey. By this time the weather was so foul, the conditions prevented anything but aimless, blundering movement, and visibility was too restricted to learn anything from what was happening: we marched back miserably to Douglas *via* Keppel Gate for an immediate full inspection. The last two days of battle week experience were crammed into a single one a few days later. Somehow I came through unscathed and judged fit to be a commander of men. I was 19 years old.

I learnt that after all I was allotted to the Queen's Own Cameron Highlanders as 2/Lt (P/256482); the tallest man in the British Army was (not for the first time) a Cameron and I shouldn't be thought odd. Frank Farrant, the friend from Waverley, was to be another. Even fewer than before had their first choice granted. Movement orders and travel warrants came next. And then we were addressed by our polished commanding officer. While none were ready to admit to a fervent desire to shed blood and bowels on some foreign strand, we did expect something on the lines of, 'Well, chaps, we've been hard on you, but it's been in your interest; we want you to give of your best wherever you are called, and to come out of it safe and proud. We shall be thinking of you all, and perhaps we may serve together and support each other one day. *(Catch in the voice.)* All the very best of good fortune!' Damn it, we had studied man management. Not a bit of it. The smiling s _ _ t came on the stage in his glossy leathers, glared at us, said, 'Well, gentlemen, we've finished with you *(pause)* and you've finished with us,' and walked off. We thought quietly of first war tales of leaders who got bullets in their backs.

Aim!

I reported to the ninth battalion of the Seaforth Highlanders at Cromer in Norfolk. It was a civilized peacetime TA unit, the CO Jock Douglas above all: the permanent cadre were the hard core of the older territorials, landed gentry and estate workers, supported by professional men and the salt of the urban earth, judged to be past combat service overseas but the right kind to run a drafting battalion for banana boats.

We became acquainted with the RSM, Chota Morton. We may have missed Christmas, but were in time for Hogmanay. Throughout a crescendo of learn-as-you-go eightsomes, Dashing White Serjeants, Athol Broses (ingredients hoarded for months out of limited supplies), hoochs and dirty stories in some village hall, the RSM insisted that the bottles could not be left unemptied. Making our uproarious way down the white village street to our C Coy four-to-the-room billet, discovering that there were pros and cons to both kilts and trews when subsiding unbalanced into deep snowdrifts, we were promised a late reveille. That was the third major drunk of my life; I remember no more ever of that standard. It is best to learn some things young, if one doesn't think one knows everything already. Following night saw us on recce patrols in the blackout. A week later I was on a street-fighting course in a deserted and badly blitzed part of Great Yarmouth's 'rows' by the South Quay. Yarmouth had just had its 73rd raid, only beaten by Malta; one crazed old girl outside a ruin in the frozen snow kept shouting that she had been bombed out three times from different homes. Next week's course was strafed by two Jerries, one shot down by a drifter's gun. Most nights we heard our own bombers droning on their way to Berlin, the Ruhr and the Baltic ports, and listened to inward raids on East Anglia.

Our ephemerality was obvious when Shug (2/Lt Hughie Gunn, a London Scot originally from Rogart, and also ex-166), who shared batman Seaton with me, put forward the thought that that small man of indeterminate age and depressed qualities from Glasgow, who had worked on Drumadoon farm in Blackwaterfoot where my parents often holidayed, and who now polished, buffed and bed-made adequately, was unlikely to be of value in the Western Desert, and should be placed on the Permanent Cadre (the core of the battalion in no danger of being drafted). What, we were asked, could the point possibly be of saving Seaton from hardship and danger, when we would ourselves be far distant long before the occasion arose? There was no danger of our joining the permanent cadre either. We had better attend to our training.

A little later Charles de Boinville our Coy Commander went on a three weeks' battle course and, *faute de mieux*, I was formally installed as coy comd with powers of 7 days CB. Again, much has sunk into some Sargasso of brain cells beyond dredging up. I recollect two days in Norwich, when we went to view divisional boxing contests and go to the flicks; we met part of the first invasion of boisterous Americans in the officers' club, one of whom thought his tan pants would be a 'good trade' for my kilt: our other, more proper, purpose was to attend a day of instruction in camouflage, led by Capt Oliver Messel, the distinguished stage designer. He was no gilded idiot, even if he did enliven his demonstrations by ducking behind a curtain and popping out again wearing some fantastic mask from his theatrical past, and feeding us on celery, apples and cake.

The principal event of this sojourn with 9 Seaforth was being an umpire on Exercise *Spartan*, allegedly the run-up following Exercise *Bumper* before the invasion of Europe. The whole of England seemed full of army, the roads stuffed with every kind of transport from heavy tanks to the new, rare and much coveted jeep. The invasion did not take place for another two and a half years. I squeezed in a ride back to Oxford to have lunch in college, to be welcomed by the head porter (who recognized me through my crash helmet and goggles), Tallboys the chapel caretaker, and Mobey my scout (who dearly wanted to make up a bed for me), and to swank in uniform in front of a couple of old friends who were medical students and 'reserved'; Edinburgh Accie and future poet Ian Davie emerged from St John's as I went in, and I had dinner in Magdalen's hall with my friends John Turner who had renounced conscientious objection and was about to join the RAF, and John Tavoularis-Troiano, a Romanian who resented Hungarian bushido (as he called the Magyar occupation).

A few days after returning to the greater sanity of 9 Seaforth, those of us from Dunbar had earned ten days' leave. At Liverpool St Station we were greeted by an emissary with instructions to return *ek dum*. Back in Overstrand we learnt that drafting orders had come through. Before taking embarkation leave we must be approved by the brigade commander. This turned out to be another exercise justifying the mockery with which our American cousins and French allies greet the British approach to militarism (and indeed imperial rule). Each individual posting order informed us that all had been personally selected for service with native troops in a tropical climate. Heaven knows what the brigadier would have done had he thought any of us unsuitable: the selection had already been made *en masse*, presumably in the War Office with a pin. From all over East Anglia's banana boat battalions came 2/Lts, and presumably all had the same interview as I. 'So, you are going to serve with native troops, how do you feel about that?' – 'I don't really know, sir, I'd never imagined it.' – 'Well, let me tell you, I served with native troops for many years, and I can tell you that it is an honour, a very great honour.' – 'Yessir.' – '*Yes!* A privilege! You are a lucky man.' – 'Thank you, sir.' – 'One word of advice. *(Pregnant pause.)* When you take your bath, never let your native servant see your private parts, he'll lose all respect for you. Yes. Always cover yourself with a towel. That's all. Good luck. Dismiss.' A very special personal selection.

One week's embarkation leave was divided between acquiring the minimum recommended khaki drill tropical kit and camp kit and listening to how every other mother's son had had a whole fortnight's leave. Then to the transit centre, already medically related in terms of mosquito nets and boots. Daily check-in was at 1030 and 1700 hours, ready to move at two hours notice thereafter. John Ellis, a comrade reunited from Douglas, and I visited the Tower, Tussaud's and Abbey, and my parents paid a hasty trip for more trying farewells. Then the two hours notice, and by crowded troop train to Avonmouth to be part of draft RNHZO, c/o APO 4970, embarked on mv *Highland Princess* for (as became obvious) Lagos. Most of the 111 officers were bunked three deep in the ship's library, compacting the beginning of a few friendships that were to last for many long years (and a very few hearty dislikes). I slept under John Ellis and near Tom Bibey. 20 officers shared a basin each; all bathing was in salt water.

The barber shop was full of outlandish 'candies', 'swim trunks', and striped 'boxer' underpants (our first transatlantic neologisms), real cigarettes at 1s 8d for 50 (60 US gaspers were 1s 6d), Yankee sunglasses and lighters, boot polish, paperback thrillers and other rare goods brought on at the last American landfall, all doubly attractive to the war-deprived for their strangeness. The ORs spent most of their days, PT apart, in the well-decks playing endless housey-housey.

Sweating did not come immediately. For two of our five weeks at sea we seemed headed for Iceland. The fog and chill were great. Doubtless the *Enigma* and *Ultra* wonders, of which we would be ignorant until long after the war, assured our passage the long way round, and not over, the U-boats. But it slowly warmed, and on clear days we might see not only seabirds but also an occasional school of joy-giving porpoises playing around the bows. Not that it was a pleasure cruise in uncomfortable conditions: the hard stuff had run out before we left Avonmouth, and there came the moment when the beer ran out also. Then the discovery was made that from the last South African landfall the bar had acquired unending crates of Van der Hum, the Afrikaners' peach liqueur. In short order the community had compared VdH neat, VdH and soda, VdH and tonic, VdH and lemonade, VdH and bitters with or without fizzy, sometimes with tomato juice thrown in. I have never touched Van der Hum since. Squadron-Leader Ralph Reader and his Gang Show (grown out of the Boy Scouts' annual mass concert) were on board, bound for the middle east as part of ENSA; on the first truly hot day they headed a mass conga of all ranks round the whole ship (bridge excepted), led by a piano accordeon. By mid-day it began to be sweltering, and our paltry supply of tropical clothing with minimal laundry facilities became niffy.

On clear nights the stars in the heavens were inspiring: sometimes distant sheet-lightning cozened the naïve into thinking that the flashing guns of the western desert might be reflected across nearly 3,000 miles of Sahara. It was heaven to look upwards at 4 in the morning, for those few who could find a clear spot to sleep on deck. Sharing duty on a Bofors gun with Ellis from 2 *a.m.* to 4 *a.m.* in case of nocturnal attack, we kept awake by singing Gilbert & Sullivan. One rainy day we saw through the haze palm trees on a flat shore, and realized that we were no longer part of a convoy; the remainder were on their way to the Cape, and all alone we were approaching Freetown, capital of Sierra Leone, one of the world's great sheltering harbours before air travel. On entry it looked marvellous, surrounded by jagged peaks, topped by clouds, jutting out to sea and belonging to nowhere in particular: once inside, all shrank and disappointed. Only those troops posted there went ashore, but we were entertained by naked boys and barely-clothed (and foul-mouthed) young men in canoes, singing raucous songs, diving for pennies, many of which sank to join the creatures of the sands, and shouting insults at the colourfully (and more fully) dressed mammies selling fruit. This was the introduction to Africa which almost everyone took for granted at that time: laughing, friendly natives living the simple life, taking the technical wonders of the west without much by way of hang-ups, and inviting no questioning on our part of our consequential proper place in the human hierarchy. Innocence, not arrogance, was at the heart of it all. Most of us were still young and ready to see the childlike primitive through what we imagined were adult spectacles.

Docking at Apapa, the bulk of the bodies on board had reached their destination: Nigeria. The *Highland Princess* then made her way south for VdH and then to Argentina, her regular peacetime route, to collect tins of bully beef for Britain's wartime diets, and return home with new boxer shorts and Lucky Strikes. Fate entered in, as ever: we queued up in the former smokeroom to be given our postings. I reached the second place in the line which was receiving papers marked IBADAN, when a friend called me back. By the time we got to the front again, the papers read EDE. So I was parted from Farrant, who went to 3 Brigade of 81 (WA) Division, stationed in Ibadan: that brigade (all Nigerians) was the only formation in this story which ever did jungle training before entering Burma – in southern Nigeria, where countless were infected with bilharzia (schistosomiasis) during an ill-advised river-crossing. Frank thereby became one of the enlarged Chindits, flown in by gliders near Kohima after the death of Wingate, whose idea that whole crazy but original enterprise was.

Instead I went with Ellis to Ede, south of Oshogbo, where 6 Brigade had its being. The train stopped at every station, all day and into the night. There was always fruit to buy, a crowd to stare, and a rush to get in whenever the driver and stationmaster ceased gossiping without warning, and the engine shook itself into a forward chug. Tumbling out of the quaint colonial carriage of the Nigerian railway, with its shutters, mosquito screens and dysfunctional fans, we were received in the middle of the night and trucked to various units. John and I found ourselves on makeshift camp beds, without mosquito nets in a shared tent (full of frogs to eat the insects), until a not distant dawn, to find we were now the newest subalterns of the 4th West African Auxiliary Group (Sierra Leone Regiment), Royal West African Frontier Force.

This was a large unit of carriers, unarmed soldiers ('UAS'), trained to carry heavy loads, stores and reserve supplies of the fighting units of the brigade, through terrain where feet were the only feasible transport. The men had been originally recruited as Pioneers in the WA Army Service Corps, then remustered and retitled early in the year as Privates in the Sierra Leone Regiment. They had had basic small arms drill, but were not expected to do anything spectacular by way of killing. Every 14 UAS carriers were escorted by two riflemen. This posting might forecast tolerable war for the fundamentally terrified, or it might mean defenceless disaster. Who was to know? A General Sir George Giffard had spent time on the Coast, become a man of power in the Far East as GOC-in-C of India's Eastern Army, and staked his reputation on Africans as jungle fighters, although most of them lived in savannahs; he might as well have staked it on me as a street fighter because I had been brought up in cities. Giffard was the man who ruled (unavailingly) that since their new Europeans would never learn native languages, all Africans must be taught to speak English: any Europeans who spoke native languages to their troops should be disciplined.

Our baggage arrived that first morning, amazingly intact. I commanded a platoon of a hundred and fifty-six black strangers, wearing slouch hats with a blue cloth triangle signifying Sierra Leone, slightly reddish collarless khaki blouses, long shorts that came down over the tops of their khaki knee puttees, and bare feet. From all the tribes of Sierra Leone and surrounding French territories, they communicated in pidgin, based on the Krio creole of Freetown. There was nothing for it but to pick it up through trial and error. The first word to pick up was 'chop,' for any comestible, including the chicken, eggs and groundnuts which were the unbroken staple diet of every European. One learned fast that the most senior African Other Rank was junior to the least British private (not that there were any in Ede), let alone a British Non-Commissioned Officer. It wasn't true, of course, still less legal. We also learnt that we served, not with native troops, but with Africans. It being assumed that the distinctions of lieutenancy were too much for illiterates to master, all subalterns were called 'Captain'. Captain Clark had a cocky BNCO to support him in his vast new command, and the company had its British CSM and CQMS. The latter two had clear duties, but my British serjeant would have been better out of the way.

Fortunately I did also have Serjeant Johnny Limba, who seemed to enjoy introducing me to Africa at War. 'Dey one tief man for captin sef patoon. Make me show massa how we catchim.' This is true: a soldier had a packet pinched from his bedding, and Sjt Johnny identified a juju man in the platoon, who took a bunch of feathers and I knew not what else with which to prance up and down the lines, shaking the fetish and mouthing silently. Eventually he stopped opposite a bed, and therein was the booty. It is unlikely to have been a put-up job to bombaze the new white man: the culprit was charged and sent to the company commander, where he confessed and was duly sent to the CO who dealt with him via the provost serjeant. Our company clerk, Moses, knew the regimental numbers, names, tribes, alleged religions and characters of all 650 men in the company, of whom seven were at all literate.

I was reinforced in my arrival in a new world by the company cook, who presided in unacceptably but incorrigibly filthy shorts and apron over great vats of porridgy material, which I ventured to taste on inspections and pronounce to be 'fine chop past all', indeed 'past corn beef', as they would say. One day he produced a lump of apparent mud, which he broke open like a fossil rock: inside was a quivering grub of immense size, or perhaps a queen insect. Watching me carefully but without any hint of insolence, he popped it into his mouth, chewed and swallowed with evident pleasure, rubbed his grimy hand round his hairy and protuberant tum, and pronounced it 'Fine chop, sah! Better medicine!' Some of the men kept pet monkeys in their huts; the company provost had a foot-long baby crocodile in a biscuit tin of water, which also he said would one day be 'plent better chop'. 'Dey don catch fear for bully beef', to my surprise, 'fine past' though it might be – because it had no bones: this led to laborious explanations, leading in very long run to elementary pidgin descriptions of dehydrated food, which found them totally incredulous (they were to get used to it in Burma). So conservative were they that they refused maize, 'chop dat na no good for African, but for animal sef lone'.

CO Lionel Holloway held the army's second most enviable gallantry medal from the first war, the DCM; years later I would see him again as head of the Technical College in Kaduna. His 2i/c Topper Brown starred in our medical overture as the blackwater survivor. My batman (I was not too keen on the pidgin expression 'boyboy'), Ali Tamara, had been the previous MO's personal servant. I judged that doctor's lifestyle by my discovery that I was the only captain to be awakened with, first a cup of warm water 'for wash mouth, sah,' then a slice of raw citrus 'for clean mouth, sah,' and only then, and finally, the necessary pint mug of tea. Ali's first demand was that I buy long bars of washing soap, manioc starch, a charcoal iron and the charcoal to burn in it.

Training never seemed to leave the parade ground, although I did venture into the forest, finding nothing but creepers and small creepy-crawlies. The men had their first, overdue, training in rifle-handling other than for drill parades, but they also sharpened their matchets lovingly. There was one exceptional exercise, when I realized how unbeatably skilled bushmen might be: cutting 'sticks' from the forest with their matchets, they could turn the inner bark into strings, wind it three-ply into rope, and then eight-ply into veritable hawsers, to carry bamboo duckboards across a stream as a suspension bridge in almost no time. PT was mostly surrendered to vigorous tribal dancing, in which it was entertaining to participate; they learnt white man dance (the Lambeth Walk) from me, and I think I won their hearts.

Four pints of beer a month were each European's mess ration, with a free issue of 50 Players and two boxes of matches a week. The theft of £7, which my juju man failed to solve, left me broke until authority came through for us to draw allowances, plus something called customs rebate, from the field cashier; real pay was still going into the Oxford bank. The exoticism of local markets soon wore off; 90% of the imported goods on the stalls and rush groundmats were German or Japanese in origin, which told a tale, while it was distressing to see bottles of Sloan's Liniment bought and *drunk* (followed by an appreciative rubbing of the abdomen). A plethora of bananas, pineapples, mangoes and limes, unknown at home, left one thirsting for apples and pears. Recreation, apart from an unreliable mess radio, was restricted to a dreary drinking hole in Ede town. A lorry trip to the town of Ibadan, the largest purely African city south of Cairo, was gloomy. The occasion was to bury a British serjeant from the Gambian battalion whom I had never known, and who had died in the military hospital from a grenade accident; but I did see a worn Gaumont-British newsreel there of my father escorting Churchill round civil defence workers on Edinburgh Castle esplanade.

When only a few days had passed, all the brigade's officers were assembled to be addressed by the brigadier, J Hayes (Joe or 'Jeyes'), a mature and much respected man. 'I cannot say where you are going to go, gentlemen,' he said, 'but I can tell you this. *(With shades of Tommy Trinder?)* You are very lucky people. You are going to fight the Japanese.' It was as well we never knew then that he had no faith in the task assigned to him. The rumour that had gained credence was that Africans were to occupy Madagascar, to relieve real soldiers for the real thing. To be told that we were going to deal with the real thing received mixed feelings. Not too many of us British fancied ourselves as heroes. Lack of familiarity with our troops, and the unconvincing nature of the brief training they and we had been having, had not persuaded newcomers that this was an army for a modern war. We thought we knew all about the Japanese. They needed damned great tanks, damned great guns, planes with damned great bombs, damned huge bulldozers to flatten jungles, and incarnations of Lawrence, Biggles and Marlborough in the van, to batter them into the ground; not the virtually naked led by the largely clueless. Never mind, it might never happen; after all, we were very lucky people. Nevertheless 4(WA)Aux Gp SaLR was bidden to entrain for Apapa to embark for Freetown, there to transship (without landing on its own home soil) for Somewhere in the Far East. At the very last moment it was decreed to be slightly over establishment and that the two most junior (easiest to spare) officers should stay behind and join The Gambia Battalion. Clark and Ellis were fingered. Some of my platoon wept, bad for my character. The CO went twice to brigade to try to keep us, but for whatever reason Ellis plus one had to go: I was seen as his mucker, and was then asked to volunteer, so it was best we go together rather than I seem a cad. We went down to the ship to see them all aboard, and came back disconsolately by truck to Oshogbo.

Battalions at this stage had a reserve company, which would theoretically stay behind the main war front to provide replacements for casualties. The two youngest arrivals in the 1st battalion of The Gambia Regiment joined its 'R' Coy. They were a very different unit from the Sierra Leonean carriers. Even more than in the Nigerian and Gold Coast units, a large proportion could only speak French besides their own tongue, coming from territories like Sénégal and Soudan with mixed motives: some sought paid and clothed employment with a higher standard of living than desert bush offered, some sought excitement, some followed relatives who had gone ahead and recommended what they had found.

One man in my new platoon had served in the French colonial army since 1938, had been in France until 'Vichy', and got lost on a patrol for 6 days during the *blitzkrieg*, had made his way from Marseilles via Oran to Dakar, been demobbed with 1,000 francs (his monthly pay had been Fr15), and joined the Waff for 1s a day. Most were practising Muslims, although the animist underlay still showed through, not least their trust in amulets containing Qur'ânic texts, that would protect against shot and shell. Such a small country had 14 tribes to populate it: mainly Mandinka, Fula (the nomadic Fulani or Peul who spread in the Sahel as far as Nigeria), Wolof, Jola, Serakule, and others. Some at least of these boasted organized warriors in their ancestry, rather than the well-intentioned but chaotic mayhem expected of combatant forest-dwellers: despite recent history, that is not a put-down of the usually jolly and occasionally enthusiastic Sierra Leoneans. The Gambians were more serious:

Sierra Leoneans giggled when poked in the belly and called 'Bushman!', but Gambians were insulted by such presumption: though even they were still happier going barefoot than when cownosed for important parades in Boots, African Colonial Forces, For the Use of (to which we shall revert). There was little chance to get to know a new, more normal sized, infantry platoon of 34 fighting men (when up to strength), because within days 1GambR was also off. The whole division was to go in the same convoy that 4 Aux had begun to fill (having for whatever maritime planning reason transshipped at Freetown, they had just arrived back again at Apapa in a larger trooper).

So the convoy, including the troopship *Staffordshire,* sailed on 11 July on another month's voyage, with various other units besides The Gambia on board: she had been designed to be a pre-war trooper to India as well as a passenger liner, a little less cramped and beastly than the *Highland Princess*, but the official OC Troops was the stereotype. Every man of my platoon came up to see my 'house', as the four-berth cabin appeared to them. Down below, they kept the hammocks and decks cleaner than had the British Other Ranks (BORs) on the *Highland Princess*, although different diets and habits made the scents distinguishable. As we were units, not drafts, organization was more effective.

Valiant but ineffective attempts were made through lectures and cramped physical activity to keep fit and to prepare for the future. The convoy docked in Cape Town on 21 July, under shelter of the mountain. Those granted shore leave enjoyed boundlessly generous hospitality from the inhabitants, with cars queuing up to carry parties off for rides into the beautifully coniferous countryside, and for food and drink at home afterwards; for this they used their private petrol rations, 200 miles-worth a month. Ellis and I were swept up by a Mrs Joan Lefson, whose husband was in the western desert in the SAAF. We found ourselves trying to communicate with her two children in pidgin when they asked me the usual questions about my kilt (the RWAFF having no recognized temperate uniform for us). The Del Monico nightclub (the Demon Alcohol or Devil's Moniker, as christened in ship's cabaret later) and the city botanic gardens, museum, library, parliament building, and gallery all had patronage, while shops sold Swiss wrist watches that Britain had not seen for years. My Rotary cost 65s, and I replaced my cracked civvy spectacle frame.

One joy was a vast route march through Cape Town's suburbs, after a spell as ship's 'security officer' alone on board. In Nigeria, marches had been through bush, and at the usual half-hour fall-out after 90 minutes on the path (temperate climates enjoyed ten minutes after 50), the bush had been convenient for everyone. In South Africa, nobody thought ahead. 1GambR fell out on an esplanade with a dwarf wall overlooking a pleasure beach, marked

'For whites only'. Before a breath could be taken, nearly a thousand tapes were loosened and an equal number of small torrents fell on the golden sands. One didn't know where to look, but the battalion was hurriedly marched on long before ten minutes were up. A small, chance, deluge against apartheid before the Malan era.

After five days, a peaceful transit followed to Bombay. The Indian Ocean was calm, the skies rarely quite blue, and it was a soggy journey into August. The chaos of landing somewhere not far from the Gateway to India, of entraining on the dockside, of passing the horrid housing estates on the fringes of Bombay and of arriving Somewhere in India said to be not too far from Poonah (we carried no atlases), all is jumbled in a fuzzy mind: but the new smells and mendicancy, and the apparent squalor and filth of the dirty grey soil of the sub-continent compared with what already began to seem a primitive idyll in the comforting rich red dusts and brown mud huts of the dark continent, remain only too clear. Another first, partially false, impression to grow out of. I was now all of 20, and thought myself mature enough to stop smoking. It didn't last.

Nasik, a holy town (therefore filthy and beggar-ridden), proved not to be very near Poona, nor Dhond where West Africa's advance party (O2E, overseas second echelon) had first settled, but fourteen miles from Deolali. A brilliantly caparisoned pipe band of Indian Engineers in scarlet, blue and white, escorted us from the station to Masrul. Col Laing was much ashamed that our Gambian fifes and drums could not compete: besides, our bass drum had been punctured on board. The camps prepared by contractors (the civilian involvement in everything military in entrepreneurial India was something rich and strange to us) left much still undone, although hard standing for a few tents and one or two wooden huts for principal messes and offices were welcome. The battalion officers' mess was abandoned, and companies set up their own in EPIP tents (European Personnel Indian Pattern mini-marquees). Roads, latrines, cookhouses and incinerators were all half-made, and gangs of ragged coolies, including women with babies on their backs, shocked our troops, who rapidly decided that these were an inferior race.

New livestock became familiar: kitehawks, scraggy cows, water buffaloes and bluebottles with red noses. Adaptation to being in India Command began: the Africans were issued with their first mosquito nets, since they were accustomed to and carriers of MT malaria, but strangers to the BT, quartan and other fevers of this continent. We were promised early issues of olive green (OG) tropical battle-dress to replace our KD (khaki drill) and long puttees, and ordered to dye any clothing that was white or light – quartermaster serjeants could only find magenta and indigo dyes in local markets, with weird results. We were issued with brown mosquito nets, and I rid myself of effete pyjamas. Many of us replaced what we now saw as shabby UK-issue KD with better quality Indian material for tailored slacks and shorts. Those who had hoarded UK 3d stamps from Nigeria to stick on forces' mail home were caught out: we now needed 4 anna stamps with the King Emperor's crowned head. We were poorer than in Nigeria because, not being in a colony or a war zone, we had to buy all our firewood and kerosene, to pay mess fees for our food, and pay rent to the contractor (the ubiquitous Wazir Ali) for our tent.

The climate was not unpleasant, coolish towards the monsoon's end. We were in a plain near a holy conical basalt hill, with one temple at the foot and another two-thirds up, reached by 500 steps (each two foot high). The priest-in-charge hawked bananas and oranges in his spare time. Some of us climbed up, finding what we thought to be numerous 'Buddhist idols', shabbily whitewashed. I watched devotees bathing in our nearby holy river, diving in to be washed downstream in the millrace of narrowly concreted banks under three culverts, and racing back to do it again. A Hindu festival was celebrated soon after our arrival, featuring bullocks with bright red-painted and brass-tipped horns, gilded rings through noses, coloured baubles and bells, white cows, donkeys stippled with green and red, and gaudy rainbow toy farmyards. This confirmed us in our schoolroom picture of the 'real' India, and made it harder to come to terms with tawdry industrialism, bolshy journalism, popular films and records, and culture that revered sex but offered it to the prurient west as smut. Gandhi, *Quit India!* and Congress meant little to ignorant incomers. We met no intellectuals, and few of the better educated above the shopkeeper or babu classes. British and African alike, we were dismayed and revolted by the perpetual cry for baksheesh: even sitting in the backs of the gariwalas' tongas, on the way to and from the town cinema, one was pursued by piteous calls of mendicancy.

I delivered myself of a sermon home: it reads curiously 60 years later. My father had wondered what I felt about Empire. I was doubtful of the policy of enlightening, civilizing and lifting out from supposed mire primitive peoples under our benignly guiding sway. Democracy, trousers, Christianity, sex-equality, cigarette-smoking, birth-control, Sloan's Liniment, were all very well for us. We worked these out for ourselves within the parameters of European historical progress, but hadn't had them thrust upon us. We had contrived, with 75% success, to give 'coloured people' a sense of our superior mental capacities and outlook, so that some thought they could achieve our standards by aping our outward effects. Many foolish people encouraged such copycats,

42 Gambian officers at Masrul: 2 would be killed, 1 to die of blackwater, 8 wounded (1 thrice), the CO would be replaced, the 2i/c medically boarded (as was the man in the very middle).

not so much by actively encouraging them in those conceits (unless out to exploit their custom and make money), as by passively doing nothing about it. The Indian babu's FBA (Oxon.) ('failed BA') was likely to be imitated in Africa. We should do what we could to help the native to higher standards of living, health and happiness, *but in his own way*. All his traditions were being lost because either we laughed at them or missionaries and misguided zealots tried to implant our own to their destruction. We were succeeding in debasing a large section of the populations into a degraded state, and antagonizing the few who had the western education and initiative to think for themselves in our frames of mind. Nothing was more pitiful than the half-western-educated native who compared himself with his village peers and saw himself as the cat's eyebrows. If we were determined to Europeanize them, let us do it 100% thoroughly, but it would be a pity. I even wondered about the wisdom of stamping out cannibalism and human sacrifice before something equally spiritual had fully taken their places. I wanted them to make their own progress, not trail along in our wandering wakes. India might be a different kettle of fish (it is curious how that separate Empire was always differentiated in our minds from Colonies; an imperialism where we had been for three and more centuries had nothing to do with colonialism [whether settled or protective] as the word is used to-day). Very well, I was confused.

Pundits in the town's military offices and clubs, not destined to exchange KD for OG, told us, 'Burma? A cinch! Cleared by next April.' We began to be conscious of Americans in the area: they ignored the 'For Officers Only' notices in caste-observing restaurants and cinema circles, which was easy because the GIs' uniforms were as smart as our officers'; they squeezed our men out of everything they patronized, ruined the market by never bargaining, pushed the gharry fares up, were full of themselves and anti-us being India's rulers, *etc, etc, etc,* as all the stereotypes and clichés had it. Their black soldiers were ill at ease, and the Waff was ill at ease with them. We lost the British CQMS of D Coy to a sten gun accident, always an unreliable and dangerous weapon. Next day the div comd Maj-gen Woolner inspected us, and the very next day after that all the Europeans of the division were assembled in the largest camp marquee, to be addressed by a real bigwig. This turned out to be the current corps commander, a Lieut-Gen Slim, who took off his Gurkha hat with the staff insignia in front and said, 'I want you to take a good look at this ugly mug, because it's the one that is going to be buggering you all about before long.' Bill Slim won our hearts. We were not told that a little later he watched one of our brigades with all its carriers strung out in line; it proved independence from transport, but was a wonderful target, and he turned his back in horror.

Training continued in a field area from 30 September, while the rains failed to end, and there were still many colleagues and men to get to know. My absence for a fortnight in Deolali was recounted in the opening chapter. On returning Paul Ward, a knowledgeable subaltern and future principal 'cellist in the Boyd Neel and Halle orchestras, lent me his gramophone; he had 78s of Tchaikovsky's first piano concerto and Toscanini's Beethoven seventh symphony (I hummed the slow movement of the Beethoven almost nonstop when we became active in serious matters). The rains finally did end, and the sun came out with its vitamin D. We overcame the pallor of dank climates and mepacrine discoloration and 'got our knees brown'.

In October the end of the beginning became apparent: Div HQ disappeared eastwards, presumably to spy out the land. We had to fill out our wills from the officers' blue equivalent of the ORs' brown AB64, and to send them off to 2nd Echelon for safe-keeping, and all but our mimimal baggage was packed to be stored with banks in Bombay. In November our whole battalion went at last on a three days' stunt with the Sierra Leone battalion. I think it was part of what was suitably called Exercise *Headload*, around Lake Tansa, Bombay's reservoir. To make up strengths, I was posted from reinforcements to C Coy (Ellis to B), and it became obvious that we were about to move. Yet another lot of colleagues and men to get to know, at the very last minute, including a new batman, Babukar. I wonder what they thought of having to get to know a stranger, so soon before mutual confidence would matter so much. I still missed my Sierra Leonean pals: it is odd how first loves, however brief, stay so firm. My platoon, No 12, was up to strength, 34 men in three sections with a bren gun each, including the serjeant and three corporals and three lance-corporal 2i/cs, the rifle bomber with his cup-discharger, and the BNCO's and my orderlies.

My new coy comd was a Seaforth piper, Major Godfrey Oliphant who, in a more gentlemanly laid-back way than Col Laing's, made it plain that if anything went wrong, it was the supervisory European's fault, never for a moment an African's. The other officers were congenial. His 2i/c, Bob Pusser, was the junior captain, rather on his dignity. Two of them had just spent their fourth year with The Gambia, compared with my three months (one whole week with my platoon), waiting mostly to resist a Vichy invasion or contemplate an attack on Dakar. They *knew* that to 'understand Africans' required complex years of close association and study: I, not having four years to spare, depended on what the African Other Ranks (AORs) appeared to be thinking of me and of the other Europeans, and on individual approaches and reactions.

My platoon serjeant was a big bearded Bambara whom nothing fazed. The other two whom I remember most clearly were my orderly, Abu Silla, with a wonderful smile and a heart and will of gold, and Corporal Keramo Fate, i/c No 7 Sec, stocky, cheerful, a manager of men and a pillar when things were shaky. Keramo had been a DC's steward boy, regularly hauled in to oversee officers' mess functions requiring understanding of how to lay tables and cutlery, and to serve food and drinks without anyone's embarrassment. Ending as RSM following (I think) a spell as Provost Sjt, after the war he was major-domo and mace-carrier of The Gambian Parliament. When I lost faith, these were the three (aided by the Beethoven *allegretto*) who could restore it, more than any other comrades-in-arms. None of the Gambians had ever seen hills, let alone mountains, like the Western Ghats over which we did that week of training, 50 miles distant from our Nasik camp. For a Scot who, city-born but not confined, knew his own country, this breath-taking scenery, the plunging gorges, the dramatic hills and valleys, thick forest and ridged paddy fields where cultivated, were a tonic. At night when 'in harbour', without a flicker of light apart from a little moon and stars, it was heavenly. One day we halted at the top of a hill, where the Indian village band came out and played spontaneously for us: their instruments sounded like party cracker squeakers. I have no idea what the exercise actually taught us, let alone the staff.

Among the platoon commanders I was the least but one. 'Ham', who had been up at Balliol in the year before the war, a classical 'first', was an unforgettable man of colossal energy, with the shortest of fuzes, ever ready to point out what was not right about things and to whom to attribute the cause: he was to become a schoolmaster of note, and also the volunteer historian of this little war of Gambian Waffs as part of 81 Div,★ whose invitation to scrape the barrel of memory was the *origo* of this chapter. Jock Morris was very much a lowland Scot, enjoyed a good girn, knew his rights and had the best of natures; like Ham, he is a friend to this day (they have corrected the grosser of my false memories). My appointed mucker, Ellis, was becoming nervy, quick to show anger with the troops. P had doubled round the Meadows trees in the STC with me; he had octu'd at Barmouth with my school friends and was to go with me into the colonial service, but to Sierra Leone. Q was plump, self-confident and good value in small doses, but doomed. R was an Errol Flynn lookalike with a hot head, but amicable. S was an ex-regular drum-major, who had learnt how to get away with anything, and wasn't going to forget. T, a little older, was a nice guy with bad feet. U (in dock with malaria while we were mustering) was efficient and companionly. V was a little effeminate but friendly; doomed. W was quiet without being self-effacing. X, the ack-ack platoon commander, was also assistant adjutant, and desperate for his third pip. Y was small in stature, Z was a Londoner, and I recall no more. Since

---

★*War Bush: 81 (West African) Division in Burma 1943-45*: John A L Hamilton, Foreword by HRH The Duke of Edinburgh; Michael Russell (Publishing) Ltd, Norwich 2001; ISBN 0 85955 267 5.

nowadays it is so very important, it is curious to reflect that most were probably virgins.

Fire!
What the next months taught me was that however much one might wish to be elsewhere in another time slot, and however wickedly or thoughtlessly authority might have planned that one be where one was, if there were no practical alternative to making the best of whatever worst was to hand, then one simply got on with it, for as long as flesh and spirit could cope. It helps to have a job and responsibility for others. Even if unconvincing, one is also helped by the fear of being thought to be fearful. These aids take the mind off things. At its very lowest, in jungle (and, presumably, in desert) there is nowhere to run away and hide, even if lectures have been given on survival and why The Jungle is Your Friend, with all its access to strange edibles and potable water inside bamboo stalks. It may be different in street and open country warfare. At its best, Dr Johnson has said it for us. I cannot look back with pride, but I may do so with some twisted gratitude that my understanding was immeasurably widened of things that few of to-day's generation can comprehend – even when I had no conception of what was going on around me, which was almost always. I can now look askance at ideological politicians who send young folk to real war without the background of having faced fire themselves.

Organized chaos got the brigade on to trains for the long haul across India, stopping at stations where sahibs might eat in a certain comfort in the buffet. The Gambia went in two echelons, detraining at Alipore station on 29 & 30 November 1943, and we made our way to barracks somewhere not far from Howrah, Chowringhee, Fort William and the *maidan*. We had read about the Bengal famine, which had hit the sub-continent's administration hard: at least, as Kipling-readers knew, there had been tried and tested routines long laid down for action and relief, and these were in train so far as war priorities permitted. Yet it was difficult for a wartime civil service to prevent hordes of villagers from the *mofussil* pouring into grossly overcrowded and starving Calcutta to add to the horrors. In our brief stay we were hardened to the sight of emaciated children, and became used to stepping over recumbent figures on the pavements, who might be alive. Some of us were detailed to load corpses on trucks and take them to mass lime pits at Dum Dum (I wasn't.) The feelings of our Africans were not easy to judge; but whatever our own embarrassment when consuming our daily rations, we could not but wonder how many children might be fed on the day's dole of rice, bully beef and biscuits (delicious local Shakupara, not ship's cabin) issued to an AOR, or on our British Troops rations. War has its own priorities. (Decolonized Africa suffers famines that our empire never knew.) Soon enough we embarked on another troopship, on the banks of the Hooghli. I was with the second echelon on the TSS *Nevasa*, which observed an unresisted aerial Japanese bombardment of the river from a safe distance.

Sailing across to Chittagong, on 8 December we found low-lying and dank countryside, with small rises around the villages and farms, full of spiritless Bengalis. A short march brought us to the Assam & Bengal railway, which had a narrow metre gauge spur to Dohazari; thence by bus to bivouac at Chiringa, where we stepped down to stand on the feet which would carry us for many months to come. It was all jungly country, in spades. It is salutary to recall that 81(WA)Div had only been conceived on paper nine short months before (when French West Africa's black governor-general Éboué having declared for the Allies, our colonies were no longer threatened by Vichy). The 3rd (Nigerian) brigade had been removed to support the Chindits' LofCs (our 6th 'international' brigade from all four colonies was followed by the 5th Gold Coast brigade). We had never trained as brigades, still less been exercised as a reduced division. We had not trained with, nor liaised with, the light batteries with their 3·7" howitzers who were to back us. We had understood there to be light ack-ack-cum-anti-tank batteries in support, but they were not suited to our proposed long march. We had heard of our Recce Regiment, but they and their bren carriers had been detached to support the main corps down the coast on the west. We had no machine guns heavier than the section brens. None of our divisional top brass had had any more experience of this kind of terrain or warfare than the rest of us (as already said, 3 Bde did have brief forest training in southern Nigeria, but an alarming number of its strength had gone down with disease picked up in water-crossings entered contrary to RAMC advice). As ours was not to reason why, none of this was fully appreciated at the time and did nothing to demoralize us. We vaguely knew that we were repeating on a very large scale the first Chindit campaign, air-supplied with no protected lines-of-communication, and very possibly with no aerial evacuation either, in country like theirs. We should of course have the wonders of wireless, if it worked.

If the reader has no conception of what was going on all the time, that is because, as we know, my mates and I had none either. Nor is there much to read elsewhere: before Ham's book, the formal histories and most of the personal memoirs in commercial print ignore the fact that there were 96,000 African troops in Burma – a substantial figure against 36,000 deservedly famous Gurkhas, the 120,000 British troops of the Forgotten Army, and a quarter of a million Indian Army.

We understood that the division was to protect the left flank of 15 Corps, commanded by Sir Philip Christison, and pose a threat to the Japanese rear, by moving down the Kaladan valley, the principal channel dividing the Chittagong and Arakan Hill Tracts from central Burma. The challenge was to get there. We would be like microbes traversing corrugated cardboard. There was a 'coolie track' trailing across three major and three lesser precipitous north-south ranges of up to 3,000'; this coolies' way led up the Sangu river from Dohazari, past Mowdok to a big stream called the Pi Chaung. Thence the Kaladan river made its way down to Akyab, the target port of this part of the Burma war. All the big stream gorges were called chaungs. The Kaladan was tidal from shortly below where we should reach it. There was an Indian infantry battalion of the 5/9 Jats at Mowdok who had been pushed back there by the Japs, and were to see the monsoon through, backed by scouts from Tripura Rifles, supplied with difficulty upstream on the fast-flowing Sangu by country boats and *khistis* (local canoes punted through the gorges by river people) – road-building on its banks was impossible.

Our div comd was Major-General C G Woolner, CB DSO and three Great War MCs, who was a sapper to trade (staff officer to Engineer-in-Chief in 14-18 France), senior by service to his superior lieutenant-generals. He saw that the mountains were soft sandstone, susceptible to being cut into a narrow track. The wonderful new vehicle the 5cwt 'jeep' could tow the guns on it, and carry loads beyond the capacity even of the Nigerian Aux Group Munshis, trained to lift 70lbs worth of dismantled mountain guns (Kipling's screw gun). Everything and everyone else would go on foot. Beyond that, he could only look at the maps and hope. There was also V-Force (British or Anglo-Burmese intelligence officers accompanied by local hillmen), who could try to tell us where the Japanese might be, and which of the few villagers who would not flee from intruders might be trusted.

We were given enough jeeps for twelve 3·7" howitzers and essential heavy loads. The Commander West African Engineers recced on foot all the way 'straight across' to Mowdok on the Sangu, since even a jeep track could not be forced up the sides of the Sangu gorge, while the Jats' supply dump was enlarged at Mowdok. We should reach Paletwa on the Kaladan by 19 January 1944. 4NR went ahead, putting out a company to protect the 'front' at Daletme inside the Burma frontier, higher up the Kaladan. Early December Field Company sappers, backed by local paid labour, began work on the first twenty miles of the notional route, marking out the traces for the sweating PBI to hack out, preferring their traditional matchets to the effete European picks and shovels. We, the rest of 6 Bde, the Gambians and Sierra Leoneans, were behind them (Div HQ and 5 Bde followed a fortnight later, the light batteries by Christmas). Our job was to carve out the tracks both sides of Mowdok; the Gold Coasters to work towards us from Chiringa on the Matamuhari river.

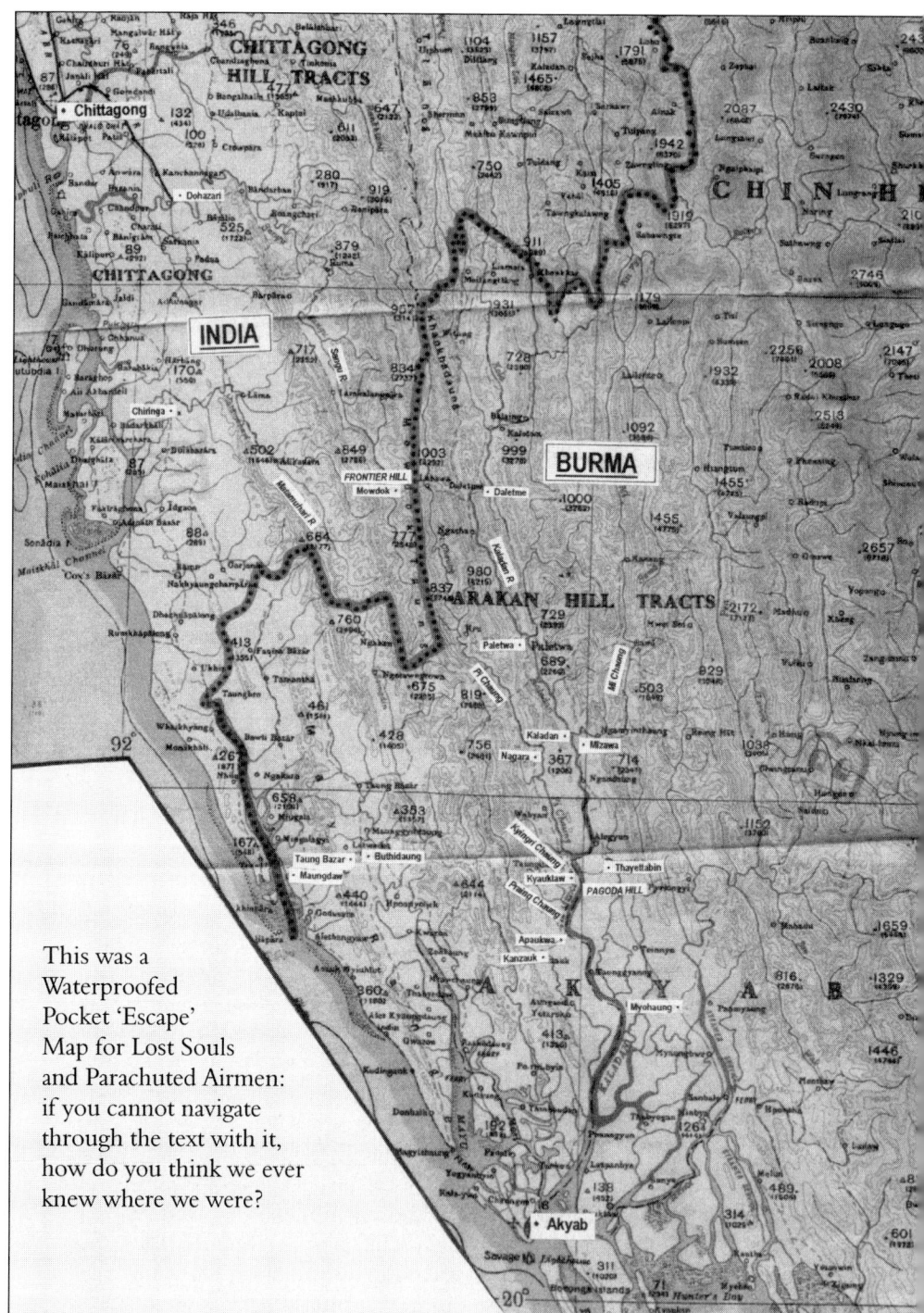

This was a Waterproofed Pocket 'Escape' Map for Lost Souls and Parachuted Airmen: if you cannot navigate through the text with it, how do you think we ever knew where we were?

There seemed to be an Indian RIASC Mule Coy (by coincidence, No 81) involved in the Mowdok supply, which everyone wanted to replace with our jeeps. Speed was of the essence.

We discovered how little introduction we had had to WT (wireless telegraphy, not weapon training), apart from voice procedures, even when terrain and equipment allowed attempts at intercommunication. To add to the initial miseries, there was an outbreak of cholera, and out of 72 cases 44 soldiers died, 15 of them in our own unlucky D Coy. About now I heard that schoolmate Colin Oliphant, who had been a staff captain in Delhi, was a lieutenant again and serving with divisional signals on the main front to the south-west; whilst another school contemporary at home had done 30 days for some offence connected with becoming a conscientious objector overnight. John Ellis had joined our C Coy at this very last minute, replacing a malarial casualty.

I was coming to terms with jungle existence: I had had my bellyful of the vegetation and the hill-climbing, the foot-slogging and splashy tramping through rivers, and the ubiquitous bamboo overshadowing everything from the cool dry season sunshine. One could admire the local village skills in building *bashas*, beautifully sturdy erections of bamboo scaffolding with criss-cross interwoven flattened bamboo walls and floors, and heavy leaf roofs; regularly rebuilt, they seemed healthier and more pest-free than mud huts and thatch. Despite the absence of mosquitoes during the dry season, there were always flies and ants, but one could be entranced by lovely butterflies, and by the vivid emerald dragonflies, especially the red ones with blue noses. There were no visible birds in the undergrowth, although they could be heard twittering in the treetops, not least those with the unending song of delirium, or the rainbird's cuckooish tinkle of a bell. Bats swirled round the trees at nightfall. Sometimes a barking deer would surprise us from across a valley, though we never saw him. Tree frogs sang to us. So did the politely-named air-blown *Tuck-too* lizards, whose repeated belches we crudely capped with a 'Tuck you, too!' (or something like it). They were no relative of the *Tock-tock* birds, who sounded like little geologists hammering on little hollow rocks. There were also the howls of the jackals, almost domestic, and the squeals of baboons and cries of the langur monkeys. Not that the 12-14 hours a day digging and cutting, not all supervisory by a long chalk, left much opportunity for nature study or contemplation. Bully, tea and biscuits occupied most spare time, and sundown spelt the end of any activity, except restoration of the tissues during a cold night, for more track-building soon after dawn and a hurried breakfast. Sometimes a mist would come down at the bottom of a valley, and the bamboo leaves might then drip their condensate upon the sleepers, leading to an intensely chilly wakening in the dewy morning. The cold at night was the greatest strain on the AORs; they slept with every stitch of clothing on, as well as blanket and gascape wrapped round bodies and heads. They couldn't have feared cold feet too much, though: many had already managed to 'loss' their boots, which they had found hindrances on slimy hills, in streams and up steep obstacles. God made us barefoot and hoofless, after all.

Christmas Day 1943 is our one day off. At half past six Babukar brings his master his mug of tea; he has at last learnt not to add sugar. 'A Merry Christmas, Serjeant Ballance!' From a nearby equally makeshift but tolerable bush bed of bamboo and sticks, surmounted by a green mosquito net, comes, 'Same to you, Sir!' His servant is an alleged Wesleyan Methodist, my only Christian in the platoon, so I wish that youngster the same and turn over. Breakfast arrives (bully and biscuits, but to-day with jam), thanks to the uncomplaining company cook, and at half past nine I rise. Beginning to shave, I decide, just to see what happens, to grow a moustache until we return to civilization, if we do; Wingate has told his chaps to get five minutes more kip a day by not shaving, so some of the less prepossessing of us are letting beards grow, with tacit permission (nobody has ever stopped our Africans from having hairy faces if they so choose). Next begins a succession of winningly hopeful visits from 'my men', each looking for their 'Christmas'. Explaining that even if I had brought the bank with me into the jungle, and that even if my bedload had been overloaded with 'small-small tings' to 'dash' them with, I am puzzled at what Christmas has to do with them, I politely rebuff them all. However, I have managed to purchase a small sack of rice from an amiable bare-bottomed local Mugh, and with Ballance 'won' some extra sugar and bully beef, so they don't do badly later in the day.

I send my orderly away down the track to the neighbouring platoon, to offer Lt Ellis seasonal compliments and the *Essays* of Francis Bacon on strict loan. I am still getting into Boswell's *Life of Dr Samuel Johnson*. We hope for a bottle of beer to commemorate the Saviour's birth, but are only promised the possibility of a rum ration (distilled in Nasik, and thought the least treacherous of Indian spirits). There has been no home mail for ages, which leaves more time for removing ticks from parts of the anatomy. Somehow I have scrounged a Burmese *dah* in a nice leather case, narrower and squared off, but serving the same purposes of hacker-tool-weapon; I try it out in competition with my orderly and his issue matchet at cutting open bamboo stalks, to find out whether there really is drinking water inside – there isn't. Ballance and I discuss the great event of a few days ago, when a unit a mile away was challenged by an angry elephant. The last meal of the day, before sundown, has a double dishing of tinned fruit: it doesn't make us think better of the QM. Funny thing, there's no sign of felicitatory intercommunication with Bn HQ.

In the first week of January 1944 the first airdrop parachuted down, and from the middle of the month the division was wholly supplied by air. Woolner was able to jeep all the way past Frontier Hill to the Kaladan (some descents were so steep that not every vehicle was able to return back, even in reverse, unless it had a winch built in). We had completed the 73 miles of switchback jeep track to the river on time. It was immediately dubbed 'West Africa Way'. I doubt whether anything quite like it has happened since Hannibal took his elephants across the Alps, but nobody knows about it bar the few remaining who were there. We finished our company's specific part of the jeep track on 13 January, where the CO unveiled a memorial to the cholera dead.

Jeep-track building gave way, among more warlike occupations, to clearance of dropping zones for parachuted loads and freefall of (theoretically) unbreakables. 81(WA)Div was the first full formation to be totally supplied from the air without ground LofCs, and that includes the original Chindits, who lived off the land. Unarmed *Dakota*s (DC3s), British, Canadian and American, flew successive runs at as little as 300' over our DZs (dropping zones) between the escarpments. Occasional parachuteless 4-gallon kerosene tins full of 'compo' rations ('bully beef bombs'), and many double-sewn sacks of cereals or clothing, were hazardous free drops: three soldiers were to be killed by them, including our own Lt QM. Each compo held a day's food for eight men, capriciously discriminating for European, Hindu, Muslim and, in theory, African troops; everyone appreciated having another race, religion or creed's approved sustenance, making an interesting change when mistaken allocations arrived. American K rations would come, for use by patrols, with such necessaries as candy, gum and lavatory paper included with the chew-bars; occasional Yankee D rations were seen, which explained why doughboys loved our bully and we their spam – anything for a change.

Things now became serious, and a combination of muddled memory, less informative letters home surviving to jog the muddle, and the sketchiness of anything more official to consult, mean that my own undistinguished part will be disconnected, and probably inaccurate even in sequence. C Coy with the rest of the battalion went from Mowdok down the Daletme Chaung which split in two (we took the eastern fork). During our trek down the river the Europeans were enabled to do target practice with their sten guns at kerosene tins floating past. For the first time I fired my personal weapon (or any sten gun at all, for that matter); it was nice to know that it worked. On 21 January C Coy went down another chaung, the rest down its parallel sister, where Hunt was fatally wounded in the stomach. We harboured in a hamlet, while a patrol led by CSM McGuiness captured two miserable little Japanese (McGuiness ended as RSM and retired near Blackpool, where he organized the local children to wear sacks for kilts and to drill to his bagpipes, collected RWAFF and other military memorabilia in every corner of his house, including in his bath, and kept Gambian reunions going until his death.)

Considering the remoteness, and that years would pass before satisfactory air photography would be possible, the maps from the old Indian Surveys were surprisingly good. The valley was beginning to broaden, with room for fields and villages on either riverside. 5(GC)Bde were behind us at first. What might have been thunder, but probably was gunfire, could be heard across ridges far to the west, the Japs giving 5 and 7(Ind)Divs a hard time at what was to be the notorious Admin Box action. (Nobody heard exactly what happened to Colin, said to be destroying codes in his signals HQ when 7 Div HQ was attacked hand-to-hand near Taung Bazar and wiped out.) I do remember being held up in front of Kaladan village: it was here that I saw my first dead soldier, an African lying by the side of the path near the river. My own men looked at him without much open emotion, except for my serjeant, who said, 'He good man – he die, him body no smell.'

When and where the next memorable event took place, I am unsure. My platoon found itself facing up a defile at the side of a chaung, advancing against a presumed enemy defending Kaladan village, twenty miles on from Paletwa. Everywhere there were chasms, waterfalls and cliffs, hindering our intent to outflank it from the spur shown on the map to its west. Short of scarpering back, there was no way to go but onwards and upwards, single file, through the familiar map legend, 'dense mixed jungle, mainly bamboo'. Ham in B Coy, below us on the dry bed of the chaung, has a similar memory to mine of the precise event: a whistle blew from some vantage point high on the cliff-like hill above, following which the 'throp' of a mortar firing was heard, and a few seconds later the severe crack of the bomb exploding much nearer. Ham tells me there were several in a progressive enfilade from our right, but I only remember the one that landed (I swear it) three yards away from me and, shall we say, deafened me but did no other harm; Sjt Ballance was less lucky, although further off, and was wounded, as were Godfrey Oliphant the company commander (I suspect it was one of the other bombs that got him) and one or two AORs. Oliphant was no relation of my poor school friend Colin.

The incident encapsulated for me what I at my lowly level later diagnosed as the Japanese policy – let us move forward to some difficult situation; when we were in the most difficult environment let us have it while we were in confusion; then quietly dematerialize in order to repeat the performance a good many miles further on; until they were quite ready to turn the tables and wrap us up in kinder country. There had been nothing approaching hand-to-hand fighting, nor was much to come. What left the most impression was that within seconds of my personal explosion, the only two humans I could detect in the vicinity were my Ballance and, visible and audible, Oliphant. Where my platoon and the other wounded had gone, Allah alone knew. When the confusion and the casualties had cleared up enough to realize that indeed the Japs had withdrawn (possibly they thought they were severely outnumbered for a long haul) we reassembled somewhere, very confused, and arranged to continue towards the village; then 12 Platoon sheepishly reappeared out of the blue. I was wondering who would be to blame if I had been given some offensive order and found nobody to pass it on to or share it with. I was not wondering about my, and my soldiers', lack of relevant training and inadequate knowledge of each other; I was wondering whether the idea of using African peasants in such a war was not misguided. Yet we needed the manpower to cover all the theatres that had opened up in the world. I never for one moment questioned whether we, *and our Africans*, were right to be fighting the war, both to defeat the totalitarians and to save the parts of the Empire that they had taken (or intended to take) from us: nor have I ever since.

We were shocked many weeks later to hear from one correspondent that Hunt's personal effects had been sent home, and that his mother had opened the sad bundle to be faced with his bloody and bullet-ripped OG battle dress. Was this also about the time when another major got it too, in 'the groin'? We heard various scraps of news of the outside world: Maungdaw had been recaptured, and Churchill had publicly revealed the existence of Fourteenth Army. We still felt Forgotten. During the month I had changed my batman, for the better; my new personal servant, Alisan Djibba, who resented having to do 'woman work' but carried my 20lb bedroll and '08 pack as well as his rifle, built bamboo beds wherever we stopped for more than one night, shared my slit trench, and did for me generally, with what one may only call faithfulness and loyalty. He had the unfortunate experience of a disagreement with a local Burmese, who he unaccountably thought had been passing our whereabouts to the enemy. I came back from a patrol to find that he had been caught by an officer smiting the villager, and hauled before the CO, who had wasted no time on protocol 'While On Active Service' and had him promptly whipped, 'twenfo fo harse', by the provost serjeant. 'He near kill me,' Alisan told me when asked what accounted for his obvious gloom. It is a token of relationships that I felt personally involved, even if I felt the summary justice deserved: I complained to the officer witness that he should have awaited my return and as the 'boy's master' left me to take primary action to secure discipline and any retribution. I got very short shrift.

The benighted country now had a sickly smell everywhere, its cause dubious. It lacked the magnificent scenic compensations of the switchback ranges over West Africa Way's summits. As it opened out into clearings and paddy we realized how protective jungle cover had actually been. The river was now wide, deep and tidal. The 11 (EA) Divisional Scouts, from Nyasaland, had joined us somehow at Paletwa, and were also to the front on the east bank: they were even more lightly armed than ourselves, spoke no English, had been mustered as lightly disciplined tip-and-run guerrillas and spyers-out of land, but not as infantry, and were led by splendid Europeans out for adventure but not materially equipped for the hard slog. Our light batteries had caught up with the division on the track at Mizawa, just up the Mi Chaung which entered the Kaladan river opposite Kaladan village.

I now saw my first live Jap: he was a lad, looking bewildered beside his captors but otherwise expressionless; the Celestials alone knew whether he regretted being left behind by accident and should commit *seppuku*, but he was amenable despite getting a hard time from his black warders (I had missed seeing the two who had surrendered before Paletwa – I never knew what we did with such strays, unless they were flown out for interrogation when there were spare seats). It has always been surprising how much nasty thick jungle warfare can be fought without actually seeing the foe.

This was a strange time to receive at a place called Nagara the Edinburgh Lady Provost's comfort parcel. It contained some heavy writing paper, a Christmas card from the Lord Provost himself, a copy of Graham Greene's *Brighton Rock*, a five shilling postal order, a stick of shaving soap, a tin of Gibbs' dentifrice, two Gillette razor blades and 24 Kensitas cigarettes. Perhaps that was what induced me to remove the moustache, which had not been admired. I lived for a whole day on Japanese food; we had found some of their hard rations abandoned in a *basha* – muslin bags filled with tiny biscuits, very like our old HP biscuits, mixed with little sugar-ball sweets and tinned fish (a mixture of salmon, prawn and crab), all tasty. Europeans were now issued with tins of face cream for camouflage: a dirty greeny-brown paste made by a famous cosmetic firm as its 'war work', it left the troops in stitches, thinking we were trying to look like *pukka* black men.

Meanwhile a difficult hour had passed. The CO Laing had come round the companies and assembled the Europeans. It had come to his ears, he said, that expressions had been uttered of distrust in our troops. This was no more than the truth, in varying degrees. My experience of losing all mine into thin air had not been the only one. When it came to my turn, as ever throughout life I shot my mouth off without considering the consequences: I was not sure that I would have faith in them if we were again suddenly presented with an unexpectedly alarming situation requiring them to stand fast and await a command, or words to that effect. Laing was livid: look, he didn't want to send me for court-martial, he said. Idiotlike I mildly replied that I thought that he had asked us an honest question, and I had given him an honest answer. Ellis foolishly but stolidly then said that he quite agreed with me, and our CO looked daggers. An unconvincing pep talk followed, and after his departure several subalterns and serjeants said I had only given word to what they all thought: but the acting coy comd was silent. We were still pretty young. It was the mob effect that was worrying us: I still had real affection for Abu Silla and Keramo Fate, and for batman Alisan Djibba.

We continued our advance. I remember on 20 February reaching the point where the Pi Chaung was about to flow into the Kaladan, but have no recollection of how we crossed it on the 22nd, nor of crossing another chaung at 1330 on 23rd and being under heavy fire all night, and losing all contact because our 48 wireless set battery was flat. We took the outpost and entered Kyauktaw village unopposed on the 24th. I knew the place names, but many have been suppressed as they could mean nothing now without a map.

The weather was hotter and stickier, and sleeping out on bamboo beds with only a groundsheet above the mosquito net was pleasantly cool. Although the Plough now dipped under the horizon, we still saw no Southern Cross. The few villagers seemed reasonably but not rapturously pleased to see us, but we were advised to ca' canny. For a few peaceful days I occupied a deserted *basha*, the first roof over my head since Calcutta; there I had a bizarre parcel from Mona Cannell in Douglas, containing brilliantine and a Mabel Lucy Atwell calendar, and found that my precious bottle of Quink had leaked all over my haversack and writing paper, reducing me to pencilling letters home on flimsy field message pads. Wondering what might happen next, I was sent with my orderly on some errand to divisional headquarters. My message delivered, I was asked by a kindly staff officer whether I would like to sit in on a GOC's briefing session that was going on, and for the first and last time got something like a whole picture of what we were supposed to be doing. I reported back to Col Laing, who seemed offended that Little Me had been made privy to higher thinking.

We could see the 350' high Pagoda Hill, topped by its principal pagoda shining with gold leaf, dropping sheer down to the far bank of the river, which was about 450 yards wide. There were tales of the presence of an INA (Indian National Army, known as the Traitor Army, deserters or POWs who had been 'turned') battalion of the Subhas Chandra Bose Brigade, named after the Bengali nationalist who had seceded to Tokyo; I never saw hair nor hide of them, although others reported sighting a motley brown mob in reach-me-down uniforms. The Nyasa Scouts, making do as best they could to substitute for our phantom third brigade, had got that far, and were handing the Hill over to 4NR, while they went east to patrol a road to Myohaung from Thayettabin. My unofficial HQ briefing may have named Myohaung as the division's prime target to occupy, thereby cutting the only effective Jap LofC in central Burma. The division was still diminished in its essentials, lacking its third very light infantry brigade, but arrival on the plains' edge enabled the Dakota-borne arrival of encumbrances taken for granted in a regular formation: Bofors guns, folding-boat equipment and outboard motors, motor transport now amounting to about 40 15cwts and 140 jeeps, not to speak of an Indian Inland Water Transport Company to paddle or power the growing merchant fleet of river craft. The crowning glory was an Indian Divisional Pack Bullock Company, 74 handsome and bulky white cattle (daubed in khaki camouflage dye), presumably to carry whatever trucks, jeeps and aux group carriers could not lift: as no such loads existed, it was no surprise that one by one the unhappy clumsy creatures suffered strange injuries requiring them to be put down (throats). By masterpieces of engineering improvisation Div HQ and all this paraphernalia crossed to the west bank by 27 February.

I now read that at this moment smiling Christison suddenly changed Woolner's orders: he was to concentrate on occupying the western line between Apaukwa and Kanzauk, thus threatening the Jap LofC on the Mayu river between Akyab and Buthidaung, and also to keep the Japs guessing as to his intentions – while still holding tight to Kyauktaw and Pagoda Hill. An Indian battalion, 7/16 Punjabis, was to be put under command, which would be concentrated back at Paletwa. 4NR left Pagoda Hill to the Nyasas, crossed and pushed south on the west towards Apaukwa, DivHQ being behind them, south of Kyauktaw where we Gambians were still in reserve around the main airstrip. They took it on 1 March, with us listening to the light battery firing in support. Meanwhile we were told that there had been trouble up the river, where a defenceless CCS (casualty clearing station) of medicos on its way down had been mauled, and Col Hubert of the Punjabis had lost his boat during a shooting match, making his way back to his battalion after a liaison visit to our bosses.

Here I *really* became confused, and nothing read since reduces the confusion. The official records by people who were not there write of our disaster and demoralization as a formation. All I can testify to is muddle while trying to do the impossible, and that at the end nobody, West African or nervous European, had done anything shameful that I was aware of. We had heard artillery fire on the east bank, where the East Africans were all alone, suggesting that at last the Japanese were coming back instead of continuing phoney, let alone tactical, retreats. Once we were in open plains, it was the obvious time and place for them to counter-attack. Late in the evening of 1 March Woolner took 1GambR effectively under direct command and warned us to be ready to plug the gap. One company slipped over at dead of night, and the rest of us followed at first light. The Nyasas had fallen back on Pagoda Hill during the night, and had met our leading company at its north end. It was obvious that Pagoda Hill, jutting out of a plain with no cover on the east all the way to the motor road and Thayettabin, needed a brigade and heavy machine guns to defend it against serious attack, not a scout battalion. The Japs were serious: they had a 150mm howitzer, which had done moral and physical damage to the Scouts overnight and was now aligned on Pagoda Hill. D Coy was posted to a tiny village at the north end of the hill. By mid-afternoon my platoon found ourselves near the north-east side of the hill, Ellis's slightly towards the south on the same side. I think another company was intended to occupy the top, but for some reason the intent was unsuccessful.

We dug in, but our slit trenches were far from reassuring. I have no recollection of where the rest of the battalion was, nor of having close contact with any other platoon, still less any HQ. We were looking out over a mass of long grass at the plain or paddy towards scrubby bush and hillocks round and behind Thayettabin, and the hill range behind it. The advance company was, I understand, sent down to the south at dusk. We spent the night by the light of the moon, awaiting we knew not what, but assuming it would be an assault. We heard many shots and much shouting.

Why I got a message from a runner (the first and only word from higher up since digging in) to withdraw at a fixed time in the morning, I never knew, but I well remember staring at the minute hand till the precise moment registered on my Cape Town wristwatch, which had been synchronized at the previous day's O Group. It was just after daybreak when I gave the order to up and away in a southerly direction. As we moved off, none too slowly, down a chaung to rejoin the main battalion south-west of the hill by the river, we heard crackling noises of bodies moving through the dry grass behind us: obviously they had crossed the plain in the dark and had planned a dawn attack. Had they made a night offensive, in the absence of any other orders (and there were none that I recall), we should have had to stand firm and resist; why instead under orders we withdrew at first light without a shot was not evident. That it was intentional was only ambivalently evident when Bul (Capt Bulkowski) welcomed Ellis and myself at our rendezvous with the encouraging news that he had never expected to see us again, and that we should both get MCs. 'But Bul, we never opened fire! We retreated, strictly as ordered, before the enemy arrived!' There was a mittel-European gesture of nonchalance. The battalion, or most of it (some, including the mortar platoon and parts of D Coy, were cut off) moved downstream to meet the Sierra Leonean battalion. They had been sent over to back us up, but been stranded on an uncharted sandbank and arrived too late. Tales were exchanged of how one company had seen some untidily uniformed INA, of a Japanese officer riding down the road on a white charger, and of the African who had been captured and deprived of his uniform, but escaped, in nothing but the PT shorts which he wore as underwear, after seeing the 150mm gun being towed by a 'horsecart'. 'Cellist Paul Ward had had a finger shot off at Lammadaw: praise be, it was the right hand, leaving him as capable of wielding his bow as before.

I have read that on 1 March a massed congregation of British and West Africans held a commemoration service on the banks of the river to celebrate the first anniversary of the division's formation. Pigs have flown. I have also gathered, more credibly, that by late on 2 March Christison had changed his mind again, possibly hearing premature or mischievous rumours of our alleged disintegration: Woolner had been told to hang on to Pagoda Hill and Kyauktaw at all costs; the rest of 6 Bde was to have crossed back east to support us. As may appear from my uncertain account, 1SaLR had come too late, 4NR was too distant to follow up, and the hill had already been abandoned anyway. Gambia's 2i/c told the sad tale in no very coherent fashion to Div HQ in mid-morning of 3 March; shortly afterwards he was evacuated, suffering from fibrositis. Our general recognized that with Japs on Pagoda Hill overlooking everything for miles around, and enjoying heavy artillery and machine guns, despite a modest air strike (which we cheered) Kyauktaw was indefensible. He promptly decided to concentrate the whole division (for the first time ever in a single locality, it may be said) in the area lying between the Kaladan and the Pi Chaung where there was cover; he dubbed this mesopotamia Iraq.

The heavy stuff which had so recently arrived, conceivably helpful in a further advance downstream to Akyab, was now an embarrassment; new jeep tracks had to be hastily cut out to hide them and enable eventual terrestrial or aerial evacuation. 6 Bde was reunited on the west bank by a nocturnal river crossing on 3/4 March, which received no attention from Japanese guns or patrols, and made its way to welcome cover on the Praing Chaung, whence the sight of Pagoda Hill being shelled by our 3·7s and bombed and burnt by RAF or IAF *Vengeance* dive-bombers was cheering. There had been a few previous dive-bombings to watch on our way down, boosting morale; the aerobatics of the planes curvetting round jungle peaks and valleys virtually shouted the aviators' skill and courage.

Covering the withdrawal of our brigade and divisional HQs, we made our way next to yet another chaung, west of our old acquaintance the Pi Chaung, and finally to a ridge at the north-west corner of a meander of the Kyingri Chaung. This formed a three sided loop suitable for a divisional defensive position, an 'Admin Box' with a *Dakota* strip in the middle and the ridge for the fourth side. There were significant changes in leadership. Our Brigadier Hayes, no chicken and under the befogged cloud of Pagoda Hill, gave way to one Cartwright, a fire-eater who was before long to keel over and die. Two battalion commanders went, one being Bob Baillie of 4NR, another imperturbable middle-ager whom I should serve before long: he was in charge of a column ('Bailcol') to make its way out on 25 March, back up West Africa Way on which we had all come in, with all the now superfluous transport and heavy equipment that was jeepable (not the edible bullocks) and the latest casualties. The 7/16 Punjabis, whom I never saw, were still at Paletwa. In The Gambia we had a further upheaval. For reasons which I forget, the relics of juju-demoralized D Company were redistributed among the other three companies; a new company had to be formed, with presumably higher morale, under the former adjutant Walker. X Company was its not too encouraging title, and I, with most of my men, was told off to join it later in March.

Patrolling restarted, and when this discovered something in need of attention there might be an airstrike in support: the outside world was helping us in other ways than just bringing the groceries down the chimney. I remember two of my patrols, and one strange incident, at the Kyingri Loop. I was sent out on a recce patrol into the bamboo-clad hills to find what might be there. As we crossed an unavoidable wide open patch of dry paddy, a machine gun opened up from the ridge opposite and I gained my only war wound. No 1 Scout and No 2 Scout trampled me into the ground, and I never knew whose was the boot whose nail tore part of my left thumb-ball open: I bore the scar for years. Picking myself up in very short order I galloped back to cover, arriving by far the last. 'Well done!' said Major Walker. Despite my report, another patrol went out the same way next day; Lt Brown went 'missing, believed killed'. A day or two later Sjt Turner (my new platoon BNCO) and I took two sections on a standing patrol to watch one of the re-entrants on the edge of the Kyingri redoubt, a place covered with dry and whitened dead bamboo at every possible angle, and overlooking a near-precipice: he regaled me with the life of a Nottingham miner, and I learnt some poems from Palgrave's *Golden Treasury*. It was an idyllically peaceful 24 hours, and our AORs slept them contentedly away.

A few days on, I was on watch in our harbour in the middle of the night, when Armageddon began. An observant African saw what he imagined to be a torchlight in the dark below our redoubt. He opened fire at it, the rest of his section followed, and within a minute the whole battalion was firing wildly. Racing round my own platoon, I realized that most were firing up into the air from their slit trenches and that nobody had a target. I was reduced to clouting their heads with the butt of my sten gun to stop the waste of ammunition. We never knew what had sparked it all off, but my bet was, and remains, a cluster of fireflies, which were not uncommon. Our CO was replaced by Tony Read, a Gurkha one day to be a full general. Laing did not say good-bye. Blameless Woolner also left his division.

Soon afterwards I left the battalion, as in Chapter 1. John Ellis had been shot ten days before, losing the 'terminal phalanx' of the fourth finger of his right hand, and suffering damage to the little and middle fingers, the only casualty in a patrol (I wondered whether this would affect draughtmanship in his intended profession of architecture, or like Ward it would make no odds). The following night Johnnie Rose had stuck it out with his platoon on a rise in the same area, surrounded by heavily firing Japanese whom he successfully repulsed despite his wounds. Rose won an 'immediate' MC. The battalion then joined Hubforce, commanded by Lt-col Hubert of the 7/17 Punjabis, which was to cover the division on the south side of its retreat north, while deceiving the Japs into thinking nobody had left at all.

I went out in Murcol, the column commanded by Lt-col Murphy; I was with the Field Ambulance part of that outfit, which crossed the Kaladan on the nights of 7 and 8 April 1944. Alisan Djibba stayed with me, carrying my bed-valise all the way. He was a caring and thoughtful young soul who instinctively knew what circumstances needed. Some Gold Coasters in the column fired at a troop of monkeys in the Matamuhari gorge, and ate those they hit. Alisan was appalled: 'Man dey eat monkey all same man dey eat person,' was his commentary. I began to smoke again, and continued for another 19 years. I made a new friend, Ted Hubbard, who had been what was no longer called 'shell-shocked.' We reached Chiringa on 27 April, and the base hospital at Chittagong a few days later. We were too late to hear Vera Lynn, who had been singing a week before, but I listened to the first music apart from my own humming for almost six months: *Iolanthe* on the hospital mess radio. I was concerned for my stored kit: a munitions ship exploding in Bombay harbour had destroyed the godowns containing, amongst so much else, everything we had deposited with our banks. I might have lost every valuable except my valise, my watch, my pen and my skean dhu (which in my absurd BOP innocence I had stowed in my ammunition pouches, in case I might heroically and stealthily slit the throat of a Jap sentry on a patrol). I was able to have a full oriental haircut and shampoo, to exchange my green battle dress shreds for new, and above all to unite my sliced-open cownoses with proper size 13 boots. Private Alisan was almost as lucky; not least, he was given Indian Army boots, which fitted his African feet perfectly instead of his cownoses. I was also able to contemplate my navel.

I could not deny relief that I was out safe. Nor could I deny that this was tinged with self-reproach. The jungle experience had certainly changed me. I had found myself losing respect for people of whom my upbringing automatically inspired awe. I had lost the schoolboy's reverence for those whose special attribute now seemed superficial – 1st XV colours, or a Blue, or a 'First Class Honours,' or some unusual gift or skill, if that was all that they did have. I had lost any sense of embarrassment, such as at wearing boots with the caps carved out through *force majeure*. I had learnt scepticism, if not perpetual cynicism (I still hoped). I had little to be proud of, but imagined that I had done better in arduous surroundings than a few others in a campaign that was almost over for the season, even if less well than most. Above all, I concluded that it was time for me to be planning my own future.

CHAPTER 4

A Soldier's Life is Terrible Hard

As an old soldier I admit the cowardice: it's as universal as seasickness, and matters just as little.

[G B Shaw, *Man and Superman*, act III]

Retreat

I FOUND MY WAY in trucks and riverboats to No 2 Wing of the WA Reinforcement Camp in Comilla. Alisan Djibba rejoined his countrymen in the battalion, and mess chat hinted that my future lay in 'admin', or 'instruction in jungle warfare', for which I was so marvellously equipped. Pondering whether to send for a textbook on physics, so as at last, after demob, to embark on medicine from scratch, presumably *aet* 23 +, I heard that my company commander Johnnie Walker had been shot through his lower jaw, which brought me back to earth. First, some leave. May meant monsoon – raincoat was ashes in Bombay, gascape somewhere in Burma, groundsheet in the hands of a Bengali thief at one of the staging hospitals we had passed through. My slouch hat was an umbrella of sorts. A trip down the Ganges, later recalled by Jean Renoir's film *The River*, was an eye-opener, leading to 14 unromantic days in the Grand Hotel, Calcutta. Personal morale was low, its overt symptom a temporary aversion to Africans (except the much missed Alisan, and such as Abu & Keramo), even more to Indians, and especially to the swarming Americans, with stars and stripes on their backs for 'friendly' recognition if shot down over China.

I was booked temporarily to Dacca (as it still was, Bangladesh itself being unknown), while my future was determined. The job of assistant SSO, mentioned in Chapter 1, involved signing countless meaningless memoranda wherever a babu told me to write my name, and sending off seeds for 'Grow More Food' gardens in strange base units. Then I got a real job, reported in full in the opening chapter, the trip with Vera Lynn to Bombay (Mumbai also still unheard of), a cleaner city by far than Calcutta. Censoring British Other Ranks' letters (part of OT for sick officers) made me realize how banal my own letters home must now be, after the decision not to go into any more mother-bothering details. The fall of Cherbourg to the British Liberation Army was good news. It seemed unlikely that BORs would have any stomach for coming east to finish off the Japs after Europe, but could Indian and African troops do that on their own? Americans might deal with occupied China, which their missionaries had recreated as the USA's substitute for our Indian empire, but hardly with recovering the British Empire.

I have no memory of how I got back to Dacca. Passing through Calcutta, I went to see Major Walker in the BMH Barrackpore, where also was the Rhodesian major shot in the goolies. Paul Ward, my 'cellist friend, had now been shot in the arm in his first action after recovering from losing his finger. The buzz elsewhere was that Noël Coward was in Bengal, in the wake of Vera; most British troops agreed that he was the hardest worker of all the big ENSA names. In Dacca they found what to do with me; this was to send me back to the West Africans, at Ranchi in Bihar, to reinforce No 1 (WA) Leave Camp, a new 'shower' c/o Adv Base PO 10. Real soldiering? My mind was kept occupied by the Oxford Books of Latin and Greek Verse (in translation) and Wavell's *Other Men's Flowers*.

I shared a bulbless compartment on the antique Bengal & Assam Railway with American GIs, rated for first class travel, unlike our own BORs, who if lucky might go 'Intermediate'. The Yanks' overseas tour amounted to two years: ours was still five, though the current aim was to bring it down to $4^{1}/_{2}$, then four and eventually perhaps three. We discussed our uniforms: they were rightly pleased with their superior quality of cloths, but in two minds about not generally wearing shorts in the tropics (although issued in some US Pacific stations). I suggested that their superiors might think that adults in 'short pants' didn't look grown-up, which adolescent Yanks were already always so desperate to become a.s.a.p. Some demurred, so I asked why American films about India and Africa always showed their own film stars in slacks, and only the actors in British bit parts, usually effete or comic, were costumed in shorts. We gave up on our differences, but it was so sweaty before we reached the plateau that they envied my bare knees (I was shy about wearing olive green battle dress when in no danger of needing camouflage). They had no envy of my curious toeless boots, which squeaked embarrassingly however much linseed oil was applied (I had kept them for travel).

Consolidation

I arrived at the leave camp in July 1944, unexpected and unknown. Ranchi at 2,500 feet was high enough to have a tolerable climate, a flat town ranked as a 'second class hill station'. Rickshaws, cycle-rickshaws and bad smells abounded. Coarse grass covered any bare parts, but for miles around the top of the plateau there was terraced paddy, punctuated by one or two small pimples like the Laws of the Lothians. The camp lay in a quarter of a square mile, two-and-a-half miles outside the town, down an avenue of low poplars leading off a hedged highway, all surrounded by orchard forest. The buildings and grounds belonged to the Maharajah of Chota Nagpur, everything being consumed by white ants and populated by mosquitoes (*aedes*, not *anopheles*). To the left of the entryway were a football pitch, hockey pitch and tenikoit court, with a powerhouse in the corner and a cinema at the far end, where Motor Transport was parked. The central office had been the maharajah's summerhouse, its ventilators the homes of many finches; all rooms opened into each other, surrounding an open courtyard. As well as finches there were breathtakingly beautiful white pigeons. Another main building, 'Africa House', sheltered the doctor's MI room, a canteen serving tea, buns and curry, a grocery store, clothing shop, games room, sports store, book stall and African serjeants' mess. Behind the MT was a higgledy-piggledy array of tents for one of the Sections responsible for the leave drafts, with a reading room, latrines, wells, dhobi facilities and miscellanea. Beyond the cinema were two more Sections (one to be mine) in better apparent order.

The theory was that the unit should have a second wing, each accommodating 1,500 African soldiers on leave, with a small permanent staff; the soldiers on leave would normally arrive for one or two weeks with one of their own officers, who would share their oversight. Meanwhile one wing was notionally ready. Initial reorganization was still in progress, under command of Major Bob Baillie, recently Lt-col, CO of 4NR and head of Bailcol that had marched out from the Kaladan with surplus bods and equipment before Murcol and me. The MO, Jack Ratcliffe, had been on the mv *Highland Princess*, and had found a pony and royal-blue-gilt trap for transport. The adjutant, an elderly Irish lieutenant, was already demob-happy. The quartermaster was a plump regular, on his umpteenth foreign duty. One lieutenant was a barrister's clerk whose family ran Ye Olde Leatherne Bottel at Goring-on-Thames, with a stack of good gramophone records; another was a reserved man with an interest in bird-watching who would one day be a single practising barrister in northern Nigeria. I was junior subaltern but one, and youngest. The orderly room serjeant would cut my hair at a posh Princes Street barber's after the war.

Mango trees abounded (as did iridescent green mango flies), local urchins and sweepers stripping the fruit before it ripened, though our own men and boys tried to compete. White ants built their tunnels and walkways of mud and sand wherever they needed a highway. Mud-wasps laid their young in every available orifice, not omitting razor handles or whistles. The charpoy beds harboured stink-bugs. During the rains tiny frogs abounded, which we hoped, fruitlessly, might eat the mosquito larvae and white ants. Cockroaches flew into faces, and after every shower of rain winged ants rose in clouds for the 20 minutes of flight life granted by nature. Lizards congregated under any light, to chop the insects attracted to it: their babies had a certain charm, with their huge heads – snakes might be less repellent if they had legs (we killed one 7'2" outside the mess). As the seasons changed, a freak thunderstorm always arriving just when the dry spell seemed permanent, so did the pests – mango flies and mossies gave way to eye-flies, tiny silent bee-like swarms that entered the head's cavities and settled in huge clusters on any hanging string (I sent a pile home in a letter), and to big wiggly earthworms. Rats and cockroaches abounded, succumbing to no chemical attack (the former consumed tubes of 'Ratto' and Ratbane biscuits with apparently as much enjoyment as they did any exposed lead piping), but only to traps and squashing respectively. A cockroach squashed at the start of writing a letter home would have been dissected by ants by the end, the legs and antennae the first to disappear in the nest's direction. This tended to take the mind off the war, though nobody had the gall to suggest that the hardships were up to Arakan standards. The camp developed its own farm, with pigs, goats, hens and some vegetables in the sandy soil.

The immediately important personal discovery was an official Officers' Shop in the town, which not only sold a WWI pattern trench coat to keep rain off, but bliss – real size 13 *officer's* boots. My heavy kit, safe with Grindlay's when the Bombay dock blew up the other banks, arrived, unharmed after a year or more. Duty? I was put in charge of one of the three No 1 Wing sections which took care of the groups of leave-happy AOR visitors. Their idea of 'leave' was 'mammy palaver', pursued while the Military Police looked elsewhere in darkest downtown Ranchi, which was of course *aftaban* (out of bounds) but kept Ratcliffe's sick parades busy. I was put in charge of a leave draft returning to its unit via Calcutta, and on return made to take over as President of the Mess Committee, for which Ted Hubbard (the peacetime accountant from BP I had met in Murcol) would instruct me in double-entry bookkeeping. The acting unpaid mess corporal Ibrahim ('head boy', I suppose), one of the countless men from Biu in Nigeria's Borno province who migrated to domestic service, would reappear in my future life as a senior office messenger in the Governor's Office in Kaduna.

So how did I, for one, spend so many days of the next year? We endured a spectacularly hot dry season, followed by a torrential wet that brought back the blue mould and Turkish baths under the nets (and disastrous floods to ruin Bengal's crops and return cholera to Calcutta). When the really cold season came I wore my kilt all day, the first time since Cape Town (The Gambia's seniors had not approved – it now invited amiable discussions with Africans about curious cultural customs).

I was brought into HQ as ack adj (assistant adjutant), still junior sub but one. The reason became clear when the adj was boarded with amœbic dysentery. Baillie, now a Lt-col again, commanding 'Leave Camp (Overseas) West Africa', as our new inflated War Establishment entitled us, told me to put up a third pip as adjutant in November. He must have favoured an ex-Kaladanite. By now the truly dry weather had arrived, vegetation was temporarily bright green, and it was pleasant to walk around the paddies. The HQ office was comfortable in the early mornings, keeping the previous day's warmth going through the night. The new responsibility involved going through the day's mail, drafting answers for the CO to sign, filling up returns and 'casualties' for O2E (Office of Second Echelon in Jhansi, where records were kept), phoning to Movement Control, hospitals, writing up the War Diary, compiling the Intelligence Report, submitting endless Returns (Vehicles, Stoppages for Losses, Traffic Accidents, Sabotage [!] *et al*), all as if we were a fighting force; there was a tendency built on harsh experience to stay on after office hours in case someone rang in to say that x AORs had arrived at y station, z miles away, and what was I going to do about it? Had I only known, it was a first step in teaching oneself to be an administrative officer, and one day to run a colony and its civil service.

For the first time in life I played tennis and badminton, but also squash at a court in the local hot weather Government House. A second best was make-do chip and putt golf in the local paddy. There were cinema problems. The Army Kinematographic Service would not entertain troops stationed less than three miles from a commercial screen, but the Indian contractor setting up a facility in the camp had technical difficulties, just when we were praying for competition for our soldiers against the downtown brothels. We had our own drum and fife band, somehow, who played all day every day. November 1944 was cause for celebration – the Africans' expatriation pay of tuppence a day went up to sixpence.

I was reckoning on soon inheriting the adjutant's brick house with bed, table and two or three chairs, which I should embellish with curtains and a bush carpet, but the two majors who came in to command the two expanded wings had priority. Then the news broke that they would leave Ranchi and rejoin 81 & 82 divisions; when exactly, was unclear. One elderly subaltern to go home because his 'age & service group' qualified for early 'Class B' release was the son of an Edwardian comedian. He was replaced by a former policeman by whom we could tell the evening time: like clockwork, if there were a drinking session, at 9 *p.m.* he would tell us tales of catching queers in public lavatories. He expected a quick Class B release himself, for his priority 'reconstruction' occupation. Distinguished inspectors included Auchinleck and the emir of Katsina.

By July 1945 I was virtually alone, nursing a feverish cold and in sole command of our imminent move south. Staff outnumbered men on leave by three to one, and a cyclone flattened every temporary erection. Most of the unit's time was spent on writing letters home. Lt-col Baillie had seen No 2 Wing on its way to Sandoway on Ramree island off the Arakan, back in SEAC and the Burma operational area to serve 82(WA)Div, whose sign was two spears thrust through a carrier's headpad. He had then been summoned back for his repat ship *en route* Rhodesia, and seemed unlikely to be replaced. Leave Camp (Overseas) West Africa was permanently split in two. No 1 Wing's major was on leave at his Kenyan farm. Packing and clearing, dealing with the loose ends, records, imprest account, movement orders, organized chaos, all almost made me put in for the cushy vacant job of WAEF's PR man. We were ready at last, but still did not know when we would move. However the 22 days during which I was OC No 1 Wing, before VJ Day, were one day more than the minimum span for a wartime temporary captain to be eligible for an acting majority, and to have that rank engraved on his Defence and War Medals. I bought the crowns as souvenirs, but could hardly wear them in arrears. There's glory, however tarnished. Self-righteously leaving it to others to assess my eligibility for the Burma Star (I had to do this for everyone else in Ranchi), of course I was only entitled to have 'Lt' inscribed on the upgraded 39-45 and the Burma Stars. Very few 14-18 ex-servicemen had had more than three campaign medals. There's inflation for you.

Amidst all this year or more there was time for brooding. Looking back on what I thought then, while war still raged, and comparing it with the new millennium of to-day, irony is strong. My youthful standards allowed subjective introspection into the real war being fought elsewhere; into *weltpolitik* as I presumed to understand it; into India; into what I truly felt about Africans; and into where I thought the UK was heading. Take these in turn, remembering that this is what I thought then, whatever I may believe now.

Some shocks made me question, yet be shamefully grateful for, my cushy billet. First, the confirmation that Colin Oliphant was now officially 'missing, believed killed'. Then Michael ('Midge') Blair, his contemporary, had died of wounds in the Second Front with the Recce Regiment: described in Chapter 2, this was the saddest waste, he could hardly not have achieved worldly greatness. And then my second best school friend, Craig Mitchell, also in Normandy, with the Black Watch. Difficult letters to write, and guarded replies that wished one a safe personal outcome. It was not hard to transfer a few resentments. One noticed that the Americans must be the first to enter Paris, and contrasted the slow but sure advances of our own Fifth, Eighth and Fourteenth Armies with reported panicky reorganization of Japanese ARP when six Superfortresses reached Nagasaki. When it seemed possible for the European war to end in 1944, had lengthening lines of communication and still-blocked channel ports not slowed supplies down, it was cheering that the Finns and the Balkan collaborators were getting out of line. Hope remained of reaching Berlin before the Russians, through airborne troops leapfrogging the Siegfried Line; yet when the Arnhem offensive was launched it was an 'Allied' initiative, but the setback following suddenly became 'British', and American troops were moving in to save the day: not so very different from Burma's 'Forgotten Army'? Who then would be allowed to reach Berlin first?

What effect would victory in the west have on our eastern war? When would reinforcements arrive to bolster Fourteenth Army and let the old sweats go home? British rank and file thought that, after Germany's defeat, everyone serving in the far east could be relieved by mid-1945, since after two years in the tropics everyone was drained (but not, one might ask, the Japanese?). I guessed that repat might come down to three years, for married men. An army conjured up from a never-never-land might after acclimatization finish Japan off in Mountbatten's hinted 'ninety days'; but might not Britain's army be half-demobbed after Germany's defeat, and those out here, largely imperial, be held on, to demonstrate what a mischievous critic had described in a letter to Roosevelt as our 'token assistance' to General Joe Stilwell's brilliance across the Hump in China? If we believed American PR, 85% of the Chindits' achievements were to the credit of the USAAF; but if we believed the WAEF PR, 80% of the Chindits were the Nigerian Brigade, helped by a few Cameronians.

We heard of Hitler's death and the German surrender the same day as the re-entry into Rangoon, and soon the atomic bombs: my immediate reactions were that these weapons meant either the end of all wars or the end of civilization, and to pray that Truman, Attlee and Bevin would not give Stalin any help towards making one himself. This was journalistically 'A Time for Greatness', but we might be embarking on a series of terrible disasters. The Japanese did not comprehend surrender, and unless this new bomb were used against ground troops in the Pacific, Mountbatten and the problematic Chiang still had harder tasks to face than MacArthur. The founding of UN had seemed appropriately to be performed at San Fiasco. Two flawed but great men, Winnie and FDR, succeeded by pigmies, no longer counterbalanced Uncle Joe. Had we known that we were going to use the bomb, we should never have encouraged USSR to join the Pacific War. That dog would bite the hand that fed it; would it grab Manchuria, Korea and bits of China? I was surprised at how little overt emotion I felt: apart from the promise of an end to slaughter, I was simply worried. Nostradamus's most recent interpreter had found that eternal peace would come in 1953 – could that become true because no human world would be left to be peaceful?

The Japanese were not victorious, but had not as a people been vanquished. They had three weeks to tuck things away before the Yanks landed in their homeland. We heard of Japanese still firing on US planes, and wondered whether MacArthur would repeat the gesture of walking their seaside from a landing craft. The Emperor's surrender led to speculation about where the shipping would come from to carry the occupation forces, to the detriment of our own repat and demob; our regulars took it for granted that we wartime bods would do at least another 16 months abroad. How would we dejaponize the Pacific territories that the Japs had colonized? Mental confusion reigned. In a broadcast service of thanksgiving for peace in St Paul's Cathedral the canon-in-residence gave interminable thanks to the Almighty for everything relevant, except for the atomic bomb which had won it. Were we in an unholy muddle?

As for our temporary home, India, there was no joy abounding. Most of our mess agreed that we would depart and that Hindus and Muslims would fight it out for another couple of hundred years of mutual disaffection, or until some future USSR, USA, China or Japan decided that enough was enough and stepped in to take over where we had left off. We saw no satisfactory solution, since they were too intermingled to partition, and indeed thought a quasi-federal imposition as no more possible than a European Federal Union would be.

I still contrasted India, dusty grey and depressing, with my brief experience of West Africa, earthy red, bustling and laughing, each reflecting local human characteristics. I began to want to go back to Africa, as I reassessed my opinions of its people. The process had begun in Murcol: I pictured again and again 18 smallpox cases being carried for 80 miles on head-borne stretchers across Burma's country at its most heart-breaking. Nine survived: several stretcher-bearers caught the disease, and one of them died. Memories of unheroic behaviour were set against memory of how black and white had shared the same lack of joint training, lack of mutual familiarity and experience, and lack of inspiring leadership. The more understanding, the more forgiveness. In the leave camp, even the 'savvy boys' began to enjoy themselves more as we stragglers, pitchforked into an unexpected job, taught ourselves from scratch how to organize 'rest and recreation'. When soldiers caught pneumonia in the cold weather, the cheering hospital visits became a worthwhile duty. As one began to observe the half-way cultural problems of the Eurasian Anglo-Indians and to hear of half-black illegitimate American-Europeans, one occasionally wondered about the future of the Afro-Asians that were undoubtedly being fathered in the shadows.

And what did one feel about home, the UK? Today's legend conflicts with what I reflected at the time. Few believed that they would return to the world they had left, dearly though parents might want it. Yet I feared that our sterling working class was not about to be taught that no brave new world could come about without years and tears of toil and discomfort, which they themselves would have to provide and shoulder: even the more mature would not get back to fireside, slippers, dog and pipe, just because of Beveridge. We had not won the war on our own, 1940 notwithstanding, and the Americans, Russians and Commonwealth did not owe us a living because of the Battle of Britain or El Alamein. I was unhappy that alone of the United Nations, big and small, we seemed be careful about antagonizing others. If our new leaders were determined that we should be finished as a world-leading nation, then let us be well and truly finished, but at least let us go out with a sound bang of the door, not a smarmy buttering of the hinges.

The arrival of Army Forms B2626 to register our votes had not aroused enthusiasm in our environment: we could airmail our choice for MP, or appoint proxies (some did because the mail was run again by the civilian post office). After swithering over an Independent on principle and a Liberal because it sounded middle-of-the-road, and rejecting outright SNP, Communist and Labour, I eventually plumped for a Unionist. Discussion flowed with parents about my future: they tended to suggest the law, while after a momentary flirtation with architecture I toyed, not for long, with the church – it seemed to me that if all the Christian sects became one, we would end up without all faith. A circular about post-war opportunities in Home Civil, Foreign and Colonial Services made it clear that if one was capable of a second class honours degree, had a knack for languages and was prepared for a year of university training, the colonial service might get one released almost at once, but there would be great competition for the few vacancies (and a £4 entry fee). The Home Civil seemed unattractive under the new government. 6 or 7 years' medical training was intolerably long. Nor did I expect a Class B release: I might in my dreams have aspired to a First in factual Honour Mods, but had not won it: I never thought my philosophical ingenuity would get me far in Greats. I wrote to Magdalen's Dean, who replied that after two terms one might take a 'special' exam and earn an unclassified 'War Degree'. Sending an advance party off to the Madras area, after which everyone confined their working hours to writing letters home, seems the right point at which to cut short brooding, dredged from almost 60 years ago: whether it has helped to explain what I was to turn into, a reader may judge.

Regrouping
I had been for all practical purposes, and would remain for the rest of the year, in sole charge of HQ and No 1 Wing of our shower, as my seniors waltzed in and out after Bob Baillie's demob. One result, which only ex-servicemen would understand, was that I developed a strong and unlikely affection for a unit, 'my mob', more than the sum of its fundamentally inferior and damaged parts. It was more than pique that upset me when we were beggared about by people who took us at face value; but one thing at a time. We left Ranchi in two halves, our major (just back from leave) and I in the second party, taking four days in shocking Indian Railways troop trains. 3rd class meant hard wooden benches, jammed to rooftop overflows with humanity, much of it ticketless; 'Intermediate' was better; 2nd class was choicer, while 1st was about as

comfortable as UK 3rd's corridorless carriages on remote suburban runs, but much dirtier; bunks rarely accommodating well-nourished Caucasian bodies. We avoided Calcutta, grateful for the good behaviour of our AORs, all of us living on K rations – those American stop-gap emergency cold meals in waxed cardboard, half good, half inedible. We Europeans got cooked meals at some stations *en route,* sharing our carriage part of the way with the good company of some IAF officers who had just become RIAF.

After one change, Madras was our first major stop. My 'boy' Moma Kano went astray in the city, and we parted company when he went off for his 14 days' jankers, to be replaced by John Ohaka from Onitsha, a quiet lad who got on with things without whingeing. The last rail lap, to a hotter and stickier climate, was enlivened by a crowd of hostile babus sharing the train, racist about both Europeans and Africans. We camped for ten days with 4AuxGp, which had seen some changes but still had remembered faces from Ede in 1943. By the time we settled in our own area, Nagari, housed in bashas with a vague promise of electric light, 60-70 miles slightly NW of Madras on terrible roads, we had been joined by a welfare BNCO. He brought an array of equipment, generator, radio, amplifier, record turntable and speakers to wire up a large leave camp: he said Delhi was the best wartime shopping centre outside UK, doubtless barring the States. Our transport and personal kit turned up much later, with all my bumf about post-war resettlement. In some way never made clear to me despite my place in things, our establishment was conglomerated with that of the dispersed Recce Regiment as a repatriation group, and the former G2 became our Lt-col; he brought in a would-be regimental Anglo-Indian captain as adjutant. Our major had compassionate demob, and someone spare in 81 replaced him, so I reverted to plain captain.

'R&R'
There being no future in it (a cant phrase of the time) as spare part in the disassembled toolshed of an *ad hoc* shower, I wrote to Ted Hubbard in Rangoon, whither No 2 Wing was just moving, knowing that his Age & Service Group 27 was coming much closer than my '47'. He stuck tongue in cheek and advised 82 Div that it might be convenient if Clark, who knew everything that was to be known about running leave camps, were to transfer across as 2i/c, with a view to succeeding him in due course. Three calendar months of acting as major made one a war substantive captain. I then saw no danger in asking for leave, since further change behind his back could hardly disadvantage the sole oarsman of a burnt boat. It was the first time in my life that I remember trying to organize my own future. The obvious place to seek rest was four weeks in the Nilgiri Hills.

I packed my text book, and the half-encouraging, half-critical tutors' notes on the few essays I had submitted to my Bombay Institute of Engineering Technology correspondence course on chemistry. I missed seeing Gielgud in *Hamlet* in Madras, which he was playing in repertory with *Blithe Spirit*, while I did unit bank business for the Imprest and browsed the streets, market and bookshop. I scraped my lip and began another moustache. The RTO had booked 3 Wrens and 5 men in a 4-berth compartment of Madras & Southern Mahratta Railways' Blue Mountain Express. The sight of two RAOC officers with a rare bottle of Haig and two glasses caused the Wrens to decamp, and the eighth man was a 'no show'. The Haig became vague, and solid sleep enveloped the four, until 12 hours later a change had to be made to a narrow gauge rack-rail rising 1 in 12 or 13 from 1,200' to 6,000'.

The Dunmore Hostel at Coonoor was surrounded by beautiful wooded hills, waterfalls and streams, with eternal spring breezes, ideal for battle dress blouse and kilt. A town photographer insisted that his grandfather had taken a photograph of Clive of India. Ootacamund (Snooty Ooty) was 1,500' higher, an hour and a quarter by bus on that rare substance, tarmac. The promise of nothing but reading and corresponding on chemistry for a month was soon broken. In a thirty foot circle round the hostel were rose bushes, orange trees, bananas, strawberries and the greenest, springiest lawn. The large bungalow on a ridge (nothing was flat) loomed over small annex houses. The next-door house held some attractive cage-birds, including a mynah with a repertoire of 'Raja! Ram Krishna! Good morning!' The countryside was like the Downs: except that, sitting at an outside café, one could send out for strawberries, and within minutes have a 4lb basket for four rupees. The butter was tinned Polson's, but edible. Nothing was rationed but everything else was expensive, and the chemists were full of rare patent medicines.

I chummed up with two people over an expedition to Mysore: an Indian Signaller from Rangoon and a garrison engineer. Several RAPWLs (returned allied prisoners of war on leave) unsurprisingly talked about nothing except their sad experiences: the exception was an elderly Australian RAMC Captain, who had been in Singapore's Changi prison. He had spent 30 years on Malayan rubber plantations, and only wanted a ship to get him back to start all over. He had had 2,000 78 rpm records in KL. He was an attractive old-fashioned socialist, and would happily strangle all teachers of English, with their passion for cramming the grammars of deceased languages into innocent heads – what a difference in Russia, where a whole people had been re-educated in 20 years. Harrumph?

The weekend in Mysore was reached by 13 miles in a taxi and 99 miles in a bus. On the Downs past Ooty we skirted the kennels of the Ootacamund Hunt, which pursued jackals in pink jackets, but by 3,500' we were nigh to a jungle warfare training centre, looking at concrete-like termite hills, baboons, monkeys and lemur-like creatures. At 2,500' we reached plains again, still thickly wooded. Arriving in the cleanest town yet encountered in India, we saw the grand palace, not the usual flaking whitewash plaster but real marble: but His Highness Krishnarajendra Bahadur would not permit visitors – not because (unlike his father) he was strongly anti-British (though a devotee of western music, soon to sponsor HMV recordings of Medtner), but because he was tired of Congress demos in his gardens and durbar rooms. He was a plump and pasty grey 26, permanently on shikar, since until he had shot 100 tigers he would not sire an heir: meanwhile his wife had gone back to her parents. There were two 'European' hotels, full and unhelpful, although the Resident adviser was probably the only British inhabitant of the city. We were used to the press picking on anything, however petty, to pervert and exaggerate – clearly the British were generally hated by the educated classes. We were barely tolerated because we acted polite and friendly, wore no badges on our green drill, and might be Americans. Not but what taxi-drivers, hotel servants, bearers and soldiers, the ones who might be losers when we did quit, behaved differently, yet not obsequiously. We ended up in a 'Modern Hindu' (Brahmin) hotel, sleeping on hard boards and eating in the station restaurant, and found it acceptable, reading liberal posters that said, *'Bread is a noble food – treat it with respect – break it with your hands, do not cut it with a knife'* and *'Do not nibble at the food of the poor'*.

In the afternoon we wandered about to see an up-to-date hospital, the palace offices, all the modern developments that we expected in civilian India in 1945, but not seen elsewhere. There was extravagant floodlighting to celebrate the Maharaja's birthday, a pleasant park, gilded statues, and a colour-lit fountain. Strangely, no Indian seemed to be appreciating them, nor another European enjoying them. In the evening we taxied up a hill whose crest was outlined by lamps, past a fantastically lovely guest palace, allegedly built for the Prince of Wales's visit; at the top, shoes off to enter a Hindu temple, where baksheesh to a priest allowed us six yards into the first court – further was forbidden to Parsis, Muslims and Europeans. We did see a finely carved stone tower, disfigured inside by gaudy cheap coloured glass and a lack of fresh distemper. The taxi took us on to tour the Maharaja's summer palace, the front gate opening automatically whenever the front tyres tripped a contact. Finished in modern hotel style, it boasted western baths, sandalwood dressing rooms, bedside switches controlling everything. There was a spectacular view over Mysore city, all lit up, with the famous great stone bull Nandi half-way down the hill. After dinner we took a tonga ride round more of the town.

Morning brought real coffee in a coffee shop, and another tonga ride to see the royal elephants and camels, and the present ruler's great grandfather's palace; this was now a tawdry museum, sporting a splendid gauge-1 silver-plate dining table railway to carry the curry side-dishes round the guests. Then a drive through mulberry bushes to the government silk factory, where Hungarian and Swiss looms demonstrated what local enterprise could do, and to a sandalwood oil factory, where I bought an ivory-tipped sandalwood swagger-stick with which to swagger between covert sniffs. The afternoon brought us to the royal garages with their 65 vehicles, including an electric brougham, lorries, Rolls-Royces and wireless cars to keep in touch with the beaters on shikar. The stables were more attractive, 70 horses including some white beauties bred locally: one barbary brute took a bite out of my OG blouse. Next morning we patronized the market, buying tiny beans with six minute ivory elephants plugged inside, and remarking how much less baksheesh was being sought here than in British India. The bus home took five hours, the second half of the journey freezing cold, with a stop for eggs and chips. We wondered what view the anti-British were taking of the Auk (GOC India Auchinleck)'s divorce, much in the news.

Unsurprisingly I had read little of my correspondence course texts, was still convinced that I could never face 'Greats', and harboured regrets about medicine. Some East African Port Artizan Works Company officers who had expected to clear Singapore docks seemed to think little of their east African troops, who were restive over the uncertainty of when they would go home. This was nothing new. Current rumour had it that British A&SGp 40s would not be home for another year. Brooding again, I turned to pipe-smoking, possibly subconsciously to match the moustache. I failed to enjoy it. The lady who did our catering had a Dalmatian, and said that puppies were available, especially wire-haired fox terriers and dachshunds. I almost fell for a Sydney Silkie, but the threat of six months' quarantine saved me. Thinking of peoples, I concluded that despite the stereotypes of the gallant, loyal and upright 'martial races' of India, and of the weak, fawning 'missionized' tribes, I had found the Madrassi Christians the worthiest of Indians: unlike the African 'savvy mission boys' whom I had seen in the RWAFF's extra-regimental employment (taught literacy at school, but rarely a vocation before enlistment), these converts had remained simple and unaffected; they brought us all nosegays at a Christmas Day tea-party in Coonoor, without hope of any reward beyond a smile. This had followed a huge lunch, at which the 3-year-old son of the lady superintendent had handed out presents (mine was a pair of initialled silk handkerchiefs). I had earlier been brooding on imperial attitudes, identifying stereotypes: the memsahibs at their most memsahibery, and their awful children, with the bogus club life, that often put me off earning a living in overseas service (unless one remained a single man in the highland wilds and then went barmy or became a lush). I now saw another innocent side, as there is to everything, not least in the following grand old-fashioned Christmas party, with Consequences and community singing, all natural and unforced, games with bottles, matches and chairs, and record recitals.

Return to Pastures New
Back at the ranch on New Year's Day, about 7,000 AORs had already gone home, but tens of thousands still waited. By now 4,000 BORs were going home by sea each month, and 10,000 by air. At this late date a new shoulder formation flash for non-divisional WAEF troops was approved, the RWAFF palm tree badge in yellow on a green backing (the officers' version, woven, was very posh). Mid-January saw my transfer to Rangoon settled. I now had too much kit to fly from Calcutta, but Embarkation HQ Madras found a ship with a spare berth sailing by the 27th. In the end I embarked on the 24th from the Transit Officers' Hostel in Madras, having given my 'boy' John Ohaka and orderly Etonge Mongo (a sweet-natured French Cameroonian) the run of the town the day before. I was sorry to leave all but the two interloping Europeans at Nagari, but my morale was obviously rising as I thought of new faces, scenery and occupation.

HMS *Persimmon*, a Landing Ship Infantry, converted from a merchant ship while on the stocks, was a slow mother ship for assault landing craft, which hung all around her. The interior décor was duck-egg blue, her Tannoy relayed loud jazz all day, and the naval routine was relaxed. My two Africans could/would not be shared with the IORs on board, but after an intervening fuss by me they were installed in a forward hatch and served BORs' chop. The Indian Ocean was smooth as a mirror. I was awakened at 2 *a.m.* on 25 January 1946 by a ship's cat miaowing on my pillow, one of the many pets on board. We anchored at noon and left at 3 in a Landing Craft for shore, where we were met, despite not being expected for another week.

Rangoon was still war-scarred: little seemed to have been cleared in the nine months since reoccupation. The Japs had not checked the spread of weeds and jungly bushes; everything, however ramshackle and unkempt, was (if marketable) expensive. The city was crammed to suffocation with military HQs, offices and units beyond description. The civil power was in charge, but the military thought this six months premature. Officialdom was not happy to see the army's numbers falling, and unhappiness was increased by dacoits in the wilds and the Chinese in the north showing every sign of staying put. Heavy spraying of DDT made the capital malaria-free, but it was a depressing, spoilt, battered place with no apparent future, in contrast to the possibilities that trips to the countryside were to suggest. I bought several silk *lungyi*s which served me for slumberware for many years to come.

Our camp was 7 miles from both the centre and the docks, with a holiday-like vista looking over the edge of Victoria Lake; but it was only a small space off the main road, otherwise surrounded by a 3rd echelon workshop, an artizan works company, an infantry battalion and a provost section, none of which gave a leave camp any sense of getting away from it all. Our leave drafts, mainly from units beyond Rangoon, spent all their time up to mischiefs in the city. We had electricity, when the generator was operating, and untrustworthy kerosene pressure lamps, but for all ranks, unless going to the flicks or exploring red lights, 'early to bed' was the norm. Eventually we acquired a good radio, and could enjoy Tommy Handley's *ITMA,* and fantasize about the proposed BBC C programme, which promised wallpaper culture. The first lavatory pan I had enjoyed since leaving UK had no mains inlet, and had to be flushed with a bucket: it occupied a quarter of a 6-foot square 'bathroom', meaning that the tin bath had to be used in the 'sleeping accommodation'.

In transferring across the Indian Ocean I had lost adjutant's pay, with the hope of gaining a crown. My experimental moustache added a conceivable ten years to my appearance, but I had to concede to myself that it made me feel itchy and unwashed. I wondered whether it might be thought that I only grew it to look a less unlikely major, and therefore be seen as as bogus as I undoubtedly was. If I couldn't make the grade for what I was under the surface, then bother it: I shaved it off. On 1 April Ted Hubbard handed over to me.

My new rank caused me to have difficult, but successful, negotiations with CWAEME over the write-off of a water cart that another driver had rather bent. I was less successful with CWAASC, who found that I had successfully indented for OG shorts and hose-tops for my unit in a tick-free area. Another failure was to get most of those AORs, who had originally come out in units now booked to get home earlier than we, posted back so that they would return with their own folk, and not mope demoralizingly on the quayside. I did get two or three Gold Coasters back to their chums, including my own driver, a very nice 'savvy boy' Jonathan Oko (I had chaperoned him to his confirmation by the Bishop of Rangoon in the cathedral, and shared his first communion at the altar rail of this modest but badly damaged church, stripped by the Japs, and now jury-rigged for its true purpose).

It was impossible to explain to African troops the thinking of 'higher-ups', and I was grateful for hard lessons in not losing temper, when insisting for the umpteenth time that the ships that had brought them out were in a queue to take numberless troops to many other places as well. It was teaching me that 'public service' means getting things done, not talking about it; but also that sage elderly advice and youthful energy did not easily gel, since youth once given responsibility uses it without looking for advice. The BOR custom of naming their vehicles after their womenfolk, or painting catch-phrases, inspired me to ask my replacement Gold Coast driver, Afful Oseku, what his wife was called: he was not pleased when he found NIMOTA ADUKE painted below the windscreen, as he didn't love her any more. I told inquirers that it was Wollof for CCL ('Couldn't care less') or Mandinka for 'Roll on that boat'. I was on my fourth bush hat (I had vomited in the first UK issue, lost the second in one unheroic retreat, had the third irremediably squashed by Moma Kano in a valise, and they were not too easy to replace in an officers' shop).

We got about. There was a GI cinema, besides our own. There was a Burmese *pwe* (theatre), performing a slow, leisurely and long dance, followed by what was probably comedy, makeshift but colourful. Our RC Padre took me to the Convent of the Good Shepherd, where there were still two sisters, for my first hot buttered toast for years. The Japanese had kept searching for the sisters' husbands, certain that something subversive was going on in this strange establishment. On one return visit to the Shwe Dagon, content to remove shoes but not socks, a saffron-clad monk solemnly, without a hint of a wink, showed the very steps that Queen Victoria had ascended on her famous visit, unrecorded in the official registers of Her long and glorious reign. A RC RAF padre, friend of our padre, took us 50 miles up the road to Pegu, to see the famous reclining Buddha, 130' long by over 30' high, under a vast hangar-like canopy.

ENSA brought Tommy Trinder (*'You lucky people! But they don't put anything in my tea!'*), who repeated the Carmen Miranda routine that Tom Bibey and I had seen when waiting for draft RNHZO to leave Marylebone for the Coast. A visit to the Royal Engineers' Survey and Map-printing mess gave me waterproof maps of Burma and silk 'escape' maps that remind me to this day of these times; they were listening-in to a cup final commentary, angry when it was interrupted by a news bulletin. I went to the cathedral for monthly communion, still briefly wondering, not for long, whether I had a vocation: the CofE SCF to the division struck me as rather wet when he once came to our leave camp church (non-RCs were looked after there by an African Methodist from the WA General Hospital). Reading was enriched by the first of many comic novels by Caryl Brahms & S J Simon, *A Bullet in the Ballet*. A major change in lifestyle came when for the first time the rationed bottle came, not of what I had found unpleasant *Canadian Club* or *Four Feathers* whiskey, swappable for gin and beer, but of real Teacher's *Highland Cream* Scotch; with a greater proportion of malt than most blends, it has remained my tipple ever since.

Meanwhile, what were the Russians getting up to in Persia and Manchuria, and would the US poach all the Japanese technical skills for their own benefit alone? Lease-lend had been cut off pretty sharp like. The world might have shrunk, leaving no room for 18th century masters of all trades, but there was a lack of even mediocre leadership evident when the propagandist slogans trumpeted 'A Time for Greatness'. Would Russia simply walk out of UNO, before the democracies had been able to form a convincing anti-totalitarian bloc within that phantasmagoria? Russia, Ukraine, White Russia, Poland and Yugoslavia had just united against some simple proposal at the peace conference. At home all that seemed to matter was nationalization, with an Edinburgh neighbour who understood accounts becoming a very senior National Coal Board manager without (unlike my mining engineer uncle) ever having gone down a pit, and Bevan's oratory about the National Health Service leaving me unsympathetic with its organizers but glad, not that I would not be becoming a doctor myself, but that I should not be joining the unfortunate doctors who would man it.

My 'boy' John Ohaka caught otitis and was replaced by a Michael. We had progressively become less and less a leave camp and (like Nagari) more a holding unit looking after residual HQ 1 Bde, some WAA, a few WAAMC bodies and our RC padre. Our last leave drafts came at the end of June, and the div comd troubled to tell us that our camp had been a great success. The office tent moved to the tiny lakeside area that our permanent staff numbers and 'residue' merited, while the monsoon belted down and blue mould spread. Eventually, we evacuated our bungalow and the office doubled as mess, with minimal furniture and most of the files burnt. The announcement of the War Medal, awarded to almost everyone for almost anything, renewed some cynicism about tinsel (The Defence Medal equated 3 years fighting the London blitz with one year in New Delhi; the Burma Star equated 6 months in Calcutta, while others were retreating from Rangoon, with 6 months boxed in at Kohima). However, I jumped the Q queue and acquired eleven feet of the riband, which we got mounted and ceremonially distributed to all eligible among the troops under my dubious command. By now everyone had one thought, apart from studying 'compassionate repatriation' leaflets: when shall I go?

In my own case, I gathered that clothes-rationed Britain saw those without demob suits happily wearing worn-out canary jumpers with cast-off red corduroys. I planned to wear my Camerons kilt. First, I had to re-establish contact with my college. I decided to ignore the circulars about 200 reconstruction vacancies in the foreign service, or the home and colonial offers: I should at least collect a 'war degree' and let university resharpen my mind enough to be in with a chance later. I wrote to the secretary of the tutorial board, Eng Lit don K B McFarlane, explaining that the thought of the NHS

The senior of two orderlies by tradition wore his commanding officer's home regimental cap badge; nobody had heard of skin cancers in 1946 (cf Chap. 1).

had put me off medicine, and had a non-committal but encouraging response. My Mods tutor, Brink, never replied. If nothing transpired, I was looking forward to seeing more of west Africa, to help judge better the attractions of colonial service. I was becoming closely attached to the Africans. This was in small part because an excellent Yoruba schoolteacher on strength had been teaching me (somewhat barracky, but appropriate) Hausa, whose use on parade and in chat eased relationships considerably with most Nigerians and some others. I might be fed up with end-of-story army life, but it would be a break to part with most of these black men.

If Magdalen did not get me out under *Bees* (class B), then the chances were, if I could not hang around in Africa until A&SGp47 was released under *Ajax* (class A), estimated for December, that I would spend 3 months in Austria, Italy or BAOR, with the danger of becoming 'deferred, operationally vital' there, while regulars reinforced the peacetime units based in UK in case of trouble elsewhere in a funny old world. It allegedly took 2-3 weeks after the Ministry of Labour processed any request for an undergraduate's release for the offer to arrive in India, so a return for Oxford's Michaelmas term sounded improbable. Shipping schedules were pored over ever more closely. One to UK was scheduled for 3 August, while that for September would be too late for start of term. News broke of the notable *Highland Princess* which had brought so many to Nigeria three years before; it would leave with us for Lagos between 31 August and 5 September. Alas! She was diverted to carry illegal Hebrew immigrants to Palestine away to Cyprus instead – but maybe the *Derbyshire* would collect us on 9 September? I now took it for granted that I would be on it.

All were perky at a true prospect of going home. The incessant monsoon apparently ended as we marched into the marshalling area, to return in brief torrents, leaving the camp awash, just after my last major hollow square parade, presenting (in Hausa) long service & good conduct medal ribands to two serjeants. The last message before the telephone was disconnected on 29 August, was an IMMEDIATE War Office signal *dated 12 July*, authorizing a Class B release for Major A T Clark. When it came to the point, I could not bear to watch my people embarking, but said goodbye to them all in their tents and handed the tiny office with its austere stationery to my Number Two.

Curtains
Yes, but how and when would the release eventuate? Nobody undertook to take charge, and I forget which brand of Movement Control I approached. The target of 'home by mid-September' would be hard to hit. It might be best to start off in the opposite direction – by *Sunderland* to Singapore, whence there was a regular RAF air-trooping *bandobast*. I could leave my excess over 65lbs of baggage to the Military Forwarding Officer. OK, but having had only 24 hours' notice I missed the Monday plane: there were 16 passages a week, and I should have priority after any compassionate cases. Once in Singapore, it would 'only be 3½ days' *via* Karachi and Lydda to be home. So they said. My parents were talking of a Swiss holiday (I still had the latch key of our back door). I did get the next plane, and found that the *Sunderland* had been converted into a BOAC *Hythe*. It was the most comfortable plane I have flown in: four armchairs with wide arms faced each table, two-by-two. Taxi-ing downriver until lift-off was exciting, and the views down the western Malayan coast to Singapore striking. This VIP treatment ended at the wharf, whence we were trucked to the officers' transit camp (at Bukit Timah), where I learnt that the RAF *Yorks* (*Lancaster* frames with seating) left early every morning. This meant rising between 3 and 4 *a.m.* to break an elementary fast, truck into town to the Air Booking Centre to be documented on to the day's flight, then the other way to Changi airfield to embark at first light. We followed this routine every day for a week, sometimes being belted into the *York,* sometimes no further than the

assembly area, sometimes halfway – there was always a last minute fault to be found in our plane. We wondered whether we would ever get away and whether the plane would survive the effort.

On the eighth day we did, admiring eastern Sumatra before crossing the ocean to Ceylon's RAF station at Negombo. Something else went wrong. The extra night allowed a screening of *The Young Person's Guide to the Orchestra*, Malcolm Sargent conducting the LPO in, and narrating, Britten's variations on a theme of Purcell. Next day we took off, and half-way up India noticed oil spreading over the starboard windows; we understood that the pilot considered landing at Bombay Santa Cruz, but bravely battled on to Karachi. We were not surprised not to have to embark early next dawn, but courage prevailed and, at hottest mid-day, the latest artificers enabled us to be put into an oven-baked fuselage and (to avoid overheating the engines) be towed by tractor to the end of the runway, from which we rose in the general direction of the Gulf, eventually landing at Basra, nightstopping without further anxiety or entertainment. Another day brought us to Heliopolis, close enough to Cairo to have had a snatched aerial view of the pyramids; and another to Luqa in Malta, an island that from the air seemed to be solid desiccated sandstone. By this time we were confident that 16 days after starting the promised $3^1/_2$ days journey from Rangoon to UK, we should arrive home without incident. We almost did. The weather was clear and beautiful across the Mediterranean, across France (where we flew over Caën, like a volcanic crater, a flattened city surrounded by half-demolished suburbs as the rim) and across the channel. Just as we began to look for greenery and pleasantry, the clouds descended. RAF Lyneham, our destination in Wiltshire, is barely 60 miles from the coast, so after half an hour's 'stooging' through murk it was surprising that the plane began to fly low under the cover and pass over several airfields before landing after over an hour on the right one. It was patent to pongoes that we had been relying on visual navigation and had got lost: the pilot's excuse, when we twitted him at reception, was that it was terribly easy to do, old boy, 180 degree error in our bearings. Some believed him.

I had pictured a straight run home, King's Cross to Waverley and, the Almighty permitting, a rare taxi home with my back door key. Nothing so simple. The train from Swindon was as packed as the Indian railways, and in the corridor I sat on and broke the handsome turtle-shell cigarette case I had bought in Negombo. Movement Control ordered me to nightstop in the Marylebone District Centre whence my travels had started, and then to report to my regimental headquarters to be demobilized before going to the centre for civvy kitting out. The Camerons, whom I had regrettably never seen despite my uniform, were at Fort George, beyond Inverness. I passed many uncomfortable hours, in supposed first class, past York, past my home, over the Forth and through Perth and the highlands, to spend twenty minutes saluting an adjutant, filling up some forms and rejoining a train through the highlands, Perth, Edinburgh, to York – my highland comrades had wryly informed me that the authorities had just closed the demob centre at Edinburgh's Redford Barracks, and that the nearest was now in York. There were no standard grey pinstripe suits to fit me, so I opted for a bespoke tolerable tweed (the tailor had never measured the inside leg of a kilt-wearer before, and decided to guess – when the suit arrived six weeks later, it included the only trousers ever that were four inches too long for me). My arrival home needs no embellishment. This may serve as the wrapping up of my tale so far, where not already covered by the chapters on health and learning. I did write to my MP (something never repeated) about bureaucracy that could not demob and kit me as soon as I reached Marylebone. He gave me the answer that I might have drafted myself years later. *Tough!* No wonder I ended up a unionist Tory.

CHAPTER 5

Baptism of Colonial Fire in 'The North'

In imperialism nothing fails like success. If the conqueror oppresses his subjects, they will become fanatical patriots, and sooner or later will have their revenge; if he treats them well, and 'governs them for their good', they will multiply faster than their rulers, till they claim their independence.
[William Ralph Inge; *'Patriotism'*,
Outspoken Essays (First Series), 1919]

WHY JOIN THE colonial service? During the late hostilities, as we have seen, I had been selected for service with African colonial forces, first boy scout fun with adolescent Sierra Leoneans; and then seriousness (when not frightening) with solid Gambian soldiers (many in fact from 'French'). Many black and a few white youngsters (enjoying minimal training and mutual understanding) learnt the hard way to support each other and to mature. In safe quarters I had looked after the welfare of thousands of Africans from the west coast, and (with the help of the Yoruba schoolmaster clerk) learnt enough Hausa to talk to those puzzled that ships which brought them east could not take them home on VJ Day. I had come, after doubts founded in youthful ignorance, to like these black men, whose natural quotas of intelligence, wisdom or ignorance, cunning, devilry, honesty or criminality, humour and patience were as equally distributed as among Caucasians, despite contrasting cultures and faiths. They would need help in a fast-changing world.

Friends envied the 'winter cruise' on *mv Accra* from Liverpool. The ship was 11,600 tons, carried 256 1st class and 24 3rd class, and rolled like a fishwife, the smoother the water became. We had tea in bed, a large breakfast, beef tea at 11 (once in tropics, ices substituted), lunch, tea at 4, dinner, and sandwiches at 10 *p.m.* – no wasted moment. The most surprising thing, $3^{1}/_{2}$ years after peace had broken out, was the whiteness of the bread. Rationed UK had forgotten what it looked like, even if Woolton had improved its vitamin content: soft, new, snow-white rolls provoked thought. Olde worlde deck games were played, with deck chairs for basking after leaving the Canaries, when the swimming pool opened. Cigarettes were 2s 6d ($12^{1}/_{2}$p) for 50. A memorable day in Las Palmas included a hair-raising taxi ride round the island, driven by a madman ('Look, no hands' while brushing curly hair back under his greasy cap before every hairpin); he had four words of guide's English: 'Oranges', 'Tomatoes' and 'Bananas groves'. I expected greenery, but it was Arabian, all erosion, sandy rock and dust. Franco's régime was evident in the uniforms, but inhabitants seemed as poor as Indians and Africans, while not resenting us for being British; the children, begging for pennies in the take-it-for-granted way that eastern baksheesh had been implored during the war and after, were happy and pleasant. We saw families living in caves.

At sea, spirits were raised by dolphins leaping around the ship's bows. Sierra Leone's Freetown, the 'ultimate projection of empire', looked more attractive than the Canaries, but there were now fewer Kroo-boys diving for pennies – nothing under sixpence worth retrieving. The end of the great troopship convoys had knocked the bottom out of their market. A telegram in the library told us where we were posted – for me, Bauchi. The Gold Coast's port of Takoradi had not changed, but the 'happy colony' had had its first political riot a year before – were people looking at us quizzically with bare tolerance and condescension? Were we on the defensive in the administration of an 'unhappy subject people'? This would be a setback before even starting a career. What rude reception might await us from the more sophisticated 'dock-rat' types at Lagos's Apapa wharf? Reassuringly, they were tame, and accepted refusals to tip excessively with no more ill grace than a BR porter or London taxi-driver. The customs officials showed a mixture of obstructionism and bumbling inefficiency (cutting down to size any sceptics who thought burra sahibs were the oppressors), but the only dues were on guns and musical instruments (sport and culture). The governor and chief secretary were away, so our batch were distributed among senior secretariat officers for advice and entertainment (tea, surf-bathing and drinks) before joining the boat train at 9.30 *p.m.*

Arriving in Jos at the week's end, we were corralled by the ADO of the provincial office. Our little group had three days to spend in the Hill Station rest house, run by a redoubtably retired education officer with duffle-coat and cigar. We were each prompted by Ibrahim, Hill Station's chief steward, to employ a cook and steward, whom he introduced from his makeshift employment exchange (most, like himself, came from Biu, but some came from the plateau). I was joined by Adamu from Biu as valet; Ousman Foram from the plateau was chef, who rarely took the easy option of opening a tin of fruit when preparing puddings. After a night in Bauchi, the provincial capital, 80 miles down a rough road from the plateau, spent with Mike Hollis, in charge of the provincial office (the Resident of the province was away on tour), there were another 132 miles north to Azare, my destination and HQ of Katagum division, half way between Kano and Maiduguri, which are on most maps.

What did I find? Memory has distortions after half a century. Katagum division was 'holy North', little aware of the 20th century, and dubious of what it saw thereof: one largish emirate, Katagum itself, savannah tapering towards desert; one modest scrub-bound emirate to the south, Misau; and one tiny

On leave, with the Laird of Glen Buchat.

emirate westward across the Bunga river, Jama'arc. All had chiefs of the second class, rated from their forebears' flag-bearing place in Usman d'an Fod'io's *jihad* – the first was new and inexperienced, a former works foreman; the second experienced, intelligent and well-thought of, a member of the house of chiefs; and the third a vain, silly, amiable man with an aura of crookery. The DO, Captain McKenzie, was a shootin' and fishin' Scot, looking forward to retirement in September when he would be an old man of 55 (tradition still thought imperial masters, from governors downwards, to be worn out by heat and fever at such an advanced age). He hailed from Glen Buchat in Aberdeenshire, and was universally thought to be 'The Laird' thereof. At a time when true whisky was 'rationed' to a bottle a month (issued by the store one patronized – nobody could afford to run accounts at more than one local supplier), newcomers who did not (yet) drink the barley bree promised gratifying economic exchanges. He no longer fell back on a strange Dutch spirit, Maltky, which was in good supply for lack of demand, but still left any newly emptied Scotch bottle upside down overnight over a glass, where a teaspoonful dribble of the true craiter would be found in the morning.

Also in the station was Syd Smith, an inspector of works who oversaw Katagum's native authority works yard in Azare, a rough diamond with a heart of gold in the mixed mineralogical metaphor. Dr Afolabi Alakija, the MO, had been to an English grammar school, but his ten years qualifying at Glasgow university had left him with a Clydeside accent, despite being the son of Sir

Adeyemo, a distinguished Lagos figure. Immensely likable (he 'beered his cross' with us in the evenings rather than read the *BMJ*), Labi was proving slow to acquire professional self-confidence. His Vauxhall was already falling to pieces. We all played tennis. The fit-as-fiddle-at-55 Laird chose his stance and played every shot so that he need not move for its anticipated return. The dispenser and works mechanic (both Africans) made up our fours. The most memorable local people were Daudu the Spiv (the lorry-owning Mister Fixit), and Sarkin 'Yan Doka Ibrahim, head of the NA police and the sole true *évolué*, known to us as SYD. *Syd* Smith lost no time in driving me out to see a deserted tsetse research station at Gadau, the HQ towns of Misau and Jama'are emirates, and to Foggo to see new market stalls being laid out (where one day a road bridge would open up a new route from Bauchi to Kano), and to introduce me to the farmers' scourges, baboons. The harmattan wind and dust was blowing hard, and as I was quartered in a virtually unfurnished round mud rest house, the overlay of sandy squalor on every possession was recompensed by not having to pay even half rent (Ken Johnson, the other ADO's arrival six pre-emptive days before me had won him a half-rent building). The local postman, a former Nigeria Regiment steward, would cut my hair when essential. When the DO's out-of-date newspapers and my Penguins from home ran out, I had Sutton & Shannon on Contract and Winfield on Tort. There was an examination to face in June on *Financial Memoranda for Use in Native Treasuries in the Northern Provinces,* known as 'FMs', which would bear practical study.

For this the Laird sent me to check the Jama'are native treasury ('The *ma'aji* [native treasurer] will show you what to do' – besides knowing what it would be wise not to show me, he had a cleft palate). The hired NA kitcar bouncing on the corrugated laterite road was a shaking introduction to modes of transport when and where vehicles could not go.* I visited small Jama'are and Misau villages, my Union flag flying outside the village host's *zaure* (porch hut), and sitting in my director's chair with Bargery's Hausa dictionary weighing down my lap. After a few weeks I was adjudged capable of organizing Misau's agricultural show, six months too late: by now the best cattle had been sold and, so far into the dry season, the rest were simply scraggy. At least there were exciting races, with riders 'swording the pumpkins' on poles which they galloped past. I regularly met a missionary couple at Hardawa in Misau, the Sandersons, who were making no converts but felt justified by simply being there and ready to discuss anything with the inhabitants, including faith if it cropped up in casual conversation.

---

*Some scientist calculated that the rhythmic wheel-and-suspension movements interacted in a mechanical way with the grains of ferric soil to build up the succession of rippling rises and falls across the road; principally created by the heavier lorries, they defeated any engineer, however often road gangs might recover the surface with fresh laterite from the 'heaps' collected by contractors, or beat the results down level.

When the rains started I learnt to cross the racing river to Jama'are naked with thoughtful escorts, leaning on a calabash for water-wings. I had also been bamboozled into mounting a steed, the first time since aged 13. I was not happy. Nigerian horses seemed a creation apart. I may have learnt the elements of changing gear, so to speak, but Hausa hacks didn't work the same way, reins, stirruped feet or slapping hands having no effect on them (at least, not mine, not that my entourage looked any more comfortable). Each just did what the horse in front did, all the time: I dared not find out how one might lead a cavalcade. Those in front performed a bone-shaking motion that moved them forward no faster than a walk, but too fast up and down to rise in the saddle and cushion the blows. By the destination every bone and muscle in the body ached, certain parts were raw, and the only recourse was to the Hounsfield bed. I asked a lad to walk in front, not that he would control the brute either, but once this appalling back-break started at least he could clout it in the snout and give it cause to pause. I wore ever sweatier and greasier flannel bags, thinking riding breeches presumptuous if one was unlikely ever to risk polo, but pined for the moment to change back into clean starched and airy shorts. I thought of finding a horse and groom that might be moulded to my needs, but budgeted that the £3 monthly horse allowance would not cover the outlay while I was still paying off my initial household and touring equipment.

The Laird had pressed for posts & telegraphs wire to be extended to Azare for ten years, but the war had got in the way. He got me out of the way again for several weeks in Misau, to supervise its town plan. They could not understand why I wanted them to retain, indeed to restore, their ancient defensive mud walls as a part of their heritage. They did not mind that the mud native treasury building would disappear, nor really did I.

There were diversions. A hunter collected two three-week-old lion cubs after frightening their mother off, and brought them to the emir of Katagum, who sent them to the GRA (government residential area) for information, not for necessary action. I misunderstood for a couple of days, thinking I had been presented with adorable equivalents of a white elephant, and wondered how to give thanks, but still more what to do once they were weaned off condensed milk. Fortunately they were reclaimed: ultimately the enlightened provincial education officer Robert Wright named them 'McKenzie' and 'Umaru' and found them a home in London's zoo. Then the emir of Jama'are sent the DO a letter through his scribe, dated 24 March, saying, 'I am very much enjoy to lat you know, we are going to make fishing on Friday 25th/March/1949. please imform ADO Mr Cluck and Mechanic to come and take photograph of peoples while they are fishing. Kindly acknowledge receipt.' However little the notice, how could one refuse? The *sarkin kogi* (lord of the Bunga river) had by custom forbidden fishing on a length of stream towards the end of the dry season, had blocked off four of the wettest parts, and was waiting for us (and camera) before letting the populace loose to crowd in, stripped to their *bantes* (little triangular loincloths), with nets, calabashes and screaming vigour to capture masses of the *giwan ruwa* (water elephants, the Nile or Niger perch) and the mud catfish caught in the pools, both of which made exceedingly good eating. This was a version of the famous Argungu fishing festival, which attracted fame and distinguished visitors to Sokoto province every year. When rains resumed, the waters began to rise. Soon the road to Jama'are would have to cross an Irish bridge of stones and matting, until that was washed away and one would again have to swim. Syd (not SYD) was posted away and left me his small red monkey, which was entertaining but mischievous: Ousman called her *Dattijo* (Reverend oldster).

Sunday was Azare's market day, where one might ponder exotic medicines such as monkeys' paws, special birds' wings, and of course fish, dried or still fermenting, and what would become over the years the familiar selection of decorated calabashes, woven baskets, embossed terra cotta pots and dishes of all shapes and sizes, and pretty grass and reed mats. In impoverished early years these decorated the walls and floors of junior officers in their 'temporary buildings'. For tea there might be chocolate biscuits from someone at home, which the climate rendered inedible excerpt by spooning the contents from the silver paper. There were mangoes, dates and limes in season, but the expected tropical fruits (bananas, grapefruit, oranges, pineapples and coconuts) came by monthly lorry from distant parts via Jos. What ran out before the next delivery simply ran out. Before the rains there would be bush fires, one in particular starting between the GRA houses, when the *d'an doka* (NA policeman) on guard at the office dozed peacefully, until the blaze warmed him to raise the alarm. There was a visit by a silent mobile cinema, whose operator gave an *ad hoc* running commentary in Hausa on dated newsreels and Disney. Camel trains sometimes passed through laden with potash from the farther north, but the usual beast of burden was the donkey.

I contrived a visit to Potiskum, eastwards in Borno province, where I first met an ADO who had served with the lovely hill peoples in the Burma political service, and a 'veterinary development officer' and his wife. This was my first meeting with one of a group that was to grow in numbers and importance: officers paid from colonial development funds, with initiative, maturity and personality but lacking paper qualifications, who supplemented the work of the pensionable permanent staff flaunting degrees. As a treat McKenzie sent me west on a lorry to Kano to supervise collection of emergency supplies of petrol and works stores, going out on one road, and returning on another, neither of high grade. The famous walled city impressed, and a colleague from Oxford who hosted me in a temporary building, little more comforting than my own in Azare, depressed me (his father had governed two Indian provinces, and to tour Kano districts had not the same cachet). It was enlightening to see the pyramids of groundnuts awaiting rail transfer for export, what time the beetles ate the crop. Sheet lightning gave promise of rain on the journey back, and the increasing humidity brought out carpets of unexpected wild flowers on uncultivated roadsides. I began to notice the birdlife that some colleagues would see as the greatest joy of living in west Africa. Most impressive was a solitary Greater Bustard, a fine big fellow; the Abdim's Storks, evidently designed by Disney's studio, who arrived in large numbers 40 days before rain; and the Crown Birds (*gauraka*), very common crested cranes, awkward, raucous and accustomed to fly honking around the heavens in pairs. The Ground Hornbill (*burtu*) would settle at night in the middle of a laterite road, and its sleepy, impoverished aerodynamics when trying desperately to flap into take-off speed before the approaching monster's headlights pounced upon it were a wonder to behold. All this so far was an eye-opening start, crammed into little more than four months of having been plunged into the deep end. First impressions never leave one.

I was summoned to run the provincial office in Bauchi for the Resident Geoffrey Payton, a cultured man, dubious about speedy political change, and unhappy because his wife did not join him. He thought my predecessor Mike Hollis should be exposed to bush, and I to paper. The NA lorry covered 132 miles in five hours, including a quarter-hour farewell to Sarkin Misau, half an hour for a cold lunch, 10 minutes having a beer and 10 more halted because of a deluge of rain. As flat desert gave way to real hills, so green returned. Bauchi was 2,000' above the level of the sea from which it was so far. On arrival I took over Hollis's comfortable bungalow before sitting (and passing) the FMs exam. I should have to afford a garden boy (eventually, after an old, respectable but incompetent old man, I took on Buba Gur, a newly graduated Elementary 4 son of a Dass hamlet head, who very publicly bade me to beat him if he misbehaved, to the evident approval of the company). The house was known as *gidan aduwa* (the house of shade), surrounded by mango and other trees; its wide entry verandah was covered by glorious *corallita* creeper, with bougainvillea bordering all, and the ubiquitous *canna* lilies that ringed most expat quarters. None of this required expert horticulture. To the north the outlook was upon a picturesque rocky outcrop.

As 'ADO(O)' (O for Office), after tea in bed at 6.15 *a.m.* with the agreeable whisper *lokacin tashi ya yi* (time to get up), office from 7 to 9.15 and 10 to 2.45 *p.m.*, I learnt about filing systems, annual reports and returns, vote service ledgers, permits, the single telegraph wire to Jos, the duties of aerodrome control officer (and by tradition of bar secretary of the club), and how much depended on a southern clerical service who had good memories, dedication to routine and suspicion of change.

The offices were mud-built, although the Resident's, the DO's and provincial office had corrugated iron ('pan') under the thatch; Bauchi divisional HQ was here too. In 1949 the club boasted 13 Europeans at the hub of a district half the size of Ceylon, with over a million people, including one white wife (the vet's). There had been a mud squash court, before it collapsed, and a golf course, now hidden under the new residency and an extension to the airfield. The memorable officers were the great Robert Wright, who now had two ostrich chicks, 18" tall, as well as the lion cubs; Ernest John Butler the agricultural officer, playing Scarlatti on his huge EMG horn gramophone (brother to an equally redoubtable Irish HQ education officer Herbert George); Humphrey Tupper-Carey, a former senior district officer re-employed in retirement as a forest estate officer (the Duke of Gloucester had been his fag at Eton), whose redoubtable spouse and former army matron Marjory ran the catering rest house with a rod of iron; and the unidentifiably mittel-European Dr Frishman with his worship of Bach. Robert went on leave soon after my arrival, and lent me his kerosene-powered Electrolux fridge and 6-volt car-battery-powered Bush short-wave radio. Wireless news was a welcome change from my portable 78 rpm gramophone and the case of 50 shellac records.

The Resident was sociable, approachable, and a classical scholar as ready to discuss Creech Jones as Leslie Henson. His working dress was blue shirt, navy blue shorts and stockingless sandals, a fashion from wartime shortages that banished forever the caricatures of the helmeted, belted, cropped and booted authorities of anti-imperial fantasy. He offered me the province's sole annual permit to purchase a kitcar (a 29·4 hp Chevrolet 6-cylinder pickup truck, BY 4753, which my household would scrub and polish on Sunday mornings while, in as few clothes as they, I cleaned the engine, checked the plugs, pumped the tyres and greased the nipples). It cost a salary advance of £520 (sterling devaluation was imminent and the next Chev on offer would be £707). The works yard built a wooden cover with canvas blinds over the back, for the cost of the materials, sheltering loads and bodies surplus to the two, sometimes three, who shared the cabin seat with me.

So began three tours in Bauchi division, ending as DO in charge, the longest an administrator had spent in one district at this period. Not the only HQ not to have electricity and piped running water for years to come, nevertheless Bauchi prided itself on being 'the last gentleman's station'. It was long before I appreciated that it was the epitome of the North, not too holy, with something for all tastes. The emir of Bauchi was a first class chief, a Muslim but proud of his Gerawa ancestors, pagans before conversion in the not too distant past. There were several outcrops of pagan people under his rule, mostly innocent of all but the minutest clothing. Ningi was a modest third class chiefdom of three districts, part animist, with an unattractive chief. Dass was a tiny chiefdom in dramatic rocks, with Islamicized headmen but undeveloped peasantry, and a jolly, unpretentious leader, too unimportant to be allowed an official car. Neither Ningi nor Dass had been given flags by Sarkin Musulmi during the *jihad*. After growing their own food, chiefly corn and millet, the farmers' main produce was cotton and groundnuts.* A healthy amount went out each year. Probably the equivalent of the whole Kongwa (Strachey's infamous East African Groundnut Scheme) crop of groundnuts could be bought within a few miles' radius of Bauchi (certainly of Azare) town, but we did not try unsuccessfully to grow sunflower seeds on the side. There was no commerce, the big internal African trade apart, and little mining, although this was on the increase as the plateau fields to the west showed preliminary signs of being worked out, and our smaller easterly deposits became relatively more attractive.

The atmosphere was of Hausaland. All the leading figures were sincerely practising Muslims, but broad-minded tolerance prevailed. Nobody, except for a lorry-owning merchant Musa d'an Matori and the emir, was markedly rich, and true hardship only came when locusts arrived, or cerebro-spinal meningitis struck, or fussy bureaucrats distorted the balance of life with annual tax counts or a decennial census – I encountered them all. NA officials returning from a British Council visit to UK uttered surprise at factory employees working for hours without a break, and everyone in the streets hurrying somewhere: Europeans evidently neither sauntered nor just stood (these northerners had never experienced Onitsha in the south). The first four Penguin prints (an innovation now long forgotten), including a Paul Klee, went up on my living room walls in wooden frames made by works yard apprentices. 'Small boy' Jibir (sometimes 'Jibirin') kept the cold water tank filled from a well for our running water, and brought the hot bath water in kerosene tins from a wood fire. I sent him to an adult literacy class three times a week, balancing my own three hour long Hausa conversation sessions with a mallam (the word for a literate man, extended to a polite equivalent of 'Mister' for the less sophisticated).

Meanwhile Dattijo was taken by a nocturnal leopard. My Bacama office orderly from Rangoon, Gumi Mikah Lamurde, had heard that I was in Bauchi and made his way from Adamawa, partly on foot, perhaps hoping to join the Nigeria Police, but in effect to look to me for help. Gumi became head

---

*To underline how socialist bureaucracy bedevilled colonial development schemes, how better than to quote verbatim SR&O 2 598 (1947)(xix)(5bb) para 16: 'In the Nuts (Unground)(other than Ground Nuts) Order the expression 'nuts' shall have reference to such Nuts, other than Ground Nuts, as would, but for this amending order, not qualify as Nuts (Unground)(other than Ground Nuts) by reason of their not being Nuts (Unground); and the expression 'unground' shall exclude such Ground Nuts (Unground) as do not fall within the scope of the expression 'Nuts (Unground)(other than Ground Nuts)' by reason of their being Ground Nuts'. Verb *sap* or *sat*.

gardener and extra hand in the house, another set of uniforms to have tailored (I never dressed my household in dreary khaki: white for day work, a cheerful colour for evening hospitality). Foxy (and Rosie) Cole arrived as acting Resident. The development officer who checked and advised the Bauchi native treasury (in theory relieving Cox and me for more constructive duties) was Lt-col W D Holt OBE; he had been a regular cavalry officer, temporarily blind for two years, an acting brigadier AG in a phantom 12th army designed to fox the Hun in north Africa, and a cousin of Sir Stafford Cripps – we knew him as 'Colonel Chinstrap' from the BBC ITMA show, where that character's line, 'I don't mind if I do', was trotted out whenever he was offered a 'coaster' at the club bar (a 'coaster' being a pink gin & soda with a few pearl onions rising and falling with the bubbles).

Marjory Tupper-Carey had never condescended to take quinine in her life; she fell foul of a fever and was eventually convinced by Frishman that mepacrine was essential. Paul Waters, a close friend, was principal of the Teacher Training Centre at Yalwa, south of the airfield under the shadow of Bule mountain. Bunny Hicks, with a Spanish wife Carmen, arrived as rural education officer, to run a teacher training annex for candidates from undeveloped areas, attached to the TTC. I acquired a black male kitten, part Persian, named Diabolo. By Christmas Cox had gone on leave, the first DO for many years to have spent his whole tour here; he lent me his bookcase, but not his dog, which had seemed likely, nor the fridge (Robert would soon be back to reclaim his). Cox left me with the task of persuading the NA to stop building £100 elementary school 2-class blocks entirely of mud and thatch, which collapsed every couple of years and had to be rebuilt. I was to recommend £400 buildings, with cement floors, an office between the classrooms, shutter windows, zinc-bound roof trusses, and if possible 'pan' under the thatch which local labour would still provide, together with the mud and rubble for the walls, now held firm by masonry pillars. When the provincial education officer Wright returned, and with his NA assistant, a Malam Abubakar, as joint advocates, we succeeded.

I sat the lower standard Hausa exams, being passed in the oral by F W de St Croix, known simply as 'X', a learned, modest and loveable ex-public schoolboy who had spent his life in the bush among the cattle Fulani; he firmly failed a tongue-tied friend. For part of the written exam the NA education assistant (former middle school headmaster), whom I now knew as Malam Abubakar Tafawa Balewa, read the dictation. Thus tightened one of my strongest bonds, a growing friendship with Abubakar, prime minister and martyr in making. I came to realize that he judged younger administrative officers by their ability to resist taking powers out of the hands of NA officials, and by their willingness to get out of their offices and on tour. Someone else who came to talk things through with Abubakar was Jack Davies, general manager of the United Africa Company in Nigeria: this led to UAC selling its rights to mineral royalties 'back' to the Nigerian government, I learnt. I found more mundane matters to discuss. Abubakar was engrossed in G M Trevelyan's *English Social History* (bought by me in Rangoon), and we found common ground in lauding the work of the well-sinkers, two of whose expatriate inspectors I admired as rough diamonds. I was not so sure of his sophistication when he insisted that for all the surveying and prospecting of almost half a century, there must be untapped mineral resources in the North that would enable it to prosper without relying on the south for anything.

My earliest success was a 1950 study that convinced the emir (and DO, Resident and secretariat) that the Jarawa pagans should have an overall chief recognized in a district of their own, separated from Sarkin Kudu (chief of the south) Malam Sani, the *évolué* Muslim district head (DH) who presently stood between them and the emir. Sani had been favoured by Robert Wright when he had been DO Bauchi; he was the model of a modern, well-educated DH, keeping a flower garden as well as a self-sufficient farm, and would have been a leader had he not been responsible for people with whom, embarrassingly, he had little in common. The Hill Jarawa lived south of the road to Jos, at the western end of the division marching towards the main plateau. I began my inquiry at the vernacular elementary teacher training centre at Toro, inspected the dispensary there, thence to Tilden Filani where the plateau mining community had its furthest eastern link, and heard my first structured complaints from Jarawa people. They agreed that they had been under the suzerainty (hardly their word) of the emirs of Bauchi for 140 years, but they no longer recognized the authority of Sarkin Kudu, whatever his merits, and wanted a district head of their own who would answer directly to the emir (to whose family Sani's incidentally posed potential rivalry). Changes in the air had woken them up.

I travelled round the hamlets in between harvest and ploughing, when the main occupation was the drinking of local beer (not undrinkable, I tentatively discovered), and found ways to avoid the presence of the emir's official representative, a 'detribalized' Bajari himself. The north's highest mountain, 5,841' of it called Shere, was close by, and it could be very cold. Unencumbered by wrappings, the Jarawa often kept warm by dancing, playing on their cane whistles and strumming on banjo-sounding instruments like small seven-stringed clarsachs. Through eager interpreters, mostly teachers, their shamans told me, in palavers lasting three hours or more, of how since slavery and tribal wars had ended with the arrival of the British, they were beginning to spread into the surrounding valleys and plains. The older men still wore their penis-sheaths (gourds, in fact) even when also covering their loins, but the younger generation was ceasing to have the characteristic facial scarifications carved on their cheeks as children, or to wear the gourds underneath their *warki*s (whole goatskin loincloths). Ready-made market shorts and the Hausa *'yar ciki* (sleeveless short shirt) were now not unknown, and this had little to do with mission influence.

The Hill Jarawa were unanimous, and my report endorsed their felt needs. Four months later I returned with an approving emir of Bauchi to say that everyone agreed. The Resident (by now Humphrey Gill, the Coles having been recalled to Kaduna after eight months) recorded that 'the report had been a very creditable effort, particularly for a cadet in his first tour'. I sent my father a copy: he responded with wonder at the responsibility laid on young shoulders – could he ever have believed that Major Me had commanded a military unit?

I chatted with the NT accountant Yak'ubu Wanka, a future federal legislator, saying that the Jarawa were now at the happiest stage of history – peace prevailed and slavery was forgotten; they had a dispensary and access to medical care; their crops were better fertilized; their children were being educated to at least primary level and possible upward progress to the middle school; with their own court and access to the DO's supervision justice had improved; lorries were taking their produce to markets; and they did not yet know enough of the wider world to become jealous and discontented. 'O, no sir, no sir, they still do not have proper clothes and are superstitious'.

The next task was to reconnoitre Yuli district, a part of the division to the south-east, ostensibly to judge suitability for cotton-growing. We wanted the development board to finance a road in, for ease of exporting market produce, hoping *sub rosa* to get closer administration into places not toured for five years, nor for three years before that. With the NA's senior agricultural assistant Malam Ahmadu, Buba Gombe a splendid government messenger, and the train of carriers and my staff, we left Bakoreji, where a well-sinker from Gombe obliged me with a haircut, and headed south. It was very backward; we saw lion, giraffe, hippo, bush-cow and two 12' dead pythons, but were at a loss to see any of the water that wildlife, let alone people, must surely drink. Robert Coulthard, the veterinary officer, and Tupper-Carey had their eyes on declaring the part of this bush, already gazetted as a forest reserve, as a game reserve. Our tour was the basis on which the yet-to-be-named Yankari Game Reserve, one of Nigeria's tourist attractions which I would enjoy 38 years later, would be founded, with little disturbance to local settled population.

Back at HQ Jibir, to my great disappointment, pilfered from the bags of corn I bought for the household. He was succeeded by another Elementary 4 product recommended by his headmaster; Audu d'an Dada was a bright lad with promise. Part of the test for applicants was to *run* round the central flower bed bearing the tea-tray without spilling anything. Nobody had been appointed to succeed Payton as overseer of the club library, and when *in absentia* I now was: few suggestions for fresh titles came in, so I ordered the new Everyman's Encyclopaedia, so unwelcome on arrival that in honour bound I paid for it (it faces my desk to-day) with the gratuity following success in the Hausa exam. There was no cash reward for passing the laws, but that did mean (with FMs in the bag already) that with good conduct I should be confirmed in appointment at the end of next tour. A baby duiker, confiscated from naughty boys, imprinted itself on Gumi, who called it Binta Daji (bush girl).

So back to bush, to tour Duguri in the west, which had once been independent of Bauchi. The dry-season drifts over river-beds were dicey by this time, and there were latent worries about whether one might get the kitcar back across if the weather broke – abundance of scorpions was always an indication of the coming wet. Cerebro-spinal meningitis was abroad in the dust, which rains would quell, and I found myself 'treating' two cases in isolation camps, following whatever instructions Dr Russell Aliyu Barau Dikko gave me. He had succeeded Frishman, and was a half-Fulani brought up in the CMS mission, the first Northerner to qualify as a medical practitioner. He was also president of the Northern Peoples Congress, a cultural body which (as the Indian Congress before it) was to become the North's first political party: as a government officer he had then to resign, but Abubakar Tafawa Balewa, a native authority official, remained a stalwart. This last major tour before leave, after overseeing the opening of a postal agency at Kafin Madaki, was with Bauchi's *sarkin daji* (lord of the bush), the senior forest assistant. For three weeks we rode round the forest and notional game reserve north of the road to Jos. He was accustomed to Tupper-Carey's 30 miles pony trek a day, and wondered why I took things slowly, liaising with beery pagans round the edge of the delimited reserve. Apart from a rare forest official they had seen no European officer for 20-30 years. They certainly wore gourds under their goatskin *warkis*. Their ladies fashioned their hair like unto American military helmets, and carried wooden discs in their bored ear lobes and lips, progressively exchanging these for ever wider inserts until the ear-rings rested over their shoulders and their mouths were unkindly interpreted as 'duckbills'. In our palavers I told the men versions of Hans Andersen stories, with the invitation to cap them with their own folklore tales: our mutual Hausa just sufficed. All I saw of game in the reserve was some elephant dung and an ant. We crossed one river in a dugout log, while our ponies were induced by their grooms to swim. One book I took to read was Robert Graves's *The Isles of Unwisdom*, which I found unenthralling, not seeing 22 years into the future.

We came home to hear that war had broken out in Korea. Ex-servicemen had officially been released to a reserve, liable to recall – I hastened to tell the War Office that I was in Crown service elsewhere, and it duly took note that I 'appeared to be overseas'. Binta disappeared one night, having grown to 15" at the shoulder; sadly, we were visited by hyenas. There were now 27 expatriates in Bauchi GRA, including more than one wife and a couple of children. I celebrated my last day in Bauchi with a tea party for all the NA mallams and clerks I had worked with, involving elementary politics in elementary Hausa. The postmaster wore, as usual, a golf cap: I had long ceased to find cultural idiosyncrasies, whether rivers chiefs donning top hats or district heads wearing laceless gym shoes, as patronizingly funny. I had taken to market flip-flops, and even a *bante* for filthy and sweaty car maintenance, myself. My household dispersed to their homes; their travel costs and half-pay retainers committed them to return, draining my depleted budget. I drove to Kano, where the PWD took my kitcar into store on bricks, battery unplugged and radiator drained. The standard 13-15 days' sea passage did not count against leave, and to encourage us to spend less time away, we were awarded an extra week each way if we elected to fly in one day, which I chose to do.

My first leave began with a visit to Paul Waters, already home, much resented by my mother who thought nothing should delay an immediate flight back to the nest. During a coach tour through France, Switzerland and Italy, with a nip through the edge of Austria, using our permitted £25 a head foreign currency, my parents and I were blessed by Pope XII (with countless others) during an outdoor audience at Castel Gandolfo, and met Robert Coulthard in a restaurant by the Roman catacombs. My parents and he did not quite understand each other. In Paris we saw Gounod's *Mireille* at the Palais du Chaillot in the Trocadéro. A memory of that holiday was of the American lieutenant-colonel from their judge advocate-general's department who, towards the last day of savouring Europe's cultural heritage, refused to get out of the bus; 'All we ever see is old, old, old! I want to be shown sumpin noo, noo, noo!'

I visited the Laird at Glen Buchat, where he seemed lonely. Edinburgh's festival for the first time featured Sir Thomas Beecham, now forgiven for having prophesied failure in 1947. The city fathers who attended church once a year, at the kirking of the council in S Giles cathedral (better known by them as the High Kirk), expressed horror at the opening Sunday concert being billed as Beethoven's *Messe Solennelle* ('A Mass? On the Sabbath? Before The Queen, the lay head representative of the Established Presbyterian Church of Scotland? No way, Jimmy!'). Tommy had to substitute the *Choral Symphony,* but got his own back. He performed Elgar's arrangement of the national anthem, very slow, all three verses, 'knavish tricks' and all, dragged out the final chord as only he ever could, turned, bowed to the Sovereign still at undaunted attention, and walked off for an unscheduled interval.

I ate dinners at the Middle Temple, and had lunch with Malam Tukur who had done so much to make my Hausa fluent and intelligible, and with Robert Wright at his London club. A very surprising sight was a yellow-labelled gramophone record turning ludicrously slowly on its turntable in a London record shop, playing music then almost unknown, Vivaldi's *The Four Seasons*. Shellac had its marching orders, and long-playing vinyl was about to conquer. 20 weeks expired and I reduced my accompanied air baggage from 70 lbs to 'near enough' 44 by filling my raincoat pockets with books, toiletry and footwear; I flew back on new year's day 1951 to learn at the Kano railway guest house that I was reposted to Bauchi (and to remember that I had failed to surrender my ration book at Heathrow customs – would my mother be arrested by a snooper?).

Another reappraisal. I enjoyed my work and saw no reason to abandon it. *Pax Britannica* meant that politics had little meaning for the people at large. One authority might make for as much good and ill as another. The two great needs were roads and water. Without communications to evacuate primary produce, progress would be small, and without decent water health progress would also. In 1950 I persuaded myself that we should declare a moratorium on schools and dispensaries until there were enough real roads and good wells everywhere. Physical infrastructure should precede social reorganization. Unfortunately, railways now cost too much (had Colonial Development & Welfare been invented at its present scale long ago, it would have gone so much further when labour earned 2d a day).

A jejune opinion that would change ere long was of the prevailing faith, which travels among the animists had done much to nurture. Muslim towns reflected the culture: people jealous of their privacy, and wary of letting their women into another's sight, surrounded every compound by a high wall, with entry through a *zaure* (a hut forming a gate-house). This seemed symbolic of a generic refusal to let their hair down, open up and become part of a wide world. The most emancipated still clung to the forms of purdah, not noticing the lack of sunlight and fresh air, with complacency little different from deepest obstinacy. I found pro-Islamic prejudices hard to follow, even though the alkalis' courts seemed to administer a *shari'a* that was understood without question, being the application of the will of the Almighty to what had been ordained. Yet one could not but be moved by the unanimity of public confession when a town's whole population turned out to pray behind the emir before the mosque on Friday. One day I would respect a corporate way that seemed more real than the self-regarding pseudo-humanism that has been reshaping the convictions of two western millennia. It was a respect which, remembering the peaceful times we spent in the decolonization of Nigeria, might have survived the excesses, largely heretical as I understand them, of today's resurgent fundamentalism. The heart was that there could be no distinction between the religious and the secular in life, least of all in law. Stability without doubts still has strong attractions.

Another staple of the time would be reviewed regularly wherever colonial administration was being weighed, and which becomes more topical at home as standards of public service degenerate through expansion – corruption. Many of the traditional authorities through whom we carried out our 'indirect rule' were, by British civil service standards, corrupt. Custom that we abhorred had been part of life throughout Africa since time immemorial, kept in check by methods that we equally abhorred, whether in major kingdoms with hierarchies or in small extended groups. Perhaps things were not always so bad, certainly not so evil, as high-minded thinking suggested. It might not be for me to say that there were occasions when the time-honoured excuses for letting the lesser, and broadly speaking more harmless, rackets continue must wear thin. The most common was, 'Who would you find any better to put in his place if you did sack him?'

I collected the kitcar, met the Hardawa missionaries, Sanderson, now fully occupied in Kano with a retranslation of the bible into Hausa, and set off on the dry season road to Zaria. Arriving weary at Bauchi, I found that the Resident Gill was as silent as ever, Laurence Giles was divisional officer, I was to be temporarily housed in Robert Wright's house out at Yalwa, and that Frank Farrant was expected. Immediately I had to organize a stall at an agricultural show to induce farmers to use superphosphate on their exhausted soil, and was made by Giles to sit as magistrate on overloaded lorry cases, since he was dissatisfied with the paltry fines imposed by the alkali's court. He was probably the best Hausa-speaker in the North, a double first in classics, and had had a fascinating war 'spying' on Vichy French across the borders. His nickname, said to reflect his stature, was 'Afo' (Hausa for 'three-ha'pence', but he preferred it to be the Fulani 'Ahu', younger brother). I greatly respected him as well as finding him friendly, and we shared amusement when the Hausa newspaper *Gaskiya Ta Fi Kwabo* ('Truth is worth more than a penny') suggested sending a juju-man to UK to help discover the Stone of Destiny, which Scottish Nationalists had stolen from under King Edward's coronation throne in Westminster Abbey.

Lere district, largely peopled by the Seyawa around Tafawa Balewa ('Black Rock'), its HQ, had not been toured for long enough. Thither I was sent, but not to reorganize an animist majority out from under a Muslim DH. The fine black rock jutted out, which I climbed, despite warnings that its guardian the *Sarkin dutse* ('lord of the rock') fed a python who presided on top. Missionaries active here were American lay preachers, not trained theologians. I found myself delivering a lay sermon to a large group of mission youngsters, conscious that their mentors would later label me as pro-Muslim, pro-pagan, anti-Christian, since I recommended mutual tolerance and respect. Returning home, taking breakfast in the catering rest house before unpacking, it was astonishing to meet my old classics and VIIth form master from Edinburgh Academy, 'Cod' Rowe. He was now teaching classics at Achimota college in the Gold Coast, and was on his way back from having driven a small Austin all the way to see Lake Chad. He was as surprised: he did not believe in medicines and did not take anti-malarial pills, so that it was shattering to hear a few weeks later that he had collapsed and died from cerebral fever while playing tennis in Ibadan, his next major halt after Bauchi. Some days later I was back in *gidan aduwa,* sometimes visited by fluttering flycatchers in the living room, what time an outbreak of rabies was met in part by calling in a group of animists who ate dog flesh, which they were skilled in acquiring without fear of being bitten.

For two months I was alone in the division while Afo/Ahu acted as Resident. When he went into hospital, he left me to 'answer for Resident locally'. Little study or recreational reading was possible. The forthcoming indirect general election promised to offer a daunting two months of worry, so it was essential to start now. In between organizing district electoral colleges out of the subordinate hamlet and village choices, who would choose their representatives on the emirate college *en route* to the provincial college (thence to the regional assembly, which would select upwards to federal legislative council), there was the annual return of native court corporal punishments to be compiled for the interest of the prurient, and of those MPs obsessively interested, such as Reginald Sorensen.

A dry March and April gave way to a May when rain fell in such unending sheets that all the thin topsoil was washed away and little water sank in to irrigate undersoil and roots. The deluge did not last. The farmers delayed planting in case they did it too soon, and then worried that they might have left it too late. When weather did build up, it always seemed to fall somewhere else. We were promised a locust visitation, but again, not yet. After the latest rains for years, in November the *harmattan* wind returned with the Saharan dust to coat everything that was not wiped down twice or thrice a day.

Admin officers had to engage in a whirligig of tours, explaining the incomprehensible new constitutional election system to puzzled villagers twice a day till the division had been covered. Few of those under instruction could imagine what and where a province, a region or a federation might be, let alone why chosen representatives could or should be weeded out at successive levels upwards. After several days, our spontaneity withered. If the plane to Johannesburg flew over, their flimsy concentration evaporated. Bush villagers would only choose a favoured hamlet head to speak for them, wiser than, but as illiterate and unsophisticated as, themselves. We tried discreetly to encourage selection of brighter commoners, easier perhaps in town wards. By September the primaries were over. Another month weeded out the provincial unsuccessfuls. After so much talking, all but the few still in the running had lost interest, and not till the new year would anyone know who would end up from the regions into the Lagos house of representatives. *Id el fitr,* the 'big' *salla,* was a welcome semi-holiday break.

A visit to Jos for repairs to teeth and kitcar allowed a visit to Dr Walter Miller, the renowned missionary who had reached Kano before Lugard, now peacefully retired aged 79 and 8 months: he was interested in a younger generation, and inspiring. Ousman decided around now to return to the plateau, and Paul Waters's 'small boy', Garba from Hong, asked to be tried out as the cook whose skills he had been acquiring by 'watching Nelly'. By now only Wright and Butler among the Europeans had been longer in Bauchi than I, and it was less than two years since I had come from Azare. What above everything persuaded me in my conceit that I was now accepted by the local people was that Bauchi's town alkali invited me into his home, through the *zaure* porch where most visitors, especially infidels, would be halted, and into his sleeping room, where his principal wife was lying: she covered her face with a bed cloth, but I knew that I had been truly honoured – and trusted. Many years later my wife was taken in to meet the wives of an important man whom I was interviewing, but this was a unique and unforgettable gesture for me. None of my colleagues had such a privilege, to my knowledge at the time.

An adventure followed, to have lasting consequences. 'Chad', E R Chadwick the eastern administrator who had introduced 'community development' to the more 'get-up-and-go' parts of his provinces, had gained renown by inspiring a documentary film on the subject, *Daybreak in Udi,* widely circulated among those interested in African development. This interest attracted Alec Dickson, who had observed how best to re-employ Gold Coast soldiers on demobilization, using their war-learned skills to improve villages with well-tops, incinerators, simple buildings and other cement-and-timber embellishments of mud. Dickson founded a community development training school at Man o' War Bay (answerable to the Lagos ministry of works) near Victoria in the southern Cameroons. It offered three weeks of physical and mental toughening on the lines of Outward Bound, and three weeks of exemplary community development works in a bush village to light the path for local people to follow. All provinces were asked for volunteers, and I elected to go, with native treasury scribe Fate Dass, son of the chief of Dass, hoping that it might give him ideas for his own little patch.

My Waziri came to look after me, but managed to get in on most activities. Officers were expected to share a full active part, but also to act as advisers, mentors and whippers-in of the Africans who were the true candidates. The chief instructor was Bill Fuller, seconded from the original Outward Bound school at Aberdovey. Dickson's wife Mora filled the gaps of matron, motherly care and softer concepts. During the day we learnt to row, did hearty PT with logs, studied elementary potting on a wheel, and exerted ourselves physically at general rover scout camp chores and occupations. The unspoken purpose was to bring arrogant or conceited youths, who thought that education and office work should set them apart forever from humbler physical toils or challenges, sharply down to earth. Their usual voluminous gowns, smart tailored suits and patent shoes were packed away, and they made do with PT shorts, a T-shirt when not sweating hard, and possibly gym shoes or flip-flops. As with school uniforms, their status became invisible until they showed what they knew and what they could do, but lack of dress sense was hardest on the Northern mallams. In the evenings there were competitive dances between the cultures, quizzes, lecturettes, amateur dramatics (with a side-splitting mimicry by a Yoruba teacher of Mora Dickson, pre-Maggie handbag and all) and music. Alec taught us all to sing what would be the ANC national anthem, *Nkosi Sikelel' iAfrika,* inappropriate to settler- and Boer-free west Africa, but no matter.

We had a tragedy. The end of the first three weeks was to be marked by half of the course climbing Mount Cameroon itself, 13,353' high, what time the other half rowed a lifeboat under Bill Fuller's hearty and no-nonsense skippering. I was one of the rowers (so was Waziri), and we began to wonder whether we were bound for America before he relented and signalled a return to harbour. Later we heard that during the preceding night one dormitory had been disturbed by the nightmares of a local candidate, a Bakweri, who had dreamt of the evil spirits his people believed to haunt the mountain, and swore that he was going to his death. In fact an Igbo, Hyacinth Nnaji, did lose heart in the cold mists, wandered astray and was found dead of hypothermia; the Bakweri also gave up under the strain, but was found, yet he clung hysterically to a shrub, screaming to be left alone, and despite all efforts expired. Both had been let down by mates, for the strictest instructions had been given that nobody in a file should go forward if he could not see the next in line still following. The minister of works, Abubakar, visited the next course, and when one Hausa youth jibbed at the climb, was told directly by the minister that he would go, for the honour of the North, and he did.

Then we were off to a small village on the Bamenda plateau, camping out in the village school. We showed the inhabitants how we built an incinerator and classroom block, as well as constructing a veritable suspension bridge across a gully, from local vegetable material. The implicit lesson was that with proper leadership the compulsory labour intrinsic in undeveloped culture, recognized in Hausa as *gayya* ('voluntary' communal labour) need not become unjust feudal conscription (or 'forced labour') once education introduced 'modern' ideas of rights and duties. It would work better in those parts of the North where paganism was a recent memory than in urbanized societies, but Malam

Fate did try to sell the idea to some of his Dass people as something different from a directive from his father. Returning home I chanced to meet an Oxford colleague at Mamfe, where the MO was caring for a charming stray baby chimpanzee, Wendy. No wonder European ladies can give up their lives to studying the great apes. Wendy was a real person, although a child.

My last sortie to Ningi on this tour was to watch their *salla* celebration, walking eleven miles barefoot from across the Bunga drift, since their NA kitcar had broken down. Come February I was due to go on leave. I applied for the 2nd Devonshire course, half-hoping that a year in UK would soften my mother's antagonism to my vocation, but was not chosen. Mike Hollis would succeed as divisional officer Bauchi, although Giles was adamant that my unbroken service should give me local priority. The GRA buzzed with a rumour that Abubakar Tafawa Balewa, who had made it through to Lagos, was going to host a drinks party, the first return hospitality from the town's establishment to European invitations. I was visited by a lad who said that the *baturen makaranta, shi bak'in mutum* ('the "white" school man, that black man') expected me at his home at 5 o'clock. I donned a tie and long trousers and went down, to find the chief scribe, the native treasurer, the chief alkali, the town's district head and head elementary teacher sitting in a circle round Abubakar's *zaure* with a vacant deck chair – for me: there were no other GRA guests. There was an open whisky bottle, water jug and glass for me ('You'll know what to do with that'), and the rest had Abeokuta squash. I was a guinea-pig, but honoured by the gesture. We talked about how the failure of the groundnut crop had left the railway with no freight to carry, how difficult it had been to find literate as well as intelligently experienced candidates for the election, and whether Churchill's age and health mattered more than his experience and symbolism. I knew when the time for prayer would prompt me to 'make the first move'.

A few days later The King died, and a deputy director of Nigeria's education Tony Shillingford, in charge of the north, was inspecting Paul Waters's elementary teachers training college; with Paul's assistant Mary Robson and the woman education officer Mary Kinton, all came round to my house to hear the 77-year-old Winston Churchill give his historic broadcast of mourning and celebration of the new young monarch. The local people were all genuinely sympathetic with Britain's loss, and only a little uncertain of how to come to terms with the notion of a female monarch. Resident Gill led an open-air memorial service based on the 1662 prayer book, the first time for me to wear my newly arrived uniform and Wilkinson sword, after confirmation in my appointment, now amounting to all of three years. A friendly wife had sewn me a black armband. Sarkin Bauchi Yak'ubu attended, a little distrait, but

Abubakar was attentive and moved. Leave came, and I left my kitcar in the Bauchi works yard, Giles having said that surely I must be coming back.

Early that leave I went to Jenners in Edinburgh for my first professional haircut for over a year and a half. I recognized the spare man in the next chair, and ventured after the gowns had been swept from our chests to say, 'Excuse me, sir, you won't remember me but … ,' only for Sir John Macpherson, with his viceregal gift, to say, 'Of course, Clark, it was in Bauchi'. To be remembered, after being only one of many at a drinks reception on a residency lawn in the twilight, helps morale: not all the great and good have this regal ability and interest to identify and tuck away in the mind. I remember little else of that leave. There was little fun to be found in family life. My very good friend Mary Kinton visited us at home, and my mother, suspecting the predatory worst and lacking faith in my innocence or judgment, made the atmosphere none too happy. At least the Edinburgh festival brought the Hamburg opera, with Elisabeth Grümmer, Anneliese Rothenberger, Gottlob Frick and Peter Anders in Weber's *Freischütz;* Frick, Anders, Grümmer and Otto Edelmann in Wagner's *Meistersinger;* and Anders, Martha Mödl and Lisa Della Casa in Beethoven's *Fidelio*. Barbirolli also led his Hallé in Sargent's arrangement of Brahms's *Four Serious Songs,* sung by a very serious young man beginning his international career, Dietrich Fischer-Dieskau.

My return was to immediate chaos: five months of bat droppings had to be cleansed from the kitcar, which at last needed a new battery, the original having lasted twice its expected life span; the front springs were also weakening. There were so many new faces that much of substance was overlooked. Giles had left, under a cloud for approaching a minister directly in support of his anxiety to promote cotton production and marketing, and been reposted to the middle belt before deciding to resign, a huge loss. I met what seemed genuine African pleasure that I was expected to stay in Bauchi. Terry Hopkins, the new SDO, had only just arrived, and I was to revisit the ADO schedule until Frank Farrant returned in a couple of months, when I was to be the province's special duties officer. A new ADO, whose father had run Kew, sought no induction or mentoring. I was adjudged the only person with the altitude to measure the ETC sports pole-vault athletics. There was a new medical officer, Norman Williams from Lagos, rotund and hilarious, whose private practice had earned him a Jaguar which he had lost in a disastrous fire with all his valuables, none of which had been insured. Mary Kinton was posted to Maiduguri, leaving the progress in starting a Bauchi girls' secondary school slower than ever. My Diabolo had been put down, nobody being willing to take him on when I went on leave, because a wife accused him of eating kittens: I found this incredible, considering how many welcome kittens were attributed to him. The Hopkins's dog Rags, of unidentifiable breeding, began to embarrass me by coming 'home' to me at lunchtime. I was made club secretary, with the right to use its sole pewter beer mug, which I privately thought inferior to my own.

The Gills had 31 guests inside the residency for Christmas dinner, with gramophone dancing outside. I celebrated the club Hogmanay by blacking up again. The previous year I had painted Leichner's make-up on all my and a very short friend's exposed skins, while he wore overlong, and I very short, NA policeman's uniforms. This year I found a hunter's *burtu* (ground hornbill) head-dress, indigo *'yar ciki* and *bante* with bow and arrow, and crawled round the floor, nodding the beak as the true professional did to kid the prey he was stalking. What to-day's racism-conscious righteous would think of this bears no contemplation. The simple fact is that the NA police themselves found it totally hilarious, and the hunter complimented me on my imitation of his movements. The blacking-up was a major part of the joke to them, and to my household and the southern club barman, who were in stitches. O dear, o dear, how easily innocence may be destroyed by the intelligent. Then our health sister, Mary Houghton, ran a play-reading, Noël Coward's *Blithe Spirit*. Only afterwards did we realize that she had produced a staged version everywhere she had been before coming to Nigeria, and this was her testing of the local waters. Robert Wright gave a dinner party 45 miles away in the bush, with dancers and wrestlers for cabaret. Such pleasures were sadly overcast when a well-liked colleague who had been ADO(O) in my last tour, Dave Colman, with an American wife Joy and a dab hand with his Leica which had cost him a quarter of his annual salary, was killed on an unprotected railway level-crossing.

1953 opened with news that Farrant would go to Kaduna, lessening any likelihood of my being sidetracked to adult literacy and superphosphate propaganda. Nurse Houghton had fingered me to substitute for Cecil Parker in *Blithe Spirit* (Rex Harrison in the film version), performing on the residency lawn to Tilley lighting. A party of miners came across from Jos to play cricket. They insisted that we repeat it against strange scenery in the theatre at Bukuru. The Senior Resident, Plateau, Rex Niven, saw it and reviewed the production for the local mines paper. We had our 15 minutes of localized fame. I was cheered to hear that I should have to stay in Bauchi division to cover while Gill and Hopkins took their leaves, and that A N Other would have to do 'special duties'. Come 1954, I was not only the divisional officer, but entitled a District Officer: my uniform gorgets were no longer a midshipman's stripe, but the smallest cluster of oak-leaves. I planted a dozen graft citrus saplings in my garden in their honour, and a new hedge of bougainvillea, but the dozen guavas were drowned by extraordinarily heavy rain. Diabolo was succeeded by a new kitten, another entire black male but with a white throat, Beelzebub: he had to be nicknamed 'Imp' for the convenience of local tongues. I encouraged my household to grow groundnuts round my garden where bush grass grew wild, to serve as cash crop and fire-break.

What do I remember most about my third tour? The coronation to celebrate. For this we had a circulation of shiny new *aninis* (the ¹/₁₀d coin) and planted an avenue of flame trees. There was a public parade on the primitive racecourse, at which Resident Gill and the emir gave loyal addresses, which I relayed over loudspeakers, fed by car batteries, to the crowds. There followed horse races, comic school sports, feast and dancing around a bonfire, and fireworks which the provincial engineer and I, with two assistants, erected. As a provincial HQ we had been awarded £100 worth (divisions had £25, Kaduna noticeably more), with Brocks's instructions on ignition and sequence. I reckoned that there would be more impact in half the time, if we let off two explosions at once, instead of in turn, and even in *ramadan* the Bauchi public yelled in joy. The PE and I were singed, not very badly.

There was the by now triennial constitutional meeting, as well as a commonwealth meeting at Carlton House in London. We heard about them, but never felt involved, least of all informed. The uninformed buzz was that the North was being talked at and into what it did not want (reflected in Britain in Europe long after). The British press sounded incredulous that the North did not join in the 'SG56!' (self-government by 1956) cries of southern leaders. It was a great success if one believed the editorials and the woolly commentaries. Oliver Lyttleton and his officials did not appear to be trying to keep politicians' feet firmly on the ground, with results that appeared chaotic in unsophisticated northern bush. Final agreement might be difficult when they reassembled in Lagos. Malam Abubakar told me on return that to his (and my) surprise the only 'European' he had spoken to properly, who seemed intelligent enough to understand Africa truly, was Sir Roy Welensky of Northern Rhodesia. We were shown none of the related newsreels, but a 20 minute colour film of the coronation filled the gap. Meanwhile in Kaduna plans went ahead to set up semi-executive ministries, replacing the departmental headquarters to which ministers' private offices were attached. A circular came round for a volunteer to go as Government Secretary to St Helena. My seniors said they would recommend me. It was not that I was sure an older man somewhere would be found that made me say, thank you, but no.

The changes were eventually disclosed to those at the coal face. Our lieutenant-governor would become a full first class governor of our Region (no longer just Northern Provinces). All subjects not reserved to the federation under a governor-general as of national and international significance would be dealt with by the regions, with panoplies of ministries. The Northern Peoples Congress was by now our inevitable ruling party, with 'Hausa' urban malcontents supporting the Northern Elements Progressive Union, and non-Hausa provinces showing sympathy with the United Middle Belt Congress.

There were smaller groupings, and wide swathes of indifference, yet all seemed distant from reality in Bauchi, despite the growing importance of our own central minister, Abubakar. He made time to write to congratulate the Bauchi administration on the firm stands we were taking in the emir's council meetings.

When the rivers had gone down, we enjoyed a visit by the Nigeria Regiment for bush and field exercises, and for recruitment. Their corps of drums gave the chief of police and myself an idea. We planned to send a squad of Bauchi volunteer constables to the Kaduna police college to learn to play bugles, fifes and drums (I was at their passing-out parade during my next tour). I mentioned this intention to Laurence Cox, who had looked in from some travels, learning that I had indeed been booked for Kaduna in my third tour, and only discovering my fate to be 'special duties officer' had withheld the lieutenant-governor's hand. Talk about causation. I should then have avoided one contretemps. Yak'ubu Wanka of the Bauchi NT had been elected a parliamentarian. He was now the proud owner of a motor car and, subject to the DO's signature endorsing official duty, entitled to buy his petrol at the internal-freight-free rate allowed to government officials. Yak'ubu found me at the gate of the prison early one Friday morning. He flourished the form at me rather importunately, interrupting chat with town head and warders, and I fumbled for my pen. Unfortunately, there was no desk, nothing to rest the paper on but the otherwise empty air. I made a clownish gesture, and signed – on Yak'ubu's shoulder. Everyone, I thought, giggled appreciatively at the informality, all friends together. I never gave it another thought, and Yak'ubu left, apparently satisfied. Ten days later, a bemused Hopkins showed me a signal from the lieutenant-governor asking for an explanation and apology from the administrative officer who had humiliated a legco member in front of NA officials by signing a paper on his back, causing him to bow down. I was appalled, but sent a crawling explanation and apology. When I met Yak'ubu Wanka on a rare appearance at his place of work, we made up; he mumbled about how fellows had decided that a stand must be made about relations with British officials and had made a joint approach to Sharwood-Smith – his was a minor addition to graver accusations. The local witnesses of my enormity told me that they were shocked by how soon he had acquired pomposity. But it was more than a straw in the wind. I was as shocked when in Kaduna I mentioned the incident to the governor, who claimed that one of the most vociferous complainants had been Abubakar Tafawa Balewa. I only hoped that he thought my part was lesser than others'.

Entering 1954, I began to find the bouncing of the hard-seated Chev kitcar on corrugated roads as back-aching as Wofi's idea of trotting. Five years was the time to sell a car no longer new. I had the wild idea of seeking a permit to purchase a north American saloon with slightly softer springing and much more room for long legs. Having no wife, I could squeeze 'boys' and messenger in with my touring kit, with the heavy kit on a roof rack. It was presumptuous for a Class III officer, but my local master forwarded my plea, and Kaduna sent me a permit for a Canadian Ford *Customline,* with a V8 engine. I sold BY 4753 for £30 more than I had paid for it, but I had fitted it with a cigar lighter for the *Pirate* and *Player's* cigarettes I indulged in, and also a trumpet-like hooter that gave mightier warnings than the original squawker. Local leave followed in Ikeja, where my senior WAAC pilot cousin helped to collect the car from Joe Allen's and let airline mechanics make sure LA 5280 was fit for the drive north. The car gleamed black with shiny chrome and windows all round, until the dust coated it. My household saw it as reflecting (when washed) prestige upon themselves – it was not 'mine', it was 'ours'.

What else marked these years? Creating trust and friendship with NA officials; gentle nagging to improve NA central offices, treasuries, courts, police forces and prisons; pursuing the hobby of designing the emir's flag, and uniforms, badges and buttons for local services; introducing street names; complementing departmental officers' influence on health, education, works, natural resources; one had become part of the system, and advice under indirect rule was seldom interference, because those advised had played parts in formulating the advice. By the time I was to leave Bauchi, a consolidated teacher training college, a provincial secondary school, marriages and filling of new post-war establishments had in one way and another, on far higher authority than mine, quadrupled the 1949 baker's dozen of HQ expatriates.

And so leave. Memories are nearly all of the festival, one of the greatest, directed by the local boy made good, Ian Hunter. Verdi's *Requiem* was repeated by Barbirolli and the Hallé, dedicated to the memory of Kathleen Ferrier, who had died of cancer far too young. The soloists were two Britons and two international names, Elisabeth Schwarzkopf, Constance Shacklock, Richard Lewis and Hans Hotter. Degas, Renoir and Cézanne were the visual arts. Wartime newsreader Alvar Liddell recited the first performance of Rawsthorne's *Practical Cats,* which may have given Lloyd Webber an idea to popularize T S Eliot. The operas were truly great: Glyndebourne's Rossini *Le Comte Ory* (Sari Barabas, Juan Oncina & Ian Wallace), the revised version of Strauss's *Ariadne auf Naxos* (Sena Jurinac, Mattiwilda Dobbs and Richard Lewis), and *Così fan Tutte* (Oncina, Geraint Evans, Sesto Bruscantini, Jurinac, Magda Laszlo, Alda Noni). Stravinsky's *Soldier's Tale* (Michael Flanders, Moira Shearer & Robert Helpmann). Sadler's Wells danced Diaghilev's *Tricorne, Oiseau de Feu* (with Margot Fonteyn) and *Boutique Fantasque* (with Michael Soames). The Comédie Française performed Molière's *Bourgeois Gentilhomme,*

and there was *A Midsummer Night's Dream* complete with Mendelssohn's music and Shearer and Helpmann playing and dancing Titania and Oberon to Frederick Ashton's choreography, plus Stanley Holloway as Bottom. There was an Offenbach *Soirée* with Germaine Tailleferre, one of *Les Six,* at the piano. And much, much more, not forgetting Dennis Brain and Isaac Stern. Weep, moan, to-day's intendants and aficionados! Coming 'home', as it seemed, on the *Accra,* with Sir Bryan Sharwood-Smith, about-to-be-sworn in as governor, and his PS Hugh Patterson, I mentioned that I had enjoyed the volume of 'Philip Mason''s *The Men who Ruled India* that the lieutenant-governor had had sent to all provinces for admin officers to study, and had bought the set for myself. I added that I did not know where I was bound for. Sharwood told me to come to Kaduna.

I have failed to show how I evolved from the fascinated neophyte, learning first and fast from being made by the Laird to just go and do something without anyone breathing down my neck or issuing instructions – into the Resident's willing right-hand man (repeat of being a 'hostilities only' adjutant) – into the number two performing the less prepossessing duties of a succession of seniors who knew the virtues of two-way loyalty and delegation – and into the divisional administrator in his own right, in his pompous pride trusted both by his trusty masters and by the endearing people he was supposedly chivvying in the direction of self-sufficiency. However exciting, funny or irritating, it was the routine of a rewarding job. Did I change any history, even the most local and insignificant? No, I had administered without affecting the economy much, but a generation later it seemed I must have left a small mark. And it had taken little more than five years. *Na gode wa Allah.*

CHAPTER 6

Confirmed in an Imperialist Faith

Trifles light as air / Are to the jealous confirmations strong / As proofs of holy writ

[Shakespeare, *Othello*, III.iii.323]

WHEN THE CHIEF SCRIBE voluntarily divulged one's unflattering Hausa nickname, one knew that acceptance of one's place in the division was willing. The record thus far shows small achievement, with no iconoclastic innovations; I may have left some marks on manners of organization or 'man-management'. Thirty years later old folk remembered the DO who wore Fulani sandals, made much of him, and a heart pumped faster. Because we were living real lives, I tried to make my monthly intelligence reports readable, by painting close descriptions of the individuals concerned, and entertaining, without relying on gossip. These had attracted Sharwood-Smith's attention, and I was at last posted to Kaduna for my fourth tour, to work in the 'security and defence' section of the newly created governor's office.* By the time that *Accra* had arrived from leave at Lagos, and I had flown up and driven down from Kano with my car, the governor had already been sworn in. 'S&D' was full. I took over from Pat Grier as clerk to the executive council instead (now retitled deputy secretary to the executive council).

First things first, I inherited Pat's heritage bungalow in 8 Sokoto Road, between government printer Dennis Cornish and the similar building that had long been S Christopher's Church. Waziri and D'an Dada found their way to Kaduna to rejoin me, and I found a new cook. Ali Waterworks came from Kano: when he had enlisted during the war the recruiting serjeant refused to sign on yet one more 'Ali Kano' and had demanded another place of origin: his last job had been in the Kano NA waterworks so … He had a beard, was slightly grizzled, and cooked for me to mutual satisfaction for the rest of my Nigerian days. I gave a farewell party to Pat, and knocked his wife Anna out when we essayed a fast waltz on the terrazzo floor of the main room – that luxury was more slippery than the cement floors of bush houses, even if they had been shined weekly by the junior retainer with red or green Cardinal polish. There was not much of a planned garden, and Audu D'an Dada did his

---

*Indeed in his old age he remembered me as an intelligence officer, rather than as the cabinet minute-taker. I certainly was more than a club drinking associate of John O'Sullivan, who headed Northern special branch.

best on top of his domestic chores, until the day when a Chevrolet saloon swept into my drive and the bachelor financial secretary, Peter Heathcote Guillum Scott, told me bluntly that it was my duty to do better than that. Scott looked disapprovingly at my big, black Ford, much above my station, which sometimes flew a small St Andrew saltire, but on the offside wing, not from the radiator.

Kaduna differed from what I had known before. It was an artificial HQ town, widespread and with room to spread much farther, nothing but offices, quarters and a commercial area for the stores, with a thriving, noisy *sabon gari* attached to house the many junior classes from all parts of the country. There was a growing industrial area for the new factories of textiles, bottling and such to the south. All was set in what had once been open country, sparsely inhabited by Gwari animists who owed threadbare allegiance to Zaria emirate. All roads and streets were well laid out. A whole avenue of two-storey villas for departmental and ministry head officials was dubbed the 'Abbey Nationals', while the latest bungalows for the lesser were 'T63s', dubbed the 'shoe-boxes'. However, closes were also beginning to be formed of a variation on the T63 – entry-level senior service bungalows with surrounding walls and enclosures; these were thought to be more acceptable to new Muslim officers with purdah traditions (they turned out to be more popular with expatriates who sought shady walled gardens).

Lugard Hall was an impressive building housing the legislature, there was a large open racecourse (and a pretence of a golf course), and the relatively new secretariat buildings formed a noble surround, with deep verandahs, to a major courtyard, putting the original brick offices to shame. (It was at a premier's reception in his State House that I would share with the Igbirra minister of works, George Ohikere, amazement at the little light of the first Russian sputnik passing far overhead.) The true change for me and my retainers was the proximity of UAC's Kingsway stores, and all their rival canteens: shopping was no longer a monthly and unreliable order by lorry, with possibly two or three times a year a visit to Jos. The club was suitably adjacent to the racecourse, with a biliously decorated 'men only' second den known as the Cads' Bar. Social life was as bright as one chose to make it, although professions might seem to stick together until one knew better. There was an army swimming pool south by the river, which civilians could negotiate the right to share.

My first boss was Oliver Hunt, a war hero (his DSO with the Recce Regiment in 81 Div, in support of 15 Ind Corps, was for his rank a not-quite VC) and brilliant polo player. A bachelor, he later married Terry, a spirited expat lady official. Oliver went back happily to bush as an SDO, and was succeeded by Gordon Wilson, already of the post's Resident rank; the gentle Gordon irritated Sharwood by interjecting comments during exco meetings, and in turn returned to a province. Next came Iain Gunn, a hearty and bibulous northern highlander, of enormous fun and with a feisty wife; he pretended to have no intellectual qualities, and was also happier when returned to run a province. So we soldiered on until 1957, with an interval when Sharwood-Smith was on short leave and Zaria's senior Resident Conrad Williams acted in GH, and nothing happened of note. Then came a change.

Bruce Greatbatch had been a powerful figure as a senior district officer in Sokoto, where Sharwood-Smith had ruled for long: it was common belief that the stairway to success was to have served there with Sharwood, who trusted those he knew directly more than those he had only heard of, although he was not averse to finding out for himself. Bruce co-ordinated all aspects of the Royal Visit in 1956, which has been well covered in every piece written about Nigeria of the time; my whole-time duties precluded me from playing any direct part.

Bruce was brought in to succeed Gunn on accelerated promotion, and without doubt to learn all about the centre of power in time to move sideways when that should begin to move away from the governor's office and into the premier's office. His first act was to ask for my exchange with Tony Whitfield, who was Assistant Secretary (II) in the civil secretary's office. Tony was a would-be barrister (and ultimately on DPP's staff in UK), slightly older, intelligent if a little heavy in manner, and my leave relief as church secretary. I did not want his job, and he did not want mine. I mentioned our disappointments to Peter Scott; he passed the word on to Kenneth Maddocks, the decent but unflamboyant civil secretary; Maddocks had succeeded the last 'Secretary, Northern Provinces', H R E Browne (known as 'Phiz' from his forebear who had illustrated Dickens's novels), just after my arrival in Kaduna. He in turn summoned us both. I have no idea what reason Bruce had given for wanting the change, but when the CS heard that neither of us had worked for Bruce before, he left us where we were. Bruce never discussed it, and we got on well together, for all that he was anxious to have 'hands on' in matters which were new to him but now meat and drink to me. Tony and I wondered what he might have heard of us on some grapevine, unless he wanted a deputy who could not point out precedents.

All my time with exco my 'confidential clerk' (PA in all but title) was Barbara Pott, sister of a Resident, except when she was on leave and relieved by a contentedly mature Muriel Johnson. Barbara had a damaged leg and a strong mind of her own, but produced immaculate paperwork for the cabinet office, always ready to button lips and postpone her bridge party when crises required overtime. I also had the services of a succession of palantypists, young

Northerners graduated from the Zaria clerical training centre (this was turning out replacements for the southerners who had monopolized the clerical grade since 1900; it would be the nucleus of a staff development centre, that in turn would be at the heart of the Ahmadu Bello University as it itself grew out of being the Northern branch of the tricephalous Nigerian College of Arts, Science & Technology).

For over four years the executive decisions of a government passed through my hands, from the tentative formulation of a proposal for a new policy to the ultimate decision and the follow-up confirmation that it was happening. Greater folk produced the ideas, my job was to get the petty details right on authoritative paper.

What of the wider pond in which I was now a minor, however central, minnow? All the regional deputy heads of department had been upgraded to heads in their own right under the 1954 constitution. I came to know them all in varying degrees. Their ministers were supported by administrative officers as secretaries, but they themselves were still in control of their own services and personnel. Agreement had to be reached between the politician and the professional man before a minister could well initial a memorandum to the governor-in-council, but there could be differences of balance and trust. Tony Shillingford (with Robert Wright as chief education officer) and Aliyu Makaman Bida at education, and Dr David Mackenzie with his minister of health Yahaya, made it work well, and both Shillingford and Mackenzie became lifelong friends.

The governor himself presided over the house of chiefs, but the assembly was overseen by that retired senior Resident, Rex Niven, whom many (not least himself) had thought more likely to end in Government Lodge as lieutenant-governor, and in Government House when all was upgraded. Niven had studied Westminster closely and compromised his Speaker's dress – no wig or tights, but a green silk gown that blended well with Northern fashion while allowing the inevitable cynics to think of Toad of Toad Hall in Grahameian splendour.

Niven gave me a naughty opportunity. Whenever the assembly was ending he would throw a drinks party at Lugard Hall, and was accustomed to using Basil Phillips, an old friend of mine from Bauchi days, now AS in the ministry of local government, to arrange everything, from ordering the liquid and small chop to hi-jacking friends' stewards and retainers into serving the dainties around, and seeing that all was cleared up. Basil accompanied a party of ministers to Pakistan to study political and judicial advances (noting that there was still a British officer in most major offices holding the pieces together while the local head held the public eye), and was rewarded with a return to the bush. Niven asked me to replace Basil in his butler's duty ('He did it so well, I'm sure you could too'). Gratuitous is the word that springs to mind. When I became Secretary in my own right, he still expected me to serve on, but I had the last word. 'My deputy, Malam Ibrahim Dasuk'i, is learning the ropes of my last job, I am sure it will be good experience for him, after all, we are speeding on the handing-over process?' He could not say no. I also knew that Ibrahim, a Sokoto Muslim, would know better than I how best to instruct the stewards in dealing with the *manya manya* (great & good) who demanded *Krolan zamani* (the local Cola of the *zeitgeist*), which was Coke with an invisible dollop of brandy or whisky surreptitiously added. The more bashful 'dry' intelligentsia might take straight *Krola* but quietly unscrew a miniature inside their *riga*'s vast sleeve and tip it in when nobody was looking.

Most senior administrative colleagues in secretariat and the growing ministries were easy to get on with and devoted to their work and (with few exceptions) to their ministers. The ministry *for* local government, under the Sardauna, was the future powerhouse. The Sardauna's secretary at first was Dick Greswell, who had served in the RWAFF and Sokoto, and knew how to flatter Bello. Hector Jelf was mentor of Makaman Bida, and a man with a cutting tongue, a sense of what was risible and a determination to get things right. I saw little of John Baker at health with Yahaya Ilorin at first, more of Paul Fletcher, an import from Aden, at works. Ministers without ministries or portfolios had no official private secretaries beyond what their closest native authority might offer them, so *faute de mieux* depsec exco filled the gap: thereby I was a member of the 'Kettle Club', the highly informal grouping of administrative officers who were secretaries or private secretaries to ministers, dubbed 'kettle-carriers' as the equivalent of the boys who followed respectable Muslims round with kettles of water ready for the ritual ablutions before the five set times for daily prayer. Ronnie Jacobsen, permsec of the minimalist ministry of Northern Cameroons affairs, designed green ties with little silver kettles for us all, and mine survives.

NRCF has to be mentioned in a little detail. Until teleportation becomes real, air travel was the last useful method introduced of communicating bodies and goods to, from and within Nigeria. Imperial Airways, BOAC, British Airways, WAAC (Nigeria Airways) all have their histories elsewhere, but little will be found in libraries about the Northern Region Air Communications Flight. Before the second world war a governor, Sir Bernard Bourdillon, and his administrative secretary, one Jock Macpherson, had overseen a ploy whereby a former RFC officer, now Local Authority Kano, one Bryan Sharwood-Smith, should in his spare time set up a flying club under the chairmanship of the Resident, one John Patterson, a club which fifty eager volunteers promptly sought to join. They would train in DH *Tiger Moths*, a second club would follow in Lagos, and the nucleus would be created of a feeder service to Imperial Airways' weekly west African link by 12-seater De Havillands to the Short *Empire* flying boat service down the Nile and on to South Africa. Lord Trenchard, ex-RAF and now of UAC, would look kindly from on high on the project, and air travel would become as common as it already was in east Africa. Alas, not for the first time, a financial secretary, blaming the fall in world oil-seed prices, announced that the scheme could not be afforded. It was not forgotten. During (now Sir) John Macpherson's last months as governor-general, the Northern governor (now Sir) Bryan Sharwood-Smith had been actively planning a regional air service. Not only posts and telegraphs were slow. Routine journeys by ministers and senior officials still involved days of tedious travel by rail or launch, and government must become more mobile.

Work began on clearing sites for airstrips in the more remote parts of the region, and then Lagos was tackled. There was no trouble there, since the funds for what became vulgarly known as 'Sharwood's Airline' were produced by Peter Scott (to the dismay of his unenthusiastic deputy John Taylor). The director of civil aviation (a subject not devolved to regions) was enthusiastic, and the federal minister of works responsible, Abubakar Tafawa Balewa, was a total ally. Recruitment of pilots, ground staff and indenting for planes had priority. Sir Bryan in his memoirs could not remember who the first passenger was, supposing that it would be the Sardauna, fearless of weather and terrain for emergency landing. It was in fact this member of his own governor's office, who was on paper in administrative charge of the flight. I accompanied the chief pilot Eric Minshaw to Lagos to collect the first aircraft, a single-engined Auster *Autocar* with fabric body and wings. Invited to try the controls on the way home, and to aim for a prominent hill, the passenger realized just in time that he was descending in a downward curve that would collide with the hilltop, before pulling the joystick back. In time a second Auster arrived, with a second pilot, and the pride of the fleet later was a twin-engined Piper *Apache*, streamlined metal, which could carry one or two more passengers. Applications to book flights passed through me, and I became the channel for hearing misunderstandings, in both directions, between both the pilots and the engineer in their coming to terms with a civil service on the one hand, and the would-be passengers on the other, who thought of them as a taxi service. My visible input was to have the junior ground staff at the airport, where I inspected the hangar's contents as a matter of form, wear the uniform of my office drivers. We were not accident-free. One of our permanent secretaries, Dermot Russell, was almost scalped when an emergency landing on a main road resulted in an overturn. NRCF was nevertheless an innovative leap forward.

Early in my second Kaduna tour I had the telegram of my father's death. I

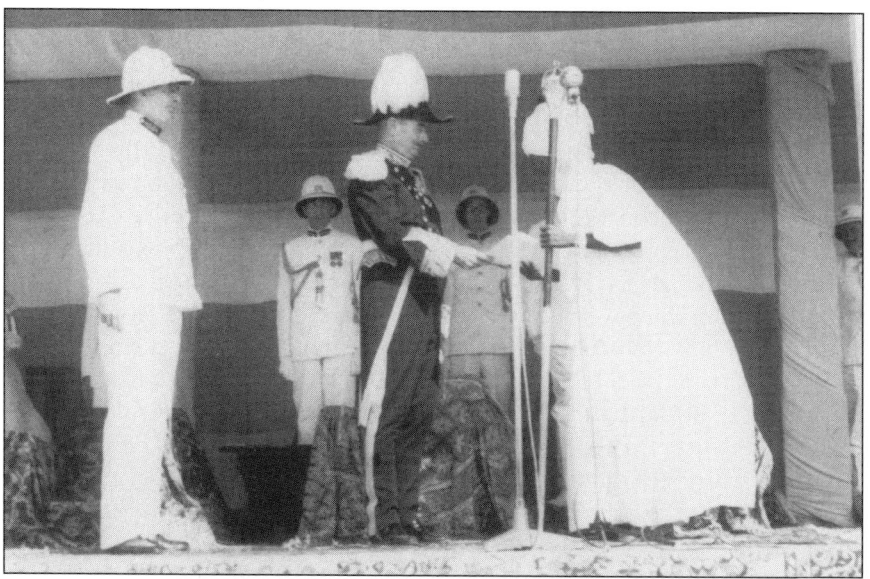

Governor Sharwood-Smith installs Adamu Jumba as First Class Chief of Bauchi (with his former DO, a visiting guest, mid rear).

was given a fortnight's compassionate leave, and contrived to play my part in putting him to rest while unable to convince my mother that I had not earned long 'recuperative' leave. My father was sadly missed by his professional world (he had only had four years of retirement, after being made president of the Scottish and UK societies of Medical Officers of Health, a King's Honorary Physician for Scotland, and finally CBE) and by many others: the main chapel of Warriston crematorium overflowed. The demands on me by my mother were beyond all that was natural and healthy. If I had surrendered, I should never again have been an individual, nor can I imagine what my second vocation would have been. The psychological chains remained, and I only remember one bright moment in my next full leave (abbreviated by compensating for the compassionate break, and paying off the extra passage by instalments), when Sir James Learmonth (my father's friend and colleague, The King's surgeon, to whom I had poured out my unhappiness) told me firmly that I must put my career before sentimental affection.

One of my more vivid memories is of the new emir of Bauchi, my old Yankari companion Adamu Jumba, coming to see me in agitation after a pep-talk to the assembled chiefs from the Sardauna about *mulkin kai* (self-government). It was an occasion in 1955 when the governor was keenly aware that the leading chiefs were increasingly unhappy that a commoner minister *of* local government, even the aristocratic Sardauna, was to be in a position to take decisions affecting 'native authorities', whether as local governments and or as chiefs in their sole right. Sharwood-Smith determined to address the house of chiefs in informal session, explain tactfully the way of the world, confirm that still he alone had constitutional responsibility for their personal affairs, and then leave them to discuss the future wisely under the certain leadership of the Sultan. The premier had insisted on addressing the emirs himself next, without the presence of the governor, who had made it clear that they owed primary allegiance to him as the Crown's representative, not to an elected politician (in which all of them would have agreed). Needless to say, the Sultan then held his tongue, gave no lead and the gathering dissolved rather mulishly without further guidance. Sarkin Bauchi held up a coin to me and asked in Hausa, 'How can we govern ourselves when we cannot yet strike our own coins?' My suggestion that they could still be bought, from the foreign workmen who already made them, cut no ice.

The governor more than once used me as a go-between with the visiting prime minister when he wished to avoid the appearance of a viceregal wish being a command, such as joining in a GH dinner party. I was managing to keep up my contacts with Abubakar as the federal minister of works or transport, and then as federal prime minister, whenever he passed through during my Kaduna years. Among the books I lent him now was Joyce Cary's *Mister Johnson,* on which his comment was, 'I did not know that the old DOs understood us so much'. He found Walter Bagehot on the British constitution 'very interesting', and once when comparing Nigeria with what he was learning of the size of other territories commented that if chief commissioners could become full governors, why not Residents too? After a visit by Abdulla Bey to Lagos, Abubakar told me that the Sudanese leader had said, 'Do not make our mistake, of getting rid of all your British officers: we thought we could replace them with people like Americans and Yugoslavs, but they only came for the money and would not go out on tour. Now, when we try to get our old officers back, it is too late, they have all found other jobs. After the next election I shall ask if we can come back into the commonwealth'. That was not to be, and some now refer to the Sudan as a 'rogue state'.

I once wrote to Abubakar after some heated scenes in exco had exposed incipient gaps between more radical ministers and civil servants striving to remain impartial. This had worried me about prospects when the Sardauna would have no restraining hand hovering. He wrote back to me from his hotel at the 1957 London conference in these terms: *'The conference has now ended. First, you are my personal friend and I take whatever advice you give me as purely personal and I never publicize my friends' advice. Rightly or wrongly we took what decisions we took, but I want to tell you one thing. You people (the Scots) in particular worked hard and suffered to establish the Empire and I would expect that you as a Scot and a young man would regard the new situation as a challenge to you. You raised many points in your letter which I hope to answer when I see you in Kaduna ... Kindest regards. Your friend* [etc]. *PS Please excuse the terrible writing I am terribly busy.*' I never forgot that, which is why years later I tried to tell his story when so many of Africa's charlatans had been celebrated and he was being forgotten. After that conference Abubakar wrote in distress to Robert Wright, his mentor, and to his confidant the Northern governor: he was tired and disillusioned with the tribalism and back-biting in Lagos, and he wanted to retire to his farm, and take up a little teaching again. Both reassured him that he was irreplaceable and that the country needed him. Both came to feel that they had sentenced him to death less than a decade later.

When I was writing my life of Abubakar, I was told by a member of the Northern Nigeria History Committee who had taken me under their wing that it 'served no useful purpose' to mention reservations I was expressing about the Sardauna. I never doubted the sincerity of British colleagues, mostly ex-Sokoto veterans, who admired his charismatic personality and frequent gestures of generosity, both material and psychological, to which I might give minor witness myself. Bad temper was not infrequent, although there was usually a quick recovery and rueful half-apology or forgive-and-forget exchange. His ambition was however unending. It was clear that no bond, however taut and just, would deflect him from maintaining his position at the head of the only part of the world that mattered to him. This was the Muslim Northern region, bonded to its historical unbelieving followers, whom he would eventually fold into the true faith. This was the present commission: the unspoken next step would be to succeed as Sultan, Commander of all the Faithful west of Borno and far into the sub-Sahara. For the present he was showing religious tolerance, but it was not deep. His attitude to the middle belt executive councillors was polite, even hearty, but patronizing. It was cautionary to notice that after the Suez 'crisis', when to general surprise in Whitehall and local relief the emirs and other leaders showed no sign of disloyalty or doubts about a British attack on a secular but essentially Muslim state, the premier subsequently commented harshly during an assembly debate with an intemperate aside on a minor Israeli assault on an Arab settlement somewhere around the Golan heights, which was barely relevant. Worse later was during a debate about possible changes in the legal system: after an almost regretful reference to the fact that 'cutting the hands of thieves' no longer took place, he muttered something about there being no sources of slavery any more either, and added '*Suna nan kuwa*' (and they're still here!). The Hansard editing was tactful in both cases.

It is my personal belief that one of the background reasons for the 1966 mutiny of southern army officers was the Sardauna's major proselytizing tours of the 'pagan' North, to which he expected his local civil servants to contribute missionary zeal: apart from their fear of being outnumbered in ruling bodies, and their one-sided intolerance of ministerial corruption, the mutineers foresaw a successfully militant Islamic North carrying a *jihad* to the sea.

I admired Sharwood-Smith for his knack, after all his years in Sokoto, in handling the Sardauna's tantrums and excesses that threatened to unbalance something vital to the unity of what in our innocence we saw as the multi-faith, multi-cultural North. That strength was of course an obstacle, once independence was about to be a fact. Sharwood knew that he was right to go when he did, although there was handwringing among those who admired the Sardauna for much of his generous nature, yet feared what might happen once no hand could restrain him. His leaving came when the latest triennial constitutional changes removed CS and FS from exco, the former becoming deputy governor, a minister of finance being appointed, and incidentally my acting as exco's full secretary. It would be gross presumption to suppose that it had similarly been right for me at my level to have left Bauchi division after so long when I did; but the change struck me when, at my briefing of Sir Gawain Bell for his first exco, I said that such-and-such was in fact the case that had been deliberately blurred in a ministry memorandum, and that he might feel it useful to ask such-and-such an awkward question. 'I could not do that, I have to act on the advice that my minister tenders me'. By 1958 he was right, although he did not block his ears to sound information: nevertheless, the cynical John Taylor, permsec finance, commented, 'Tinkerbell has cast himself in the rôle of Mountbatten, and he's playing it to perfection'.

Perhaps a word or two on extra-mural enjoyment is proper. *Blithe Spirit* on the Bauchi residency garden had whetted another small appetite for self-promotion. The Kaduna Players had been an unincorporated body for a long while, and I found myself drawn towards them, encouraged by Dick Latham, a finance boy who like myself had looked back with wonder at being a major at age of 22 (he in Java), and his wife. I trod the boards as a Wilfred Hyde-White part in *Affairs of State*, a play about US politicians, where we refrained from attempting American accents (mine was perhaps faintly Ramsay Macdonald), and as the amnesiac Ralph Richardson in *Home at Seven*. Amateur theatre brought army people into a civilian group, which was good for both sides, although one officer's lady went physically frigid whenever she and I had to entwine ourselves emotionally, chilling my own dissembled ardour on the spot. Tact led to recasting, and I found Elizabeth Reed, wife of the high court registrar on the way to being Lady Reed, wife of a senior judge, mutually compatible on the boards.

My career in buskins ended abruptly when we essayed *The Importance of Being Earnest*. I had read the text of the 'missing' scene (with an extra character, the gardener) printed in *The Listener* and had written to Mervyn Holland, Wilde's son and holder of the copyright, seeking permission to include it in our intended production, probably a world première, certainly outside London. He graciously granted permission and confirmed where it should be inserted. Mike Hollis's Rosemary, a gifted artist, designed the set and all that was left was the casting: John Dunn, head of Kaduna broadcasting, and I did not mind who played Ernest/John and who played Algy, but we wanted them to be us. We reckoned without the producer (we did not yet call them directors): Alison Wilkinson, wife of Johnnie who deserted the admin for broadcasting and ended as secretary to the BBC, was unable to accommodate my height – 'You would completely unbalance my stage picture!' John also failed to meet her specification, so on the first night he and I sat in the middle of the front row and stared at every move of our replacements. Army officers, sadly they played very well. Another target missed was when Jim Sanders, a competent musician as well as administrative officer, tried to put on a production of G&S's *Trial by Jury* at the trade centre, where there was a piano. I was to be the Learned Judge, patter songs still within my vocal competence. Finding a willing chorus was the obstacle, and it never happened. There was the alternative fun of driving out into the bush at weekends, if the swimming pool's relaxation had become too familiar, and picnicking after a stroll around or on a rocky outcrop. Boredom was unknown.

After four and a half years I was again thought to be a fixture, but Sharwood-Smith's ethos survived: he told me he had left a strong recommendation for promotion. During my next leave I hesitantly entered the first Burlington House 'house party' to select four HMOCS for admission to the foreign service: one was accepted – they were looking for qualities that might differ from what the overseas service favoured (a truth reinforced decades later). However the new deputy governor Waddle Weatherhead (Maddocks having left to govern Fiji) wrote to say that I was now an SDO and was going to Okene in Kabba province, the southernmost division in the region, where (he said) 'many reputations had been lost'. My friends wondered what I had done to earn a punishment station. John Smith handed over, introducing me to all the eight education officers, the only other expats, in the provincial secondary school and teacher training centre. I had to clock in with the acting Resident in Lokoja, whose children pestered me until I suggested that they go into the garden and eat worms. I did not dare to look the mother in the eye when they returned for tea with mud all over their faces. Then back to Okene to build upon John's run-down of personalities and problems. He tactfully retreated to a rest house on the Kabba boundary for the few weeks before he was dragged away to drearier duties. Ali soon came, with Yak'ubu Tiraka who was promoted into Waziri's place, and I found a 'yellow' lad, Shu'aibu from Kano, to succeed him.

The preliminary survey was an eye-opener. I hit a bull unwittingly within days. Doing my introductory wander round NA departments and talking to their heads, who were forthright and quizzed me as much as I them (something new after gentlemanly Bauchi), the supervisor of works Mr A R G Ozigis asked where else I had been. I said I had started in Azare, and to make conversation added gratuitously that my first DO had been a Captain McKenzie and, not quite truthfully, that he had taught me all I knew. I'd cast an unwitting spell. The word went round that (although only Igbirra literates spoke Hausa) *'Dan Kyaftan Makanzi ya zo* (Captain McKenzie's son's come)'. Thenceforward I could hardly go wrong. He had been their DO a generation before, this man who couldn't be trusted with files, who had been followed by countless others who had gone on to great things or lost their reputations, but all utterly forgotten: they still cherished the memory of this paternalistic dinosaur who had cared for them. It was touching and a boost for me, which I was glad to report to Glen Buchat next leave.

Their history was hazy. My new responsibility, the 'hill' Igbirra, may have been of Jukun origin, migrating here through Idah. The relationship of the 'plains' Igbirra of Koton Karifi was doubtful, although the core may have been there during the unsettled early 19th century. By 1850 the hills of Eganyi and Okene were settled in positions defensible against the Fulani of the North and out of reach of the southern Binis. There were four major and two minor clans, but none seemed to have a recognizable social organization beyond a priesthood, in which the Ohindase of the Okengwe clan was vaguely seen as superior. When the British arrived this chief priest lay low, and a successful warrior called Omadibi tried to deal with the strangers, being accepted as the district head of Igbirra until 1917. The Ohindase then briefly succeeded, but was deposed and replaced by Omadibi's grandson Larama, who later became Ibrahima on embracing Islam and adopted the title Atta, with a linguistic nod in the direction of the Ata Igala, chief in Idah across the Niger. It suited the government that he unite the tribe and build up a central administration. He was a 'sole native authority' until 1952, when under Sharwood-Smith's reforms Igbirra NA became the more fashionable and less superficially autocratic 'chief-and-council'. Reaction against perceived oppression grew, and the Atta inevitably 'resigned' to retirement in Igala. He attempted a return in 1956, there was a riot, and he was formally banished. A council with elected president was experimented with for a couple of years, but there remained a popular demand for a chief, a permanent figurehead to identify his people. A form of selection chose a son of the Ohindase, the candidate of the emergent Igbirra Tribal Union, and he was formally installed as chief in 1957. Gross misrule continued, led by two partisan councillors who were removed in 1958, to be replaced by three government nominees, with a severe final warning to the chief from governor and premier. Day-to-day control was by the chief's executive committee, and there were finance, tax assessment, watch and establishment committees, the whole council being formed from elected members of the eight district councils, special interest co-options, nominated district and village heads and three government nominees, totalling 25. This was where I came in.

The Igbirra had and respected no privacy. The division was the smallest in area of the North, as well as the most southerly. There was a fine water reservoir, where Nile Perch and other fish had been stocked for rowing anglers approved by the divisional officer to catch, under the watchful eye of its manager. There was, uniquely, a small swimming pool which the DO had to keep sweet; equally unusually, the DO's garden had grown to the extent of government thinking it an official amenity, which the gardener Idirisu maintained out of official funds. The Roman Catholics were well established (on the point of completing the creation of a hospital with government funding), Canadian Holy Ghost 'White' fathers; there was competition from the SIM; but when the old Atta Alhaji Ibrahima became a Muslim back in the 1920s, he had assessed where future strengths and alliances would appear, and about half of his people had superficially followed his lead. From court records of how witnesses were sworn, I deduced that 32% swore on '*Omu*', still essentially animist, and 14% on the Bible. 90% of the officially counted 143,000 lived within 5 miles of the town itself, 1,500' up and relatively temperate, in largely two-storeyed houses with pan roofs, developing outwards in ribbons of simple tracks. Far from their farms (where they only lived when sowing, tending and reaping their yams, beniseed, cotton, oil palm and cocoa, in tiny country huts), they found little to do most days but to sit and discuss 'politics', which to the outsider were purely a matter of personalities. Economic progress demanded higher taxation than the people would contemplate or indeed the productive economy yet justify.

The politicians' Igbirra Tribal Union, that had brought down the former Atta, had split into two 'wings', one largely but not wholly Muslim and conservative, and the other tending to be Christian and modernizing, but more concerned to rein in the new elected chief (the Ohinoyi, Sani Omolori). Number One wing tended when it suited them to show loyalty to the Sardauna's NPC, of whom the most public was 'Robin Hood' (a part he had played in a school play); Number Two was stubbornly independent, led by

Joseph Ohiani and Willie Omo (handicapped by a withered hand), often quite absurdly brushed with favouring the western region's Action Group. Each side came conspiratorially to me as mediator. 'No 1 Wing is going to start a riot in the market on Tuesday'. Tut, tut, better have a word: I hear you're planning something for Tuesday, is it true? 'Good gracious, no'. No riot. Later, 'You ought to be warned: No 2 Wing will have a demo outside the jail Thursday week, and the cycle-hirers are arming themselves'. O, thank you for the tip: I'll see the chief of police. But then also to the others, surely you realize that the NA police must have heard, and will have had their batons issued? 'What's all this? Never in your life'. No demo. There was also a loose cannon called Salihu Tijani, who complained and stirred but did no real damage. So thanks to the memory of a passed-over dinosaur I never had to face what Bill Ferris faced a decade before, when winning his MBE for gallantry. Thinking of the Burlington House experience, I agreed with what a predecessor had recorded in a file, 'A diplomat would have much to learn here'.

A distraction from my plunge into 20th century anthropology was my mother's decision to spend three months in Okene while desultorily seeking a permanent home in UK. It went much better than I had feared. My household and so many of the Nigerians in government and the NA made such a fuss of this unique visitor that her emotions responded, in relating to people at once so strange to her but so warmly welcoming. As well as those I worked with regularly she was taken up by A B Makoju of the PSS and the wife of R U Omoruwa, the agricultural superintendent from Warri. She never confessed that she might now understand my own attachments to such folk, but it must have made its mark. The Ohinoyi gave her a fine cloth for Christmas (the wicked old Atta had introduced weaving skills copied from the Gold Coast's *kente* cloth traditions, another of the modernizations for which he must never lose the credit, let alone his fathering of several children of great national distinction). She had another from the titular head of the ITU Umaru Adegbenro. I managed a flying duty visit to Kaduna for a few days, where she met many of my closest friends, and we hired a governor's office station wagon to bring us back.

Another break was occasioned by the governor-general's visit. As if bringing the seat of government with him, HE and his entourage took over the senior government quarter in a station as GH *pro tem*, and the incumbent was banished to the spare room (if there were one) as guest. The PS, ADC and head household staff were crammed in wherever there might be a vacant space, and the vice-regal crockery, cutlery, napiery, glass and silverware and of course everything to produce and serve food and drinks replaced the humbler possessions of the sitting tenant. Despite the upheaval, the visit was more than agreeable. Sir James Robertson played his unconvincing act of the simple bearlike peasant turned prince, and his Lady made sure that any unlikely

It was backs to the wall for the flag in Okene.

appearance of pomposity was promptly pricked. Wanting to see the NA at normal work, HE excused me my palm beach suiting for guidance round the offices and institutions and introduction to the NA staff, while I stayed on the edge at the secondary school and training college. Our well-sinker took 'John Willie' out fishing on the reservoir, where after losing three bites he brought in a fourth (served for breakfast, Lady Robertson again chose to cut the victory down to size: 'The first one you've caught in 3½ years, and it had to taste muddy!'). I had a charming handwritten bread and butter letter from Sir James after his return to Lagos, and years later in retirement, first in Edinburgh and then by Loch Tay, he remembered his Okene visit and the Igbirra well.

A dissatisfied Kaduna suspended the NA after much deliberation, instructing all the elected members to resign. I thought it had come too late, and that in fact all concerned were beginning to improve and demonstrate some sense of balance and breadth of mind. However all the powers of Igbirra NA were vested in me, who had not sought them – on the verge of independence a divisional officer was given more direct authority than any since Lugard: unnecessary, but for a short time an amazingly popular move among the NA staff and ordinary Igbirra people, who were weary of their leaders' internecine shenanigans. Now that my every word was law, provided that the census and tax registers were trustworthy, I could soon announce that 89% of the eligible population had registered on the electoral roll.

I had been conducting a campaign on paper, official and also improperly behind the scenes with our Igbirra minister in Kaduna, to insure that I was relieved by John Smith when I left: it seemed essential that the next divisional officer should be one who knew the Igbirra and whom the Igbirra knew, to avoid the historical inevitability of every little difficulty going back into the melting pot and being refashioned from the faulty old moulds. By ill luck John had a car crash at this time and broke his arm. This brought the instruction that he would not take over from me in September and that I must extend till the election was over. I have sometimes wondered whether a full tour in Okene, instead of the 'staff' appointments that came his way, would have led to a different future from what he was to enjoy (in more than one sense).

Changes were beginning. Several education officers were replaced. One new British teacher, Eric Clark (no r), was young, enthusiastic and positive, anxious to know and understand the people, and a counterbalance to those John Smith had called the 'suet puddings'. My excessive self-esteem was reinforced in retrospect when years later I discovered that Mrs Ozigis (the wife of the NA works supervisor who had first welcomed me) had written to my mother at this time, 'Mr Clark is still doing his best to improve Igbirra division as far as he can, and in this he is becoming successful through his hard-working and pains taking throughout all the time without rest. He is another God sent person to help Igbirras in all aspects and we pray that end well with success amen. My husband is in fact doing his best in his capacity but our people here do not appreciate honesty in most cases. Except that he has had a very strong support of your son he should have overthrown away. Thank God in His mercy has sent Mr Clark to safe him once more, and so like many other workers under Igbirra NA'. I blush, of course, but it reassured me that I had not wasted all my life in a now despised career.

My remaining paternal uncle had died, and my mother had just been knocked down by a car, but not badly hurt, and the domestic worries were renewed. I had by now asked the colonial office to take note that whenever Nigeria needed me no longer, I should like to transfer to some other dependency in the dwindling empire with some prospects of a remaining career. I had joined Special List A, who would serve independent Nigeria as long as wanted, and then rely on HMG's good offices to find us alternative employment. Yet one could not trust that at the precise moment of separation that alternative would exist. I was immediately offered Hong Kong, the one place, unique, that I had not expected. Having imagined that the North might keep me for a few years yet, I quibbled but was told firmly by a mole to gather the rosebud while I might, offers rejected were seldom repeated. I was sad, but looked forward to a continuation of a happy and rewarding life, even in a totally different culture. Dr David Mackenzie from Kaduna was now director of medical and health services in Hong Kong, sent there because the colonial office thought his reputation was what that colony needed; his message was encouraging, so long as I wasted no time in following him as changes were in the offing (this was unclear, but I dared not suggest to my mother that I ought to shorten my leave). A visiting US vice-consul from Lagos said he envied me what his service considered to be a plum posting.

I was privileged to have a huge official send-off at the end of my tour, apparently the first such for many years. My ceremonial handing over of my staff of office (to loud and merry applause, the substitute for this mythical bauble was a prison cane) to my relief, a mature New Zealander, featured in the Lagos press. That intrusion of the media, unknown in out-stations till the 60s, was a reminder that the days when colonial administrators were in control of what was placed in cleft sticks, for the selective instruction of higher authority and the outside world, were over. On my last morning in Okene I went to say good-bye to the NA central office staff, burst into tears and could not face going round the other offices: I bundled my 'small boy' Shu'aibu into the car to drive to Lagos, where he stood amazed at the ocean and tasted the salt water with a bitter giggle. The prime minister (who had just accepted his knighthood, to be announced on 1st January 1960) was on tour in Kaduna, so could not fulfil his offer of hospitable accommodation, but he gave me a select lunch party when he returned on the second day. 'John Willie', the governor-general, added me to his lunch reception for Dag Hammarskjöld, UN's secretary-general, who was on his way to the troubled Congo. Arrival in Hong Kong was to differ from departure from Nigeria. There was no Hausa farewell blown by police or military bugles as the good ship *Calabar* sailed out of Apapa, but I had not earned it.

What did I think I was leaving behind at the time? A federation led by one of the few heroes in my life, one of the two or three politicians of integrity known by me (the only time Enoch Powell ever spoke to me, he interrupted my conversation about Abubakar with others across a club table to interject, 'It is impossible for a politician to be an honest man'). A federation that I trusted would be held together by a civil service that had learnt from us to be the bridge-builders and fence-menders between differing peoples, people whose loudest spokesmen might be imbued with mutual hatred but whose followers could muck in with others when needs must and the devil was driving. A federation that would set bench marks for Africa. A federation with a thriving commercial and productive economy. A federation that would be a credit to and pillar of the Commonwealth. A federation where the intellect of the North would soon be as well educated as the other regions; where the stability of the North, based on organic adaptation and evolution of tradition, might begin to influence the iconoclasm, but not the ebullience, of the rest through the leadership which numbers in a democracy gave it. I might think it. If a combination of oil and mutiny has destroyed most of the work of past administrators, at least much of what professional departmental officers and the expatriate 'traders' built up as 'infrastructure' has survived in some form.

My fondest, absurdly sentimental memories are of the oval verbal misunderstandings that fed me porregg, hamalegg, omelegg, marmalegg, chutlegg, cutlegg, curregg, salegg, turkegg, and many others such (not to speak of the surfeits that have left a permanent aversion to chickegg and caramel custlegg); of my longest-serving steward, Waziri (childless when I left the country), who became a part-time 'contractor' and had stayed in Kaduna – many years later he brought a selection of his offspring to meet me for several successive nights when I revisited the capital: 'I have had twenty children, and seventeen are still alive!';* of his successor, Yak'ubu, who was told by my host's servant in Zaria, the same many years later, that that *bature* whose photo Yak'ubu kept in his room was here – and who came running over breathless from the hotel where he was now the cook; of inducting a future sultan of Sokoto into drafting cabinet minutes; of the waking cries of the poultry in early mornings, and the smoky scent of the evening cooking, throughout all the villages where I had spent the night on tour; of again meeting Yak'ubu's predecessor, D'an Dada, who had gone home from Kaduna aged 16 with a reference chit to learn to drive a lorry, and now many years later had become mechanical superintendent of the Bauchi works yard; of the swish-swish sound of the countless little grass *tsintsiya* brooms sweeping dust and leaves from floors and drives; of meeting the forest guard Yahaya Ningi whom I had sent to Man o' War Bay, thirty years later the managing director of a successful business, who told my wife that I had been his 'godfather'; of sleeping under a discarded Resident's 12' x 6' Union flag, supported by a camera tripod, when my servants forgot to pack my mosquito net on tour; of the sheer joy of freedom whenever, though no horseman, riding out to bush knowing that nobody knew exactly where I might be, and that I was for a brief spell man and master of my own fate; of dog-sitting for my Resident's 'Rags' when his master was on leave, but rather more of my successive welcome house guests – two black cats (not in succession), a chameleon, a young red monkey, a tame gazelle, and a friend's visiting eagle owl; of watching a lunar eclipse from the little boat on Okene's reservoir; of the amazing Royal Visit; of giving gramophone concerts in the Bauchi club, which our Igbo barman enjoyed more than the SDO; of climbing the Miya animists' rock stronghold and watching their ebullient dancing; of being trusted by household to do something practical about it whenever ailment or misfortune overtook a member; equally, of knowing that when

---

*Hilary thinks he said he had had 31, of whom 10 boys and 16 girls still lived: but then there were four wives.

one's own things went wrong, one's boss, one's colleague and friend, and one's subordinate would nearly always give support; of being part of a great family and community, and of having friends of all kinds; of the preponderance of well-mannered smiles and classless belly-laughter; and not least of having been a friend and welcomed guest of a great man, the often forgotten but irreplaceable Abubakar Tafawa Balewa. Memories of comrades, still here or passed on, are warm – but memories of so many Africans still make the heart pound.

CHAPTER 7

Stranger in Paradise

'There's a Stranger, 'Eave 'arf a brick at 'im'
 [*Punch*, xxvi.82, 1854]

SAILING ON *Peleus* into Hong Kong harbour on my 37th birthday, peering through a dank mist hanging over an island dampened by summer humidity, I wondered whether I hadn't made a mistake. It felt unwelcoming. One of the other 11 passengers, wife of the manager of Holt's Wharf, had been friendly, and warned me of how stuffy the government sector was, from the viewpoint of the wealth-creators. The self-styled mandarins were conscious of status; wouldn't let me wear shorts to the office; didn't like to change their ways; only socialized with wealthy Chinese, and so on. I must beware of the *t'ai-t'ai*s, the memsahibs who wore big hats to The Queen's Birthday garden party at Government House, though it always rained. I began to believe it, when I realized why my poet school friend Ian Davie, when a civil servant in the War Office, had disliked the Hong Kong secretariat officers he had had to deal with. This will be a destructive chapter, originally written to meet a narrow purpose, by and large chronicling personal failures. The following chapter will more happily shed sunlight on twelve years in Hong Kong, an experience impossible to regret.

In Nigeria, 'cadets' (the apprentice title for new administrators who would not be confirmed in service till their second tour) had been hosted on arrival by senior officers. They were introduced to the Governor and Chief Secretary before going to their first stations; there they would be allowed a week to settle into a quarter, start recognizing unfamiliar physiognomies and dress, organize domestic staff, learn the geography and civil facilities, and take breath, before anyone suggested going to the office and looking at bumf. Those who had come to us in the northern provinces from Palestine or India, or from the Sudan or Gold Coast, were welcomed for their fresh perspectives and for what they had learnt about the ending of their private empires. Here the amiable but morose colleague whom I was to relieve took me in a taxi to Victoria hotel to dump hand baggage in the foyer. He then walked me up Battery Path straight to the Colonial Secretariat, where he showed me the curious files being left for the new Assistant Secretary (General A).

After lunch in the Volunteers' Mess he took me round the offices on the sixth floor, where most of the Assistant Secretaries worked (every one an expat), to say hullo. Everyone asked the same thing. Had I worked in a secretariat before? The subliminal message was that anyone from Africa would be unfamiliar with files. Modified reassurance emerged whenever I repeated that I had worked for some years in a Governor's Office as secretary to a cabinet of actual ministers. Only one asked me to sit down: Bill Dickinson had been translated from the Gold Coast on its becoming Ghana three years before, and I noticed with relief that he was wearing shorts; they were even khaki (Hong Kong's General Regulations in fact permitted shorts, stockings and open necks in summer, except for formal meetings, but the ambitious liked to look formal). Bill and I understood each other, and had some 'useful exchanges'.

On the élite fifth floor I was taken to pay respects to the Deputy Colonial Secretary, David Trench. He had done time in the Solomon Islands, spent part of his war with the Coastwatchers, spying on the Japanese in Guadalcanal, and won an MC. He was warm and interested, and sat me down (the first to do so except the Gold Coaster). My spirits rose: but when he introduced me to the Deputy Financial Secretary, who was visiting with a file at a side table, and I told the latter that his younger brother had been my platoon serjeant in the school OTC, all I got was a grunt. It was days before I had a brief interview with the Colonial Secretary himself, and I never had any with the Financial Secretary, although I would occasionally cross his path in the corridors or take a file in to his secretary.

My final port of call was with the Establishment Officer. He was civilized, and glad to know that I had 'secretariat' experience. For the first time I heard the words which Nigerian ideas of welcome had led me to expect: 'What are you doing to-night?' I explained my position, and he said, 'Perhaps you'd like to come round for a meal?' – 'O, thank you, that would be very nice.' – 'Of course, my wife is expecting a baby shortly.' – 'Well, if it's at all inconvenient, you don't have to, really.' – 'No, well, I wonder, yes, perhaps it had better be another time. But *(the crunch line)* never mind, you'll be all right. There are plenty of cinemas in Hong Kong.' Dumbfounded, though a film buff, I spent my first night in the hotel, selected for being close to the secretariat, feeling that I had made a dreadful mistake, not knowing that it would be six months before the EO renewed the invitation, and unimpressed by the roomboy's inquiry, with a sweeping gesture over the bedcover, whether I would like him to bring me a girl. I had left an administrative service that was a family: I had come to a service that thought it was a corporate business. Fortunately the Director of Medical & Health Services, David Mackenzie, let me have his house and amah to 'leave-sit' for some months when he went off a few weeks later. A house (with a garden) seemed more like Africa, and broke me slowly into a decade of flat-dwelling.

My predecessor used volunteer forces contacts to give me a helicoptered bird's eye view of the colony, which revealed that the concrete jungle where almost everyone worked was (in 1960) not all that should affect one's judgments and lifestyle. Socially, things improved, but slowly. The DCS alone among my seniors took a real interest in the latest 'interloper' as, I quickly discovered, such as the Gold Coaster and I were known. In his flat I met his boisterous and amusing American wife Peggy (a naval nurse during the Pacific war). They took me to the old and characterful Foreign Correspondents' Club for a T-bone steak, and put me up for membership. There I met a handful of the more disreputable of my administrative colleagues, earlier interlopers from Malaya and Borneo; they had fewer problems because they were assumed to have some awareness of the Chinese, even if only the Overseas varieties. We got on well, as I believe I did with my juniors, who like all bright young men were sceptical of our bosses. Mention of juniority brings up another issue: seniority. A piece of self-pity, for the record. I had had accelerated promotion in Nigeria, to Class II (Senior District Officer or Senior Assistant Secretary), but when I arrived in Hong Kong the picture had become very different. They had promoted several officers with less age and service than myself, and inserted me in the basic class. Nobody had told me of the effect of a restructuring between my acceptance of transfer and my arrival (Mackenzie had hinted, but not defined). They thought I was blessed to have been accepted at all.

This knock back coloured my opinions. After some weeks I was bidden to lunch at Government House, where I set eyes on His Excellency, Sir Robert Brown Black, for the first time. I thought it nothing strange, but colleagues who after two tours had yet to receive such an invitation expressed surprise. HE was an upright Watsonian with Malayan training, who had been brought to HK as CS and then governed Singapore for three years before coming back as Governor. He said the right things about those who had been nation-building in Nigeria, but emphasized that here we must not rock the boat. He did not define how best not to rock it, nor indeed what that philosophy required of its functionaries: he did have other guests to look after. It dawned on me that nobody else was going to tell me either. My predecessor's files had no handing-over notes, summarizing where we had arrived in each, and why, a standard practice in Nigeria; I had to go back through them to pick up each running tale and decide without a compass what minute to write, draft to offer or reply to send. My subjects were health, education, welfare, fire brigade, post office, Secretariat for Chinese Affairs and New Territories Administration, narcotics, labour and unions, prisons, City Hall, printery and publications, information and Radio Hong Kong, and UN agencies. I made appointments to talk to the heads of departments on my schedule and tour round their interests to get to know their people: they were amazed – they expected to have to come to the secretariat if face-to-face clarification were needed. How and why Hong Kong worked, and why we thought we were there, was left to discover through osmosis. Being inherently loyal by nature (I believed) I wanted to be told the party line by an authority, but as I never was, unsurprisingly I continued to see through mainstream colonial spectacles and find the vision distorted.

At my first Christmas I pondered this new life. This is what I told those in my address book, now that I was in the Pearl of the Orient, not Nigeria. So different – but by golly, how similar for townies at HQ, always the downside of any colonial story. The people in Lagos who never crossed Carter Bridge to the mainland, except to go to the docks or airport (or to buy cheap fruit and veg at the 'frontier'); the middle-ranking who forgot that a 'secretariat' rule was not an end in itself; wives with obsessions about their housing entitlement, and the gossamer partition between their shallow racialism and unadmitted snobbery; the wording of the petitions of the humble; the queues of cars holding one person each; 'duty' parties with more guests than chairs; the grateful reaction of 'mere' clerks to any minor show of personal interest; resentful dismissal of any mention of 'how it was done somewhere else'; locals' ambition to pass external examinations by correspondence course; reactionary women of the people; bogus drawing-room cultivation of local culture to demonstrate 'commitment'; humourless second-rate academic minds trying to do a Bentham, Marx or Hardie, and quoting Durkheim; St Andrew's Night with top table full of Anglo-Saxons; dreary expatriate commerce and finance convinced that the place would collapse without *them* (rather than their institutions); HQ officers and district or departmental folk despising each other; no ceremony without long speeches and somebody's wife decoratively involved that nobody off the platform knew existed; grumbling at Treasury rulings; servants' wages going up all the time – of course, there were worthy exceptions. It was much the same here, as in the developing world all over, and afforded as much cynical amusement. The unreconstructed Lagosian would be at home, although wondering why he had to be paid so much more.

It was not the whole story. What held the old ways firm was less the strength of the old hands than the lack of thought about how to change anything without 'rocking the boat'. Nobody dreamt of independence here, nor of involving the population either. Nobody dreamt at all, working so hard to make money made sleep heavy for all when it came. The first word that newcomers heard most often on ferry, tram or bus was *man*: 'dollar'.

The civil service worked longer hours than Whitehall. The psychology might be wrong, based on the grocer's mentality that advised policies. Yet keeping the government shop open all day didn't make it more profitable, though it left little time to think and be constructive. This suited the real grocers. So did the air-conditioning that sealed every office off from reality, conned people into wearing suits and ties in the foul mid-summer weather, cutting them off from the herd, while forced in their warrens into conspicuous consumption of tea and gossip. One might think that we were there to make the world safe for shippers and bankers – the grocers on whose advice and by whose consent the ordinances were made that the secretariat concocted, from departmental or section briefing, and the legal department drafted. I fantasized that if the entire entrepôt trade upped sticks to Manila, though we would lose our upper crust and poshest households and Brightest Young Things, night clubs might close, the government might no longer afford air-conditioned offices and the roads wouldn't be dug up so often – but (Mao Zedong still permitting) there would still be a very lively and worthwhile Hong Kong left. Lip-service was paid to the industrial revolution of the 1950s, and to the workers and Chinese bosses who had to be induced by commodity controls, overseen by our own economic agencies, in effect to work less hard, so that their products (mostly now of quality) didn't undersell manufacturers in Lancashire and the USA: but the grocers still got the jam. Praise of Hong Kong's successes was taken as giving credit to those who had only earned it in part: criticism was taken very personally. I felt open to persuasion that all those energetic, thrifty, friendly, prolific people did prefer to tolerate rule by grocers and to shirk responsibility themselves. Then I should be assimilated and feel that I belonged, but I remained unpersuaded. That was not the choice: if we, not the grocers, were to go, Mao would assume all responsibility, our workers would share less than ever.

Although there were clear doubts of my reliability, my clerical skills and past cabinet and legislature experience were adequate to let me take over from the ex-Gold Coaster as Clerk of Councils after about nine months of settling in. Perhaps the acting pay (Staff Grade C – the substantive rank did eventually come, but not quickly) would soothe me. The schedule included subjects new to me, additional to the familiar prospect of being secretary to the Executive Council and supervisor of the Deputy Clerk to the Legislative Council – civil aviation, immigration, nationality, urban council. The Hankey-Downing Street fashion of Cabinet Conclusions was anathema to Hong Kong: what was wanted was a crisp decision, agreeing to a specific proposal, suitable for the secretariat to interpret as would seem appropriate later – 'Council advised *such-and-such*: His Excellency concurred and ordered accordingly.' No record was made of digested points made pro and con, much less any flow and ebb of discussion or debate; let alone any dissension, although I maintained my Kaduna-Downing Street tradition of fullest possible notes in a private notebook. This sat sacred in the safe as evidence for an indeterminate future: suppose that some Honourable Member broke his Oath of Secrecy and that a judicial inquiry might require the official recorder to refresh his memory of what was said in fact by whom. As for Legco, the Deputy Clerk's most arduous task, apart from helping visiting MPs to shop for jade and suits, was to dictate the play script for the next meeting: honourable legislators depended on it to know when to stand up and read. He sometimes drafted their speeches for the Unofficial Members. Apart from making life easy for the 'Hansard' reporter, the justification was that by handing the scripts out to the press, 'the journalists wouldn't get it wrong and misreport us.' If anyone adlibbed, chaos overtook civilization and gave the shorthand recorder conniptions (she was usually my PA, an ageless lady of original, quietly vespoid, character; her leave relief was a forthright secretary of volatile temperament – both enjoyed character-assassination sessions and were wonderful supports).

The post had advantages for an inquisitive interloper. Apart from admission to the Consular Corps's social list for National Days and the osmotic major public shindigs, it was possible in Exco to observe the Governor, the Colonial Secretary, the Attorney General, the Secretary for Chinese Affairs, the Financial Secretary, one other (usually silent) senior administrative head of department appointed to maintain the voting strength, the DCS (silently ready to interpret any woolly secretariat memorandum which he had approved for submission), and above all the Unofficials. Clerk of Councils sat at a small side table, not (as in No 10 or Kaduna), at the president's right hand, and could study all the faces.

One problem was to understand the relationship between a governor and the Honourable Members. He could get rid of them whenever he wanted. He also seemed at times to accord them deference beyond the call of good manners. The latest term of the most senior member, a knighted Chinese doctor, was expiring. Renewal was taken for granted. HE and CS felt that age and change had brought the time to say goodbye, but were at a loss how to engineer an Apotheosis. The file was on my list. A pre-war circular despatch laid down that Nominated Unofficials might be granted a second term of office, but only with express justification a third; a fourth was not acceptable. The despatch had never been cancelled. It took little effort to draft a valedictory letter in which the SofS would express HM's great personal sadness to see him go for constitutional reasons. Claude Burgess, the CS, called me in to thank me for solving what had seemed insoluble. HE congratulated me 'on a masterly draft.' In a silly moment I regretted that I had not suggested raising the retired Unofficial to the peerage. Many a jest foreshadows truth: it did happen to another retired Unofficial, Lord Kadoorie, some years later.

We had not yet been made to allow the death sentence to fall into desuetude. Mandatory sentences for murder were referred to the Governor-in-Council for confirmation or reprieve. These sessions sidelit the consciences of members. Virtually all Chinese agreed that to repeal hanging was out of the question – in theory. When it came to the decision that someone should hang, equivocation and prevarication took place. The judge's report to the governor (like that in the UK to the Home Secretary) was submitted, and the Attorney General gave his opinion on the law and how it affected the facts proven in the case; an administrative report from SCA or District Commissioner, New Territories, was received on the views of the local community. After discussion, members were asked, in upwards sequence of precedence, to advise HE on whether the law should take its course or whether commutation should be considered. One *taipan* invariably said crisply, 'The law to take its course,' without much sign of having thought about it. Chinese members wriggled in discomfort before making their decision. Almost every member agonized before giving a sincere opinion. HE reserved the decision for further thought: constitutionally it was his and his alone.

Colonial governments were closer to the American constitution than to Westminster. Governors and Presidents descended in direct line from British executives presided over by the monarch in person. Only the early George's lack of perfect English had (legend unreliably says) led to the office of a Prime Minister, as opposed to a First Lord of the Treasury *tout court*, emerging. An appointed 'house of lords,' replaced on independence by an elected senate, and an assembly elected on a limited franchise, reflect both Washington and the Caroline-to-Victorian colonies. Hong Kong followed the streamlined evolving practice of lacking a second chamber. Bills prepared by rulers obviously require no revising chamber to make them perfect.

The reason for not following the post-war imperial urge to induce dependencies into electoral democracy was that it would inevitably lead to the CPC and the KMT fighting it out on the streets of Hong Kong. The agonies suffered by officers in Commerce & Industry and the Economics Branch over Multi-Fibre Agreements, textile quotas, or tariffs raised because low labour costs could be represented as the result of sweated exploitation and not devoted hard work, went to show that Hong Kong's true enemies were in the western democracies.

In everything so far learnt, the missing link was awareness of the foundation on which the edifice stood: Mr Wu, with his *t'ai-t'ai*, his *tsai-nui* and his rice-bowl. There is no suggestion that Honourable Members were indifferent to the conditions of the population; they knew about typhoon and fire disasters, they put their hands in their pockets for relief, they voted funds for resettlement of squatters washed off hillsides, as refugees flooded over in successive waves to find a better life than in Mao's China; but there was seldom a rueful acknowledgment that if it were not for the labourers, the skilled workforce, the clerks and overseers and middle managers, the colony's growing prosperity (especially their own) would have been a mirage. They knew it in their hearts but, as in their social and leisure pursuits, *few ever uttered it.*

I self-righteously refused to accept nomination for the Hong Kong Club, whose Chinese members were those sufficiently *papabili* to aspire to Unofficial Membership of the Governor's Councils: in Nigeria, as long as I had been there, any Africans of 'senior civil service' status in commerce, local government or professions (or chieftainly rank) had been eligible for nomination, if they had wished to share the rather limited luxuries of west African clubs and their denizens. When the barrier lowered, I remained po-faced (although I may now enter the Hong Kong Club without a fee, as member of affiliated British clubs). I found allies in unexpected places. One senior officer was different. He was immensely intelligent and a born scholar. Like many such he had committed social errors. One of the few of those who after being 'in the bag', interned in a prison camp by the Japanese, had managed to emerge with few psychological scars, he had been a gentleman and done the decent thing. A Chinese lady from the north had been his pre-war girl friend, and she had at risk continued to smuggle comforts in to him. When peace and release came, he married her. This cut him off from certain groups of society, which would have mattered little had she not come to make use of her place as consort of the District Commissioner, New Territories, to meddle in land disputes, and make unwise promises. This inevitably banished him to backwaters, however valuable (like census and statistics), and lowly honours. He was the man who said that the British Colonial Administrative (like the Indian Civil) Service was the nearest to the perfect form of apolitical, paternalistic government that the world had known, to wit, the Imperial Chinese Mandarin Service. Each was recruited on élitist principles and sent to the furthest ends of their empires, to administer incorruptible justice to strangers in whose personal affairs they would have no interest. Once they became too comfortable and susceptible, they would be posted elsewhere. This man of quality argued wisely about loyalty: when transferred between regiments, one must find a new loyalty without weakening the old one held in memory: but, yes, loyalty was a two-way process, it had to be earned and not presumed upon without welcoming initiation.

Another senior, not quite such a scholar but equally a Sinophile and more of an initiator, much admired all round for his activity in the British Army Aid Group behind the Japanese lines in support of the Chinese KMT Allies, had married a comely and gifted lady. He ought to have become the next Colonial Secretary when the CS in office when I arrived left in a hurry; but CSs act as governors, the prospect for full-blooded Chinese Honourable Members and their *t'ai-t'ai*s (and for some expat wives too) of having to kowtow to a Eurasian

Acting First Lady in Government House, however civilized and characterful, was in the early 60s still too much to bear. Those seeking less offensive excuses for his disappointment hinted that he was given to self-indulgence; any truth in this could be attributed to that very disappointment. He had pulled a shattered hierarchy together when a disastrous fire destroyed the shacks of many thousands of squatters, and authority had despaired of what to do. He organized an imaginative scheme of resettling them in hastily built tenement blocks, with only the most basic facilities and minimal living spaces, but at least secure roofs over their heads and, with modest rents to pay, some direct contact with a government that promised better oversight of an amorphous population: and he had rightly made a name for himself as the administration's star.

Institutionalized racism as a sidekick of snobbery did not last long past the 60s, for the obvious reason that the colony's steady growth as an industrial and financial centre, where the Chinese were making all the real running and true wealth, made it as impractical as distasteful. And so it began to appear where the genuine power lay, and light was at last shining on that strange relationship between the governor who proposed and his appointees who disposed – not least when one considered those Chinese who must have been sounded out but had politely, presumably, declined high unofficial office. Not that all this left much mark on those remaining Ladies of the Peak whose manners with domestic servants or shop assistants had nothing to learn from some of their Kenya sisters of the 20s. (An Australian journalist working for an American news agency included them in his cabaret songs written during the cultural revolution. It would then only be four years since one of the most senior and kindly heads of department had tactfully advised a brilliant junior to lay off the charming Chinese girl he was courting, a sweet lass who had been Edmund Blunden's star student at HKU: he should think of his career. Not unnaturally my friend resigned and went happily married into academia.)

Leave seemed a suitable time to complete the eating of dinners and taking of exams for call to the English Bar. It might be good to show more than past success in Africa. The establishment branch was persuaded to extend my leave by a month (to come off the next furlough) in order to go to a Chancery Lane crammers and be brainwashed through the last paper in Part I (real property – how a sober, usually pragmatic, people like the English had come to saddle themselves with this imaginative mixture of philosophic concepts, faeryland feudalism and virally poisoning complexity, was historically explicable, but had proven a stumbling block in my part-time march to the qualification). This would be followed (I hoped) by the Finals, all at once. Others had been given study leave with all paid to acquire specialized diplomas, so why not ask for something towards the fees for this? A cadet with a legal qualification must be more valuable than one without? Those concerned saw no reason to help with something undertaken without their encouragement. When I commented that I could imagine how smugly they must have reached this conclusion, it was salutary to be told that this only showed up my own arrogant superiority. Doubtless the messenger was justified, but he might have been less triumphal.

My second tour was in Social Welfare Department (semi-affectionately known as 'Swid'), as No 2 i/c admin. A different world, remote from the DCS who was glad to see me go, and not of my choosing. It introduced me to what present-day Brits may consider the incompatibility of temperament that allows an educated and trained Chinese official to show both understanding compassion and a heart that does not bleed the tiniest drop. There was no welfare state. Charity was almost entirely the concern of voluntary agencies. The government made provision for dealing efficiently with natural disasters, but relied on victims wanting to get away from soup kitchens and temporary shelters as soon as possible, to make their own way in the world once more. It dealt with feminine (rarely boys' and never men's) lapses from morals and virtue so far as its statutes required its officials to intervene, but left rehabilitation for religious and social organizations, that had the centuries of wisdom behind them, to offer. It oversaw the law of adoption and wardship (with some heckling from the SCA over traditions), but left day-to-day negotiations to voluntary bodies of standing. It ran a probation service and approved school, while encouraging independent institutions that took in orphans, strays or the naughty before they embarked on crime. It kept a weather eye on old folks' homes. It advised the Royal HK Jockey Club on where best to spend its vast charitable donations and projects, and was the channel for funnelling Treasury grants to welfare bodies subvented for the purposes of good policy and stability. There was no dole, income support or 'benefits', but a little cash might supplement relief in kind for those who had sunk to the very bottom and were for the moment past self-help. The department got the blame whenever a recusant street-sleeper, determined not to be tidied away, died from cold on a winter's night. *Laisser faire* it was not, but the most that was offered was seen, and almost invariably accepted, as a temporary crutch. In the Chinese tradition the key to survival was the family, to whom governments and authority meant nothing but trouble.

One enlightening contrast was that between two ways of approaching wayward boys. The Prisons ran a couple of Borstals (under other names), where naughty, sometimes vicious, youths were confined, disciplined and taught trades by order of the courts, and appeared on public occasions playing such martial instruments as bugles, fifes and pipes in uniformed bands: the Commissioner, unusually cultivated for the head of a disciplined service, dealt with offenders in the modern way by 'withholding privileges', never with a schoolmasterly cane, which he supposed would have to be administered after strapping the stripped delinquent to a formal frame, as Singaporean and Malayan prisons do to this day. An ex-Royal Marine Colonel ran the HK Sea School, a voluntary agency which took in waifs and some barely incorrigibles from the streets, and trained them to be hardy seamen able to row into the open sea and produce button boys, as well as boxing compasses, learning all the knots and flags, rigging overall and thoroughly modern morse signalling, diesel maintenance and ship construction: their winter uniform was scarcely more than their summer gear, and their inspections to justify their subvention were done by Swid, especially Swid's probation service (which kept its distance from its social worker colleagues with their funny UK or Canadian ideas). When a Sea Cadet wandered astray, the colonel applied a plimsoll to his *derrière*. More than a few 'borstal boys' became recidivists; the shipping lines fell over themselves to recruit Sea School cadets, and some of them went on to get their mates' or masters' tickets.

Service in a spending department was not a good way to absorb the vision of the Hong Kong Way and Purpose as understood by those who, never having served elsewhere, were ignorant of alternatives; nor to gain the trust of the Financial Secretary. Looking back upon an impoverished west African territory, where the 1950s tap of technical assistance from Colonial Development & Welfare Funds was hard to turn on, rulers and ruled alike had made the best of things, and had been surprisingly content (when a score of years later independence and newfound oil riches had enabled huge technical advances and kilobyte increases of corruption, most were enjoying a gaudier lifestyle, but with much unhappiness under military sway). Hong Kong's circumstances gave promise of combining material advances with social comforting, through a loosening of the purse-strings, which might lessen any tendency to bribe one's way to satisfaction.

It was to take another fifteen years, after an interlude in another territory totally surrendered to a cargo cult of entitlement to First World taxpayers' handouts, and a return to Britain morally and economically destroyed by its own post-war perversion of the cargo cults, to recognize that that promise would have been the first step on to a very slippery slope; and that for all the personality faults our FS and his long-term views had been just. He could have justified them at the time, had he taken the trouble to explain in comradely terms to the interlopers. He saw it as beneath his dignity to explain it at all to people who must just be bloody fools. The proof lies in the contrast between the stabilities of dependent Hong Kong and Eurerast Britain in the late 1980s: the one wealthy, fully employed, low-taxed and with very few *misérables*; the other struggling to maintain standards of living, its creative employment largely emigrated to younger economies, heavily taxed and supporting a growing underclass of the demoralized and alienated (both circumstances have changed since). Without the intellectual leadership that might open eyes to the future, however, HK's interlopers working close to the less fortunate were bound to think poorly of colleagues thirled to the interests of those living artificial lives at the top of the pile.

Working in Swid led to friendship with a group of people in the Anglican Bishop of Hong Kong's 'Social Justice Group'. Bishop Ronald O Hall was another of the few great men whose paths I had the privilege of tripping over. He had drawn a line in the sand during the war when, as Bishop of South China as well as Hong Kong, he had through *force majeure* ordained a Chinese lady as priest, having no other priests to carry on the church's work and no way of getting Lambeth's blessing anyhow (he may have doubted Lambeth's likely approval, but his conviction of the Spirit's guidance was firm). He was unabashed that the many church primary schools he succeeded in founding came to be known as 'the bishop's Communist schools', because his head teachers were unemployable lefties, rather than Christian proselytizers. Other members of this social justice group included the editor of the *China Mail* (an English-language evening paper); a 'cadet' who was amazed at the concentration of power in so few hands and believed that Hong Kong watered the seeds of its own destruction (he was to resign and become an MP); another cadet and his sociologist wife, interested in local research that might gain publication; an economist at HK University (who would one day adorn Patten's kitchen cabinet), with a social worker wife who had similar academic interests; and a highly intellectual but warm clergyman. We met in the bishop's house, where he promised financial support for anything practical we might achieve (nobody could unravel Ronald Hall's capacity for inveigling funds out of unknown pockets). The cadet made me join him in a confessional visit to the DCS, so that our participation should be above board: but 'social justice' was an offensive concept to our purse-lipped boss, suggesting subversive thinking, and our openness probably did not make us seem more reliable. The group renamed itself, grandly, the Hong Kong Institute of Social Research, and spent the bishop's money on the first issue of its *Journal*, containing academic work of the sociologist and the economist which presumably no other journal had accepted. The enterprise died, divided between those who saw it as an expedient for academic publication, and those who saw what the bishop wanted but doubted how to achieve it through an artefact.

Swid did not seem the proper place for an administrative officer. I gave birth to two concepts which my director (ex-Ceylon, and therefore not one of the Inner Circle) forwarded upwards. The first got short shrift: it suggested that the urban areas should have District Officers, as did the New Territories, to take responsibility for co-ordinating government services in their bailiwick, for looking after the inhabitants and listening to their views, and incidentally for intelligence reporting on internal security, policies and public figures – from Nigeria I knew that an administrative officer picked up matters and nuances that coppers, however specialized, would miss. I expected opposition from vested interests, but intelligence was only complementary to co-ordination. These urban DOs would have minor executive duties which required the public to know where single-doorway offices were, so that they would not be remote and inaccessible: a doorway to seeking licences for popular occupations might be worth exploring, without withdrawing existing powers from Urban Council, Fire Brigade, Police *et al.* Bicycle licences?

What floored me was the DCS's incomprehension when I was summoned. 'What would a DO *do* in the urban areas? The departments look after the roads and drains, the parks and abattoirs, the clinics and community centres, the housing and communications, and very well they do it. We couldn't have them meddling with land matters, the secretariat has to look after them.' He could not see that indeed departmental officers dealt with services, but only teachers and medicos met the individuals who used them. He was disconcerted by the thought of junior cadets discussing high policy and important men with the common people. As for land usage, which the NT DOs managed almost as their prime duty, the thought that the secretariat lands officer should have his urban plans and schemes trodden on by administrative officers, as well as the PWD on the ground, was unbearable. The idea was sat on. Three years later, in the wake of troubles, it was acclaimed when it was reborn as the brainchild of officers unsullied by service elsewhere.

The second suggestion was that the most senior administrative officer serving in a professional or specialized department should submit monthly intelligence reports, covering the ground proposed for urban DOs, opening up paths for material not always accessible to Special Branch. I was summoned to GH, where it was clear that there was sympathy from a man who had learnt his initial trade as a traditional DO. Authority arrived to submit such reports from SWD on a three months' trial. There were two drawbacks to this: one was that Swid's contacts with the outer world were limited to narrow fields, it being wiser to widen the experiment to several departments at once; the other was that welfare officers, the channel for most of the information gathered, took time to appreciate what was wanted, what was petty gossip and not wanted unless it proved some wide public misconception, and what the point of it all might be. Three months was not enough, in SWD at least (it might have blossomed in Commerce & Industry or Labour). The DCS gleefully reported that HE felt that the trial had not turned up much not already well enough known.

My third HK tour, surprisingly, saw me back in the Colonial Secretariat as an acting (fairly soon substantive Staff Grade B) Principal Assistant Colonial Secretary, taking over the General Branch. Six years before, this had been the largest, if not the most influential, branch, including not only the schedule that I had first arrived from darkest Africa to assume, but all the social services and miscellanea, varying from the secretariat's own management to protocol. There had been changes, as the powerful Economics Branch swallowed up subjects from other branches that had even a tenuous claim to influence the economy; and the social services had been placed under a new Assistant Colonial Secretary, ostensibly answering to me. The Cultural Revolution was also beginning to be noticed. But I was not to join at once. The colleague whom I was to relieve was in no hurry to go on retirement, and I was farmed out to the Resettlement Department as the senior of the Assistant Commissioners. This department had been formed to cope with housing the squatters and refugees made homeless and destitute by the disaster already mentioned. Their housing was basic, but each successive estate had been upgraded as ever more new estates required to be built, to house waves of refugees smuggling themselves in, the hillside and rooftop dwellers, or the boatpeople whose moorages were needed for reclamation. This was lowest cost housing: official Low Cost Housing was provided by the Housing Authority (essentially the Urban Councillors under another name). Official cross-memberships brought me for the first time into contact with these bodies, except when acting DSW I had sat silently on the Urban Council as a Vote, defending embarrassing questions about welfare. When the first resettlement blocks were built the costs had been calculated around a basic 27 square feet for each adult tenant; a later Director of Public Works, architect by training, had literally on the back of an envelope worked out that at marginally greater costs the layout of new multi-storey blocks could be rejigged to afford as many as 35 square feet.

The first challenge was to tackle the standing orders of the department's many officials. By spelling out how every duty should be performed, implicitly they denied the right to take a decision for oneself. The need for staff to exercise initiative suddenly impacted. Hong Kong watched with concealed trepidation the tumult of the Cultural Revolution, and the demolition of tradition and education by the Red Guards. The first rumblings had come with the well-orchestrated and absurd 'Star Ferry riots', supported by expatriates who should have known better: the first class fare was raised from 20c to 30c, but the 2nd class remained at 10c. Neither workers, nor those rich who preferred to avoid having to climb up and down stairways to the glassed-in cabin, were disadvantaged. More serious Troubles followed.

Diplomats in Peking had been barricaded and their buildings stoned; the British consulate in Macau plastered with 'big character posters' and the consul forced to wave a Little Red Book for hours under a blazing sun. One day our embassy in Peking would be burnt, which would affect all future FCO attitudes to Hong Kong – nothing could be allowed to spark a repetition. It all began to wash over. Riots, stonings, planting of small bombs (and hoaxes) in carrier bags at tram stops, mass demonstrations, loudspeakers chanting Maoist slogans from mainland-owned buildings, insults from assistants in Communist-owned emporiums, all have been well-documented, in imaginatively frightening detail. Less well so the dedication of the great mass of the people, who still emerged in spotless, starched office clothes from their shabby resettlement blocks and tawdry tin hillside squatter shacks, and made their way to their workplace on time, leaving early and making long detours whenever the radio had announced troubles *en route*, or wherever a clattering helicopter overhead marked unrest below.

Doubt was raised by a colleague at an early departmental meeting chaired by me (the Commissioner was absent at a conference; he had learnt his trade in Scind before India's independence, and as a marginal interloper was another excluded from the inner circle of Staff Grade A seniors): should we not protect our staff by withdrawing them from estates where pro-Communist trouble might be expected? After all, we did not know which tenants were 'reliable'. This was appalling: our duty was to the people of Hong Kong, so many of whom lived in our estates, and practically all of whom paid rent on the nail for the bare services provided. Our staff were part of our duty and our service, and were also people of Hong Kong. On the contrary we should strengthen our visible presence in the estates, and show whose side we were on – all the more likely then that they would *all* be with us. This view prevailed, and most staff, from the Commissioner down after his return, spent time on visible visits, walkabouts, talkabouts and shows of confident goodwill. An ex-African had found the voicing of that doubt unnerving: it had sounded like our merely being 'there to administer the colony' – in blinkers. Ostentatious inspections of the estates were as invigorating as hoisting the flag in an African village for the night and finding out what was worrying the farmers and villagers – but for faltering Cantonese instead of fluent Hausa.

The PACS(G) whom I was to relieve refused to handover anything, saying that I knew everything already, which was flattering (FS and DCS were unlikely to agree): nor did he let me into the office until midday on a Saturday, when he had spent the last minute of his last day ('These establishment people, you can't trust them, if you don't work out the full month they'll calculate your pension factor one-twelfth down'). In retirement he set up a lucrative industry with New Territories craftsmen making fishing flies. I found the ACS(SS) had been left to deal with the social services on his own, often by-passing his

Showing the flag with staff to tenants during The Troubles.

supervisor when submitting files upwards to DCS 'to save time' (which suited the DCS, but not me who would carry the can if the ACS went astray). More depressing was the ease with which some of my *bêtes noires* had crawled invisibly into the woodwork during the troubles. The jealously protected experts in financial, establishment and lands matters who had spent happy hours frustrating other departments' and branches' ploys were now there from 9 to 5 on the dot, but almost inactive. The Governor had appointed a second DCS with little secretariat but varied departmental experience, for the special duties of dealing with the emergency and its challenges. This encouraged some to send routine files to him, bolting on a trouble-ridden attachment, in order to get quicker and more frequent approval without nitpicking queries.

This DCS(SD) had a reputation for down-to-earth thinking, tinged with class chippery, and was the right man to stir up a resistance morale in modern Hong Kong; his touch with the sometimes bogus *echt*-Chinese of the olde worlde (and with the worms in the woodwork) was not always so sure. When presented with specific proposals he was quick with encouragement that one should get on and do it, but less able to press the case with the old guard who might have to help in providing material resources or legislative support. He was however a breath of badly-needed fresh air, and presided over two active committees which in the guise of overseeing external public relations (arguing Hong Kong's vulnerability and need for diplomatic and trade support to the rest of the world), and internal public relations (combatting Communist press dissidence, devising novel ways of expressing government policies and practice, and dabbling in black propaganda on the side), gave more pushy middle grades the chance to say the previously unsayable. It was a joy to sit on the latter body, which included a lively and creative deputy to the titular head of Government Information Services, and a couple of British army officers, seconded because of their stated experience in winning hearts and minds and handling security problems elsewhere. A large meeting of senior officials called by DCS(SD) filled the legco chamber to overflowing, at which the DCNT rocked the boat by declaiming that what the colony had long been lacking was Leadership. Nobody denounced him.

It is strange that the most uplifting time for some officials in Hong Kong should have been when its stability and future seemed less certain than at any time between the Japanese occupation and the negotiations looking towards 1997. A chat with Whitehall's chief spook in Hong Kong led me to theorize that Britain might take a clandestine policy decision, to plant and water seeds of thought, through discreet education curricula and brave economic acts; these should (changing the metaphor) feed a virus into the Chinese bloodstream, too powerful to be killed off when ultimately the motherland reclaimed the colony – after all, China's revolutions in modern times had all started in the south, in Hong Kong's backyard, and this would only invigorate what was already happening in small ways. The security man smiled, sympathized but commented that I had been reading too much Ian Fleming or Le Carré: Whitehall had far too much on its plate, too little time for thought, and too little imagination to go in for CIA-style melodramatics or long term plots. Change was essential, and for the moment those opposed to it were silent. Local change smothered my growing hopes of playing a useful part. A recently appointed DSW was transferred to be Defence Secretary. The man it was proposed should relieve him had gone on leave, and the gap had to be filled. Muggins's turn.

The pay as Director of Social Welfare was 'acting', but the appointment was substantive. It was not hard to assume command. I knew everybody already, and there was no boss to fuss when I reinterpreted social work jargon into English in public reports. The professional and administrative assistant directors were Chinese friends. The offices had moved but were almost as near to the municipal squash courts. Through chairing the Social Welfare Advisory Committee (who were surprised that I expected to receive unsolicited advice as well as comments on what the department referred to them), and much liaison with the director of the Hong Kong Council of Social Service, I made many

Formerly invisible bureaucrats were taught to give public interviews.

new relationships which in my last period were not available to the non-professional assistant director. Yet I felt marginalized from the colony's real action.

During this spell there was another typhoon, with the customary storm damage, destruction of people's wretched makeshift homes and need for relief. All government's services went into customary top gear to clear the roads and drains, get injured to hospital, restore cut telephones and electricity, and so much else (after a direct hit HK looked almost normal 48 or 72 hours afterwards, where most disaster-stricken countries take months, even years, to clear up). Swid had responsibilities of its own. A wealthy Chinese businessman rang me up and promised a substantial cheque towards the usual appeal for charity donations in support of human victims. We were delighted to accept, but as frantically busy in the departmental HQ as our workers out in the streets or hillsides in co-ordinating services; so when he turned up in the office with his cheque, he received profuse thanks from the top brass hurriedly assembled, coffee in proper cup and saucer with biscuit, and an informative rundown on what everyone was doing to restore normality, as if he had been HE himself. Then we saw him off to his car and got on with things. A few hours later a miffed Deputy Economic Secretary (one of our best respected colleagues, not a *bête noire*) rang to know why we had not informed Information Services, called in a photographer, summoned the press and made a public ceremony of it:

didn't I know why the cheque was being given? Well, of course, but it was a matter of urgent priorities, and we'd done the best we could – a little patience on his part and later we could have called the police band in. But it wasn't good enough.

A friend rang in hysterical embarrassment: a wealthy Chinese businessman, whom he knew well socially, had asked in confidence whether someone could tactfully suggest how much in cumulative charitable donations would qualify for the award of, an OBE, say. My giggling friend didn't want to offend someone he liked, for all his naïvety, and felt he had to give some answer. We cooked up a formula: this was not the way things happened, but a lengthy record of public service in charitable bodies, voluntary efforts beyond the call of duty, known support for the administration, openness with officials and other such Confucian behaviour, not to speak of close relations with the SCA or NTA, had placed some feet on the first rung, the MBE, and that monetary donations would no doubt be unostentatiously noticed in the course of events. You couldn't buy it. Not exactly.

When six months of temporary glory were ending and the real DSW (a renowned cricketer) was imminent, something unprecedented took place. The chairman and some members of the Council of Social Service waited upon His Excellency with a humble deputation. They wanted to have me retained as the permanent DSW. I knew nothing of this, and would not have wanted to be stuck there, happy enough though relationships with everyone in that world were. It was not my scene, as they used to say. When the leader of the delegation told me what they had done, and that HE had kindly explained that this was not the way things happened in HK, it became evident that while the Governor might have noticed my acceptability in one quarter at least, the 'establishment' felt that my new friends were not the unofficial world that mattered – quite the reverse, and not to my advantage. On returning to the Secretariat the DCS said bluntly that I was not universally welcomed back.

Peking had woken up to the disorders which its followers in Kwangtung had stirred up in Macau and Hong Kong. For all the media hyping of 'violence', there had been far more noise than injury from beginning to end. Yet loss of confidence might threaten to bring colonial control to an end sooner than the CPG was prepared to face under its own timetable (it was generally thought that Peking would let the pimples on its backside grumble on until it had settled the one real carbuncle, Taiwan). Almost within days the challenges and disruptions dwindled, although it was months before foreigners began again to patronize Communist shops or to receive civil attention from their assistants. There were of course still sporadic fake bombs, malplaced firecrackers, stone-throwing and affrays by a small stage army of union strikers, left to tire themselves out.

However lessons had been learnt, and revitalization of the information and broadcasting services went ahead. Senior officers were for the first time to accept personal publicity, to give interviews, and to be trained on how to appear on television. The most obvious changes came in the SCA, where sound and trusted officers, headed by the excellent man who would never be substantive CS, came up with the unheard of idea of City District Officers, to complement and upgrade the liaison officers who had traditionally drunk tea with traditional community leaders on behalf of the SCA (which should now be known as the Secretariat for Home Affairs – as daft as some outsiders' misconception that the SCA dealt with diplomatic relations with China was the cosy PR thought that the SHA would deal with 'people in their homes'). Impractical heresy from one source became wholly reasonable from another. Alice in Wonderland *déja vu* pervaded introspection, as well as regret that 'unsoundness' had kept one out of departments where earlier thoughts of constructive change might have had some effect.

The virtual self-determination of the social services section, coupled with further depredations by the powerful Economics Branch, turned the formerly distinguished appointment of Principal Assistant Colonial Secretary (General) into the least regarded of senior secretariat posts. A timid suggestion that a minor rationalization of structures might justify its oversight of the non-Council duties of the otherwise lone independent ACS, who was also Clerk of Councils, produced strong reaction in defence of a self-governing little empire which I had ruled myself six years before. A chance meeting with the FS, who had hardly exchanged ten words with me since my first day in the colony, did little to cheer me up. He expressed not unkind dismay that I did not yet seem happy with much that I saw.

I tried to explain why I appeared to look at many things, but especially at the local people, through different spectacles from those who had gone up the escalator from Hong Kong's painful but vigorous post-war reconstruction; those who battened unconsciously on to the ethos of the Bank and the Shanghai entrepreneurs who had sparked it all off; those who did not confess that all that thrusting and risk-taking would have gone for nothing without the backs of the artizans and lower middle classes who had borne the brunt of the weight, and the hungry refugees from communism who had done the hard labour. I understood how the Unofficials were where they were and had the power they had, even if some did not deserve respect by every criterion; I accepted that free enterprise was the strongest engine for making wealth and progress; but I did not understand why so many of my colleagues in authority might collect jade and snuff bottles (as investments as much as for their artistry), speak good Cantonese or affect to appreciate calligraphy and Chinese opera, and yet show so little convincing empathy with the folk in the roads and markets; why they approved of commercial enterprise but wanted the doleless hawkers off the streets because the juices of their wares ruined the tarmac; why they took their splendid standard of living for granted; why they differed so much from colleagues out of the same drawer who had been elsewhere and seen other ways. There was more to it than the unique difference that we were not guiding towards self-government; not least, what *were* we expecting to happen when the leases ran out in thirty years? I got another grunt, but also, 'I am sorry you see it that way.' That was, I suppose, the last chance of getting the most powerful man in the establishment to regard me as potentially a friendly junior ally with an alternative perspective on the same goals.

It was no disappointment to be put on to special duties. The troubles were dying down, and Peking seemed to be thinking twice about whether anything had been achieved. It was my final chance to prove credentials as a valuable member of the policy boys. There had been severe criticism of the Immigration Department and policies towards illegal immigration, and a review was needed. My first DCS had made a name by reviewing the Fire Brigade, and here, it was hinted, was my opportunity. I blew it. I had been familiar with immigration when ACS(C) and Clerk of Councils, while the senior Superintendent of Police who ran immigration as part of the Police Force had prepared his report on civilianizing it as a distinct department. He had become a friend. I had been out on the border, watching in astonishment a large body of refugees literally pushing down the wire fence that kept them from Kowloon's gold-paved streets, during an earlier major incursion when Peking's eyes had been turned the other way. I had watched Gurkhas rounding most of them up in the New Territory foothills, and had heard the police admitting that those who got through the net, most clutching a paper with the address of relatives in the colony, won the race if they could get to the registration office before being picked up. I knew all about the so-called self-balancing quota, which allowed 50 Cantonese to cross to cultivate their ancestral lands daily, and 50 to go home again, identifiable by little more than their *lingua franca* (the trouble being that few ever did go back).

That had not been the first, nor by far the last, occasion when Hong Kong had decided that the cure for an unsatisfactory service was, not to get its boss to make it satisfactory or to put in a new boss, but to set up a new department, only to find that the new chicken hatched new eggs and the new problems were greater. My trouble now was that in opening a Pandora's box, inside was found a set of Russian dolls. One inquiry kept leading to another. In one direction, the question of how many men should man the immigration desks at Kai Tak airport could only be answered by deciding how acceptable a wait should be for disembarking passengers from the average long distance service. Since the FS had been at the heart of the call for the inquiry, I asked him: he said that was not his decision to make – nor would the DCS ask the CS. This was unhelpful towards making recommendations, based on alternative figures all drawn from the air, in the knowledge that it would be easy for a senior, or for exco, to reject a proposal, but embarrassing to admit how that proposal had originally been suggested. In another direction, the preventive service (HK's Customs) could have suggested how many back-up immigration staff would make their raids and searches more effective, and how they might best co-operate: but nobody was prepared to quantify. My recommendations would be my own, unsupported, and easily disowned.

A similar problem was that, although hived off, immigration still had to co-operate with police – intelligence concerning illegals, marine and border patrols looking for smuggled refugees, and so on. There were disaffected criticisms from coppers who thought the new department a mistake, but there were examples of poor communications and bad blood. Then there was corruption and morale. The public perception was also important: the change of uniform and titles had made no difference to applicants' impression that they were dealing with the same brusque, often rudely arrogant, officials they had expected in police stations. One unturned stone led to another, and I was unhappy with what I found. It would be useless to advise on numbers and structures, detailed policies and presentation, using my own judgment, if the management culture remained unchanged.

As drafting began, every chapter in its first form was sent to the Director of Immigration for him to comment and criticize. He was a senior member of the Executive Grade who had been promoted to the new post, in terms of salary the same as my own; but I was a secretariat officer with supervisory duties commissioned to review matters in the name of the bosses. The nearer the end of the drafting approached, the more uncomfortable the Director became, because the clearer it was that I thought the problems started at the top: his criticisms became less helpful towards a balanced final version. Finally he refused to comment further but complained to the DCS that he did not like the way the inquiry was going. When I submitted the report, there was a hush for a few days, and then the DCS told me that I had gone far beyond my terms of reference but, worse, I had presumed to criticize a Head of Department. 'I can't circulate this, even secretaries might see it!' The thoughts were put back to him that this was not a very senior Head; that secretaries had undoubtedly typed, let alone seen, criticisms on confidential files of other officers of equal, let alone higher, rank (such as me); that there had been no logical point at which to stop following up answers to questions, in order to respond to the purpose of the inquiry; and that the only intention was to recommend an efficient, economical and happy, well-run part of the government. Personalities should surely not prevail over principles. Two solid months' work was buried, a colleague was told to produce something brief and uncontroversial, and the problem remained tinkered with. Only myself to blame, in retrospect, but there were colleagues with local credibility who would have been listened to had they done the same: and they agreed with my opinions when I discussed the affair with them.

Apart from Hilary's surgical needs and my mother's demise, the last tour in Hong Kong was the happiest, contrary to expectations, and so coverage will be brief in this iconoclastic and selfish, but abbreviated and selective chapter. Urban Services, and dealing in the central areas (excluding the New Territories) with the Urban Council, had never seemed glamorous. It was fun, as well as basic. Once more I found a vast manual of departmental standing orders, by the same draftsman over whose tablets I had stumbled in Resettlement. A page illustrated how a street-sweeper should sweep his street (the wording may not be exact): 'Hold the brush with left hand uppermost; facing the oncoming traffic, advance the right foot along the pavement edge; sweep forwards, moving the left foot behind the gathered rubbish ...' and so on (with Chinese translation on facing page). There was this to deal with. The director was an excellent man, who had censored letters in the HK Post Office as a private in the Royal Scots, being shipped off to Officer Training School in India a fortnight before the Japanese occupation at Christmas 1941; he had served in Force 136 in Malaya, meeting the Chinese communists, led by Chin Peng, who were saboteurs behind the Jap 'lines' (and terrorists in post-war recovered Malaya); after the war he had been in British Military Administration Libya, and briefly in Northern Nigeria (where he had not found a Resident's use of an ex-lieutenant-colonel as a cadet very appropriate), before engineering a return to Hong Kong. He had not entered the charmed circle, but was able to deal wisely with the strange group of Unofficials who were the members of the Urban Council – being official Chairman took most of his time, so his deputy was in effect the 'chief executive' of HK's municipal authority.

Half of these Unofficials were appointed by the Governor, as for Legco; half elected by ratepayers. There was a handful of Official heads of departments thought to have interests in common with the Council. Two political parties, so-called, provided most of the elected members, though with little in common with the masses of HK. The Reform Club was headed by a sweet-natured barrister of a liberal turn, Brook Bernacchi, brother of a Pacific Resident Commissioner, who was supported by expatriates from the professional or superior minor commercial worlds; the Civic Association had Overseas Chinese leadership in Hilton Cheong Leen. Both had Chinese membership, their policy differences were insubstantial, and they counted for little in the scales weighed in Lower and Upper Albert Roads; but only the crudest of cynics would sneer at their sincerity. The most notable, or notorious, member was a missionary lady who might once have featured in *The Inn of the Sixth Happiness*, but had lost the convictions of her faith. She had however developed a passionately admirable sense of responsibility for HK's Chinese underdogs, the hawkers not least, coupled with a sad conviction that all government actions, and most of its agents, were corrupt, reactionary and uncaring. Much departmental time was spent in anticipating or answering her angry allegations in council committees, letters to editors or complaints to higher authority.

Some time was spent in seeking out corruption, mainly in the health inspectorate. Licensing brought in revenue that was, if not paltry, not major: but the inspection behind the grant of a licence, whether for a wretched hawker, a billiard saloon or (the most ripe for pickings of many sorts) a restaurant, was the killing field for blackmail by some proud man dressed in a little brief authority. Every call for legislative control of potential abuse, by bolting doors before the nag had had a chance to smell his oats, opened a gate to more demands for bribes, protection money and preference. The daughter of good friends (he the CO of the local RNR, she the Barry Norman of the *South China Morning Post*) opened a boutique in Central District, intending to add facilities for coffee and cakes. She mentioned to her parents the number of inspectors she had had to square – health, fire, police, building control, those only the recognizable ones – and they mentioned this to me. 'Hurray,' said I, 'the break we all wait for, a witness who will not be intimidated and will testify, where can I talk to her and get details?' No dice. If we clobbered all those, how long before their mates came round to find petty infringements and put her out of business? Better to pay up with a whistle, was her upstanding Caucasian response. She was right, of course. The regulations specified precisely x inches between the end of the towel rail and the edge of the sink in a restaurant washroom, and an error by a joiner could expose the owner to the threat of a cancelled licence unless he 'drank tea' with the inspector. How much better, one might feel, to wait until someone did get collywobbles and then punish the committed offence. But even this free country of ours now believes that, for health and safety, thousands of pages of regulation and battalions of corruptible experts of modest education but specialized training are worth expenditure of millions, to avoid a few inchoate dangers, instead of straight checks for filth, rotting food, cockroaches and poor refrigeration.

A new governor introduced new thinking. I prophesied MacLehose's appointment, knowing that the FCO would have first call on any remaining plums in the overseas service. The most striking was his fresh look at corruption. The police force had its anti-corruption branch, and the Deputy Commissioner responsible had often pleaded that the law should be changed, so that wealth, not accountable for in known salary and investments, should be evidential. This was contrary to British justice: a person had not to prove his innocence, the prosecutor had to prove guilt. Honest police were not encouraged when it was loudly announced that corrupt practices now made known were beyond all that had been thought. An Independent Commission Against Corruption was to be created, and legislation would be introduced whereby unaccountable possession of wealth would be *prima facie* evidence of guilt. The Deputy Commissioner had only just named to MacLehose two or three senior police officers whom he knew to be corrupt, but could not 'prove it in court', and now he was in effect publicly accused of failure. ICAC collared many crooks, but the Royal Hong Kong Police Force never quite recovered from not being empowered to collar its own. ICAC has in its turn had to accept internal investigations.

Another major change was superficially well judged. The entire structure of government was creaking. A small cadet service running a small secretariat and heading a few departments had kept the boat from rocking on a calm postwar sea. A decade before we had been exposed to 'management appreciation' by consultants, and told that indefinable things *could* be measured, and that one day a street riot could be controlled by a computer. There was interest in forcing commercial concepts on government; but the purpose of modern business was to create consumers – what should we make our citizens consume? The solution bruited now was to bring in yet more management consultants. Many lectures and seminars ensued on critical paths, cost-benefit analyses, MBO (Management By Objective), assessments of time spent on various duties, and much else. There were two mistakes: the first was that the consultants were not permitted to look at the Finance Branch; the second, that all the gobbledegook of the newspeak was nectar to some of the executive grade. Bureaucratic class snobbery this may be, but the process added power to those without vision.

Two things began to strike me: first, I had been in Hong Kong for a year longer than I had served in Northern Nigeria, and yet, for all my wife's wide circle of friends, and mine, in and out of officialdom, was still made by a significant few to feel a newcomer (even worse, was classed by one or two of those who mattered as an unwelcome interloper who would never understand); the second, and more important, was my perception that there were only two jobs in the Hong Kong government worth having for anyone with that 'let's have a go' African temperament – Governor and Financial Secretary, and I wasn't going to become either if anyone could help it. I was enjoying USD, but my boss wasn't much older than myself. It was impossible to prove myself in that local fast track to administrative success, the closed shop of commerce and industry, and I had no yen to leap into the dark of the business world itself, as several cadets did. A friend from Nigerian days was now FS in the Solomon Islands. He wrote to say that they were speeding towards independence, but apart from the High Commissioner and himself, not a soul had previous experience of 'decolonization'; few expats had any faith in it, still less wanted to see it. Their CS was likely to go off to govern some neighbouring islands shortly, the Secretary for Protectorate Affairs was retiring and his post was redesignated Deputy Chief Secretary: could I come and help?

I wrote to the High Commissioner, and was told that it was up to FCO to fill the post, that there was no certainty that the DCS would succeed if the CS did depart, and that the salary was half my present one (by now Staff Grade B1 – another sliced rank introduced to make the ladder taller), although arrangements for mitigation might be possible. When a saving arrived from FCO, inviting applications (and understanding that Clark was believed to have expressed an interest), my boss was disappointed but not very surprised. The DCS was reluctant to believe that I could be serious. By now he was the former DES whom I liked and respected, despite his having once wondered why I always wanted to change everything (only just true, and then only in crucial matters, I insisted). Did I not realize that I would be the next Director of Social Welfare, for which I had such obvious 'flair'? It was not obvious to me. Most people thought me mad, of those who showed any interest (I never had an inkling, now or when my time in the Pacific ended, whether Hong Kong's governor was consulted or expressed an opinion on my hopes or value). The terms, when my interest was confirmed and FCO and Honiara had agreed, were a secondment in the belief that the British Solomon Islands Protectorate would be independent in about two years' time; the BSIP would pay HK A$5,000 a year to preserve my HK pension rights against a supernumerary post; and by living simply and banking my Overseas Service Aid Scheme expat allowance I should be able to continue saving a proportion of what I was already saving in HK. Why I did not return to Hong Kong once the Solomons were independent, instead of retiring to yet another life in British local government and museums, will appear in the next chapters but one. A recap comes first, recounting the rewards of twelve years in Hong Kong. Throughout the present chapter I have never forgotten that one of my most respected seniors in Nigeria told me that my annual confidential report had mentioned that I possessed a *mens sibi conscia recti*.

CHAPTER 8

Pearls Around the Neck – Stones Upon the Heart

He who would search for pearls must dive below
[Dryden, *All for Love*]

Hong Kong's imperial armorial bearings were inspired by the heraldic interests of the DCS who doubted my 'soundness'. (The old flag badge, displaying a junk and wharfside goods easily mistaken for opium barrels, was out of favour.) They featured as crest a lion holding a pearl between its paws – the Pearl of the Orient. The symbol is apt: irritating grit causes the creature in its shell to cover the invader with emollient coats of shiny mineral, sometimes making a perfect sphere, sometimes a misshapen blob, but always a thing of value. Potential metaphors for the grit, the nacre and the resultant evolution are many. We have looked at some of the itching, now let us search out the gleams.

Within weeks of arrival younger colleagues, good friends to this day, asked me to share their weekend expeditions. I was taken for walks on Hong Kong island or in the New Territories, including ferry trips to the larger islands. I envied them their colloquial exchanges with the passing peasants, policemen and taxi-drivers, Chinese waiters and boatmen, shop assistants, foodstall operators and hawkers, farming folk with baskets and buffaloes, and their ease in tea-houses. Few seniors seemed to share such enjoyment; perhaps they had once, before marriage and status took control. My larger income and the knock-down prices meant that what had been longed-for luxuries in Nigeria were easy to acquire: better cameras, hi-fi stereo, decent tableware, soft furnishings and bespoke furniture, records from all over the world (books were expensive at a HK$ per shilling list price). Only the carefully mean remained content with standard PWD house equipment.

Rural areas were like my last home, Okene, except no palm trees and sea around. It was beautiful, and with the winding roads, steep hillsides and islands, despite the smallness of the place one gazed on an entirely different view every minute. Still, there were differences. The government was more efficient than some I might think of, principally because of, despite language, the remarkable Chinese clerical staff. The filing systems worked. Registries produced the paper in minutes. We imported numbers of young ladies who had to sit around polishing nails while complaining that they 'didn't come out to do copy-typing'. It was a question of 'face', a term pounced upon by the

European as an excuse for letting the wilier oriental get away with murder. The Chinese had given (in Cantonese) *min* since the beginning of time, which can be noble or kindly, but once translated into English as 'face' it became an object of abuse and demoralization. If you didn't have your own nail-polisher, you weren't 'in'. (I dissociate my own series of secretaries from the nail-polishing genre: Diana stood no nonsense from the man she worked for; Margaret kept the exco paperwork to the highest of standards, and remained loyal to the colony; Diana Kan in Swid never complained and never let one down; Lucy Hung was swift, reliable and 'pro-active' in the general branch, but widowed, before tragically succumbing to nasal cancer and leaving two children.)

If one telephoned the PWD or the electric company, or the urban services department, or a firm, for someone to come and fix something, someone came with celerity and fixed it – with a smile. All my UK friends knew that I had come to a realm of vice, poverty and drugs. In six months I saw less evidence of vice than in six days in London's west end. The faces were of people making the best of things, even the old women at the end of the trail, not of hopeless, resentful, spiritless DPs. One felt pity, but admiration also. There was no sharp cleft between Haves and Have-Nots, but in between there was every level of wealth on the ladder, evenly graded.

By spring 1961 I had amassed enough 'points' to qualify for a government flat, a low viewless home, spurned by juniors with the wife and children that won them priority points, but luxury after Nigeria, and independence after squatting in the residences of colleagues on leave. I inherited Ah Kam as 'cook-boy', valet and all-purpose supporter, from Trench, gaining the second best human relationship that Hong Kong was to offer, not only because he could make Baked Alaska. The new post of clerk of councils offered new fields to graze, most of which was run under Victorian legislation. By custom 'CofC' was the administrative service's representative on the Association of European Civil Servants, the expat bureaucrats' trades union or 'Bolshy Society'. Since AOs in particular posts controlled conditions of service, conflicts of interest were easily discerned. There was a fine line between inactive support while accepting membership, and ostentatious rejection of suspect disloyalty to the Establishment (in more than one sense of that word). I took the line that cadets must not seem stand-offish to other callings, but recognize that a responsible political officer had to master the art of wearing two hats, and never forget that he could only wear one at a time – and never forget which was on at that time. Tiring of trying to persuade one or two recalcitrants to join, I conceived a local Administrative Service Association, to include those cadets eligible to join the AECS's parallel body, the Senior Non-Expatriate Officers' Association (the

SNEOA AOs were less fidgety about being active in a staff association). As well as being a social group sharing the corporate enjoyment that was so lacking, we might also have informal seminar-like meetings when professional ideas could be exchanged and perhaps original thought on policy might emerge. That notion appalled some superiors and was still-borne. Nevertheless the founding of the ASA was something to cherish. Its first necktie, designed by a colleague with a high-minded view of the cadets' character, was covered with the calligraphic character *yü*. This represented the noble legendary qualities of jade (it was also associated with the characters *wang*, that represented the imperial nobility connecting heaven with earth and man, and *chu,* the lordly flame spreading virtue and light).

Although I was no longer desk officer for Radio Hong Kong, friendship with its staff continued, leading to amateur broadcasting. The head of music was amused at a party by my very personal Thomas Beecham story, and asked me to repeat it in a chat show.* There followed a contractual commitment to the roster of reviewers of new records, an appearance on the local version of *Desert Island Discs*, a series of Easter contemplations before the morning news, another series of Christmas poems of many kinds, backed by recorded carols from unusual places, and voice-over commentaries on the cathedral's watchnight services at Easter and New Year. The signature tune of my regular reviews was Walton's *Popular Song* from *Façade,* and I also used the intro to Stravinsky's *Pulcinella*. My pseudonym was Alastair Harrison (AH), but the voice was not disguised. The CS was displeased when on the desert island I mentioned Mr Harold Macmillan's 'cronies'; he had not appreciated that (*vide* Robbie Burns) Scotsmen use the kindly word for intimate colleagues, not for venal placemen. I was interviewed in a current affairs programme over the murder of Abubakar Tafawa Balewa, but no comment followed on my evident shame that Mr Harold Wilson remained silent, despite attending the Lagos Commonwealth meeting, hosted by Abubakar, a week before.

One disadvantage of being tall is that one stands out in a crowd. Being seen regularly at S John's Cathedral, I was accosted by the dean to become a sidesman. Within months my profession as a minute-taker found me a member of the cathedral council, and its secretary for over a decade. An idea

---

*I had been the sole member of Edinburgh's Usher Hall audience to applaud his RPO performance of Haydn's little known 40th symphony, which I knew well from his 78 recording, played regularly during a tour in Nigeria: I clapped after the *allegro finale* because there had been no preceding minuet & trio, but everyone else knew from the programme that it had four movements and there must be one to come. I had a very deep personal bow directed towards me in the cheap organ gallery seat, while the cognoscenti took whispering pleasure in what they saw as Tommy's silent sarcasm. They began to wonder and even look foolish when after another short wait TB walked off the platform in the still expectant silence, to bring on Anthony Pini to play Virgil Thomson's cello concerto (who said Beecham never condescended to perform modern music?). It turned out that Dennis Brain, who had a difficult horn part to play in the missing movement, had called in sick.

had been to rally the Roman and nonconformist churches to join the Anglicans in combining all their choirs, with the aim of singing Handel's *Messiah* ecumenically during the opening of the City Hall. I was landed with registering the members and keeping the vast body together, and ultimately with designing and writing the programme and posters. We had hoped to cajole Sargent into conducting, but had to fall back on local talents. It was a sell-out, and led to annual performances of great works like the *Matthew Passion* and *Elijah*, often conducted by overseas examiners of the schools' music festival students. This is how I met, first in 1962, a truly great man, Sir Thomas Armstrong, head of the Royal Academy of Music. It was inspiring to watch how in so few minutes he transformed a large group of untutored enthusiasts into a body that understood what both Handel and the words meant, and to unite their meaning. He repeated the miracle another year in Bach. He asked whether I had 'come to terms yet with Britten's *War Requiem*', and seemed to agree with my callow opinion that Wilfred Owen's clearly articulated words gave it its power.

For a cathedral anniversary I had the thought of asking half a dozen English (language) poets each to write a new 20th century hymn, with some relevance to east-west unity, and then approaching six living British (and possibly Hong Kong) composers to compose the music. Needless to say, the Hong Kong Minimal Hymnal came to naught, and not only because of doubts how to hint at the nominality of any fees that might be negotiated. Around this time I met the amiable and worthy Edmund Blunden, author of the classic *Undertones of War* and instructor in map-reading in 1941's Oxford STC, now professing English at the University which had celebrated its 50th anniversary. A meeting took place shortly afterwards at the home of the editor of the *South China Morning Post*, who had been asked by my school rector to look out for me. This former assistant editor and art critic of the *Glasgow Herald* had been asked by someone else to entertain a newly arrived physiotherapist tutor, Hilary Anderson, whose younger brother happened to have been in my class at Glasgow Academy. We began to go to concerts together.

By the end of my first tour, with Mr Wong's sleepy lunchtime tutorials, I had passed four colloquial oral Cantonese exams, some 'with credit', and with the help of a dear old gentleman recommended by Trench, the first two examinations in characters. Much of the vocabulary learnt had little relevance to my daily work, and opportunities to talk to those who knew no English were few (there were fewer walks with bachelors over the hills). I was determined to show progress, if only to smother the snide references still overheard from less intimate colleagues to Bongo-Bongo-Land, but it made little difference. Personality mattered more, presumably. I had come briefly into my own a month or two after arriving, during a visiting Nigerian Trade Mission when I was turned into an instant but ephemeral expert, without back-up. It was a boost to renew friendships with the North's head of civil service, Ali Akilu, and the federation's high commissioner in London, Abdulmaliki from Okene, and to meet the redoubtably naughty and ebullient minister of finance Festus Sam Okotie-Eboh, who was gratified to hear of my close friendship with his prime minister.

In late 1961 the political adviser's gopher introduced me to the Burmese consul at a function, and I began to hanker after another sight of his country. I had also heard of Angkor Wat. HK wealth and proximity made such visits possible. Not long afterwards Burma became virtually closed to casual tourists, but I was not unlucky in taking local leave. On the plane I found myself seated by a brusque police superintendent. He was also bound for the Khmer monuments, and we shared each other's company to Phnom Penh, still very French in atmosphere, and on by internal plane to Siem Reap. The sheer wonder and splendour of Angkor Wat, Angor Tom, the Bayon and other jungle-encrusted ruins, built without arches, need no embroidery from me. The charm of the pedallers of the *cyclo-pousses* who propelled us around was icing on the cake, and the Gallic hospitality in the *Auberge des Temples* was simple but perfect. I parted from the red-faced copper and took a long bus ride back to the capital, past the Tongle Sap lake, crossing it in part on a long causeway. The front seat was shared with two monks, who tried valiantly to talk English, and six chickens.

I managed to reach Rangoon *via* Bangkok, which was cheaper than Phnom Penh. The Grand Hotel was as I had expected. Remarkably little had changed since 1946. The Shwe Dagon pagoda had been regilded (poverty did not affect proper dues), and a vast artificial cave-mountain had been erected to commemorate a recent 2,500th anniversary of Buddhism, but apart from one block of 'workers' flats' which a taxi-driver insisted proudly on showing me, and some new bungalows around the university for overseas teachers, military rule and post-war rehabilitation had made small difference. Nonetheless, all was normal and natural, with nothing sham for tourists. Silver-beaters, alabaster-carvers, weavers and potters were plying their trades for their fellows, although I failed to see pretty girls rolling cigars or cheroots on their thighs. My old camp site by Victoria Lake had reverted to uncultivated sward. I flew to Mandalay, where the resthouse cuisine was regrettably the chicken-and-caramel-custard inheritance of imperialism. The old monuments were no disappointment, and the guides friendly. Burmese, not only the hill tribes who favoured our rule, are nice people.

By now routine patterns were set. The annual cholera jab, celebration of Liberation Day every 30 August, the disappearance of household staff for four days at Chinese New Year (Ah Kam, who had rejected an approach from the newly opening 'American' hotel, always left a great veal-and-ham pie to see one through after breakfasts), attendance at every opening of the latest exhibition of Hong Kong products, renewal of squash-playing (impossible since Kaduna), and the walks between flat and secretariat through Garden Road or the botanic garden, and between Star Ferry and the favourite Kowloon-side shops.

Social life seemed to include Hilary more regularly and comfortably. I was not sorry to leave the secretariat for a department, despite it not being of my choice. Although social welfare would highlight the Chinese facility for remaining cheerful in face of trouble, I was concerned by the preponderance of lady social workers ('social work' was quite a new expression outside north America), of whom not a few allowed their emotions to spill over into their duties. I have described how I fitted in among the probation officers and approved schools, the youth welfare officers (soon to be renamed community organizers), the child care or adoption officers, the moral guidance officers, relief officers and special welfare officers for rehabilitation of the handicapped.

A real achievement, begun in this tour, was prolonged. As a result of Man o' War Bay in Nigeria, I had on a leave pursued its chief instructor back to his roots in the original Outward Bound School at Aberdovey, and my interest had grown. The non-governmental wife who had befriended me on the *Peleus* during the voyage to Hong Kong was married to the head of Holt's Wharf on Kowloon side, and from his comradeship I realized that John Holt had had much to do with backing the Outward Bound movement ('to serve, to strive and not to yield' – or count the cost). There was an Outward Bound school in Malaya, also in the business of showing young people that nature enabled brain and frame to go that bit further than the over-cosseted mind believed to be practical, or indeed sensible. Students desk-bound by vocation and unathletic by constitution learnt how to transfer what they did reluctantly but physically into intellectual or commercial terms. Claustrophobic materialistic Hong Kong could surely benefit from some of this? The 'community organization' aspect rang a few small sympathetic bells in Swid, and we rattled the cage of the Social Welfare Advisory Committee gently. An admin friend and commercial companions joined on expeditions to find a possible site, and interest grew. The principal from the Malayan school, where he had won himself an overseas Chinese wife and two charming children, came to advise over the winter 1965-66. Eventually we had a costed business plan, with outline approval from New Territories admin, for a school at Tai Mong Tsai, and went caps in hand and full of confidence to the Royal Hong Kong Jockey Club, seeking funds from their vast annual charitable takings (out of the pockets of the colony's racing-mad addicted gamblers). We were turned down after a year's wait.

We did what many others did without shame, although it was awkward for administrative officers to contemplate without commercial back-up. We went to the governor (by now it was April 1967), set out our wares and wrung our disappointed hands. Trench was enthused, and said he would 'make inquiries'. At the next distribution of Jockey Club wealth, we got our development funds, we headhunted Malaya's principal, and soon there was a residential school with equipment for climbing and serious exercising, a ship to man and sail, and enthusiastic staff, largely local. Sir David Trench came by helicopter to open the school, and to wide alarm took off again with his safety belt flapping out from the closed cabin door. Business firms and educational establishments gradually took up all the places, and scholarships were created for the less well-off. Our faith was rewarded: many youngsters, superficially effete at first glimpse, were willing to take the chance, and were so proud at the end of the course. A '24 Hour Solo' was introduced, which entailed dropping single individuals off on successive small islands, with just enough for food and sleep, and a diary in which to write something, anything, but preferably relevant, that inspired them. The astonishment was how many had never in their whole lives been quite alone for 24 hours; and from the eternally buzzing and humming environments of Victoria and Kowloon, that spread to neighbouring islands and open spaces, had never experienced total silence. This was more scary than the challenges of hill and sea.

1964 had been a difficult year climatically. Water shortages continued. Chinese New Year was humid, and fewer fire disasters were reported from carelessly lit fireworks (supposedly illegal). There was a string of five typhoons. 12" of rain in the first did mean that we had four hours of running water every other early morning instead of only the accustomed fourth day. My third floor flat in the Albany, theoretically for bachelors, had no lift, one small spare room and a small dry room for a dehumifidier: but it had a good view. Ah Kam thought the geomancy good: Trench had had the same flat when he first came to HK. When typhoon *Ruby* came, I sat in Swid throughout. It was followed by *Stella*, when my director was absent at a conference, and I not only had to sit inside, co-ordinating welfare relief while most staff was working hard outside, but was regularly on the radio and calling for contributions to the Community Relief Trust Fund. *Tilda* just missed us, but there was another. When the director came back, I reflected how much easier it was to be a boss, even if one might have to carry a can in the end: all one need do when everyone was up to their eyes was to say 'yes' or 'no' or 'try again'.

My 'op' was described in the opening chapter. Convalescence was much promoted by Hilary, and I gave myself occupational therapy by constructing an electronic two-manual organ (before the days of chips, this included soldering many hundreds of transistors, capacitors and diodes on to printed circuit boards, and seemingly miles of wires and switches between the keys, the stop tablets and everything else – I never knew what did what). It was something different, as were the recuperative isotonic Canadian air force 5BX exercises at lunch breaks, which probably increased my blood pressure. Recovery meant that I might no longer be unexpectedly boarded out to low income idleness, or carried out to worse. I might seriously contemplate matrimony. My return to work in the new year coincided with the death of Churchill, which only too clearly brought down the curtain on Britain's greatness. We had lost our Arthur, the Once King unlikely to return as the Future King.

Hilary was a further growing part of my social life. We announced our engagement in early 1965, arranging the knot-binding for May Day. The governor and acting SCA sent good wishes, but the CS and FS did not. Unusually the bishop, who held back from uniting people who wanted to make a social splash of their great day, said he would be pleased to celebrate ours – he had confirmed Hilary who had volunteered, without a word from me, to take instruction and to join my pisky denomination and leave her presbyterian upbringing (she also decided, when discussing the order of service with the dean, to obey, as well as to serve, love, honour and keep according to the unadulterated BCP: raging feminists do not appreciate with what psychological bonds this shackles the groom). My director asked us to champagne cocktails, ending in nice hysteria when the bubbly was flat and the orange bitters overdosed the sugar lumps, but the ice broke. The first dance we had together was at the Swid senior staff dinner. A good AO friend (a future vice-chairman of the Tories) agreed to be my best man, and Hilary's superintendent physiotherapist to be matron of honour. A Chinese architect and a former eastern Nigerian DO undertook to usher. We discussed music with the cathedral organist and settled on nothing but Purcell, but *not* the so-called trumpet voluntary – on the day she played the (Jeremiah Clarke's) trumpet voluntary and Bach's *Jesu, joy*. The hymn that sticks in memory prayed not for ever resting by still pastures but for strength to live courageously, on steep and rugged pathways to boot (it seems to have been granted, by and large). Ronald Hall's little private homily about lifetime bonds of mutual support is reflected daily in Hilary's care. Her brother Ken came out to give her away, but my mother managed to make a house move an immovable obstacle to joining us. The reception was arranged by the editor in whose home we had met. It did not strike me immediately that my unacknowledged state of denial (that service career ambition was frustrated) had been permanently displaced by calm acceptance of an emotionally balanced life.

We were booked on Cathay Pacific Airways to Malaya and Thailand, and were seen off happily for our closest well-wishers to return to the club for the rest of the evening. Twenty minutes into the air, a technical hitch returned us to Kai Tak, where we sat glumly until the flight was renewed far into the night. By this time CPA's head had heard of the contretemps and phoned from the Country Club to upgrade us to 'first', with a bottle of champagne. We got to bed at the Cockpit hotel in Singapore in wee small hours, and were charged corkage on the champagne next day. In the next fortnight we saw what Kuala

Slicing into new life.

Lumpur and pink pre-British Malacca had to offer before several days in the undeveloped peace of Fraser's Hill, the sights of Bangkok, and more days in Chieng Mai, where we had tourists' views of Miao 'tribesmen', dust storms and Queen Victoria's statue in the *quondam* British consul's garden. The hotel was incomplete, and whenever something failed to function, the young staff dissolved into infectious giggles. We saw crafts in production for the markets, not just for amateur anthropologists' entertainment: paper-making, umbrellas (made from the homemade paper), lacquerware, silver-beating, pottery – and everywhere, but especially among the Miao, everyone from toddlers upwards was smoking, pipes rather than cigars. I learnt sharply not to read books at breakfast and lunch, tough on a long term bachelor.

Sirikit, our Siamese cat, was also to learn not to sleep on top of the bed behind the crook of my knees. Soon after our return Hilary, who had been a peacetime Wren in Clyde Division after war service in Bombay and Ceylon, had to do her annual week's training in the Hong Kong RNR, and to act for a few months as officer commanding the Wrens' reserve, with drills, lectures, sailing in inshore minesweepers through choppy waters (not all the Chinese girl ratings being particularly good sailors), and educational visits to the fire brigade and Cable & Wireless, the Royal Observatory and HMS *Tamar* naval base. By marrying she had lost her entitlement to accruing gratuity (or pension after ten years) and leave. As still a tutor physio she was submitted to a course on 'Methods of Instruction', engendering more jargon than technique. Such a wife still needed an Ah Kam, who broke tradition by not abandoning his employer when that bachelor wedded, and by methodically instructing in cookery and menu-concoction. The household was happy, and tea-parties for physio students complemented my invitations to office clerks (where the call had been for Elvis, not Haydn, when I offered LP music). We learnt that permicide would kill kitchen cockroaches, and to care for Queen of the Night cactus on the verandah, which bloomed capriciously and magnificently for one night alone. Sadly, our cat twice jumped on to the wet verandah rail when rain had fallen, and slipped straight over, down on to a glass frame. A broken septum eventually led to toxaemia; antibiotics and glucose feed did not succeed, and we mourned that I no longer had to curb her habit of chewing my pen handle when I was writing letters, or of leaping from shoulder to shoulder of our dinner guests at table before settling round my neck.

Not all was peaceful that year. The Double Tenth brought out more Nationalist flags than ever. A US transport plane crashed into the harbour on taking off. Typhoon *Rosie* shied off, but *Agnes* brought 17" of rain. Ah Kam had to be X-rayed for a stomach ache, but all was well. My mother came out to stay and pass comments on the passing show, and was given much generous hospitality. A salaries review commission was initiated, for which insiders tipped me to be secretary, but Bill Dickinson was chosen. A delegation of legal luminaries on their way to a commonwealth conference in Sydney included our former Northern Nigerian attorney-general Hedley Marshall, now an academic. And then came 1966. Princess Margaret, and a Lord Snowdon suffering badly from polio-induced backache, paid a visit. My director had about three weeks of thrice daily farewell functions before retirement, but earned his ceremonial departure from Queen's Pier, bearing his departmental souvenir, a jade incense-burner which his Chinese section heads had unaccountably insisted that I choose (but which they approved – face-giving or diplomacy?). The department was left in my acting hands until the heir was free to assume control. There were three days of riots: the motivation seemed obscure, although with hindsight a forewarning.

Our 1966 summer leave began with dolphins and whales in Hawaii, the indescribable Grand Canyon, and cadging on hosts. The rest was spent showing the relatively newly married pair off to relatives and friends all over UK. It was crazy, nobody supposing that we might need a rest. All this and the Ashridge advanced management course. We were worn out when we visited

In the Highlands as well, on leave.

friends at Munich on our way back to work. It did not stop us eating swordfish on the Bosphorus, or wondering at the blue mosque, Hagia Sophia, Topkapi and the Kariye Cami'i's wonderful mosaics in Istanbul, followed by Ankara, enjoying Atatürk's tomb, the Hittite museum, a picnic in the valleys and the Turkish friends of our ex-Nigerian hosts, who preferred them to their embassy colleagues. At Tehran we goggled at the crown jewels and bought a fine carpet, desperately building up strength for a stay with brother-in-law Ken and his missionary family in Pakistan, between Lahore, Sialkot and Murree. If one had to work in Hong Kong to achieve all this, it must be worth it?

We arrived back in November 1966, worn out, just in time for Ah Kam's 60th birthday, lavishly celebrated. Spending Lunar New Year at an offshore island bungalow, we steeled ourselves to the renewal of water rationing (turning the daily supply off at 10 o'clock got us into bed earlier and prepared us for HK's longest, coolest, greyest winter for years) and went to see the works at Plover Cove. This had been dammed, the salt sea water draining out, to be replaced by rainwater from conduits round the hills, creating a lake which would hold more water than all the existing reservoirs put together. A great engineering feat, and a major repositioning of villagers to boot. A hot and humid summer followed soon enough, but even with eventual rain the water supply went back to alternate days. Hilary was in charge of the physio school while the superintendent was on leave, with only one relatively inexperienced assistant, and took her charges to the Hei Ling Chau leprosy centre to learn what kind of patients they might have to treat. 400 bright young Chinese applied for the 15 places on the next course: the stigma of physiotherapists being seen as masseurs and masseuses was waning. She was, like many, heartbroken when it was decided that that among other retrenchments the HK Royal Naval Reserve was an unnecessary luxury and should be closed down. This won her an engraved cigarette box for her commanding of the Wrens, and (in an auction) the mess gavel and cigar-lighter, but something of symbolic community spirit, shared by Chinese and 'foreigners' alike, was destroyed.

The Commissioner for Resettlement went to a conference in Honolulu, and I was briefly acting commissioner and a member of the urban council. Then dismayingly the troubles broke out. Chaos, the era of the Little Red Book, the Red Guards and the Cultural Revolution, swamped the world's most populous country. People distant from Peking's control did not think before they acted, and whatever the Party's ultimate intentions for Hong Kong, local activists saw virtue in stirring the pus in the imperialist pimple. Rioting now seemed more serious. Minor left-wing labour disputes degenerated into hooliganism around Kai Tak. I organized meetings of Chinese tenants known as 'responsible' (= 'reliable'), and (as already described) we 'showed the flag' and hoped the trouble-makers would tire themselves out. In UK the undiplomatic George Brown delivered an outburst at the Chinese *chargé d'affaires*. Ambivalent observers expected what was regarded as the smug, self-satisfied and repugnant Mao côterie in Peking to react to the first plain-speaking they might have heard. I recall silence. Rioting spread to the island. The Bank of China's loudspeakers bellowed inflammatory messages, and the government information services replied with louder Peking and Cantonese opera highlights. Office-workers were distracted, but still came to work. Curfews required that they be home by 6.30 *p.m.*, yet there were few disruptions: postmen conducted only token strikes, and buses and ferries had only short stoppages. Barbed wire hastily erected around Government House was removed after two days' quiet.

We breathed too soon. One lunchtime, in Robinson Road at our *SCMP* friend's, was spent watching a major event. A large crowd gathered outside the Hilton hotel at the foot of Garden Road, charging at lines of police defended with riot shields and batons, and falling theatrically on to the ground with blood stains (from ketchup?) for the benefit of television cameras (something new at public occasions). Many of the crowd made their way up to GH, but its gates were impenetrable. With gin in hand, our host asked me whether this was the end of Hong Kong. With beer in hand, I replied that, no, I didn't think so, no, not just yet. Ah Kam's grand-daughter had found a summer job reporting to the information service on how ordinary people said they were treated by government offices, and what they were thinking; she said that there were still malicious anti-British rumours passing between more susceptible clerical workers (she went on to matriculate, to win a bursary in social studies at HKU, and to become a social worker with a BMW more impressive than my Ford before we left).

By the time six months had passed in resettlement my last task was to open a *kaifong* (neighbourhood association)'s headquarters, one of the non-statutory but essential representative substitutes for western democracy. I was saying good-bye to that milieu (and my thanks to the staff whose commonsensical fellowship I had enjoyed, not to speak of my regard for my boss – when he retired, Hilary and I were shattered to hear his wife say that she had spent so many years in HK and *hated every minute*). I could no longer accompany Hilary daily on the *Star* ferry to Kowloon. A new government language school was opening, using some but not all of the private teachers who had instructed newcomers for so long: I attended more classes regularly, from 5.30 to 6.30, aiming at the 'intermediate' level while still tongue-tied in daily conversation.

I was returning to take over the rump of the secretariat general branch I had joined nearly seven years before. Principal current concerns were air pollution, the problems of a new pathological institute for Queen Mary hospital, and the introduction of communal television aerials on multi-storey buildings. Nobody noticed until too late that Rediffusion had a statutory monopoly of passing electronic images through wires, which each communal aerial was clearly doing. The legal department and I had many a headache before we could legislate ourselves out of the morass. I was also in the middle of a tug-of-war between the education department, which was setting up a television service to bring subjects beyond the technical capacity of most schools to the majority, and Radio Hong Kong, who were not yet allowed to offer public service visual broadcasting in competition with the commercial. 'ETV' won its spurs, but RHK did become Radio Television Hong Kong.

As for the troubles, for most of HK's public the overt irritation was a series of pinprick transport strikes: the fears of a PLA marching over the border were common and real, but buried invisibly deep. We began to wonder whether the troublemakers' controllers might not be realizing that they were on the wrong tack, but would Peking be wiser? Curfews made for quieter social life and restful nights, and the police and army were less shy of arresting communist suspects. General morale was raised when a spectacular raid was made on a 25-

storey building, with police moving in and up from the ground, and a Royal Naval helicopter landing another party on the roof to work downwards: inside they found a hospital for rebel compatriots who might be injured in future clashes. Gradually routine returned with the welcome rain, as minor scuffles between coolies and border guards became the norm in security reports. This was not to be a repeat of the humiliations of Palestine, Cyprus and Aden. There had been only three or four truly awful incidents during the five months of highest tension, including the temporary seizing of a police officer and a close AO friend, who had put on a gallant display of self-discipline and leadership before unfriendly cameras, duly recognized with an honour; at the end of 1967 a peaceful exchange of peasants for constables brought police hostages back with weapons intact. 1968 opened with all this behind us, a backlog of undone work, and some new challenges as the need for true change sank in.

There had of course been determination throughout the 'Troubles' to keep ordinary life and work going. Visiting culture continued, but less of it. Max Adrian gave us his one man show as George Bernard Shaw. There was an amateur *Blithe Spirit* which I could not but compare with that in Bauchi and Bukuru 14 years before. Elisabeth Schwarzkopf cancelled, having listened more to international media reports than to balanced local advice. The year ended with a heavy blow: the editor, who had unwittingly brought Hilary and me together, and with his wife been pillars on whom to lean, died without warning of a heart attack during the night after our last meeting.

Once more I chose to brood on the future. In all constitutions, checks and balances were what counted, and in ours they were human. The long foretold confrontation had begun. Academics supposed that one could cure all by giving everyone the vote, though hedging about 'for what' and 'to whom'; economists thought it a question of keeping production costs low and tariff walls lower; grocers wanted government to be firm (*ie* use the police aggressively) and to keep politics out of the trades unions; applications for British travel documents were multiplying; capital was looking for other resting places; the many fake and few genuine home-made bombs might have been planted by some militant minority, whom the established communist leadership would dearly like to control; the mass of the population had come out in tacit opposition to the communists, but had not said much *for* the existing Hong Kong government.

Were the cultural revolution finally to spill over our border, those with anything material to lose would stand up and be counted. The older working person, with long hours and a cramped house, might not have much to lose, but knew well enough the immaterial things he would go without in a people's republic. Younger people did not know at first hand the neighbouring conditions portrayed as worse than their own, although they had learnt avidly how conditions in the western world and south-east Asia were glamourized. Youth was not generally angry, but many were ripe to be plucked by a call to some new 'idealism'.

Since Britain had lost confidence to inspire by idealistic calls, we should anticipate communism's ideological pre-emption by overbidding ourselves – some calculated, materialistic provisions that would offer more than communism's 'economics' permit, plus continued access to the depravities of occidental culture. This would not win over the petty hard core, but it could immunize the majority. Assuming that a degree of sanity would return to Peking, and they began again to tolerate this pimple that provided their foreign exchange, and as long as the process did not stick in their gullet through tactless or triumphal comparisons by us, we might quietly build up a population that remained Chinese but understood the west. It could not be a provocation were we to redouble our efforts in education, housing, health and working conditions. If we awakened ideas about economics and industry, this could be paid for by increased productivity, efficiency, innovation and diversification (achieved actively, not by mouthing the slogans of management-speak). We needed new faces, and those who expected a certain 30% return on investment might have to put up with 10% flat salaries tax rising to 15% or even 20%. In the medium term we might go on co-existing with China, administering something that Britain might still be proud of. The phrase 'winning hearts and minds' had already come to be treated as a cliché. I hoped that our UK masters, Wilson, Brown and Thomson, would appreciate that in a generation to come the world would be grateful that Britain had not done an Aden in the South China Sea. Meanwhile this was still a safer place to live in than Soho.

On New Year's Day 1968 we walked round Lok Ma Chau, now peaceful, and looked at the deserted villages being slowly drowned on the edges of Plover Cove, with patches of pathetic old possessions lying where they had been left. Ah Kam gave us a fright, vomiting blood, but they could find no reason at Queen Mary hospital, and he made his Lunar New Year arrangements for us as usual. The substantive rank of Staff Grade B was divided into B1 and B2, and I found myself again a grade further from the top. When I could see the tarmac beneath me through the corroded floor of the big Canadian Ford *Custom 300* I had brought from Nigeria, earning some flashy disrepute, it was time for a replacement – a white British Ford, *Zodiac Executive*, second hand with not many miles on the clock. I rejoined the committee of the Administrative

Service Association, and we were asked to the wedding of my former secretary, Diana Kan. Almost immediately, while still bemoaning my predecessors' failure to resist the demolition of my general branch (once the possible focus of general*ist* fresh thinking for the secretariat as a whole, balancing the finance & economic steam-rollers), I was sent back to Swid. Its present director was one of the tough but 'sound' members of the administration. New approaches were being made to the aftermath of cultural revolution, and he was brought in to be an effective defence secretary.

I was the obvious temporary substitute, not needing any induction. We have been over much of the experience already. Friendly colleagues included a Malay Chinese with his concave mirror set in his office window to repel unfriendly spirits. A local officer had succeeded in charge of probation (and would one day head the whole department). Other things being equal (they were not), it might mean finishing daily files at 5 o'clock rather than at 7, as the longest, dreariest and dampest winter in memory ended. A flu epidemic and typhoons followed, a thunderstorm with 4" of rain in minutes, and the hottest day recorded since 1900, 95.5°F (there was always something to encourage malcontents, notwithstanding positive satisfactions). A US freighter grounded on Waglan and oil slicks polluted several beaches, but the DCNT and an unostentatious but warm-hearted *taipan* often took the DSW and spouse on their launches for weekend escapes. We were close enough to the Royal HK Yacht Club to be daily amused by how land reclamation had moved it steadily inland from the tip of its original causeway and mooring berth.

As well as 'yes, no, or try again', being the boss meant membership of legislative council (swearing the oath of allegiance as 'The Honourable the Director of Social Welfare, Mr Clark'), urban council and housing authority, and various committees *ex officio*. I was soon opening a new wing of a children's holiday camp, inaugurating a new Po Leung Kuk committee to supervise an orphanage, and inaugurating a library and youth club on the roof of a 22-storey housing authority block (it rained, but the dragon dance and gymnastic display went on regardless of what the sky just above was up to). Next it was presenting gold medals to the two oldest inhabitants of Tsuen Wan, a chirpy lady of 104 and a doddery youth of 84, and attending the open day of the drug addiction rehabilitation centre. There was no end of welfare agencies to visit (remembering that the voluntary agencies outnumbered the government's direct social services). The Hong Kong Sea School seemed a good depositary for all the magazines our household and friends accumulated. Gala charity premières abounded, such as a film of the D'Oyly Carte's *Mikado*, and we supported the governor when he opened a new sports ground and was later given the 'big howl' as chief scout at a rally (As DSW I was made a vice-president of the Scout Association). There were cocktails in HMS *Albion* and HMS *Defender*.

Chief Scout Governor Trench and Vice-President DSW inspect Scouts (Baden-Powell now plays baseball).

We managed a short 'local' leave in what we still thought of as Ceylon (one of Hilary's wartime postings), staying with friends of Hilary's who planted tea, and seeing the attractions of Colombo's Galle Face, winding one-way roads up to Nuwara Eliya through jungle like western Nigeria, and of Kandy and the caves and frescoes of Sigiriya; Buddhism abounded, and the Singhalese manager of the next estate (still dressing in the sparkling starched white shirt, shorts and stockings of the departed rulers) took pride in having grown a *Blue Moon* rose bush. (It was around this time that sea-mail deliveries were interrupted by the closure of the Suez canal in both directions.)

A new chief secretary arrived, his military mien suggesting that as a former governor he was being positioned to succeed Trench. We attended two christenings: the son of close Chinese business friends was already 14 and embarrassed. The second was an uncomplaining baby son of other friends, Chinese medicos, who made us god-parents. I interviewed 30 candidates for the director of protocol post, which should have been localized, tried desperately to master a year's Cantonese tapes from the language school in three days for another exam, and acquired the piles recorded in Chapter 1. By the middle of the year we were due for leave, and decided for once to exercise our continuing right to a sea passage, since leave terms were progressively cut back in successive salaries review adjustments. We were accompanied by the successor to the SCMP editor, and by the retiring director of education, who celebrated departure by shaving off his moustache. I thought this reason enough, in the privacy of SS *Arcadia*, to grow my own second.

We disembarked at Kobe, saw Kyoto and Hakone (where we bought Hiroshige *ukiyo-e*), took the bullet train past Fuji to Tokyo (buying a *netsuke* to add to our growing collection), and saw *kabuki* theatre high in a skyscraper on the same storey as the metro, re-embarked and reached Honolulu. Here our principal woman social worker comrade had given us an introduction to a lady, who helped us to see the naval base with its Pearl Harbor memories, Diamond Head and pineapple plantations. I wore a suit on Waikiki beach, and we met a 92-year-old princess of the royal family, who asked for a whiskey sour and deplored modern hula-dancers ('We never raised our hands above our shoulders'). Colonial problems of development and progress were set in due perspective when we realized that even nails and timber had to be imported into bustling, modern Hawaii. At Vancouver we saw the totem poles in a park stinking from a garbage-collectors' strike, and at Los Angeles visited Disneyland, which was so clean, efficient and entertaining that we will never hear it sneered at. Acapulco gave us sight of the divers from the cliffs into the sea far below, a downpour that quickly swept away the blood from a sudden stabbing in the doorway of a 'café' where we were sitting, and the chance to buy tourists' silver. Balboa and Cristobal took us through Panama, whence to Curaçao, where distant relatives of Hilary drove us round the picturesque multi-distempered streets. At Trinidad it was a delight to meet my Swid deputy's family, and the Kaduna colleague I had succeeded, now in the high commission. That only left Lisbon, a fair city (like Madrid, Vienna and Paris, obviously once capital of a great empire in a way that London lacks), and Cherbourg, where we shared with fellow passengers the largest pyramid of *fruits de mer* that we had ever seen.

We were back in Hong Kong by December for what was, as already recorded, to be my last, and professionally most satisfying, tour in the colony. As deputy I answered to a trusty and decent friend who was preoccupied with the crosswinds from being chairman of an urban council that did not always have the respect it should from the central powers. I was to be in administrative charge of the colony's public health, cleansing, hygiene, pests, abattoirs, markets and hawkers, crematoria and burial grounds (always producing problems in the NT), the city hall and cultural services, parks, gardens, swimming pools, beaches, recreation and entertainment.

I had hardly begun to settle in when I had an incoherent call from my mother, international telephoning still being something rare and adventurous, but it hardly prepared me for a cable a couple of days later to say that she had died. She was 77 (possibly older, according to one relative), she had for years denied the possibility of happiness, but had not seemed physically ill barely a month before. I flew home, spending part of Christmas day in Beirut, where I was given a small potted Lebanon cedar (which I planted outside the Tunbridge Wells flat). Her kidneys had finally given out. It took about a fortnight to settle affairs with lawyers, and I locked up what was now our home in Britain and returned to work. My mother's burdens were over and only to be shared in retrospective guilt.

The police had thankfully handed over responsibility for keeping hawkers and cooked food stalls under some semblance of control to USD. My father's profession left me in no doubt that although general opinion was that our prime purpose was to keep them under vicelike control, the most important division was the medical assistant director's environmental health. The health inspectorate was a large body, some specializing in 'meat' to supervise the abattoirs, some dealing with pests, many looking at restaurants and food outlets. Their chief was the equivalent in the health world to the successful executive officer in my own world of administration, convinced that lack of university education was irrelevant to intellect and leadership – which is true, but far from universally evinced. The cleansing inspectorate was also a vital force for protection of public health, and more technical than the picture of a street-sweeper holding his brush with left hand uppermost portrayed. Its assistant director, having seen other world cities, managed to convince the providers of resources that we needed the latest street-cleansing equipment. The latest garbage trucks collected a major rubbish-creating economy's organic and inorganic products. They delivered them to incinerators that destroyed pollutants, and whose chimneys were designed to waft the residue afar, or to monitored landfill sites co-ordinated with land reclamation projects. Despite the haze that Hong Kong now endures, it is intriguing how we were, within contemporary parameters of knowledge and practicality, anticipating the west's preoccupation with pollution.

I was deputed to represent the colony at the first Economic Commission for Asia and the Far East (ECAFE) meeting in Bangkok, to discuss the regional environment. The plane was the last to take off before a typhoon closed the airport, and the pilot told us to look down at something few ever saw – that huge bowl of ringed porridge was the eye of the typhoon. I was unbriefed, new to international conferences, and assumed that I should, after quietly observing, humbly report back. It was electrifying after several prepared speeches from representatives of major countries, from India downward, to hear the rapporteur announce that 'the distinguished delegate from Hong Kong' would now address the assembly. I thanked heaven that I never stayed in my office, but had by now visited all our workplaces. After an *ad lib* description of Hong Kong's contrasting urban, rural and insular environments I described how

USD dealt with nature's and mankind's challenges, as industrialization spread its muck from piggeries, tanneries, factories and mass food preparation. I ought never again to be scared of speaking without notes to a large and intelligent audience – which is not to say that I never was. This time I seemed to get away with it. I did write a full report, of which nobody above my director took note. It would be indulgent to hope that, coupled with the forthcoming Stockholm conference, it sowed the seed that ripened into an Environmental Protection Agency after I went south. At the time I only knew one colleague who had heard of, let alone read, Rachel Carson's *Silent Spring,* and he borrowed it from me.

The pest control officer, who kept nasty reptiles in his bath, also cared for the birds and animals in the botanic garden's little zoo. Public cemeteries required watchful eyes on traditional burial grounds. The recreation division brought semi-social extra-mural responsibilities similar to those in SWD. Playgrounds and courts for ball games kept us close to the resettlement estates. The new governor MacLehose encouraged the concept of national parks.* Lifeguards did duty at the designated beaches we kept in good order. Europeans had greatly outnumbered Asians at the beach in the early 1960s, but a decade later local people began to enjoy wading, splashing, swimming and (except for most of the ladies) sunbathing. (Changing attitudes were also notable in dress: when the mini-skirt swept the western world, all were agreed that Chinese girls would never be shameless enough to abandon their frocks, let alone the unsurpassably elegant *cheong-sam*, but they spoke too soon.)

Cultural services revolved round the city hall, where more and more concerts and recitals were given, under impresario or urban council auspices. The Hong Kong Philharmonic Orchestra, from a beginning of gifted amateurs led by Dr Solomon Bard, grew into a substantially professional body with, like the Japanese orchestras, expatriate principals, becoming fewer as their back desks and pupils succeeded them. The film society and various amateur dramatic and musical groups, western and Chinese, made much use of the two auditoria, also providing conference facilities. The library offered access to books of a range and interest only available before to members and scholars of institutions. The museum and art gallery, under a Chinese who would go on to greater curatorship in America, provided exhibition spaces for permanent and travelling displays. It is no exaggeration that, despite the scepticism and

---

*I was not helped in my career by his telephoning me before his first St Andrew's ball to ask whether anyone would notice that through a packing error his kilt hose did not match his family tartan: I advised, in good faith, that there were few enough truly knowledgeable Scots around, and they would all be good-manneredly silent – but some gnome did notice and wrote to the SCMP to ask why. I was doubly ashamed though blameless, because I had mentioned to the paper's editor after HE's arrival that he was wearing an ambassador's uniform gorgets, not colonial gubernatorial, for swearing-in. It had never occurred to me that my friend would rat and print a photograph of the offending collar next to one of Trench's in the gossip column, also asking why – I was appalled and never again trusted even the most amiable of journalists.

downright resistance surrounding the concept of reviving the long demolished City Hall of Victoria's reign, not as a minor meeting place but as a cultural centre (with multi-storey car-park, another USD chore), this was the turning point of a slummy, profit-driven entrepôt becoming a world-class civilized city with (for a few more years) a fine back garden. A friend with shared interests, secretary to the HK university grants committee, was to be the moving force behind the future independent academy, the Arts Centre.

I sat in the hot seat as director and chairman of the urban council while the boss took his leave. Yet again I thought laterally. City district officers had been created and their districts defined: as before in SWD I looked at our own many boundaries. I found that not a single division, section, sub-section or service shared its outlines with another. The idea was soon accepted that Urban Service Officers should be created to co-ordinate USD services within the boundaries of each city and NT district. They would be open to applicants who were competent, regardless of initial qualification.

Nowadays it is usual for officials or employees to be given an annual appraisal of their performance and prospects. In my day this was unheard of, and only once (in about 1953, when Afo Giles had said he had rather slobbered over me, despite the *mens conscia recti*) had I ever had an inkling of what had been written in my annual confidential reports. When I first wrote initial level reports, it was never without knowing the individual. At the higher levels, I knew that the entry 'No personal knowledge' could not always be avoided. I preferred to think that silence could be damning, but that if I had anything critical to say, the subject should not have been surprised to learn it. I made it my uncomfortable duty to go to the subject's own office, often a humble place, and have a long chat: I do not suggest that no other reporting officer did the same, but one never heard of it. Reporting was indeed confidential.

We accepted an invitation from our friends of Nigeria and Turkey, now in Kathmandu, to spend local leave with them. He had while head of chancery helped Shorts of Belfast to sell a second *Wayfarer* for the personal use of the King of Nepal, and as a 'thank-you' been offered a flight to the country's westernmost airstrip with a view to walking back. We learnt of this after arrival. A hundred miles trek past the Fishtail mountain and Annapurna, slightly more downhill than uphill, took us to Pokhara and a flight back to the embassy gin and tennis that we had thought would be all. Our ex-Gurkha chaperon (the embassy cinema-operator) and five Tibetan porters were as inspiring as the Himalayan scenery. A wonderful break. Once back, friends in the American consulate-general surprised us by offering me a 'Country Leader Fellowship' to USA on our next leave: if I suggested a suitable subject to study, they would take us anywhere else attracting us. I suggested a visit to the part of the home department in Washington that dealt with America's unadmitted empire. We also mentioned friends in La Jolla and Charlotteville. There was no objection.

I was ascending the ladder of the S Andrew's Society. The chieftain was expected to present the vast and costly silver cairngorm-adorned quaich to the winner of the main Jockey Club race on S Andrew's day. This meant little to a wealthy *taipan* but would be enormous to a Staff Grade B1 officer. The quaichs came from the Asprey's of Edinburgh, Hamilton & Inches, and their value very evident: I calculated that I would be in line in a couple of years. Something to be avoided? While the secondment to the Pacific was being considered (as in last chapter's end), we continued to behave as if we would return after leave. As a follow-up to the ECAFE conference I hinted that I might attend the forthcoming first United Nations Conference on the Human Environment scheduled for Stockholm in 1972. We left USD in euphoria, cheered by a tour in a good department with good colleagues, with the possibility hovering of a fundamental change ahead while no irresistible prospect in Hong Kong itself was in the air. Much change was certain with the new governor and a new financial secretary, but the atmosphere had not yet assured me that I was wanted for what with self-satisfaction I thought I was best fitted by experience and attitude. I always wanted to conform, except when I felt like arguing with seniors who had other or standstill ideas. I was never a diplomat, and in retirement I am always having to correct a generation that assumes that the colonies were run by 'diplomats': the FCO has successfully buried any memory of a colonial office – the Westminster Abbey service before Her Majesty The Queen and Duke to commemorate the end of HMOCS with the handover of Hong Kong had little official publicity and no noticeable FCO representation, let alone HM's Government.

CHAPTER 9

Is it so Small a Thing to Have Enjoyed the Sun?

La tragedia de las islas donde faltó Salamon: esto es, la prudencia
[The tragedy of the islands where no Solomon was found: that is to say, no wisdom]
[Quoted by Robert Graves, 1950, *The Isles of Unwisdom*]

OUR LAST LEAVE from Hong Kong had been organized as if we were returning thither. We spent happy times in Kenya, where we knew the professor of medicine in Nairobi, and in the Seychelles, where we knew the governor and financial secretary in Mahé (respectively, my former boss in Kaduna, Greatbatch, and a fellow Nigerian cadet). Flamingos in one, sooty terns in the other, still fly through the clouds of memory. More thought-provoking had been my representation of Hong Kong at the UN conference in Stockholm, where I was tagged on to the UK delegation as a spare and unwanted part. The soaring sculptures in the Milles Garden, and the early 17th century warship *Vasa*, raised from the mud where she sank on her maiden voyage, were tucked away in memory against the unforeseen day when I became a museums person. Then to Bayreuth for *The Ring*, thanks to intervention at the booking office by the amiable German consul-general in Hong Kong, which Hilary anticipated with dread but found a veritable new way of life. Then to Edinburgh for the festival.

Before leave ended I had an audience with the Pacific Dependent Territories Department (PDTD) of the Foreign & Commonwealth Office (FCO), which was to loom over us. The head of department was a lady, patronizing despite not sounding well-informed. She passed me on hurriedly to the British Solomon Islands Protectorate (BSIP) desk officer, at the time a decent but gloomy fellow. I learnt little the high commissioner, Sir Michael Gass (CS Hong Kong under Trench), and my old friend from Kaduna and Okene, the financial secretary John Smith, had not already told me. The concept was firm that independence should come in a couple of years. One thing I did learn: having run a cabinet office, I presumed to ask whether there were any cabinet papers to which (with the Official Secrets Act still much respected in every level of British bureaucracy) I might be made privy, concerning policy, way and purpose for the future of the Solomons, so that I should be in no doubt of proprieties and priorities. I was looked at in horror: possibly they thought me too inferior and unimportant to be entrusted with such intelligence, but the nub of the answer was amazement that I should suppose that the future of the islands might be discussed in even a cabinet committee. They were not going to show me any documents casting light on the secretary of state's thinking, be it Crosland, Owen or whoever. Whether or not in consequence, it was discovered that, like all my past and present colleagues, I had never been PV'd ('positively vetted' to insure that I was not a spy or politically or emotionally untrustworthy or blackmailable). The colonial service had been overlooked in the tightening ructions that had followed on Philby, Burgess, Maclean *et al.* Quite a reasonable but colourless gentleman came down to Tunbridge Wells and asked me all manner of relevant or curious questions, while looking sideways at Hilary and our *ménage* without direct speech. I must have appeared loyal enough, as I never heard more. Some (far from all) of my Pacific and Hong Kong friends began to be quizzed from now on. What else was checked, of course we never knew.

We came back to Hong Kong to pack, the nitty-gritty arrangements for a secondment having come to fruition in our absence; BSIP would pay HK a suitable annual sum that would keep me on HK pensionable terms. This was after enjoying the cultural educational exchange program, which had given me a week in Washington (a most appealing, misreported city) to liaise with their black-run local government and their disguised equivalent of a colonial office; this turned out to be a set of small offices in the Department of the Interior (!) that concerned themselves with Pacific and Virgin islands, Guam and, marginally, Puerto Rico. We met more good friends, ex-Nigeria and Hong Kong, and were given trips to stay with the widow of the former editor of the *South China Morning Post* in Florida, and with the retired head of USIS in HK near San Diego: this allowed us to visit the Grand Canyon, one of the world's greatest wonders (and nightstop in Las Vegas, where we watched a large party of nuns playing the one-armed bandits in the airport). After packing we were up, up and away via Bangkok and Port Moresby to Honiara, believing that our two-year tour would cover the arrival of the Solomons at independence.

We met three points of view: one minority could not envisage a viable Melanesian nation state; another minority could agree on one thing only, that only earliest independence would introduce reality into Melanesian policy- and decision-making; and that of the many that, because it would allegedly be 1980 before the Seychelles were 'ready', and since the ethnic Fijians had been so reluctant to agree to independence when the indentured Indian immigrants (to perform the labour which the Fijians disdained, but who had failed to go home when their 'contracts' had expired) were beginning to out-number them, therefore much time would still be needed to cope with 'the Melanesian (or Pacific) Way' – in other words, their congenital refusal to be manœuvred into quick majority responses. Before 1970 an immature British Solomon Islands

Protectorate legislature had seen British heads of department in conflict across the floor with elected unofficials who, because of the dire shortage of educated laymen, included white priests, unofficial expatriates, and local civil servants junior to the expatriate officials. There was some way to go. Emerging politicians were beginning to want to take the decisions, without getting rid of all expat expertise and experience; ordinary people were not seeking to be rid of us, as long as we did not interfere with 'custom' and, most particularly, the inalienable land rights of each family 'line'. Everyone assumed that 'we' (whomsoever the expat admin was answerable to) would still protect them against foreign interference that might exploit their resources without adequately large rewards to the 'big man' who negotiated the deal.

The Western Pacific High Commission was much less grand than when it had included Fiji, the Gilbert & Ellice islands, the New Hebrides, Pitcairn, the consulate at Tonga and sundry empty atolls now merely ignored. WPHC existed on paper merely to appoint a chief justice shared by Solomons, New Hebrides and Gilberts. The BSIP's recorded population was smaller than Igbirra division, yet it was the second largest remaining colony. Guadalcanal surprised many on first acquaintance, disbelieving that although the Japanese and Americans had made such a dramatic WWII campaign in it, it had been and still was 'ours'. The tales of British admin reporting on the occupation from the mountains, with loyal islanders' support, were little known. Only those concerned knew that it had been under HBM's protection, resulting from Royal Naval interference with the 'blackbirding' of labour for the Queensland sugar fields; fewer that the Spaniards had been the first westerners to reach and name the Solomon islands, five centuries before.

After a night or two as guests in GH, noting Gass's civilized passion for orchids and for photographing them, we spent some more with Jock (and Marjorie) Bodilly, the chief justice who had been my ally as the law draftsman in Hong Kong. There was a certain aura about Jock, as he tapped away in his robes at his little typewriter on the bench; his loads had been dropped in the harbour on arrival between ship and wharf, lending a permanently salty savour to his wig and gown. Government House, the secretariat and many other offices, like the hospital, sat bravely on the seashore, facing the extinct volcanic isle of Savo and exposed to any *tsunami* that might arrive on Guadalcanal. Most residential homes sat on top of the ridges surrounding the capital, while local housing schemes nestled cosily inside the hollows. Exposed housing took advantage of the anabatic breezes which swept up from the cool seas to the mountain tops every morning, and of the catabatic breezes that poured down from the hills to the beaches towards sunset. Days without rain, however slight, were uncommon. We settled along the top of Vavaea ridge into a house on stilts, and employed a cook-houseboy called Eric. He distinguished himself at our first major dinner party, given for among others the French consul-general from Sydney (he diagnosed the wine brought from HK as Beaune, despite its rough handling and storage). Eric forgot to light the calorgas oven, that the main dish should have been roasting in, until he was told to announce that dinner was served.

Easing myself in as deputy chief secretary (replacing the title of the outmoded secretary for protectorate affairs, whose last holder had retired, leaving me gentlemanly advice and wishes), I wondered for the first time after an Afro-Asian working life whether all men were the same under the skin. Melanesians, despite superficial appearances, were totally un-African. They were not like the pagan hill tribes I had known, who had had the same but more recent experience of moving straight from stone age subsistence to mission education, competitive cash economy and technology in one very fell swoop. Here a welfare state mentality had taken some root. If west Africans had been the most loveable, and the Hong Kong Chinese the most admirable, people I had worked among, Melanesians were the most vulnerable (and unpredictable). There were marked physical differences among such small numbers – those from the western islands were very black, almost indigo; others, particularly those from Malaita, often enjoyed ginger or fair hair, sometimes enhanced with lime; some of those from Santa Isabel had very Caucasian facial features, allegedly inherited from the long departed Spaniards. Each group was intolerant of its neighbours, and violently possessive of land interests whenever a stranger affected to acquire a holding by squatting or insidiously moving in to apparently unoccupied territory, or when an expatriate element insisted upon the legalities of whatever tenancy or resource-exploitation right a piece of paper might spell out. Introspective and suspicious like many rain-forest-dwellers, though quick to return a genuine smile; sturdy like most consumers of root crops and vegetable oils; skilled hill-trekkers and bold lagoon and inter-island canoeists; decorative carvers, admirably unselfconscious about reverting to trad garb (or lack of it – *kabilato* bark-cloth g-string, and lime white decoration on face and torso) for song and dance; but graceless in deportment (their gestures, movements, postures in sitting and relaxing, strolling, greeting and quizzing, were pure pleb Brit). Yet one could not but be charmed by the way so many, rough old scrubbers as well as post-teen-age males, tucked a hibiscus flower behind an ear for show. Perhaps today's Malaitan Eagle Force and Guale Isatabu Freedom Movement terrorists still do, though they probably do not pop them into the barrels of their AK47s.

The charms of youth gave way to harder adult features in early adolescence (the women soon went to pear-shape and, unless trained for modern duties, at which they became adept, disliked activity outside the recognized family divisions of chores: but when one came to know the women who had been educated and then went on educating themselves, the Daisy Betus, Ella Bugotus, Lily Poznanskis, Elizabeth Palmers, ... the list could go on, one realized where true power and effective intelligence was to be found). Church-going had taken the place of most, not all, time-occupying rituals of the past (five main Christian denominations vied with six or seven main island groupings as a basis for national divisiveness, leaving no room for party politics based on economic theory). The emotional expenditure of head-hunting raids and nominal battles (racism, in other peoples' vocabularies) had not been sublimated into anything effective (not even the limb- and neck-breaking rugby, which sturdy youngsters embraced without first having learnt when flexible children how to bend, veer and fall without clashes between immoveable masses); and so quarrels over landholding were never definitively closed. Having no traditional stimulant of any kind (not even palm toddy, while betelnuts were a recent innovation) had left them susceptible to appalling alcoholic violence on paynights and to folly after social exchanges. There being no true equivalent in the stone age village of the simple joiner (as opposed to the élite canoe- and housepost-maker and artistic sculptor in wood with shell inlays), tailor, tinker, leatherworker or metalbeater, now it was difficult to develop technical craftsmen or small businessmen – instead, straight into the supermarket to buy readymades with inbuilt obsolescence, whether clothes, tools or even staple foods. I was assailed for talking of 'the stone age', but in truth the only metals they knew were those brought by the European explorers, settlers and military men – turning bauxite into aluminium, extracting copper and discovering tiny deposits of gold, these were all foreign innovations.

Then there was language. Under two hundred thousand souls spoke over seventy identifiable languages or major dialects. Linguists from the 'west' (mainly east in truth) looking for new research fields, and patronizing students of 'development' as a new discipline, all enjoying mixed motivations, had supported the academic legitimization of the local Esperanto: this had grown from the quicksands of Melanesian language structure and the limited illiteracy of the variety of pidgin that Chinese traders and foul-mouthed matelots had imported into the Pacific. The subject caused bloodshed between expatriates generally, and priests, intellectuals, educationists and Americans particularly, *so me fellow think think good fellow more you me lose him this fellow altogether thing belong teach him long school na church altogether belong this fellow place no more, you savvy here now eh?* By devising a simpler orthography that concealed the convoluted origin of such basic words, *tok pisin* ('talk pidgin') acquired respectability, the linguists won and it was accepted as a national language suitable for official use in the legislature.

I had always sympathized with eastern Nigerian colleagues who could not be expected to learn several hundred dialects and who found that central standard Igbo was not always adequate in Igbo areas far from Onitsha and Enugu; but then the Igbos and Efiks and Ibibio *et al* spurned pidgin for themselves after secondary school, and set about learning English at least as well as we spoke it. Since most Melanesians who spoke English officially could use it well, and since *tok pisin* was relegating historic ('heritage') tongues to extinction, while crippling the less educated by making it that degree more difficult to switch over from pidgin to an internationally understood form of English, I still regret the victory of the pidgin-worshippers and creolizers; but the academics and others who forced the pace like to claim that the indigenes made the choice for themselves. That is a respectable excuse, as it genuinely became for parliamentary institutions, but I doubt whether the alternatives were ever put to those indigenes who might have given cultural leads. My opinion is of course without worth: someone might accuse me of wanting received English to be the one world language.

Yet not distant from that non-controversy was the cry, encouraged by expatriates in academic or drop-out worlds, and indeed by one or two of HM's servants, to reject the irrelevancies of the whiteman (not of course his money, clothes, films, working hours, churches, tinned foods, government biros or internal combustion engines) and return to the golden age of *Custom*, when all was egalitarian and nobody ordered anyone about or asserted personal proprietary rights: when all was achieved by *consensus*. Consensus in an egalitarian moot was tried in the early seventies, as still to a degree under the constitution I met (founded on the inter-war London County Council, as adapted for experiments in Ceylon by Donoughmore, and in the Seychelles); this was a Governing Council which formed committees and enacted laws in public, but also met distinctly in private as a policy executive under the high commissioner's chairmanship, without ministers (whatever the pretensions of the committee chairmen towards guiding the professional directors of departments). What it meant was that everyone talked themselves dry after consulting everyone remotely concerned or completely uninterested, until an unspoken understanding of a fumbling grope after a decision emerged – which everyone was entitled to disown to-morrow. It had been thought that if the whole legislature shared responsibility, there could (and in the view of Pacific islanders and old hands alike, should) be no dominant individuals.

Still, the chairmen had to remain in Honiara to take trivial or emergency decisions: the logistics of bringing members in by sea and air from their scattered constituencies were frustrating and costly, and occasionally a committee might refuse to endorse a chairman's anticipatory decision to solve a crisis while they were absent. The successful mover of a policy in the peace and quiet of the executive might, and often did, vote against its relevant implementation by bill in the same governing council when it sat publicly as a legislature, especially where a local chairman came to preside in place of the high commissioner. This all made humble planning and administration very interesting, whatever joy it gave the social anthropologists *manqués* in certain sections of officialdom, but it had not been 'imposed'. All concerned had welcomed what they happily agreed would suit their culture by reflecting it. There was also a lack of give and take, familiar in the history of moving from bureaucratic to political control in most British dependencies, between elected members who wanted to direct departmental officials and functions in some detail, and the heads of departments who were still responsible by law and reason for how a policy should be implemented, but might still look to the chief secretary for tone, discipline and protection. It was very unlike Hong Kong, where every event of every day might be foretold before breakfast, except when the cultural revolution arrived, but it presented a respectable appearance of democracy through inaction.

The islanders did not seem to mind. Hindsight persuades me that most had squared their circle: they could live with a fundamental interpretation of their Christian denomination, side by side with their social *kastom*, switching from the love and forgiveness and neighbourliness of the one to the protective jealousy and restitution-and-compensation culture of the other without hesitation. Neither 'government', nor local councils, nor institutions of law and order, influenced day-to-day domestic actions one whit. If 'self-government' meant anything at all, it meant reversion to *kastom* without *waetman* interference. The proportion of the population who had had the exposure to white men's ways that allowed them to understand and implement European democratic practices and services, was tiny.

After a week or two I was exposed to the Pacific Way in action: I was sent to Guam in charge of two of the governing council chairmen whom I was to come to know well and care for, David Kausimae (prematurely grey, a potential chief minister, had his businesses been less confused and his roots in echt-Malaitan preconceptions been weaker) and Dr Gideon Zoloveke (Fiji-trained doctor, minister and deputy speaker to be, independent but lacking determination), to attend the annual meeting of the South Pacific Commission. This offered sights of Nauru, and Palau in the Carolines: Nauru, with all its phosphate (guano) dug out was a wasteland of coral extrusions and abandoned American motor cars (originally bought with the profits of the fertilizer), but Palau was all that a Pacific island is believed to be by those who only read romances. Guam (where America's day begins) was a pimple with an airfield full of B-52s, a Hilton and other hotels, and restaurants ranging from Mexican to French. Daily a jumbo-full of young Japanese wedding parties flew in: *en masse*, they were kitted out with tuxedos and veils, married under civil law *en masse*, given a day on the beach *en masse* and a night in the mass of bridal suites, and then back home – still cheaper than a traditional Japanese wedding, with the oriental need to invite the entire very extended family, the changes of expensive costumes and the hire of a major restaurant, let alone the priestly oversight. Once a week the Hilton put on a 'British night', with roast beef served by Chinese and Malay waiters, looking very dashing in the kilts and sporrans which suited them admirably.

My chairmen tried to socialize with other islander politicians, but did not get far. The egalitarian Melanesian 'custom' of democratic committees did little for the status of 'chairmen' when comparing notes with 'ministers'. My assessment of most FCO functionaries, based on Stockholm, was reinforced: desk officers from Whitehall regarded my companions as minor hangers-on to the UK delegation, and me as their nursemaid. The deputy under-secretary (of Commonwealth Relations origin), was not patronizing but did not try to bring them forward either. He was scrutinizing me more closely. The most depressing group to observe was the American hangers-on, persuaded that it was their duty to demonstrate how intimately they had taken to the Pacific Way, donning lava-lavas and Hawaiian shirts and purporting to dance hula travesties whenever off duty. We brought nothing of substance back from the discussions wherewith to benefit the Solomons.

I created opportunities to tour outlying districts, usually with Hilary. Nobody inducted me in anything, and a few perhaps hoped I might fall into unseen pits. Having been an interloper once, it was essential to let the dogs see the rabbit in the flesh, before rumours spread of an unsympathetic office-wallah from Hong Kong's fleshpots who would never understand what required years of indoctrination to absorb, the Pacific Way. My introduction to a Gilbertese get-together in a *maneaba* at Gizo went down well, according to our one Gilbertese administrative officer, Takoa. He was the most materially successful offspring of this minority settlement, which had been relocated here after a disaster in their homeland, before the Western Pacific was balkanized. (Gizo was a small island, HQ of the New Georgia group, on the way to Bougainville.) Eventually I would decide that Micronesians (which Gilbertese were) were the most admirable, even loveable, of the Pacific islanders I met – bred as they had been on atolls, where you could throw a cricket ball from one shore of the nation to the opposite, with no natural resources but coconuts and what the sea might offer, they became magnificent navigators in their outriggers and bounced back with vigour after calamities. They took pride in their gleaming straight black hair and had a south-east Asian tone to their flesh. Grass skirts looked natural on them.

A trip to Santa Ana, an eastern outer island off San Cristobal, which had suffered from a severe cyclone, reflected a contrast. I could not but think of Hong Kong after a typhoon: there a few days after the blow the debris had been cleared up, temporary patching-up had been done and the reconstruction already started. Here, after eighteen months, felled coconut palms had not been cleared and many traditionally built homes and 'leaf' buildings remained unrepaired because, according to a Catholic priest, they were waiting for government. He was the first RC missionary I met who did not encourage self-sufficiency and self-help, by his personal example. However one effort at community work was clearing a rough road through the bush. After experiencing the ceremonial 'challenge' several times, an alarming greeting at the village's entrance by two traditionally kitted warriors with shield and wooden spear, demanding to know who I was, why I had come, what I had brought, duly translated both ways by an interpreter, I began to get the feel of things. I envied the intimate awarenesses of those like one district commissioner (DC) of the highest quality who had been sidetracked into information and radio services (his wife took Hilary into the bush, where she was taught the names and medicinal and other uses of native plants). The grand tour of Kirakira, HQ of the Eastern district, found almost everyone from the DC downwards prostrated by squitters: alone among the inspecting party, I was fortunate not to have eaten from a bedevilled tin of fruit, and was impressed to find that 'Number Nine' (the general hospital in Honiara, so named from the ancient belly remedy of our own forefathers) had laboratory facilities adequate to diagnose the bug.

On Malaita we found the descendants of the *Marching Rule* (*maasina ruru*) anti-government movement of post-war years. Most had become respectable but argumentative legislators. We heard of the cargo cults of which so much has been written (not least those in Vanuatu, as it was not yet known, that idolized John Frum with his motor-bike, or the Duke of Edinburgh). One Malaitan variant had observed American habits and concluded that the ritual which brought cargo down from the skies to Yanks in arms had been the building of shrines over deep pits, with whitewashed stone-lined paths towards them: sadly, replica latrines brought them no more wealth than the leaf, banana stem and cornstalk control towers and windsocks beside a cleared runway brought to other cultists.

Antipodeans predominated in certain occupations, and they knew just what to expect from Poms. They did not appear to notice that on the whole the local people preferred the Poms because they were not Kiwis, and the Kiwis in turn because they were not Ozzies. I introduced myself to one stalwart Oz works tiffy, much loved for his generosity, by saying that I ought to get to know him: '*Why? I don't know about that. I mightn't like you.*' The predominance of expat wives as manageresses or counter-jumpers in shops offended me. Why should the western desire for two-income families stand in the way of training locals to do such jobs? I have already mentioned the three prevalent views on the imminence of independence, two of which were discordant with London's determination to win its freedom from the Pacific, fast.

I was offered the chieftaincy of the Caledonian Club: It seemed wiser to defer to the director of public works, whom everybody knew. Besides, he had the proper recipe for Atholl Brose, to be taken at the Burns Supper. The 'G Club', the Guadalcanal Club, where many sorrows might be drowned, offered relaxation. Here the head of special branch picked up non-Melanesian intelligence from indiscreet gossip at the bar (he also learnt about the Guadalcanal dissidents, led by the renowned Moro, from his servant, who was a member of that character's 'subversive' cult). We joined a syndicate for the club's quiz nights. We learned where to shop selectively, and how best to economize by buying excellent fresh food in the market. At work, there were economic developments to be visited and understood: coconut plantations, private and commercial, the tuna canning factory, the rice-growing scheme, logging operations, attempts at introducing cattle and mixed farming, and sea transport – requiring grants-in-aid and regiments of experts, returning not a lot of profit or local employment above semi-skilled labour.

I took a more than fatherly interest in an administrative training centre, which came to life in the hands of artist Quentin Blake's brother, from London's department of trade and industry, who had hankered after change. Much later I was to develop my own induction course for new group arrivals: whether a crowd of American Peace Corps, usually rather mature, know-all but not unwilling to learn more, or a flight of young administrative officers from UK, all heard a sermon on the favourite subjects of politics, religion and sex. The text was, 'Lay off!' Despite since Marx there being nothing that was not political, they must never, until they knew what they were doing, get involved in any political differences or concepts – the local people would work something out based on their own culture, of which newcomers were ignorant, and for a long while novices should stick firmly to answering clear questions simply, and skate past woolly inquiries. Even if God was dead in the western world, he was very alive in the Pacific, or semblances of Him, and spirits were palpable: the rivalries of denominations and the strangeness of Custom should be observed and respected, but not interfered with until the next steps towards finality were vividly mapped. Lastly, the lovely idea of Free Love *à la* Margaret Mead and Somerset Maugham should go right out of their minds: that there were, always had been and always would be, 'goings-on' was patent, but anyone embarking on an emotional or gratifying experience must accept that there were no secrets, that prudishness and intolerance were at least as common here as in our own 19th century mythology, and that tears at bedtime were frequent. Prudence and restraint were not bad recipes for overall happiness in this society. The Best of British Luck, but this was not a paradise for the indiscreet.

My elderly Ford *Executive* arrived with our heavy loads from Hong Kong; but I had had a home delivery of a Triumph *Stag*, which I had driven thousands of miles around UK for over three months, intended to replace the Ford when landed in Hong Kong – when re-routed to Honiara, it had sat in the hold of the ship in the last port of call, Kieta in Bougainville, where the Melanesian dockies had had a grand party all around it, expressing their love for the better endowed by twisting handles and mirrors off and pouring cement over the soft-top. It then sat on the wharf at Point Cruz in pouring rain before being taken into a shed, which concreted the cement nicely. Eventually the insurance (and Jerry at the garage) put most of the damage right, though hardly rendering it pristine. The nadir was when the head of customs and excise in person dug out his little book, referred to the current list prices of UK vehicles and charged me full rate on a bran new car. It was a try on, but the last thing was to pull rank to earn a (bogus) favour. He demurred at my pointing out that (never mind being more than shop-soiled) the car had been heavily used before shipping, had already lost substantially on its UK sell-on value, and was simply not new. Despite a favourable private opinion from a law officer, I swallowed and paid up. I was paying for my change of scene.

There came two other blows. The high commissioner, whom I had known and respected more than had many (resentful of interlopers) in HK, became due for retirement and rumours abounded of his replacement being a diplomat reluctantly sidetracked from the FCO mainstream. The second was that the financial secretary, who had ignited the trail to bring me to Honiara in the hope of us working together as sympathetic decolonizers, was fingered to govern the Gilbert islands – everyone had assumed that this job would go to the CS Tom Russell, which would have left his deputy in the running to succeed him. Tom was a good man, mutually loved in Melanesia, with an interest in archæology and a French wife, a quiet predecessor of John as FS, so this appointment surprised everyone, possibly even John. Yet we had made our bed, and nobody could blame John for accepting what was to become his bed of nails.

We moved into John's house on Lengakiki ridge, too broke to contribute to his past expenditure on a small swimming pool, enjoying a view not unlike that to Diamond Point in Honolulu, a guest house and a separate office-study in the ground-orchid strewn garden. A lime tree miraculously fruited all the year round. Nothing had (or needed) a lock. Hilary rapidly tired of coffee mornings, even of painting expeditions, although creative weekend mornings spent with expat and Melanesian friends chopping up a half carcase of a *bulamakau* (beef) hanging from a garden tree, to be shared among several deep-freezes, could hardly be repeated too often. She encouraged an American nun, the protectorate's sole physiotherapist, to seek a furlough after seven years' unbroken service. This brought us closer to the medical establishment: the nation had a single physician specialist and a single surgeon specialist, mentioned in our medical chapter 1.

My own professional interests were soon challenged. The establishments experts had devised a new structure, with unskilled labour at the bottom and potential permanent secretaries at the top: in between would be nine 'levels' on identical salaries side-by-side throughout the departments. A senior medical officer would earn the same as a senior education officer. This made sense to egalitarian Melanesians, but created psychological difficulties for hierarchical expats with home-based ideas of ranking rival professions. We eventually made it acceptable. The Public Service Advisory Board was less tractable. A common error was repeated in seeking an adviser on how to create a new body, and then appointing that adviser as the first chairman. The worst of all worlds produced neither a hard-working full-time chairman of a non-executive public service commission with a stenotypist aide, nor a part-time chairman of local standing supported by a strong executive secretary.

My position as virtual manager of the administrative service was clarified, with the establishment secretary as gofer and chief secretary as court of appeal. I wrote personally to every AO. They had not been cohesive, nor were relations with colleagues in professional departments always free of friction. They were all to have direct informal access to me. I wanted an end to stereotypes of those who saw 'development' as inconsistent with 'law and order', district work as antithetic to secretariat responsibility, 'open-ended progress' as an escape from 'tight-fisted control', 'admin' as superior to 'departments'; I preached 'Generalism'. We were *all* trainers and localizers, lack of material resources demanded harder and longer work. The nine-tenths of the people who did not live in Honiara created most wealth and spent little of it. Future industrialization would not all be round Point Cruz harbour, even allowing for ease of export distribution. Success in ambition must not be equated with a posting to Honiara. There was the imminence of some having to be advisers and mentors to novice politicians and ministers in charge of portfolios.

Eventually I learnt from Hong Kong, before Honiara knew, that Gass's successor was to be Donald Luddington. He had been on the same Devonshire course as myself, but gone straight to Hong Kong, where he had latterly been secretary for home affairs: on exco, he believed that he had irritated governor MacLehose by some independence of thought, and had earned the Irishman's rise which this promotion involved by being got out of the way. Whether this was true or no, it was a relief that he was not a diplomat, but a friend, a man of rectitude and integrity, to whom I could be frank about everything and everyone. He went down well, approachable and informal, ran with the Hash Hound Harriers and adapted, as a son of the Raj though often mystified, to the Melanesians who were so unlike the Cantonese.

Much of our first year was distracted from the march to independence by the imminence of a Royal Visit. Her Majesty and the Duke of Edinburgh were to be accompanied by Princess Anne and her new husband Capt Mark Phillips, and by Earl Mountbatten. The Royal Yacht *Britannia* would spend a week in the Solomons, on her way to Indonesia. My rôle was fulcrum: I alone sat automatically on all the committees that oversaw every separable item of the regal progress through the islands in 1974 from Star Harbour in the east to Gizo in the west. The same ideas were shared by every group, when arguing about what entertainment or display should be offered to the visitors at each stage: there would be custom dancing and creators of local crafts would show examples of their work. It was sad to hear, whenever a hint was dropped that Her Majesty would already have seen something very similar, not least in the New Hebrides which She would have just left, a rather forlorn admission that this was all that they knew to do. We felt it wrong to suggest alternatives, which would have looked unnatural. Fortunately there were the pockets of Polynesians and Micronesians whose contributions introduced contrasts. The advance party from the Palace, including the Private Secretary Sir Martin Charteris and the Assistant Private Secretary Bill Heseltine, could not have been more helpful, and did not bat a eyelid when we suggested that 'island dress' (colourful shirts above sulus, lava-lavas, trousers or even shorts) might be all that even local VIPs could stretch to at functions, and that Europeans should stop short at naval 'Red Sea rig' as unostentatious 'evening dress' (open neck short-sleeved white shirts, with cummerbunds and black trousers). For three weeks before the arrival I was constantly catching planes at desperately early hours to Gizo, Kirakira, Yandina and Auki, with rough sea trips (5 hours each way) to Star Harbour in the east, for plans and rehearsals.

Hilary had her share, standing in as a Dignitary at sundry rehearsals, and acting as gofer-to-be in all the GH functions, lending our amiable houseboy Ben Lison (Eric parted company when we moved house) to boost the domestic staff, and instructing island Youth in use of knives and forks for the Youth luncheon. There was to be a visit to a Typical Village outside Honiara where a Tree would be Planted, and she held the spade as a Lady-in-Waiting. There was a grand major display at Lawson Tama playground, where the young local officer who would oversee the comings and goings on the actual day, confessed at the last minute that he had not been following the timetable very closely, and no participants' running over had been cut short, because he had no handwatch, never had had one (on the drenching day itself he played hooky, but his deputy came up trumps, with a watch). The wet weather alternative programmes received the sketchiest of attentions, giving the Duke several occasions to speak with his famous impropriety – 28 years later his main memory was of John Gina's bamboo band, tuned organ-like bamboo pipes banged over the hollow tops with flip-flops).

When the real thing started, Luddington and I joined the DC Eastern by plane, and took the long boat trip to *Britannia's* first landfall. The DC was

Lord Louis, with his minder, meets old soldiers (Princess Anne talks to war hero Jacob Vouza).

Francis Talasasa, the senior local administrative officer: he had gained his reputation by being the only Solomon islander to go to Oxford for a Devonshire course. The barge sailed in from the Royal Yacht, the crew performing their boat-hook drill magnificently, and we guided the family and Lord Louis to their places, accompanied by Master of the Household Sir Peter Ashmore, Flag Officer Royal Yachts Admiral Trowbridge, the Duke's Treasurer Lord Rupert Nevill, the Duchess of Grafton (related to Philip Smiley, one of our junior contract AOs) *et al*. The occasion was noisy but fun. Donald was given a cabin on the yacht to return to Honiara: I sailed through the night and caught a plane to arrive in Honiara just in time to decide that the rain had lifted enough to stick to the dry weather programme, to change into uniform, and to watch *Britannia* sail into the harbour for the line-up of local dignitaries' welcoming hand-shakes on the wharf, with police bugles impressively blown. The visitors looked relaxed and happy. The islanders were subdued, but equally happy.

On the way to Government House Lord Mountbatten stopped off to honour the cenotaph, where ex-servicemen were lined up. It was striking to see the contrast between him upright on duty, asking questions about medals worn and showing enthusiasm and nostalgia in equal quantity, and his sudden shrinking into a hunched old man whenever he thought he was out of eyesight (as the minder, I didn't count). *Noblesse oblige* in action. He remembered where

81 West African Division had been. Meanwhile, the workers had arrived at GH for Hilary to welcome, a queer lot: the Queen's Page (a podgy 45), the Duke's Valet, the Yeoman of the Baggage, the dressers and hairdresser. They did not think much of GH, with only five bedrooms: Donald and Garry had banished themselves to the junk room with Hilary and the ADC, to keep out of the way, but would now have also to accommodate the Equerry for pre-tea naps, since he could not share with the two ladies-in-waiting (all would sleep on board at night, fortunately). Hilary offered the workers 'bush lime' (freshly pressed limejuice), but supposing her to be the housekeeper they demanded gins and tonics (at 10 *a.m.*), asking how she liked the job in this wild place, and getting progressively pie-eyed. The Page made a fuss over a large cake, which a loyal wife had baked and iced, in the hope of it being acceptable by HM. Hilary thought a Lady-in-Waiting might take it on board, but 'Hit his usally the Page oo takes a cake hinto the Queen'. A large GH saucepan was duly commandeered and it was embarked within it.

The rain returned, and the real Visitors set off for King George VI secondary school, Prince Philip and Captain Mark spurning umbrellas, to see what Youth had to show by way of sports, communal activities and social commitment. The highlight was the performance by the secondary schoolboys, our intellectuals in training, of the rather rude *bilikiki* dance, wearing *le minimum* and leaning on sticks, while imitating (to western eyes) apparently copulating birds. *All* the visitors returned soaked to the skin, and the Duke inquired ironically after the wet weather programme's state. There followed, after changing clothes, the youthful lunch. Hilary managed just in time to stop the soup going round before the soup plates had been set, and the youngsters were entranced to find unknown VIPs asking them questions which they could answer.

Hilary and I were among the forty guests to dinner in the Yacht, and the two hundred at the following reception. Most of the ladies envied Princess Anne's swanlike neck and complexion at close quarters, but what impressed those near enough to overhear, if not be party to, her conversation was the depth of her homework and awareness, that demonstrated a highly intelligent young lady with well-formed views (a generation later, she still remembered the rain, but also much else). She talked animatedly with Tom Russell (who had been here for 26 years) about Melanesian 'custom', and regretted the mission influence that militated against costume and tradition in favour of 'Mother Hubbard' dress. The Queen, who changed for the reception, told me an amusing reminiscence of Haile Selassie during her youth and, discussing the afternoon's entertainment, said that when she wrote home, nobody would believe that everyone was sitting up to their knees in water (I know one doesn't repeat royal chatter unless one is a minor politician or gossip columnist, but this is harmlessly human). Lord Louis's homework had picked up the biographical note (my work) on Hilary, which led to her discussing the medical officer on HMS *Whelp* in Ceylon with Prince Philip and Trowbridge, whom they had all known: she refrained from reminding HRH that he had kissed her at New Year after she had (spectacle-free) mistaken him for her temporary fiancé in wartime Colombo. In the middle of the function, HM having apparently accepted the cake, the Page tried to return the saucepan to Hilary, who politely asked him to wrap it up and hand over at the head of the gangway when we disembarked. I am told that I received a huge paper bag and went ashore as if I had nicked some of the relics from the original *Victoria & Albert* yacht, but the memory is blank.

Next day Princess Anne opened the Honiara Fair, most of the stands of which were the work of expatriates. Then came a flying trip to Auki, HQ of Malaita island, where Princess Anne's shoes sank into the soggy ground while doing the rounds of crafts stalls in between dancing displays, and the 'mud men', who had worn loincloths as well as red mud and equally muddy balls on strings for the rehearsals, appeared prominently starkers (strung balls apart) for the real event. I explained quietly to Charteris that this was not what I had expected, and was reassured that our Visitors had all taken it in their stride and with the best of humour.

We were bidden on board for lunch before the Yacht departed for Indonesia, and a prize-giving was held in the ship's library at the last minute, in ascending order of seniority – starting with a Royal Victorian Medal for a police driver. I followed the CP, and was asked why the crowd at Lawson Tama had laughed so uproariously when the Polynesians from Bellona had performed their dry land canoe-paddling dance. 'I suppose it's like the English sometimes laughing at the Scots, Ma'am, foreigners are funny!' Then I received a signed photograph of the Queen and Duke from Prince Philip ('for overseeing us all', as he grinned up at me), and 'I should like you to have the MVO Fourth Class' from HM. I duly and sincerely bobbed at Princess Anne and Lord Louis, and after doing the neck bow at HRH and HM, backed out into the corridor to sign up to the Order. Tom Russell followed me and was rewarded with a very substantial silver desk inkstand with the royal cipher. Donald was honoured but not knighted. The flight home was subdued but relaxed: we were all exhausted.

Tom soon left us to govern the Cayman Islands, presenting different problems as a financial haven from what he would have faced in the Gilberts. He had an emotional send-off, chief minister in tears; matters were not made easy by the lady museums adviser, who turned up at the wharf to have his cases inspected because she had been told that Tom had collected artefacts that were prohibited from export and should be conserved in the museum. Tom did not have to display the presents he had been given by willing and sorrowing islanders, but it had been embarrassing and, to the locals, incomprehensible. I inherited his job but preferred to stay in the house where we were happy.

We were introducing a new constitution to try out cabinet government, while contriving to keep the 'grass roots', to which everyone perpetually appealed, concerned. Our politicians had adopted the governing council arrangement because it was made to seem familiar. Conceding that it did not work for day-to-day government across a thousand miles of ocean, now they agreed to experiment with the cabinet model, enjoying the sweets of ministerial privilege as seen in other countries. It was not imposed; they wanted to try it, and we all recognized it as indeed an experiment. I sought from London a copy of any fresh model of the cabinet manual ('Notes on Administrative Procedure') which in various forms, based on Sir Humphrey's version for Number Ten, was used in British colonies approaching self-government *en route* to independence within the commonwealth. My reward, doubly interesting, was a copy of the very manual I had myself drafted for the executive council of northern Nigeria some sixteen years before. I felt free to rewrite it with local flavour, making clear to all privy to it that, grass roots notwithstanding, Melanesian village-style politics were not going to work so long as donations from other countries remained necessary to keep the budget balanced and provide the capital investment.

The Governing Council had become unsatisfactory to everyone before its second full year of authority ended. Some officials with experience of ministerial constitutions elsewhere, advising and listening to the more ambitious of the committees' chairmen who knew something of other emergent nations, had recommended the abandonment of 'consensus' and the introduction of at least a superficial ministerial system. Yet 'consensus' meant different things to different cultures. The proposal would not abandon the innate insistence on every Melanesian big man's right to change his mind, regardless of existing commitments; unanimity declared on a topic at one meeting could not be relied upon for long – the short-term pull of kinship would still encourage wilful withdrawals during following days or weeks. Over time any mass group of islanders might change direction, and throw up new spokesmen to voice a fresh view that had been developing.

The UK authorities, for all the briefing they received from 'the men on the spot', never understood, or conceded the limits to on-the-spot officials' power to steer events. They were desperate to speed disengagement from what one Whitehall mandarin described as a 'potty little place', but were shy of openly violating the policy that it was 'the people's wishes' (not pressure by jealous countries with ersatz ethics, or by artificial international institutions with malignant tissues) that dictated the pace of withdrawal. In the 1970s it was true that few islanders wanted independence, and that most elected representatives only wanted internal self-government, leaving defence and foreign affairs to a governor, who could still be blamed if anything went wrong. Strangers, endorsing stereotyped nationalist leaders in earlier decolonizations, powerful and immoveable at the head of cultural movements (usually tribal, seldom political or economic as understood in democracies), identified local equivalents in Melanesia: vertigo overtook them whenever the system without warning produced dissimilar replacements. Our Solomon Sunaone Mamaloni (of whom more later) was neither Nkrumah nor Nyerere nor Manley, and certainly no architect of autarky. He was a promising government clerk who had crossed into resentful politics.

There was a flaw in most westerners' view of the new system, that survives till to-day: observers, most participants, and probably the draftsmen themselves, fell into the trap of looking at superficial similarities and calling the result a 'Westminster system'. The truth was that we potentially had what was as close to Melanesian methodology as most formalized attempts might ever be, because of the factor which made it utterly unlike Westminster – *all* the MPs voted in a secret successive knock-out ballot for the *bigman*, the chief minister, with no scope for partisan 'whipping' whatever. 'Party' leaders as such were irrelevant.

Despite indigenous attempts and some uitlander encouragement, party systems, as the west has come to endure them, had dismally (or happily?) failed to emerge: not least because, with a co-operative decolonizing administration, there could not yet be much difference of opinion on policies in a culturally homogeneous, religiously-inclined, undeveloped country – only bitter landbased group rivalries. The appointment of chief minister could not be predicted, even after the constituency results were in, nor need he be leader of a recognizable group of like-thinkers. More importantly, his cabinet would be treated by the house as its servants, put in to help the chief to look after day-to-day routine and local difficulties, but bound to consult *before* suggesting any innovation, to an extent incredible to 'Westminster-orientated' theorists or British-trained civil servants (Churchill wandered in this direction in romantic parliamentary musings). The concept behind the committee system had not changed. This was nothing wrong in a slow-moving society, except to authoritarians who believe that Governments Should Govern or Make Way for Those who Will. Damage follows once the 'Westminster' misconception insists that there must be an identifiable formal 'Opposition', a potentially wholly alternative government. Everyone takes part in choosing the chief minister; it only requires a shifting clique to produce an *ad hoc* leader of an opposition.

Technical advisers were critical of the administration and mission influences for not imposing some 'discipline'. The administrative 'scaffolding' suspected that it was being charged with having failed to alter the national psyche to suit alien preconceptions. Nowadays the question is asked in a different form – whether to-day's faults are not those of the former 'colonial masters'. In 1973 a missionary, Canon Fox, who had regarded the Solomons as his only home since the turn of the century, was invalided out, crying 'The trouble with this country has been second-rate missionaries and third-rate administrators!' The root cause lay elsewhere: until the overseas aid scheme came into force, boosted by British recurrent grant-in-aid funding of capital expenditure, policy had always been that 'colonies' should be self-supporting. Aid from a 'nanny state' weakens initiative and resolve.

A main achievement in the Solomons was chairing, not the housing authority nor the scholarship selection committee, which had come with the job, but the localization committee. This had to be imposed, resistance being too strong. In my first spell as acting CS, during Gass's final leave and Tom's occupation of GH, I decided to summon the whole BSIP 'senior service' to the town cinema, everyone who could not show a convincing excuse. There was a groundswell of grumbling from sundry white faces torn away for a spell from their files, their classes, their machines or their scientific data, but I was determined to grasp the mule by its tail. With the FS and AG, we spelt out in clear terms the simple fact that world and UK policy required that the Solomons be fitted for independence without delay. Too many people, including Solomon islanders themselves, would regard that as a sham if the top posts were still occupied by expatriates. We would now be moving quickly in the direction of a ministerial-led form of democracy, and although expert advice should always be the best, and for the time being some levels of technical or specialist qualifications might remain beyond the reach of local officers, we must plan without a moment's more delay to replace expatriates in senior positions, and set about the training of Solomon islanders to take over the jobs for which as yet no local replacement could be envisaged. Unfriendly correspondents led me to be reported in *PIM* (The *Pacific Islands Monthly*, published in Oz) as 'the Hatchet Man'. One of our more bolshy local administrators, Francis Saemala, afterwards said, 'There is hope at last.'

There was certainly this committee, appointed in October 1973, represented by two governing council chairmen and a back-bencher, a senior labour inspector, and two from the private sector (including the only expatriate besides its chairman, me). It regularly worked its way through every post in every department, spelling out guidance to parallel moves and possibilities in the churches and commerce. Its 123 pages were published in October 1974, with forward detailed plans to cover ten years, past independence. It still reads well, and with sincerity: its senior secretary was a manpower planning officer who had married a local girl, and who spoke of his 'line'; he had married into Melanesia, and not she out of it. One of the well-known tribe of file-handlers who accept too many minuted commitments for much ever to get done, he was locked up for days at a time in my garden gazebo.

While constitutional change was being engineered, radical reform began of local government. The enthusiasm of generalist administrators for devolution was diluted by the reluctance of centripetal colleagues glued to planning desks, and warmly opposed by doubting technical services, suffering well-founded fears of subsequent inefficiency. A familiar colonial argument reappeared, between those who believed that no local government would accept its true responsibilities unless the district commissioner were abolished, and those who insisted that the central government must have its prefect in the field, as a friendly mouthpiece for the cabinet and capital, but also as a security longstop. Although treated in face of revenue and manpower shortage as substitute for an independent magistrate, the DC was to survive until shortly after independence as an equivocating 'government agent', an unfortunate term inherited from Nkrumah's Gold Coast. In this capacity he was the first clerk to his district's local council.

In late 1974 the governing council was reconstituted into a council of ministers and legislative assembly. The high commissioner was now the governor of the Solomon Islands. He continued to preside over the council and, although the assembly elected the chief minister (the CM then recommending the ministers whom the governor should appoint), and although as in most colonies the ministers met 'in caucus' to discuss matters out of gubernatorial earshot before cabinet, he remained as much prime in constitutional practice as had the pre-Walpole monarchs. He might dream of acting only on unsolicited advice but, given that ministers were chosen less on merit than to give voice in policy-making to every district and to each church denomination, it could not be otherwise. Coupled with the local culture, this did nothing to reduce confusion among visiting dignitaries who assumed that a 'chief minister' was not merely *primus inter pares*; or among local people who assumed 'the chief' to be somebody chieftainlike, which his own elected colleagues would not wish to recognize; or among the legislative assembly who (having been elected as a governing council) regarded themselves as being the government. Of greater import to the administration was the integration of sundry former colonial departments into a smaller number of ministries; such had been the advance in senior localization already, after my committee's activity, that half the permanent secretaries were Solomon islanders.

Another success was minor indeed. The FCO conceived that HMOCS might be absorbed into the diplomatic service. Three inspectors travelling the globe discussed equivalent comparisons with a meeting of us AOs. The governor of Hong Kong could not be equated with the ambassador to Washington, so must be grade 2. CS HK must be grade 3, and governor Solomons barely made 4. Once permsecs were inserted, district commissioners would be lucky to make grade 7, or 'executive officer'. I pointed out that like was not being compared with like. Apart from the diplomatic skills required of expatriate advisers to local ministers and local governments, governors and DCs had responsibilities that no ambassador ever had to exercise: when the natives became unfriendly, a post put up its shutters and telexed reassurances to London – I would personally have to join the CP and organize the restoration of peace, find out who had started the trouble, take action to avoid recurrence, and only when it was over have to get out my one-time pad, and with the governor encode the report to London, because we could not afford telex and had no PV-ed coding officer. The DC in his district was similarly placed, with fewer resources. This would not deter London from blaming us for not having prevented it happening in the first place. My people gave me a unique round of applause.

Luddington and I were in no doubts of 'what London wanted'. The embarrassing Anguilla crisis had seen London bobbies restoring order after a tiny internally self-governing colonial government had induced a chaos which the governor had no remaining powers to quell. Henceforward there must be no prolonged half-way houses to complete independence, no more governors carrying superficial responsibility on the Crown's behalf but constitutionally powerless to intervene with political or economic decisions or to enforce law and order. The 'reserved powers', to certify expenditure and to control security, must be retained until the firm date for independence had been negotiated, not more than one year ahead (preferably six months), during which the formal hand-over through creation of independent institutions could be completed. This made good sense. It was not what most islander politicians wanted. Their people wanted more aid – but the politicians wished to supervise its expenditure without strings; their people wanted more expatriate help – but the politicians only sought it from consultants and subordinate experts among whom they might pick and choose; their people trusted most overseas officials, and longed for the reassurance of protection against unforeseeable dangers – yet they the politicians themselves were perhaps not sorry to have the security of a whipping boy should anything go wrong in distribution of resources or in public service management; their people's weak fears were occasionally resented – but the politicians could not ignore them. The British (*sc* the FCO) target was 'to get its independence from the Pacific', but no Solomon islands reputations would be made by pushing at an open door.

A slow consensus had distilled that, provided devolution was made of the more domestic powers to local governments, ministerial responsibility did after all suit their geography and development need. Now, in exchange for withdrawal of official participation in cabinet and legislature, and transfer of public service control to an executive commission, a general election should take place in 1975. At this election the question of independence would be for the first time put to 'the people', thus satisfying the needs of UK parliament and UNO: full internal self-government (ISG) would follow, but tied to a conference to settle the details of independence, which would come within a year of ISG. Now that Mr Whitlam had determined to take Australia out of Papua New Guinea, it was hoped that electors or their representatives would be unable to deny a latent wish for self-determination. Independence by 1976 seemed probable (and my return to Hong Kong).

A ministerial visit in January 1975 upset this apple cart. Miss Joan Lestor, a lady given without warning to lying flat on the GH grass (to recharge her batteries), insisted on talking to the chief minister, Solomon Mamaloni, alone, without her own FCO advisers or suspect HMOCS officials present, 'as one politician to another.' Solomon was intriguing: founder-leader of the nebulous People's Progress Party; he had been a secretariat officer and clerk to the legislature, but thinking himself ill-treated had resigned and taken to politics and vague business deals. He liked to puzzle Europeans by giving a pseudo-Masonic tickling hand-shake, and had christened one of his eleven children Audy Murphy Mao Tse Tung. He had an unfair share of Pacific *mana* (a strange charismatic power), and could be charming, mulish or antagonistic at a moment's notice. He had had a modest majority in the final ballot, and created occasional reshuffles under pressure from back-benchers, appointing a self-styled deputy leader of the opposition as a minister without any eyebrow lifting. He cycled regularly between euphoria and depression, with sudden urges to demonstrate by instant directive who was in charge, and slow lapses into long sulks of inept silence: his major talent was that of many otherwise talentless but lucky public figures – he was an actor: every utterance and gesture was considered for its effect in the rôle currently played on a stage set by the desultory sweep of minor events. Hence, with a fluent tongue, he was more superficially impressive than his colleagues, and there have been those who thought him the only man for the job in the culture I have been limning. They forget that until his first fall, no one else had the chance to try. For all his impish charm, his legpulling and his common touch with ordinary folk, he had no original ideas, no team-leadership; he was unpredictable, and above all untrusted – he never consulted those Solomon Islanders at his own level whom he should have, and wanted to take all the decisions that constitutionally he could not, while misjudging or ignoring those he could. He reacted to events, and then pretended he had engineered them. A few expatriates believed him. But he had *mana*. (We were to get another actor, in the following chapter.)

Asked by Lestor what he really wanted, Solomon replied, 'Internal self-government, that's all'. 'Is that all? Of course you may have it, before the year's end, it's the next step anyway'. Thus was the unsigned deal duly reported to us, and all reference to assumed policy (as known to us), involving the need for a proven success of the ministerial system, an election and a strict timetable, was out of the window. When these assumptions were raised, elected members (especially ministers) could not see why they should risk their seats before the statutory end of the legislature in 1977, and jibbed at having the twelve months imposed on them, even when shiftily reinterpreted as a flexible guideline which might stretch to eighteen months to complete technical negotiations of international treaties and such. The eighteen months were treated by the islanders as the (itself stretchable) norm, UK understandings with Honiara leaders became more confused, and we in the middle, the admin, became, shall we say, unsettled. Not that London apologized for their minister's failure to stick to the brief.

After some disquiet, a cross-section delegation visited London in May 1975, without any line pre-agreed among themselves, and under criticism for not having previously sought any mandate from the electorate or legislature. It accepted a form of ISG, in which the governor would cease to preside in cabinet and a minister would replace the financial secretary; the deputy governor (former CS) and attorney general would remain, although ceasing to vote, in the legislature, but the public service (with police, security, external affairs and defence) would remain 'reserved'. The departure of the deputy governor from council and assembly, and handover of the public service (subject to powers of a public service commission) would be provided for on an undefined future day, theoretically about six months in advance of independence. The communiqué rather weakly indicated that 'in HMG's view' an election should precede independence. This was seized on by jealous politicians who had not been in the delegation, and such a commitment was grudgingly accepted. There was no more thought of this being an experiment. Ordinary people woke up to the fact that their leaders were discussing imminent independence at all. This ISG was diluted, and puzzled the administration; it increased the determination of leading ministers (and of some official advisers) that in the subjects no longer 'reserved' the governor and *ex officio* members of cabinet and assembly should only 'speak when spoken to'.

A later ministerial visit happened in September 1975, when Luddington was on leave and I was for a while in Government House. Ted Rowlands was Parliamentary Under-Secretary of State, a small Welshman with no need for sleep, accompanied by DUS and desk officers. He had a broad briefing from me (it still makes sense to me in 2003), coloured with some socio-anthropology, and seemed to accept it, but expressed the desire, like Lestor, to have a *tête-à-tête* with Mamaloni alone. I sent word up to the chief minister, and was flabbergasted to hear back that if Rowlands wanted to talk, he could come

A visitor to greet was Michael Somare from Papua New Guinea (Solomon Mamaloni glowers).

up to the CM's house himself. The DUS said that protocol and courtesy required the local man to attend on the minister closer to the Crown. I asked the secretary to the CM and council of ministers to use sweet reason. He came back with an adamantly repeated refusal. I thought it better to come clean, and explained the situation to Rowlands myself. Rowlands demurred; not too pleased, he agreed to go up in the GH *Jaguar*. I never had a report of the discussion, but it was clear to me that the desk officers were unsympathetic and indeed thought ill of a 'governor' who could or would not make a small time politician do his will.

A curious new element intruded. Some ministers' children were playing with strange new coins, bearing the head of the chief minister. They were traced to Solomon Mamaloni's house, and a tangled tale emerged. A small commercial Californian mint, the Letcher Mint, had sent its agent to Papua New Guinea, hoping to gain the contract to mint that country's new coinage on independence; it had gone so far, apparently, as to design specimens with various local wildlife embossed on the reverse. The approach had been rejected, but the same designs (of birds and beasts non-native to the Solomons) had been amended, now bearing the head of Mr Mamaloni on the obverse.

Our chief minister had signed an ostensibly binding agreement with the agent, empowering Letcher to issue commemorative self-government currency, and apparently committing the Solomon Islands to use the same mint for an independence issue also. The samples had been passed down as toys. All was unknown to the Minister of Finance, still less to his officials who were advising on deals with other mints after actual independence. This secretive agreement was incapable of fulfilment in any event. The Solomons still used Australian currency, and no legal or statutory authority yet existed for it to issue legal tender of its own in any form. Solomon had deceived himself into thinking that the profits, if put into a separate account outside of Treasury control, would have paid for a new parliament house: they might perhaps have reached to purchasing a mace and some furniture.

Rumours spread of pay-offs, and all eight ministers formally repudiated the agreement while accepting the possibility of a suit for heavy damages against Mamaloni or their government: they also forced his resignation. Ministers, even Willie Betu the calmly intelligent finance minister, themselves lacked the understanding or organization to explain to the puzzled Legislative Assembly members, let alone an ignorant and bemused public, the enormity of Mamaloni's stupidity. More disturbingly, they failed to agree on nomination of an alternative; at least one only wished to teach him that he was not an independent executive president, but most paid for their unwonted boldness. Mamaloni's rivals in the ragtag opposition failed to arrange a nomination of their own, and the only new candidate formally submitted was a very nice schizophrene who had just won a by-election with a mandate from the Almighty to lead the nation into the paths of righteousness. A fortnight later Mamaloni was re-elected by 18 out of the 24, abstentions accounting for the majority (having only won a year before by 14-10 in a sixth knock-out ballot). Betu was one of the only two former ministers to have their names submitted to the governor for the new cabinet, which included the more effective members of the notional opposition. Presumptive party affiliations and overt animosities disappeared on the promise of office. For the time being Mamaloni was muted and earned little deference from his new People's Alliance Party, which now embraced his former nominal opponents in the even more nebulous Alliance Party.

A formal inquiry was necessary, which lasted for four days in May 1976. The findings were less full than they should have been; the public remained confused. The crisis had meant that the budget session could not be held before the year's end, that no moneys had been voted for public expenditure from 1 January 1976, and that the first promised instalment of ISG could not be taken as expected in 1975, not until the governor had (uniquely) exercised his reserved powers to certify sufficient expenditure to keep recurrent services funded until a budget was properly passed. During that New Year's Day holiday there was a demonstration by Honiara labour *against* the grant of ISG. Garry Luddington and my Hilary had Hilary's car frighteningly surrounded by angry young men, banging the sides and windows and daring my wife to drive them down.

The riot was put down by the police, using tear gas for the first time. It was unexpected to hear Solomon islanders cheering the police for this violent action: 'We didn't think we had real police, now we know we do!' Nor did it seem according to the imperial book that trades unions would oppose constitutional progress. The Solomon Islands General Workers' Union (SIGWU)'s leadership had been taken over by a 23 year-old Malaitan (Langalanga) graduate of the university of Papua New Guinea. He had come home, having been taught the evils of multi-national corporations (lumping the Commonwealth Development Corporation in with Unilever and Taiyo Fishing), and bound for a political life. Bartholomew Ulufa'alu's protest was against ISG under the current leadership, and his power base was already extending into the Honiara town council and the legislature. He would mature over the years. Next day Sir Donald (as he had belatedly become) signed the notice bringing ISG into force, losing the power to certify any future expenditure, except what might be essential to maintain internal security and defence.

A broad-based travelling circus of Solomon Islanders was set up in September 1975 to consult the grass roots on a form of independence constitution. Expatriate involvement was restricted to legal advice by independent and (some said) inadequate support from the Commonwealth Secretariat. Although some British opinion was known to favour an executive presidency, the committee reported a preference for no radical change. Consensus precluded internal revolution: retention of the monarchy, with a Solomon islander representing the Crown, suggested minimal change from the *status quo*. This reassured villagers who were unashamed of their need for protection, and suspicious of where the benefits of independence would fall, and any others who valued the British connexion or found African one-party republicanism repugnant. The report was perfunctorily debated in April. Reservations were common about landholding by non-Melanesians and citizenship for mixed-race or non-Melanesians, matters that obsessed many. The interesting function of the more senior colonial bureaucrats, by way of hint, gentle prod, and assumption of contrariness, was to maintain the momentum towards the freedom which most unelected Solomon islanders, grant-aided, defenceless, remembering 1941-45, and lacking in technical resources (though not in overt self-possession), foresaw as dangerous.

The general election followed, in which independence and the report were nominal issues but, like the coin affair, ignored through lack of understanding. The district administration did what it could to explain. I sat in on open-air meetings in various islands, and could not come home comforted. As in Nigeria, the DC was inhibited from giving the specific advice which was demanded, such as whom it would be safest to vote for, or can't we do without all this change? 177 candidates stood for 38 seats, on local issues, not on constitutional independence. The only party to campaign was SIGWU's Nationalist Party, and only in urbanized wards. Two-thirds of the new house, unsurprisingly, was new, the election having again been one of multi-candidate personality selection. After seven successive ballots in July, the assembly chose by five votes a new, educated, chief minister, whom I had met in my first days as a rather sad 31-year-old administrative officer in Malaita, Peter Kenilorea. Unopposed in his constituency, he formed a mainly inexperienced but hardworking new cabinet (the only 'passenger' was soon replaced). His predecessor formed an opportunist 'opposition' with the trades union leader who had opposed his own leadership on 1 January. The balance was held by a predominance of independents, who supported the cabinet so long as it consulted back-benchers and the new local councils before making decisions. This Melanesian stasis, which created a form of stability while outsiders prophesied collapse, together with the impossibility of predicting who would be returned at any election, let alone become chief minister, should have killed the solecism of describing the constitution as a 'Westminster system'. As we have seen, it did not. Outsiders do find Melanesian politics hard to analyse.

With the British alone anxious to hurry matters, the mercurial opposition had some success. The constitutional recommendations were blocked by a lengthy, ill-disciplined series of demands that they be referred back to the grass roots whence they had come. Amendments to land tenure legislation were blocked because the subject was too sensitive. There was a threat not to let the budget through. This was abandoned when the independents discovered that the governor's powers, on which they might have quietly fallen back; had lapsed. Nevertheless the prospect in 1975, that 1976 would see a conference leading to independence early in 1977, vanished. The opposition failed to bring the government down, and the government failed to get its measures through, without threatening to resign and force a new election. One could picture the Whitehall heads wagging – surely the chaps in local charge could break the log-jam, even though they had no powers and the leaders at loggerheads could not control their followers? Who would be a governor with such people breathing down his neck? The opposition did not embody an alternative government either. The independents, more numerous than either the cabinet or the self-styled *ad hoc* opposition, could have brought the government down by a two-thirds vote of no confidence. They might not then have supported any 'opposition' leader in a bid to be prime minister of an 'independent' cabinet – they might well have re-elected the fallen chief minister to nominate an alternative team. By standing firm the cabinet gained confidence, while the opposition lost it. They also lost one strong member by death, and Mamaloni who resigned his seat until another day. Inflation and low copra prices made the rural people express relief that independence was apparently not imminent after all, while the churches were critical of the negative behaviour of legislators in general. Demands were heard more loudly, especially in the west where Bougainville's troubles were close to home, for state governments in a weak federation, which would lead to Malaitans being sent home to their own island and Honiara's alleged riches being redistributed.

The British 'scaffolding' was largely dismantled. Only two of the former DCs (now GAs) were British. Newcomers no longer sought advice from old expatriate hands, and influential Solomon islanders became more selective when in quest of guidance. The setting up of a small but interventionist Australian Commission spurred this process on. After only four years Hilary and I, the newcomers, virtually led the *ancien régime*. In this nihilistic political atmosphere, injudicious Whitehall ideas of engineering a coalition, with the purpose of superficial unanimity at a conference, resulted in nothing more than mistrust enhanced. The imported Commonwealth experts went into panic, their meddling hope of compromising political coalition for a quick get-out conference having been thwarted. The new CM and council were least likely to settle for any terms except what would be acceptable to the country's grass roots in the rural areas.

The first of two dominant personalities to enter our lives, early 1976, was an amateur, a mercurial wanderer with long legs, impish disposition, the 'satiable curtiosity of the Elephant's Child, and strength and energy derived from some Nureyev of nature, all spring lamb bounce and National Velvet stamina. He had been looking for a home, and chose us by insistently accompanying us after evening walks, having nowhere else to go. It was ridiculous – that a real young 100% Dalmatian with nicely distributed spots could become an unclaimed stray in Honiara (two expat families, one Chinese, owned breeding pairs of Dalmatians, but neither wanted to know); and that, after 30 years of refusing to own a dog because one goes on leave and gets moved, here with departure and heartbreak not far off, were we accepting an emotional attachment. Snodgrass of Baskerville ('Snoddie' for practical purposes, even after we had to entertain a Whitehall warrior whose name was Snodgrass), made our last year lighter and jolly. He gained at the end a home on an island

One dog and his man.

plantation with new fond owners. Snoddie convinced me of the 'genetic' as opposed to the 'environmentally acquired characteristic' arguments as dominant. Dalmatians were bred to be carriage dogs; nobody trained Snoddie to run beside or behind the car in the natural, disciplined way he had – no snapping at wheels. Nor had anybody trained him not to clamber on to the boss's lap and lick him or her all over with a velvet tongue, including between the toes; he kept his beauty and grace for outdoor mobility, indoors he tended to obtrude, only disappearing out of sight when we wanted him to settle down at bedtime. A loveable character who kept us fit. If we had lived on a country estate, we'd have selfishly made him go through the quarantine barrier. Living out of dustbins and the scraps of the G Club, he had been seeking affection, and found it.

I mentioned the death of an assembly member – Francis Aqorau, previously Francis Talasasa, DC Eastern. He died during a vigorous bout on the tennis court, with Francis Bugotu the educationist and future travelling ambassador, who was to die similarly years later. Hilary and I heard that a wake was being held in his home, and felt that we ought to attend. There was no other expatriate, and nobody advised us on etiquette. We took places silently round the wall of the family living room. Francis was lying stretched out in the middle, and his widow was keening, stroking and kneading his limbs and chest, with intermittent sobs of, 'Francis, Francis, come back to me, come back to us'. It was heart-rending, but we were at a loss: we had not known whether to bring any tokens, how best by local custom to express our sorrow other than to remain as quiet spectators, nor when and how best to leave. After about three-quarters of an hour we rose and left as unostentatiously as possible, hoping that our gesture had been taken as it was meant.

It brought back an equally troubling memory. When Bishop John Chisholm made way for a local head of the Anglicans, he had hoped to leave his bones in the country to which he had preached the way for so long. After death his body was flown back from New Zealand, and laid in S Barnabas cathedral before burial in the grounds. As a member of the cathedral council I paid my respects. My final sight of the bishop was not happy. The embalming had left a blackened mummy, and the lying-in-state was in an open coffin. Things were made worse by the brimstone commentary from the heavens, which opened with a cloudburst and prolonged flashing of lightning throughout the reverences before the body, the funeral service and the committal into the grave.

Another entr'acte opened with a visit from a constable, asking whether I had missed anything. We had not. Would I please check my liquor store? Nothing noticeable. Could I identify this empty gin bottle? All Gordon's looked the same. Perhaps we were one short. A prisoner had left the gaol, prowled among the senior housing, nobbled a bottle from my cupboard and returned to prison, where his mates had a party. The police commissioner, who doubled as prisons superintendent, was embarrassed, and the convict got an extra six weeks. A little while after, he got out again, came back up to Lengakiki, stole a chicken and some beer from our neighbours, ate and drank, and came on to find that we had installed our first lock. Lurking in frustration, he attracted the notice of our Ben's wife Alice, who raised a hue and cry. Up flew a cop squad to sweep the gully below for evidence (he had cast unconsumed portions down on being surprised), where they found the culprit. The embarrassed CP sent him to serve the again increased sentence in a distant island lock-up. The deputy governor considered issuing a commendation for enterprise, provided that he could engineer a passage back for a third effort.

Conceit urges me to recount experience of being *Officer administering the Government* (OaG, as Michael Gass punctiliously insisted on being called when in charge of Hong Kong, rather than *Acting Governor*). There was 'GH'. The

NZ architect had sought to make the place airy, though hardly reminiscent of any Pacific vernacular building style. He had forgotten that, apart from public uses, it was the incumbent's home. The bedrooms for guests were acceptable 2 star hotel standard, but the High Commissioner/Governor's suite was similar – a modest bedroom, with poky washroom, a small day room, and that was that. The public rooms were too large for family use, although the verandahs were pleasant for alfresco meals and lounging. The study/office was adequate, but did not impress overseas dignitaries; the coding office and the ADC's cell were cramped. The kitchen and housekeeping quarters were better, and although (unlike in Africa) I respected the servants' and their families' privacy, and did not 'inspect' their quarters, they seemed satisfactory.

The gardens were unambitious, except for the orchids lovingly tended by Sir Michael Gass. The one luxury was the open-air swimming pool, but the pump and filtration plant needed a technically-minded ADC (two RAF helicopter pilots in succession denied the knowledge, so care and maintenance devolved upon His Excellency). The gardens were tended by prisoners, in blue shorts with a white stripe down the side seams, little troubled by the red ants in the grass. An entertainment was to watch the wagtails dive-bombing the GH cat. She had her own day when the megapode birds hatched, buried in the warm sands of the Russell Islands beaches across the sound. The chicks, all feet and feathers on their first flights, came over to Guadalcanal where many flew straight into the GH windows. The cat would wait and pounce on the stunned fledglings, if nobody was on guard.

It was a good venue for hospitality. There was room for about 25 at dinner: our first saw ice nicely broken. Hilary had taught our own houseboy to make brandy snaps, strange and new to GH's cook Warren. Ben brought dozens down and Hilary showed Warren how to fill them with cream fresh frozen from NZ. As Edward and his aide in their scarlet waistcoats and white sulus passed the sweet round, Hilary encouraged the guests to take as many as they wished: half way round Edward came and whispered 'No more!' 'Nonsense', said Hilary, 'there are lots in the kitchen', but, no, there were not. Warren had decided that one each was enough, and put the rest, unfilled, into the deep freeze – so the first self-helpers had to be asked to hand their surplus over the table.

Hilary as First Lady took fascinating trips with the district nursing sister by air, canoe and tractor to Rennell, and with the Church of Melanesia's secretary in his boat to Ontong Java. We took our chance to get out and about together, with a tissue veneer of comfort. In August 1975 I wanted to look at the western 'weather coast', as the south of Guadalcanal was known: at a distant geological period of orogeny the island had tipped over so that Honiara's northern coast slopes were relatively flat, but the southern was steep and clifflike, encouraging bad seas and storms when the winds blew. We sent a Marine 'ship', the *Wainoni*, ahead with cook Japhet, Tikopian houseboy Robinson and the noble Tikopian police driver Tafaka, and next day a Solair plane took Hilary, the DC, the ADC and me over wild mountains covered with bush, divided by dramatic waterfalls and gorges reminiscent of the Kaladan valley 32 years before. It took twenty minutes before landing at a tiny airstrip by Babanakira ('the tree that has a hole, from which a bird takes an egg'). A large welcoming party waving Union flags sang two verses of *God Save The Queen*. A chief gave a speech, and I replied (preferring very simple English to pidgin) with smiles and words of friendship, through an interpreter. Then came Question Time. Only two that seemed *à propos*: 'How will independence affect us? We are frightened'; and, 'Will independence be on both a town *and* a village level?' After over a quarter of a century it hardly matters how my reassuring noises sounded. I meant to imply that their own elected leaders would surely be as trustworthy as the likes of me. I got three cheers, and everyone else got one.

Walking along a path from the airstrip to the Anglican school hall, banners read, 'Welcome to our Governor' and 'Please Governor take a few steps down': had they been told I exceeded two metres? The children assembled gave a further rendering of the national anthem, plus a second song, *Welcome to our Governor*, well rehearsed and tuneful. Another speech by the headmaster, and another small one by me to the children, and on our way again, with a long train of followers, big and small. The path widened into a proper track, where a tractor (the usual form of ICE transport on the islands) awaited. Chairs and bodies were hoisted on to the trailer, and off we went as the rain began (the ADC had brought an umbrella), in the company of two pigs, property of an islander with long matted ringlets who had never heard of Ras Tafari. Benny had lost a finger: the tale was that he spent so much time caring for his pigs that his neglected wife had in a fury bitten one off. Why disbelieve a tale just because it is sad?

We bumped along to a small hamlet on the coast called Marasa. Need I say, I was in shorts, not colonial uniform, throughout? (OaGs don't get feathers, to disappoint any would-be cartoonist.) The beach was stony, storm-tossed and under lowering cliffs; but surging up and down in the bay was the little *Wainoni*, and on the beach our well-loved Tafaka with umbrellas and his encouraging smile. Boarding the dinghy from the beach was a matter of timing, and paddling it through the surf tricky: climbing thence on to the 'ship' was a matter of sprawling across at the precise moment when a cresting wave had raised the dinghy's side to the same level as the *Wainoni's* gunwale. The captain and Robinson were eager to haul us over; a split second later one might have been back below the ship's plimsoll line (if it had one). Most of the beachless cliffs thereon fell straight into the sea as we sailed westwards, tossed by mighty waves while eating spam sandwiches on deck. As the sea turned calmer, we sailed past Cape Austen into Wanderer Bay and landed unsteadily at Sughu.

This is where a former Lord Boyd had sailed in on *Wanderer* in 1851 and was murdered – why, nobody knows, something to do with blackbirding or payback for earlier killings, with mistaken identity thrown in. Our colonial secretary Alan Lennox-Boyd and his Lady came here in 1959 and gave Sughu a fresh water supply, with a plaque over the spring, and two commemorative trees. Our informant was an anthropologist priest living in Sughu. Nobody had expected us as radio contact had been poor and the weather prevented any local canoe from coming round with the good news, so school was out. We showed interest in the copra drying shed, had a mug of coffee with the father and retired on board for afternoon tea out of EIIR crested china.

The sea calming further, it took an hour and a half to round Cape Beaufort and reach the RC mission station behind the bay at Tangarare. The dinghy ferried us safely towards a colourful crowd of young and old, standing under a large rain tree on the beach. Handshakes all round, and a procession along the shore to the mission station. Both tea and supper spoke mutely of past scraping to allow present generous hospitality: enormous spreads of cakes (imported flour), locally reared chicken and pork, beef (not local), fish of all kinds. Sister Mathilde, mistress of the hens, had been here since the 1930s, uncertain whether her birthplace was now Italian or Yugoslav; Sister Evangeline, the chatterbox, had so far only spent 50 years with the mission, but knew she hailed from Prince Edward Island – her tales were full of the war and her narrow escapes from the Japanese; Sister Sanale was from the Tongan royal family, young, charming, warm and full of fun. After supper the children put flower garlands round our necks before giving us custom song and dance. By 10 *p.m.* it was more than time for bed, but duty cheers and speeches of thanks all round before flopping.

Both parties gathered for a large breakfast before going round the station. A dugout canoe took us across the main river to see a sawmill and a small furniture factory. By eleven o'clock it was time to re-embark. Back on board for the rest of our Pacific cruise: gin, curry from a silver dish on to the EIIR china, and Robinson to pass round all the side dishes. The tail end of the Raj, on virtually a lifeboat. I was unashamed. After coffee we reached Lambie, a beautiful bay at the very end of the road west from Honiara to the western tip of Guadalcanal, where we abandoned ship and took again to landrover. At one point the local legislative assembly member joined us, to show round the clinic, agricultural office, school and RC church, which the Lambie people had painted an attractive blue. Then the rain started. Some miles further on, the landrover engine boiled over in the middle of nowhere, but Tafaka and co filled the radiator with rainwater from the puddles. Our last call was at Visale, on Cape Esperance, where all the oldest RC nuns lived: the four oldest were French, having come to the Solomons in 1911, 1918, 1923 (when I was born) and 1928, and never gone home. Two had never learnt English, but all spoke local languages. Out of their sweetness and bounty they gave us a large spread. We reached GH in time to change and welcome the Inspector General of Colonial Police. This tour is typical of what makes memories of colonial life, so recent yet so deeply buried underneath pre-digested history as now tendentiously taught, sweet, contrasting the violence, civil wars and pecuniary and intellectual corruption of to-day. The little places we visited have been the scenes of much of the Solomons' recent horrors.

A few months later, after Sir Donald's return from leave, we had a memorable experience shining through the clouds that would next year blanket our recollections. One of the leading 'mixed-blood' families in the west was led by Ernie Palmer, with commitments and interests in many directions. The most eminent was Norman Palmer, the bishop just consecrated the first archbishop of the new archdiocese of the Solomons, looking directly to Canterbury in the Anglican communion. It was a delight to be invited on his first official visit to the easter outer islands, to include Tikopia – the subject of one of social anthropology's greater classics, *We, the Tikopia* by Professor Sir Raymond Firth. It is a tiny island nearly 500 nautical miles east of Honiara, peopled by Polynesians. Barely touched by the outside world, home to two of our own best-loved islanders, we had always like many expatriates wanted to see it but never dared hope for the opportunity. We boarded the diocesan ship, *The Southern Cross*, on armistice day 1975, almost the only lay folk in the complement.

Hilary and I had one of the three 'first class' cabins. The bunks were comfortable, but the ceiling was not much higher than the upper pillow: manoeuvring in and out of the senior bed was a challenge to a queasy occupant. The first day saw a slight swell, distracted by *Scrabble*. Dawn next day found us off San Cristobal (aka Makira, home of Mamaloni), anchored off the Anglican station of Pamua, some miles west of Kirakira (our burglar's lock-up). A rocky dinghy got us ashore reasonably dry, where Archbishop Norman had a dancing reception before a communion service, including a procession of priests and students (the boys all carried dancing sticks and spears, points down in token of Peace; the girls followed, topless and wearing custom jewellery round heads, arms and ankles, and necklaces of shells and teeth): feasting and breakfast at last followed, badly needed, but not until more custom dancing had been applauded, each set repeated continuously, unwilling to make way for a successor, until someone in authority started pushing several sets out together to perform in unharmonious competition. The feast was like so many – *al fresco*, under shady trees, everyone sitting on banana leaves: anonymous parcels of food, wrapped in leaves, had to be opened to discover the contents, chunks of beef or pork (hair, skin, gristle, all the way to the bone, just as the chopper had dissected the pig), or kumara and taro potatoes, or the delicious prize of cassava pudding, which our grannies called sago.

Next day we were among the Reef Islands, passing the volcano of Tinakula, a 3,000' pyramid, evacuated after its eruption in 1971, whose inhabitants now wanted to return. On to Santa Cruz islands, to Ndende where we anchored in Graciosa Bay; somewhere near, the Spaniard Mendana (who first reached the Solomons from Europe) had landed and died, with a cape named after him. These islands looked dark and threatening, and it was raining as we took water on board through a narrow hose. Even the local people seemed sultry and unsmiling, with beetling brows and a mad look in their eyes. What a difference the sun makes, as we know so well (and so rarely) in Scotland, but rain is as frequent in Santa Cruz as in our own west coast. A full four days after leaving Honiara, we saw Tikopia in the distance, mountainous towards the north, somewhat flatter to our starboard, and then a mist set in.

It lifted when we neared the shore, to let us see many outrigger canoes paddling smartly towards us through the reef. A few men wore 'calico', but most had waist girdles of bark cloth, several with turtle shell rings or rolls of tobacco in their ear lobes, and one or two sported turtle shell nose rings. We anchored outwith the reef to be ferried ashore. Tikopia was still governed by its four chiefs, a principal, two slightly lesser and one with the smallest area. They displayed the noblest pride, and held strongly to their culture. Firth had written, 'They are "primitive" in the sense that the level of their material technical achievement is not high, and they use only very few of the products of western civilization; at the same time they have an elaborate code of etiquette, a clear cut systematic social organization, and they have developed very strongly the ceremonial side of their life'. Most still wore bark cloth, and lived in plain sago thatch huts. They maintained traditional forms of mourning, marriage and initiation. All were now ostensibly Christian without changing their basic customs. We eventually landed by launch, swept in on the surf that the helmsman somehow judged to be the right wave to catch, on to pure white sands.

Bishop Kasper led us to the tall, silvery long-haired No 2 chief, surrounded by a crowd of smiling children in their school uniform of bark loincloths. Some wore garlands and had their bodies dusted with yellow turmeric, in the middle of their initiation ceremonies. The archbishop, carrying the crozier from which he was rarely parted during this whole tour, and Kasper led us gently round the broad sandy path encircling the island, lined by tall shady trees. A group of mourners passed, the son of the deceased supported by two fellows and wailing loudly; after a death the whole island mourns, and until the proper 'oven' or feast has been held no one may dance. The archbishop's arrival meant that the ceremonies must be completed quickly, for all must dance to-morrow. Arriving at an open village, we visited the large church, S Luke's, and carried on to the next village near a lake. Every door on the island, except the main one into a chief's house, was barely knee-high. We had to crawl in and out: an archbishop and (I suspected) a full governor were the only persons entitled to use a chief's main door. The floors were carpeted with matting, hard on bare knees; the spacious but dark rooms had bags of turmeric hanging from the rafters and bed mats propped up against one wall. A priest's wife fed us, coconut shells brimming with rich coconut cream and paw-paw, and lumps of cooked taro with which to spoon the delicacies out before being eaten also. We were taken to see one of Hilary's former polio crawler patients (the epidemic had not only stricken Malaita). After crawling in, we found her sitting with her father, a former chief, upright and cross-legged with many custom tattoo marks. She had been taught to walk with crutches after much rehabbing in Honiara, but had never used her callipers since coming home – not that they would have been convenient crawling in and out of low doorways.

Next morning we went ashore to meet No 1 chief. His wife Mary was assigned to take care of Hilary during a lengthy ordination service. A big, pleasing woman, well tattooed, bare-breasted and shaven-headed with a ring of human hair, she wore a splendid *tapa* cloth skirt dyed orange with turmeric. A conch shell took the place of church bells, and we were led on hands and knees into the church for Fr Luke to be priested. Hilary began to feel cramp, while her chaperone, snuggling close up, embraced her with both arms. A girl behind squeezed all her toes. The men received communion first, but after No 1 wife had led the ladies up, she took Hilary out to wait in fresh air. At the end, No 1 chief's brother escorted us to greet him. He wore a mat tied round his midriff, like many Polynesian aristocrats, with the features and bearing of a native American 'Red Indian'. Crawling into his presence, we sat on mats in cross-legged silence, while the island nurse, who interpreted, said we should walk with the grey-maned patriarch to the other end of the island for yet another feast. An open seaside area in the village enjoyed shade trees and a space for dancing. The atmosphere was of infectious gaiety, friends gathering in groups and much bustling on the far side of the bay. Thence eventually arrived one basket of food each for every important guest. This was supplemented by a vast communal, boat-shaped, bowl full of coloured paste, a kind of starch cooked in coconut cream and heavily tinged with the ubiquitous turmeric, a treat for VIPs. The familiar packets contained, not hacked lumps of pig, but excellent white fish, taro and new green coconuts bored to release the fresh water inside. The main courses had been buried in banana leaves for months; this preserved them in best condition and meant there would always be good food in case of famine or disaster. *On dit*. Hilary's chaperone had sweetly been fanning the flies away while she ate.

It was a wrench to leave these happy, natural people. In the early afternoon the handshaking was no perfunctory affair, with many noses rubbed on our hands and a tearful Mary rubbing noses with Hilary. Lower orders rubbed their noses on the chiefs' knees. On the road back, Hilary crawled in to say goodbye to her patient and rub noses with her father. There was a huge crowd to see us on to the ship, archbishop Norman being carried shoulder-high through the surf to the 'launch'; we humbler folk splashed our joyful way through shallow waves to clamber in. Escorting outriggers joined us, full of taro, pumpkins, sugarcane and bananas for our galley. It was a sad 3 o'clock when we upped anchor, but we had a new passenger. A New Zealander had been a young Volunteer Service Abroad (VSA, NZ's version of VSO) teacher on Tikopia for three years and happily 'gone native': he had a custom tattoo on his arm and had received a turtleshell nose ring from a chief, his virtual adoptive father. He was adamant that the contented life he was leaving was due to rigid enforcement of etiquette and custom by the chiefs, which made life clear but still interesting: there was a clear contrast with the Polynesian settlers in Rennell and Bellona, where custom had lapsed and degeneration set in.

It was a rough return to Luisalebe on Santa Cruz to attend a wedding. All was still wet and dark at mid-day. Someone pointed out where a Commander Goodenough had been speared to death not many years before. I was sorry for myself, having stubbed a big toe and gashed my shin during avoidance action in a very rough spell. Bishop Kasper took us into his cement house, where his Tikopian wife Georgina and father-in-law still crawled around on knees in their old way despite the concrete flooring. Kasper had brought ashore a cut of deep frozen meat. Georgina had never cooked meat. Hilary was co-opted amidst much giggling, but the problem of defrosting remained. An accountant-in-training divided the iceberg. Hilary helped the school prefects to beat the vast wooden drum which summoned the congregation to church, but hers was an unaccustomed rhythm. The men stayed on shore for a meeting, but Hilary braved the possibility of crocodiles and waded across the river mouth to the launch, finally pitching aboardship in the arms of a brawny sailor. Stormy weather in the morning meant entrusting herself to the dinghy, the launch being unsafe. Despite the strength of the sailors she only arrived at the church at half past six *a.m.*, by which time Fr Francis and his Delilah's wedding ceremony was over, the earliest step into matrimony we had yet encountered. Torrents of rain spared us another feast, but Georgina had never made a European breakfast. Each piece of toast burst into flames while the previous black slice was still being scraped; hard-boiled eggs, coconut cream and paw-paw made up for that, but it was the last meal of our day.

From ten in the morning the sea was mountainous all the way to Makira. Silence settled while the company's sole sustenance was ship's biscuits and books: next afternoon we reached the shelter of Star Harbour to drop a priest. Then to Pamua again, collecting a passenger in the rainswept pitch dark, delivered by a long canoe paddled by six boys with glistening moonlit torsos. A final communion service in the morning preceded a peaceful sail along

Guadalcanal to the harbour in Honiara, where the GH Jaguar greeted us with the ADC and a call to lunch. This was spent discussing the resignation of the chief minister, already described, which had blown up while we were away. Things were about to change for us, radically and unbelievably, with the second dominant personality's arrival.

CHAPTER 10

The Sun Eclipsed

One cloud is enough to eclipse the sun
[Thomas Fuller, M.D., *Gnomologia* (1732)]
(Or, *Burn before Reading*)

ALL ASSUMED THAT Donald Luddington would see the Solomons into independence with an extended commission. Three years had not after all sufficed. An undercurrent of hints, indirectly received by us later and very much *sub rosa*, whispered that Whitehall did not regard him as a success – in their terms. He had been expected (and expected) to steer the protectorate into freedom. Local reality had braked the acceleration the FCO had hoped for (the promised brevity had in small part led me to seek my own secondment). Donald was universally liked and respected in the Solomons as a down-to-earth and unostentatious pillar of decency. His wife hankered after Hong Kong, and when the chairman of the Independent Commission Against Corruption sadly died, the way was open to offer to replace him, suiting Hong Kong admirably. Donald told me in confidence that he would be leaving, and asked whether I would be content to succeed him for the short time supposedly left to us. I was flattered, although promotions *en poste* were very rare, and thought to myself that the Treasury might not relish someone qualifying for an extra pension under the Governors' Pensions Act after such short service (unless, of course, another gubernatorial vacancy should occur for which I was thought fit). I may not deny that I liked the idea. I later read that the minister and deputy under-secretary concerned, both of short stature, thought that although I was 'a splendid chap in many ways', they felt I was 'a little overpowering in [my] relationships with the local people'. I might have pointed out that I had for twenty-six years contrived to talk to my local colleagues, politicians or staff, when we were all sitting down, but in the presence of UK ministers or top mandarins stood, admittedly at two metres, until invited to sit. The opportunity never arose. I know a holder of high office of equal height, with FCO credentials however; a makeshift exculpation, with another kind of over-power in mind?

The DC Malaita in earlier days had been one whom I can only bring myself to name Ichabod. He had written a paper on land custom and tenure on that island, where *kastom* and land were even stronger influences than in any other. This gave him an aura of intellectuality and anthropological understanding in the eyes of some, marking him out from warmer peers. His reward was appointment to the British Resident Commissioner post in the Anglo-French 'Pandemonium' of the New Hebrides, notionally supervised by the High Commissioner for the Western Pacific, whom he came to bypass in correspondence with the Paris-sensitive FCO.

Ichabod went on to govern the Seychelles (a series of diplomats succeeded as BRC). Within weeks of arrival he undid the good work that his predecessor Greatbatch had laboriously but amicably built up over three years, creating trust with the rival local politicians and civic leaders. Ichabod had never before dealt with ministers or parties, with or without ideologies. A friend in Mahé asked me 'what it was about [the Pacific] that could produce such a man? He was "impossible".' All that mattered, I was told, was what London *thought*.

A later message was that he never showed senior staff any communication with London. The FCO quirk of having embassy telegrams signed with the SURNAME of the ambassador, even when drafted and approved by juniors, had now been wished upon colonies, which had been used to subscribing plainly anonymous GOVERNOR (unless His Excellency was making a personal point). When the name ICHABOD subscribed a telegram or savingam covering something technical or financial which he did not understand or care for, he would personally insert, *eg*, 'From Snooks (.)' while the form was on its way for despatch. His disappointment at not yet receiving his 'K' was palpable. When independence did come, he had supported the disastrous constitutional stitch-up whereby the dependent chief minister became the independent president, and the leader of the colonial opposition became the republic's first prime minister. He was to explain this to me as his 'policy of reconciliation'. Unsurprisingly the arrangement fell apart within a year, with fire-armed violence and asylum-seeking to follow. The final news of Seychellois independence was that Ichabod crept away unnoticed, regarded as the least distinguished governor that the locals had known. If London did not know, they should have, or may not have cared so long as he had been their blunt instrument. They gave him the last colonial KCMG in the end, having fobbed Greatbatch off with a bare knight bachelorhood (not that that mattered much to him, but how authority uses the symbols at its disposal, however baublish, may be indicative).*

I took early leave so as to be back in time to cover the interregnum after Luddington's departure, and received my own bauble from HM, which rests pristine in its case: when appropriate I have always worn my father's. Sadly, one no longer needs to be honourable to be honoured: it is sadder that some

---

*Luddington eventually received his K in the Most Excellent Order of the British Empire, the FCO having reserved future honours in the Most Distinguished Order of St Michael & St George, originally created for overseas service and traditionally having its registry in the Colonial Office, for diplomats.

An Officer administering a Government.

honoured believe themselves to be honourable. Next day we had been commanded to attend the Buck House garden party, and at the last minute an indigenous governor of a Caribbean island cried off, so Hilary and I were bidden by Protocol & Conference Department to replace his slot in the royal tea tent, where we had a lengthy chat about the visit and the Pacific in general. For a brief moment we felt that we had mounted a pinnacle of glory, however artificial in the eyes of Cool Britannia.

Ichabod and I had never met. With my private Mahé briefings at the back of my mind, but hopeful of making some rapport, I went down to Rye, where he was staying after his official briefing: it was a would-be village squire in tweeds who received me in the pub, except that he was a stranger to the regulars. He ignored Hilary. It was an uncomfortable meeting: I explained the failure of the leveraged ISG towards early independence following Lestor's visit, and the consequences of the form of ISG in force. We could discuss the unreserved subjects informally with ministers and senior civil servants, using amiable diplomacy, but we had no official powers and must not appear to be directing. 'I don't know anything about that; nobody has told me anything like that'. I assured him that it was what the constitutional instrument specifically required. I sought to discuss the personalities, strengths and weaknesses of the politicians and senior officers he would be working among, but he showed no interest. He was not openly rude, but he was superior, dismissive and cold, and I returned to Tunbridge Wells very unhappy.

The arrival in Honiara did not improve prospects. After the welcome at Henderson airfield, and the quick change into helmets and whites for the swearing-in at the High Court, not a word, not even an acknowledgment of the briefing notes left with his PA. It was the start of my becoming an unperson. Hilary did little better. She had provisionally arranged lunch parties for his wife, to meet Solomons ministers' wives, the guides commissioner, the Red Cross lady and such. The first had a perfunctory acceptance and then, a few hours beforehand, a cancellation. Hilary rang to say that this would be awkward and to ask what she should explain to all the expectant invitees, some from other islands. She was told that GH had been left in such a state that it had to be cleared up. As we had just left it, immaculate, she had obviously been warned off associating with us. Reluctantly she agreed to come after all, but the social meeting with the island leaders' ladies was fraught and chilly, and nobody was sorry when it came to an early end. The children were soon recognized as arrogant and status-conscious, being driven in the *Jaguar* the few yards to the mixed Woodford school.

His previous deputy in the Seychelles, who did not know me, wrote a warning. He had served with him for four years in the New Hebrides, and as soon as Ichabod's posting to Mahé as governor was announced he had sought a posting away. Ichabod had no consistent character, but went through life as it had begun, in a NZ repertory company, playing a series of rôles: at one time he would ape the gentleman scholar, displaying an attitude of indifference to mundane matters, at another the countryman, at another the political scientist. He had been disastrous in the Seychelles, and had become progressively worse, incapable of understanding his basic constitutional position, let alone the unwritten nuances, and so destroyed his own influence as governor. The chief minister had written him off within a few days and largely ignored his existence; Mancham believed firmly that HMG was anxious to rid itself of the Seychelles, and to secure a republic, otherwise it would not have sent someone so useless in a monarchical part. Attempts to get Ichabod to see the reality of his position were usually met with a look of incredulity and no comment. He never listened to anyone's advice, but was ready to blame his mistakes (if forced to admit them) on bad advice. Whatever his stage character might be, I as his deputy, saying what had to be said, would be walking a tightrope, not trusting him not to cut the wire ('and I quote'). This confirmed what I had learnt for myself. I continued to send papers up from my office. It took a week or two to notice that many never returned, and those that did usually bore a petulant disagreement in red ink. He was recreating his own registry whence to recover control over what had been handed down to ministers. I had to guess at his movements, or rely on hearsay.

His first dinner party was the last time we enjoyed his hospitality. Protocol sat Hilary on his left, and Peter Kenilorea, the chief minister, immediately opposite. At one stage Ichabod said, loud for all to hear, 'I've only been sent here to clear up the mess'. It was news that there was a mess around us. The implicit slander on his predecessor was in poor taste on a public occasion. Interpretation came when he set the chief minister's ears flapping with, 'My business is to get rid of this place as fast as possible'. In retrospect I imagine diplomats telling him that they had hoped to see the back of this poor, curious but valueless set of islands by now, but that the administration had not succeeded in disengaging itself or persuading the local leaders to get on with it. I have made clear where the FCO failed to understand that this could not have happened under the declared policy of giving friendly subject peoples the choice. It and its consultants had stage-managed the Internal Self-Government.

After three months Ichabod had to send his 'first impressions' despatch to the secretary of state. I amassed notes on everything he might be expected to comment upon, as well as references to what colleagues had told me that he had been doing, to help him marshal his thoughts: there was no acknowledgment, nor did he let his deputy see what he had written. Since I should have to assume the administration did he suffer some disability, this was not only discourteous but malevolent. I did get sight in due course. A neighbouring post to which the despatch was routinely copied sent me a bootleg copy. It started with a *cri de cœur* that there seemed to be a 'conspiracy' to keep governor and politicians apart, a gross perversion of my steady advice and description of how we had been working, walking on eggshells whenever we discussed subjects that were now devolved, or touched on personal responsibility of ministers and their officials. Ministers and permanent secretaries pestered me over the governor summoning them to criticize this and request that. Ichabod claimed in his despatch never in his past Pacific experience to have been aware of the need for, or the validity of, 'consensus'; everywhere else distinctly identifiable, established, oppositions had emerged, and he did not recognize the situation that I have been describing. No colleague recognized his.

I engineered a frank discussion, hoping to clear the air and get all back on normal rails. It was brief, and a failure. 'Until that flag comes down, I am in charge'. This was a man frightened that things would go wrong, for which he would have to answer, but he trusted nobody, whether his staff or the island politicians. He was cunning: he set up an *ad hoc* 'National Security Council', under the guise of preparing ministers for the ultimate responsibility of assuming control of the 'reserved' subjects (which Luddington and I had already been doing, but informally, whether in council or in personal discussion). He did not include in its ranks (or inform) the deputy governor or attorney general, who held an open watching brief for these matters in council of ministers and legislative assembly. In effect he restored the old council of ministers under his chairmanship, without official ballast, and then improperly sought to direct subjects that had been devolved out of our hands, having no relationship with defence, external affairs or public service. I never saw any record of these meetings. The chief minister mentioned that we seemed to be turning the clock back, but was not confident or adamant enough to take a stand himself.

I wondered whom to consult on how to make straight a very crooked pathway. I could not protest over Ichabod's head to London without firm backing. Circumstances were against me. The chief justice was on leave. The attorney general was a temporary stopgap on contract when the incumbent fell sick: he was sound and friendly, but would avoid controversy that might affect his own future. The secretary for the public service liked to keep his head down. I was on my lonely own. Nevertheless, I wrote an 18 paragraph, 2,600 word, draft to Ichabod in January 1977: it did not lack pomposity, but said what I believe needed to be said. The stopgap AG commented, 'You've got him there, haven't you?' and said no more; but without hope of his open backing I never sent it.

Shortly after this, the cabinet had found the stalled independence recommendations broadly endorsed by local councils, so far as these had understood how to translate imported words and written aims into imaginable events and changes in the real world. A new external Commonwealth adviser assisted in a third legislative assembly debate, in the hope of agreement on the contentious issues of non-Melanesian rights to citizenship and landholding. To some hardliners even Archbishop Norman Palmer and a handful of civil servants of merit, with 'mixed blood', could never be citizens. A hasty confabulation between the adviser, speaker, chief minister and an opposition member resulted in an adjournment. An informal private meeting with selective participation agreed on an outline of a constitution. The house reassembled and voted its approval, *without having seen any text*. I never saw the text devised, despite being a member of the legislature. The adviser passed his draft to the governor, who must have hinted that the AG and I might be ignored. The provision that attracted most attention was that twelve months after independence, unless a contrary vote were passed, the governor-general would assume the office of non-executive president. This approach to the crown confused the minority intellectuals who, looking for checks on power and sceptical of legislative performance to date, had been heartened by events in Australia: these appeared to hint that although democracy could not provide for recall of representatives once elected, a governor-general might remove a prime minister who might have 'gone too far'.

At least a document was available, vaguely purporting to be the wish of the legislature. With a provisional date for a conference set for September 1977, and no certainty about the outcome of those matters judged most sensitive for Britain's fast dwindling interests, leverage was abandoned and the second instalment of ISG was dispensed on 1 April 1977. The Solomon Island politicians, nominated for the final conference that would tie up any loose strings in the established way in grand London surroundings, tried hard to insist that their governor play no part in the proceedings. Solomon Islands was to become the 38th member of the Commonwealth and the 146th United Nation.

About this time the FCO's liaison officer with HMOCS told me in strictest confidence that the shortlist for Tom Russell's successor as Cayman Islands governor at the approaching end of his commission was down to three, including me. For an illusory moment I fantasized about a return visit to Hong Kong, to pick the brains of friends in that banking world for background and underhand knowledge of off-shore banking, brass plates of phantom companies, and ways of laundering wealth. What followed in Honiara, as Ichabod might insinuate to Whitehall, would almost certainly have cast a pall of doubt over my suitability for the highest trust, so my chances were slim. As it turned out, the sensible decision was taken to extend Tom for a considerable period, so the question never arose.

Following the constitutional session there was another confrontation with Ichabod, this time unplanned by me, in the course of which I finally felt forced to challenge him openly with much of my unsent letter. If he said, as I think he did, that nobody had ever spoken to him in such a way before, I think I may have said that from all I knew it was time that someone had been honest with him to his face. I certainly ended by saying that if we could not work together, or he with me, the solution might be for me to return to Hong Kong, now ISG Mark II would withdraw me from council and legislature. 'Leave it to me', he said. This I did, with reservations. I offered him advice on how to fill the vacancy (Hong Kong must have a slot for its absentee to fill, to which commitment the Solomons had been contributing during my secondment) – a diplomatic posting might be convenient, a John the Baptist ready to transmute into the first British High Commissioner.

What Ichabod wrote to UK and HK I might learn in 2007 under the 30-year rule, but someone in Hong Kong decided to abolish my office, which would give me full pension before reaching the customary age of 55. I had a letter explaining that at 53 it was hardly worth my returning for just one year (with seniority over the explainer?). I pointed out that it was by now routine for HK's 55-year-olds to be extended, two years at a time, to 60, but this was ignored; I also asked the attorney general in HK (another old friend) for an opinion on what 'office' I held that might be abolished, since I was one of a general Staff Grade A list, available to be posted to any appropriate office but not at present holding one (someone must have been filling an acting post pending the supernumerary lapsing on my return) – he could not, or did not know how to, answer. One to put down to experience.

Allegedly the establishment secretary vetoed a finance branch's proposal to create a new supernumerary post, avoiding the most junior officer acting at SGA level having to step down: the return of one who would be in the ring for next promotion to Secretary grade (shortlisted for a minor governorship) might be unwelcome. The supernumerary post created when I left for the Pacific, and in which I had been substantively promoted *in absentia* to Staff Grade A, had not lapsed. The truth is obscure. The chairman of the HK university grants committee wrote that he could fix it for me to be its executive secretary, which was kind, but I did not wish to leave the admin stream. Shortly afterwards the visiting assistant under-secretary of state, whom I still liked despite his *mauvais mot* about potty little places, came to my office after a session with Ichabod, and said 'I really don't know what has gone wrong here', and just as I opened my mouth to let it all flow freely out, added, 'And I don't think I want to know either'. I was left to nurse my wrath to keep it warm. I was succeeded by a diplomat, who told us later how quickly he had come to sympathize with what we had endured under Ichabod.

There was much comfort of a sort. I was visited by a stream of Solomon Islanders to inflate the commiserations. I recorded what they said, and it is another conceited catharsis to append a selection of what I still keep. Grossly self-indulgent, but it helps one's 'self-esteem', so important in the modern world (especially to the young).

> Sir Frederick Osifelo (Speaker): 'But why? My word! You are so respected. You stand up for things. Without you we should never have begun our administrative training. (*Pause*) Ah – it must be personality. Is it because he is a New Zealander? (*No comment*) I have noticed this, these New Zealanders, they treat the British officers badly.'
>
> Francis Bugotu (secretary to CM & council of ministers, future head of diplomatic corps): 'But how can this happen? You have so much to do. I cannot

believe it. ('*Well, some may say it is the biter bit!*') No, but it is bad for the workers. No more trust.'

Willie Betu (ex-minister of finance): 'You are going out like Tom Russell, I know. ('*No, I am going out finish, because my job in Hong Kong is taken and someone else will come here*') Why, why? I cannot understand. ('*Perhaps someone disagrees with my opinions, who knows?*') Ah, ah! The governor! But even the politicians find it very hard to talk to him. We are losing all our good friends. We shall have no white friends left.'

Most Rev Archbishop Norman Palmer: 'My goodness! What a time to change people! It will take to independence for anyone to get to know us. We should need you till then. This is terrible. You are one of us.'

The interventionist Australian commissioner: 'This is grim news. A case of the ship deserting the sinking rat.'

Francis Kikolo (opposition MLA, ex-minister for home affairs): 'If you have no better job, why not stay to help us to our independence?'

Mariano Kelesi (minister of education): 'But your time isn't finished? I had a great shock. I tell you, all the people have more respect on Luddington than this man. The British government made a great mistake in sending him back again. They remember him from before, my word. They should have sent someone from another place like Luddington.'

A visiting Bank Line Director: 'Your new governor has a reputation of being the man who will bring independence about at any cost, whatever the cost in friendship. My drinks party was embarrassed by his gratuitous denigrations of his predecessor to strangers.'

Paul Tovua (land valuer & minister of natural resources): 'I did not know until Ben (Kinika) told me. It is very sudden. There is no political reason. I think you should stay till your time is up. I am very sorry.'

Francis Mauli (working priest & administrative officer): 'We are very sorry you have to leave us. Those of us who depend on you for advice were very surprised.'

Daniel Ho'ota (teacher, AO & minister of health & welfare): 'I was told you wanted to go. I was surprised. I wondered if ministers could have a petition to keep you.'

Colin Gauwane (minister of agriculture & lands): 'I am sorry you are going. If your term of service is not up, and we do not know who will take your place, I do not understand.'

Matthew Belamatanga (MLA): (*After a long garbled comment*) 'I was very surprised to hear that you were going, and thought that you must want to. It is wrong for you to go. We have lost too many, independence does not mean we pack everyone off. I do not know any politician wants you to go. We need your experience till independence. And after. When we have our own governor-general, he will need someone to advise him and help to begin with. Oh, I know this governor.'

George Atkin (information officer): 'Will you comment on these rumours in the town that you have chosen to go because you have been threatened?'

All those names reprove me: in writing so much about myself, I have overlooked how much of the work in the Solomons meant close and warm relationships with the islanders. Chilly remoteness was never the way of most 'imperial masters'.

Our last few days were brightened by a visit from the Archbishop of Canterbury, Donald Coggan, and his wife. He declined gently an invitation to stay in Government House, pointing out that Norman Palmer was his host, and that it would be wrong to prefer grander accommodation. Ichabod took offence, and did not even ask the archbishops for a token drink. The Coggans had arrived from PNG in a small un-air-conditioned plane, and had problems in having to arrive in full archiepiscopal raiment for a great welcome at Henderson airfield. His sermon in an overflowing S Barnabas cathedral was marked by his kindly tact when asking the countless 'maries' (*tok pisin* for 'women'), and their squalling children to reduce the clamour (they occupied according to custom the west and south sides, open to the grounds around and segregated from their menfolk). The archbishop was one of those unselfish great men who make their current interlocutor feel the only person who matters; she was a humbly modest lady with quiet charm and deep interest in all around her. Norman told me afterwards that he had described the embarrassments that Ichabod had caused to his flock, and in particular to me: Coggan's secretary and chaplain had assured him that this would be made known to No 10. I wonder. We were asked if we would take home on our boat the bulky crafts and carvings given by island congregations to the Coggans, too substantial for their small charter plane. We eventually delivered these to Lambeth Palace, and were rewarded with a tour of the archbishop's home and headquarters, impressive not least for the minimal evidence of important or valuable private possessions of the incumbent.

A Chinese trader asked whether he might take some of the ground orchids from our garden, bringing workmen with spades who stripped the beds of every single plant. The parting from Ben Lison and his family was not easy. When we embarked on the good Bank Line ship *Hollybank*, friends gathered to divide our possessions between cabin baggage and the crates which were to sit on the wharf until a cargo ship could collect them. Our accommodation, much larger than P&O A Deck, was the 'owner's' on the port side, opposite the master's on the starboard. We were the sole passengers, thanks to a director of the line whose sister had been a close friend in Hong Kong's broadcast media. The ship was abuzz with visitors to wish us well. On our last day about 70 people, a 'cross-section from all walks of life', crowded in like the cabin scene in the Marx brothers' *A Night at the Opera*, to see us off. The 'owner' had a night and a day cabin, a bathroom with a bath long enough for me, and the first running hot water since leaving Hong Kong (furloughs apart – David Trench had decreed that heaters were unnecessary in the warm Pacific, so all made do with heated showers). The WC was held together by a concrete mound – on a previous voyage the King of Tonga had sat on it: it had collapsed under his weight.

As we left in our

> Spanking Glasgow motor vessel, with flared false funnel,
> Swaying through the Islands (where the Aid Trade pays),
> Picking up copra bugs,
> Cocoa beetles, artefacts,
> Coconut oil and palm oil, in a cheap gin haze,

the heavens spoke as they had done for Bishop Chisholm's funeral, but endorsed by the underworld, for there was an earthquake. We feared for our crates out in the shaking and soaking environment (but one day they arrived safely in Edinburgh, as securely as the professionally packed chests had come from Hong Kong to Honiara five years before). There was material damage elsewhere ashore, but no major disasters. The journey home in this copra ship took nine weeks; whenever it rained loading had to be stopped, for copra has to be kept dry, and the attendant copra bugs covered every light-coloured surface. There were three officers' wives, besides the master's wife and child. Individually, we got on well with all. The journey was long enough for our nerves and preoccupations to settle, and to read the backlog of books collected over the tour. Cooking was Bengali dak bungalow style.

Each landfall lasted a few days, loading when dry or sheltering from rain. Our first stop was Yandina, reuniting us temporarily with our dear Snoddie. At Port Vila we were looked after by John Smith's successor as financial secretary, now advising the New Hebrides: the French food and wine were good, and we bought an oil picture of a mangrove swamp from Nicolai Mitchoutouchkine's studio, which dominates our sitting room (he was a Russian émigré who exhibited in Paris annually, and then came back to live with his Cook Island boyfriend, whose *métier* was to create appliqué tapestries, the most prominent decorating Vila airport; Mitchoutouchkine himself had designed all the recent French colonial Pacific stamps). Here we had a wire from our Edinburgh solicitor, canvassing our interest in a flat about to come on the market in Ramsay Garden (we were pipped at the post when the offers were closed a third of the way through the islands, but then the flat immediately above came on the market, and we authorized a repeat valuation and firm offer).

In Suva we renewed acquaintance with a colleague who had lectured in the Honiara administrative training centre, and suffered much rain while contrasting Suva with Honiara, dazzled by the wealth of shops, the colourful market and the mix of Indian and Melanesian faces. In Nuku'alofa, capital of the Tongan islands, not so beautiful as the Solomons but full of charming and friendly people, we met the British high commissioner, who had virtually become a Tongan; his driver presented us with a vast piece of *tapa* cloth which had been part of the king's carpet from palace to cathedral on a great occasion; it now papers a wall of a room. We also saw the monocled and very large Crown Prince, Queen Salote's grandson, review a superb parade to celebrate his birthday. The governor of Ha'apai, another Tongan nobleman, gave us great hospitality on his island, and loaded us with gifts, as did the governor's representative on Vava'u. In Apia we clambered and scrambled up the pilgrimage route to Robert Louis Stevenson's tomb above Vailima, and saw Aggie's hotel. Western Samoa's people looked nice, but were less friendly: prostitutes swarmed on the ship and one of our ship's wives was attacked by a female would-be thief.

There was now time for more shallow philosophy. I did not accept the happy, state of nature, picture of the Pacific that so many of the young (and elders not yet disillusioned with Margaret Mead's false pictures) thought that their predecessors spoilt, but some of the innocence in the vulnerability was still very endearing. One foresaw some successor of Moro in Guadalcanal arising to drive all the Malaitan 'settlers' out, but not as 1999 and the years to follow were to produce. What made our financial sacrifice worthwhile, exchanging unattractive Hong Kong prospects for the Solomons intellectual drench, was emergence from a materialistic rut for a while, where originality only thrived in the commercial world; and into a 'potty little place' where people were different from anyone known before. The differences would be eroded with time, but would make ploys to engraft political and economic formulas, evolved elsewhere, nugatory. One could only guide insensibly by gentle concealed pressure in overconfident patience, regarding no delay as failure. I wished that 'Britain' still thought the friendship of small, distant places to deserve the same service and care as the strident bullies. Money and technical co-operation, weighed out by economists to formulas, never won us a tenth of the influence and friendship as decent, quiet government before independence and frank honesty in all things afterwards.

Few bearing true responsibility in London or Honiara had had direct personal experience of earlier accouchements of a nation out of an originally artificial dependency. Not one of those had seen the Solomons through from start to finish. The Foreign & Commonwealth Office had never come to terms with the existence of colonial governments, dependent but distinct, which they had only limited powers to direct, or of overseas civil servants whose prime duty was to take decisions within the local Crown's policies, and only marginally, and dubiously, to fulfil an embassy's rôle of reporting, persuading, and representing on behalf of the Whitehall Crown. The ambivalent skills of HMOCS had become rarer and unfashionable with the predominance of contract officers who lacked lifetime dedication. If the empire had indeed been acquired in a series of fits of absentmindedness, its final dismantling was no more 'professional'. This strengthened the dependencies' negotiating hands, while reducing their emotional pangs; Melanesian veterans fondly remembered district officers who had watched the Japanese with them from mountain fastnesses; younger recipients of transferred power took it coolly from the hands of short-term experts. The officers they replaced now felt a sense of anticlimax rather than achievement when independence did at last come. The euphoria shared in the first Indian and African freedoms was less common.

It took eighteen days to cross the ocean, without sight of funnel or sail. It gave a feeling of limitlessness and of world problems being irrelevant. Half way across the Pacific I stubbed my toe and a leg swelled and inflamed itself. It would be diagnosed as gout in a repeat a few years later. Perhaps you read about unreceivable WHO radio medicine in chapter 1. When back in wireless contact we concluded the purchase of a home which we had never seen, one of the least wise transactions that our good Writer to the Signet admitted that he had ever overseen. Then through the Panama, as before in *Arcadia*, and home to Liverpool. We were no longer imperialists, and a new life beckoned. First I would write a frank letter to the deputy under-secretary, putting my side of any story on FCO files: I never had an answer, although the word had obviously got around, since Bruce Greatbatch wrote spontaneously to commiserate over 'how the FCO had treated' me (he did not mention Hong Kong's manipulation). When the DUSofS and I met at the reception after the Solomons independence service in Westminster Abbey, I mentioned that he had not acknowledged a letter. He looked at me quizzically and managed no more than a 'Well, … …' before changing the subject. Mancham had undoubtedly been right.

I should add that I was asked whether I would be interested in the post of administrator of Ascension Island, a dependency of St Helena. This would involve responsibility for calming ructions between the RAF and the USAF who both used this landing ground, and caring for the labourers brought in from St Helena itself. I inquired quizzically whether I would act as governor of the colony during leaves and interregna: it would have been curious to live in a GH equipped with Napoleon's furniture. The answer was, No, as indeed mine had been from the start. Nobody was surprised.

Eventually Secretary of State David Owen sent me a short valedictory letter, thanking me for my service and mentioning in particular my good judgment. I lacked any parsnips to butter.

CHAPTER 11

The Lowest Political Rung (and a Philosophical Distraction)

'I have come to the conclusion that politics are too serious a matter to be left to the politicians'
[attr to Général de Gaulle]

'Culture and the State are Antagonists, ... Power Makes Stupid'
[Nietzsche]

WHAT ARE YOU going to do?', people asked me, settled back in Edinburgh. I was to write a book, but kept quiet about that. The DIY for our new home – papering, sanding, painting, distempering, hanging, hooking, scrubbing, polishing, rearranging – would take Hilary and me months, and I usually cut off with, 'I'm going to enjoy my pension, isn't that the technical term?' They banged on, and at the friend's of a friend, the host said, 'You can't do that, your experience shouldn't be wasted, why not go into politics? You've spent all that time abroad and know places no one else does, the European parliament is always going on about aid to the "ACP" countries (*Africa-Caribbean-Pacific*), they need folk who might help to see it's not all wasted. Why not give it a try?' So I thought about it. Which party? I had learnt, from contrasting unending constitutional changes, that the more that reforming governments tried to do, always in a hurry, the worse everything became. Gradualist organic growth made best sense. Nobody got elected as an independent any more, so the Tories (Unionists) seemed the best of a poor set of choices; at least they talked about rolling back the frontiers of the state, although they had fallen for the gimmick of electing a lady as leader to replace the odiously self-righteous Heath. I had always found socialism attractive as a concept, but quite unnatural in practice outside family circles. I did not believe in eternal compromise, which many Liberals seemed to do, under the pretence of being pragmatic. I hadn't spent years participating in efforts to unite quarrelsome neighbours, only to support fissiparous Nationalists who fostered not a little hatred and some violence among their progeny.

I went along to the Scottish Conservative & Unionist Party HQ to make inquiries, and met the director, not yet knighted, Graham Macmillan. He understood the basis for my sudden interest in the European parliament, for which direct elections were imminent. He would be prepared to put my name forward for consideration, but pointed out that lack of years of working for the party rather mattered. Perhaps I might show willing locally: he understood that the Tory constituency association in Central Edinburgh (sitting member one Robin Cook) needed beefing up, and I became installed as a voluntary organizing secretary (they couldn't afford a paid agent). Central Edinburgh was a salamander of a geographical constituency, long, thin and meandering, covering a line from Meadowbank stadium to Tynecastle (Hearts) football ground *via* Princes Street. It had no core community, only small working class or lower-middle class clusters and straggling retail outlets. At the next boundary commission redistribution it became a more recognizably compact central union of some Old Town and some New Town areas, and Cook rapidly decamped to Livingston New Town. At the revision after that it reverted to gerrymandered absurdity, and I have doubted the integrity of the Scottish Boundaries Commission ever since. It is about to vanish as Scotland's over-representation in Westminster is corrected.

Meantime, what about Europe? The sitting North Edinburgh MP and junior Tory minister, the late Alex Fletcher, who had sat earlier in Brussels/Strasbourg/Luxembourg when Westminster MPs did double duty, was not encouraging – everyone wanted to be an MEP now, he said, because of the attractive salary; so someone with the smallest question mark against suitability had little chance of being selected. I collected piles of paper, but no worthwhile advice, from the EEC's permanent representative in Edinburgh, and not much more from their outlet in London. I signed up for a crash updating course at the Alliance in oral French. I looked out for others interested, to compare notes. I was summoned to Smith Square to be interviewed by Sir Marcus Fox, the party vice-chairman responsible for candidatures. After a good but fair grilling Fox said he would be prepared to put my name forward. By chance I met at a college gaudy a young man who said he also was thinking of the European parliament, and picked my limited brains before admitting that his eyes were on the Lothian constituency.

Later I was summoned back to Smith Square for interview. A rubicund old boy with whiskers met me in the lobby, saying, 'I'm Chelwood, Lord Chelwood, probably never heard of me, I used to be called Tufton-Beamish', and ushered me upstairs to be introduced to the two others of the panel: a Lady peer, Baroness Young, and another Lady, consort of a knight of the realm. Again, I had a probing, intelligent but unintimidating interview, ending with Lady Young saying, nicely, 'Mr Clark, you have had an outstanding, I may say distinguished, career, but I would advise you in your best interest to acquire some experience as quickly as possible at the factory gates, to show your mettle. There is a by-election coming up at *(somewhere in England),* and if you were to offer your services there, I am sure they would welcome it'. I went home in two minds about the whole enterprise, but before having time to think of spending some days at somewhere's gates, I received the 'Dear John' rejection that Fletcher had foretold. The heart was not broken.

However I got on with keeping the branch minutes as Central's organizing secretary, and getting to know my colleagues, who bore no resemblance to the stereotypes of Tory heartlands, but demonstrated well how only a quarter of a century before more Scots had voted Unionist than for rival parties. Apart from our candidate, the Writer to the Signet David McLetchie, who would one day be Scotland's Number One Unionist, our most active man was a hospital caterer (with a feisty wife); the most helpful in practical ways was a minor jobbing printer (with an ever-present teenage son); the one who could produce unending girlpower (from his small trichological school) to stuff envelopes, deliver leaflets and make canvassing tours look formidably large was a hairdresser (with the most intelligent and committed wife); and there were a couple of ladies of value and indeterminate age who had no social pretensions but many a social grace. There were also a newsagent, a small-time financier and a passing-through Yank. No hunters, no aristos, no landed folk, no big business, no academics, and no la-di-da accents. As long as Joe Public tended towards apathy we were in with a chance. But the boundary gerrymander favoured the sitting tenant, and when the general election came, despite our party being out on the doorsteps every night of the campaign, Cook got back in. His behaviour at the Meadowbank count fixed my opinion of him forever thereafter, without having to weigh his morals when he dumped his wife in such a public way. So sure of his success, well before the last boxes had been emptied and counted, and without any reference to the returning officer, he lined up his opponents and instructed them like a master of the ceremonies in what order to come to the microphone, what time limit to put on what they might have to say, and to know their place.

Soon after licking our (or rather, David's) wounds, a Labour regional councillor for Holyrood & St Giles division got himself into Parliament. There was a by-election, and we wanted a paper candidate. Nobody pushed themselves forward for a hopeless cause. I said I might find it fun. Sighs of relief (I think). Leaflets, posters and beadiest of eyes on expenses were something new to learn. Advice varied. It was probably wise to talk of 'experience in administration and government in a number of (unspecified) countries', rather than to say baldly that I was an ex-*colonial* officer. On the other hand I balked at being told not to waste my time going round Dumbiedykes estate, where everybody on subsidized council rents (this was still 1978) would vote Labour till death. In fact I found Dumbiedykes fascinating, and educative. 'A Tory, eh? Never seen one here before. Come away in and have tea'. 'My wain's a bright lad, I think he'd do well enough at the uni, but his teacher won't do anything to help'. 'Those tinkers down in number twenty-three, it's terrible, Friday nights he comes in shouting drunk, beats them all up, breaks all the furniture and likely enough starts a fire; then come Tuesday the Social are round replacing the damage and they're laughing'. Of course, I didn't get in, though there was the daft moment in the count before all the boxes were in when my piles looked encouraging. I did get more votes than previous Tory candidates.

 I chatted about this to an advocate I had met in some political meeting, who had parliamentary ambitions himself. He was associated with the Edinburgh South constituency, whose sitting MP was Michael Ancram (Earl and heir to the Marquess of Lothian). He said they were looking for a candidate for the district (city) council ward of Marchmont, and the selection committee was meeting next week – why didn't I come along? Nothing loth, for the fun of it, I went and to my surprise as a stranger against several locally familiar faces, was adopted as the 'prospective'. It meant parting with my friends in Central, but such is life. South had a full-time paid agent, Sue, which a successful and prosperous constituency could then still afford. It also had a membership more like the popular picture of Tory masses than Central, but still far from the English shires or Belgravia. The municipal election would not be until May 1980, so I had time (housekeeping and author's research, of which more later, permitting), to think about my 'campaign'. There was a small core of helpers, who came to life in the week or two before the election itself, but the main effort had to be my own.

 In the late afternoon of 2 January 1980 I began at the house on Blackford Hill, nearest to the Royal Observatory and southernmost in the Marchmont ward, and carried on till suppertime. By the end of April, adding in many Saturday mornings, I had knocked on every door in most streets, and on some doors in every street, and had reached the Meadows, the northern edge of the ward. The process brought home a few lessons. One was that this was the one sure way to get the fact of one's personal candidature across to the people who vote. Secondly, that I was lucky in not having to earn my living at the same time. Finally, that for a would-be MP to do the same in a constituency, of perhaps a dozen or score of wards, would take literally years. Yet to rely on media coverage, unless one already has a public persona that journalists can make copy out of, is hopeless. The proof of my own pudding's recipe was that when on the day I traipsed round the three polling stations with my rosette, grinning stupidly at those going in and out, the number of total strangers who nodded at me or gave thumbs-up signs was remarkable. I had been remembered because I had called, even though I never went back a second time to knock at doors that had not opened. I had more votes than all the others combined.

The front of a canvassing leaflet – did it garner votes?

If I had imagined that the party 'group' of which I was now the newest member would want to find out what I had to offer, and use it to best advantage, I was in self-opinionated error. The hard core that led the group, mostly members of the same old boys' rugby club, had everything nicely shared out. I was put on the recreation committee, whence I managed to get nomination to the Edinburgh Festival Council, to the chagrin of some who had imagined that this meant free tickets (it didn't – nor did I dare mention that while on the way home from the Pacific I had wildly applied for the post of festival director, thinking that a lifetime of running organizations of growing magnitude, coupled with love for most of the arts, would make it possible, if I had a few months sitting beside the retiring director Peter Diamond, to see how he worked – I wonder now at my presumption, but I still have ideas which I have not been ashamed to share amicably with Frank Dunlop and Brian McMaster. Anyway, we got John Drummond). The group leader let me 'have' the festival when I said that in return I would go on to another committee no one else wanted. My first essay in wheel and deal.

I came down to earth in my first full council meeting when, having listened to the arguments from Labour, Liberal and SNP on the siting of a 'halfway house' for social inadequates in a certain middle-class area, to which my party was opposed, I decided that the likely harm to neighbours was minimal and voted for it. I'm not sure I was ever forgiven, but I had supposed that elected representatives had their own consciences to follow as well as the whips'. Innocence was tarred again when a wily councillor (of what would now be called New Labour persuasion) later referred to this and said in debate that Councillor Clark had once shown himself to be a decent man. It didn't help (nor was it meant to). Abuse was more common, although I only once reacted, when a young opponent with ambitions referred to Councillor Clark and 'whatever banana republic he came from'. This I took as an insult to a developing commonwealth nation, and he was told by the Lord Provost to 'withdraw'. I was not displeased when years later the boy got into trouble as a junior New Labour minister, through alleged fiddling of the rent of his constituency office.

Despite (or because of) my having headed both a major local government organization and a civil service, and administered an entire government, it was never thought appropriate to put me on the policy & resources, finance or (except briefly) the general purposes committees which effectively ruled Edinburgh's municipality. Length of time in the group was what then led to the top, and in the early eighties there the old-timers stayed.

After the election, in ignorance, I supposed that councillors might as individuals make things happen. The word was that the Royal Infirmary of Edinburgh was past further modernizing and that a new hospital should be built. But where? Did it have to be outside overcrowded Edinburgh? Presumptuously I gathered the council's chief officers. Look, I said, there is a great mess opposite the Usher Hall, where there is the entry to a supposed but never progressed West Approach Road from the city's centre out towards the airport and Glasgow road, by-passing Corstorphine. This idea has blighted planning all around. Let us try lateral original thinking. Where the clapped-out carpet shop, the city's once sole Indian restaurant, and the shambles where the Caledonian railway station's sidings once congregated, there was a mighty space for redevelopment. Have you seen La Défense in Paris, a mighty block like a vast Arc de Triomphe, full of offices?

Why not design a huge hospital *over* the start of the new road west, which would run underneath with adjoining multi-storey parking, at the heart of the city? When the Royal Infirmary has moved in, let the university move next door into the nobly historic old hospital buildings, restored to glory with all excrescences removed, the wards becoming ready-made lecture rooms, its offices filled with dons and clerks? Then strip out as much as possible of what the university has done to ruin George Square and the adjacent Buccleuch streets, and restore those tenements to quality residential accommodation in the centre for the middle classes? It would 'cost', but so did much else that raised no eyelids, and would it not be good? The silence was stunned, and stunning. 'Councillor Clark, have you any idea of how many vested interests you would be treading on?' 'Probably not, but tell me'. In-taken breath, shrugged shoulders and out-stretched palms were as eloquent as any rational run-down. I suppose I apologized for wasting their invaluable time, but it was as good an idea as some Edinburgh developments that have made money for the developers. The same space has since been filled by a Sheraton hotel, an underused open square and two huge office blocks (joined by a pedestrian bridge) full of financiers and consultants who should work in the city's outlying business parks. The new Royal Infirmary squats far out in the green belt, remote from all but the residents of one ill-favoured housing estate.

It is prudent to skip most of my paper record of eight years on various committees, planning & development, technical services, personnel, environmental health, housing, benefits, licensing and more. The mind retains freshest memories of 'recreation' concerns: the row over the Playhouse theatre, which could have been our long-bruited 3,000-seat opera house, convenorship of our theatres and halls, representation on the Royal Lyceum theatre board, orphan archives and dumbed-down libraries, Commonwealth Games, …

The lasting result of involvement with 'recreation' was appointment to the Edinburgh International Festival Council, to which I was re-elected as a private Society member after leaving the city council. The festival director was John Drummond, a sort of Scot, with a track record in the BBC. He produced outstanding festivals, and introduced elements that freshened what might have become, not less in quality, but too routine a pattern. He experimented, and had good judgment of standards, but not of personal relationships. He related to those who might be of value to himself, but was dismissive of others. That the festival council was his employer and that its members, however ignorant or token, might expect a modicum of politeness never occurred to him, as some comments in his autobiography make clear in other fields. He stayed in Edinburgh only when he had to. I identified him with lesser diplomats I had observed at social gatherings: making petty small talk on auto-pilot, their eyes would wander over their interlocutor's shoulder, searching for someone more significant whom it might be advantageous to accost. After my first festival under his wing I ventured to write a reasoned criticism of what I had seen and heard. I supposed that the reactions of ticket-purchasers might be at least as valuable as reviews by paid critics. My reward for seeking to be helpful, not exactly gratuitously, was, 'Dear Councillor Clark, Thank you for your letter. I find that I am not in agreement with some of your artistic judgments. Yours sincerely'. I wasted no further time on sticking my nose in where it was not wanted, but had no regrets when he rejected an extended contract.

I found myself on the selection board for his successor, chaired by the *ex officio* festival chairman, the Lord Provost. The then new Tory group leader and I were far from each other round the table. There was an interesting list of candidates, among whom was a gnomelike, sturdy little man who was different. He had a distinguished career behind him in theatre, and was remembered for a festival Shakespeare-in-the-round on the old Edinburgh ice-rink. Some interviewers pounced on his apparent absence from the world of pure music, to which he replied that he made no claim to be an authority, but would take advice. This was honest, and I saw no harm in the director of a festival of music, drama and the arts being pre-eminent in an aspect that might have taken too far back a seat in the past. My Tory superior evidently thought the same, as well as being attracted by the man's character. While argument swayed back and forth in favour of others, we two stuck to our guns and eventually prevailed over others' disagreements.

So Frank Dunlop joined us, and proved a success, in the teeth of London's music critics who never went to the theatre. Frank's international drama imports were welcome, and their impact did not overshadow some very fine and original music – which sadly began to suffer, as the festival in general suffered, not from his lack of imagination, but by the inflationary expenses of hiring the world's finest and greediest performers. Frank, like most good directors, rarely used other people's unsolicited ideas, but had the courtesy to listen to them. After his retirement, I asked what his proudest production had been. 'The Toho company's Japanese *Macbeth* by Ninigawa!' It still is my own favourite memory from so many festivals, excepting only 1947 and Kathleen Ferrier's (and Bruno Walter's) *Lied von der Erde*. I had no part in Brian McMaster's succession, but think I established friendship with this cool, far from garrulous, knight who settled in Edinburgh and has managed to retain the balance that Dunlop achieved. He has widened the net (while giving some individuals virtually permanent 'in residence' status in the programmes) despite having no option but to abandon block-bustering. He willingly feeds amateur opinion into his round-up assessments after each year's menu. I sympathize with his frustration that a festival founded by Bing and Falconer to celebrate music, drama *and the arts* should be denied policy input into the contemporaneous exhibitions in our public galleries. I was heavily invited by the deputy chairman of the society council not to stand for re-election, allowing him to parachute in an influential replacement from a rival institution. I was hurt, because there were, admittedly greater, names on our masthead whose attendance at meetings had been negligible. *Schadenfreude* followed when the substitute failed of election. Hilary and I still spend an annual fortune on tickets, and we house many friends anxious to share our pleasure in the banquet.

To return to the city council. After a year of self-criticizing doubts, I asked the original group leader to a lunch *à deux* for a general chat. I failed to discover what convictions or abstract philosophy (or personal prejudices) informed his Toryism. His bluff generalities were shallow. I asked bluntly why he thought, while I rubbed along pretty well with most of the group (a few very well), there was evidently no swell of desire to bring me into the inner circle, where my practical past and a few outside contacts might be beneficially used. He smiled and said that he could not help it, but there was 'a feeling in the group' for which he could not account that they did not really want me in such a position. I was left to rationalize that it was unfortunate that I was not a member of Leith Academicals Rugby Football Club, that fellows might think me too much of a toff, that the leadership felt no need of new thinking, that people comfortably established never give way without a nastier brawl than I could contemplate, and probably that I was a self-regarding charlatan ill-suited to political government anyway. An objective reader of past chapters may long ago have diagnosed my personality weaknesses. However one or two other more prototypical Conservative councillors were ready to challenge, not only the self satisfied ethos of the leadership but the leader himself. There was a change after the annual group re-election practice towards the end of my first four years. I found myself in various close discussions with the new leader and the finance spokesman, not least over an opera house, but also over ideas I had for groupings together of adjacent wards, to cover recognizable divisions of the city, sharing a common office and generalist municipal manager for the whole area. Area committees would work in harness with the subject committees (shades of Hong Kong's urban district offices?). I began to feel less useless. Labour won the 1984 election, fairly comfortably, and our new leader lost interest and withdrew. I took courage to offer myself with others as a replacement, but we were outvoted by a young man (the success of a lady PM had made 'youth' another modernizing specific). This new leader said *sotto voce* that he would have pushed for me to be Lord Provost had we won, thinking that existing post-nominals would be helpful in more than one direction. Porkers have flown.

A new perspective during that campaign led to lateral brooding. A friendly member of our congregation, apprised of my affiliation, said over coffee, 'A Conservative in this church? That's a turn-up for the books!' A housewife near Blackford Hill had said at her door, 'I do not understand how any Christian can possibly be a Conservative.' I recalled Tom Lehrer, who had lyrically founded *National Brotherhood Week* with the words, 'I am sure we all agree that we should love our fellow men. I am aware that there are people who do not like all their fellow human beings, and ... I ... *hate* people like that.' There were less alienating experiences on the doorsteps: one little old lady replied, 'Ach, na, A used tae vote the SNP, but noo, A jist gang tae the kirk.' Another shook her head gently, said she would read our party news-sheet, but that only one man would get her vote – the Lord Jesus Christ. It was sad to find intelligent and civilized folk who regarded their own view of how worldly political institutions and fashionable economic managements should be arranged as prerequisite to admission to the ranks of true believers.

It looked clearer to *me* how the virtues of faith, hope and charity were strained under corporatism, while the cardinal, pre-Christian, virtues of prudence, temperance, fortitude and justice were disdained under collectivism. Within my own experience the Christian virtues seemed to be those of the individual who managed to preserve respect, and perform worship, by dint of recognizing duty to others as something more demanding than a basis for negotiation. A society gathered together of those who shared a discipline of duty might be in less need to stir unendingly the bubbling pot of 'rights', which often aggravated the thirsts of discontent and envy. It was arguable.

What troubled me were the materialist causes, claiming possibly shaky Christian foundations – abortion on demand but horror at the death penalty for the wicked; political change through terrorism; financial independence from the family (by way of financial dependence on taxpayers) at age 16; fomentation of the class war; trivialization of mysteries few of us comprehend (like the sex drive); rejection of local custom in favour of inadequately understood but fashionably attractive foreign traditions – the list went and on. All such 'issues' appeared to be irresistible magnets, not only for those who denied religion (or gradualism in politics), but also for some professed (or should I say 'professional'?) Christians: those who, for example, rather ostentatiously preached *Judge not, that ye be not judged*, and *Forgiveness of Trespasses*, as though these concepts made it hypocritical to distance oneself from the sin, while praying close by the sinner for repentance.

If God is not dead, neither can be Satan? The latter may still quote Scripture. Yet not all minority rebels are to be supported, surely, even though we may love them as ourselves (and how *blindly* do we, in truth, love ourselves?). I suspect that in the secret mind which we never open to our very dearest, few of us admire all that much of ourselves. Should we not all conceive it possible we may be mistaken – some of the time? Is it any *more* difficult to love one's neighbour as oneself while a member of one secular party than of another, granted that one first loves the Lord with all one's heart, and all one's strength and ...?

It was possible under Roman rule, in the Dark Ages and the Renascence, during the Reformation and the Counter-Reformation, the Industrial Revolution, the Age of Exploration and transpontine expansions, the Missionary Years, and it is so to-day under Western Democracy or in the free republics, one-party states and autocracies of the ex-colonial nations. I expect it remains so in the Age of the Pill and the Chip, of AIDS and SARS. Political and economic institutions have evolved throughout history, and doubtless will continue without Utopia coming any nearer or history coming to an end. We may trust that inherited Christian teaching and faith (immutable, if they embody Truth) will guide how decision-makers inside 'western' institutions of the future may reach and implement decisions. But we have to come to terms with Islam, where religious and secular affairs are inseparable, and where to question or argue with God (or Allah)'s revealed and interpreted will is unthinkable. It is not credible (to me) that mankind will ever cease to create new institutions, within which its congenital talents and activities, and its acquired skills and experiences, will discover new patterns of relationship, to challenge anew its maintenance of religious behaviour and belief. The Nation State may yet be seen to have offered no more worldly security to individuals than the extended family or the feudal village, and there may be more ways of tending to the helpless here and now than we have tried, under God's laws. I hope that we will not for ever be able to say, 'We have paid our tribute money to Caesar, let Caesar get on with the Social Work and the National Health.'

Two things seem fundamental. There must be faith that God has not abandoned us to fight out battles without His hand intervening – sometimes without our awareness; and there must be faith that we may aspire to share in His Kingdom forever and ever. When we are taught to believe that the struggle is up to us, unaided except by clashing cymbals and material support, and that any Paradise that we may enjoy in our present persons must be found here and now, then we may have to respect those media-persons and Bishops who treat Christianity as a two thousand year con-job – and the other revealed religions as no better windows on to the mysteries which we are sufficiently advanced to detect, but not to unravel. It may be more fun to be a Buddhist, it is a saving of fruitless inquiry and discontent to be a Muslim, and if all you are concerned about is the here and now, be a humanist (like those Bishops). I still feel bound to ask questions about the nature and purpose of the teaching that people seem to have purveyed to the young of our own nation.

I distrust eclecticism too, those who would temper a little bit of good with a little bit of evil. I suspect those who proffer an *hors d'œuvre* dish full of tempting morsels of Marx and Freud, neo-Darwin and neo-Luther, instant *canapés* offering painless revolution through a middle way, charted not by measured sightings but by Ologists. If we have to fall for metaphors, I suspect that Bunyan wrote the most convincing ones; but in trying to understand worldly facts I envy the various natural and cognitive scientists. The little of science's wisdom that I can penetrate fills me with awe and ultimate hope, whether I'm presently in the Slough of Despond, in the Valley of Humiliation, at Vanity Fair or in Doubting Castle – yet it certainly reconciles me to a world in which it is in sweat of his faith that man eats bread, where it is childish to start arguments with, 'It isn't fair!' A world where the most satisfactory consolations seem to lie as much in feeling that one shares with pastoral nomads, settled farmers, artizans and urbanized managers alike, a single unbroken tradition, steadily evolving without snapping any golden thread, and in unspiteful confidence into an unforeseeable but reassuringly beckoning future. When I look for people who think the same, I have found as many around gap sites and in estates as in comfortable dwellings. This must be unconvincing to those who have another partisan allegiance, blasphemy to all who have sold what they have and given to the poor, and specious to many of the remainder. Time to stop preaching and return to the main road.

The 1984 labour leader was a hard socialist with an angry attitude. With much ill-will the councillors' ceremonial robes, worn for the kirking in St Giles or when the Lord Provost presented Her Majesty with the keys of the city at Holyrood, were abolished to store. The new Labour majority neither attended the kirk nor supported ceremony. The past was to be buried and forgotten. The ancient office of Bailie, granted to leading councillors but abolished by an earlier board-sweeping administration, had been mooted for restoration, and indeed had been retained in Red Clydeside, but this revival was denied despite the title having been held by at least one prominent Labour councillor still serving. The waves of hatred that wafted across the council chamber were palpable. Yet when on a planning visit I found myself sitting by the leader, we discovered a joint love of Delius (his wife played the piano to professional standard), and I realized that although his hard upbringing in a doomed mining community had led to a politics and public manner that I believed to be myopic, it was understandable. At least if mistaken (in my judgment) he was incorrupt, unlike many around us, and I could respect him, if not like him. His sharp edges caused too many abrasions, and in due course his own party replaced him by what we did not yet know as New Labour. We had known where we were with him, but now we would always be guessing.

During those eight years the amount of direct reporting and informed or informative comment in our 'national newspaper' of municipal affairs shrank steadily to a minimum, except around a quadrennial election. Nobody cared, except tyro councillors proud of their unrecorded eloquence. Apathy had begun its remorseless march through the kingdom's institutions. I found more satisfaction in the two community councils that my ward straddled. Those local folk who found themselves on these councils might be patronized as interfering busybodies, as idle hands or as idiosyncratic nobodies – I still found them to be genuinely concerned by real local events and trends that some authority ought to be involved with, so long as 'society' believed that individuals must surrender prescription of remedies to remote overseers. Dirigistes and statists in the making treated community councils as buzzing flies at the best, to be brushed off, and at the worst as the next on the list for extinction.

There was one curious contrast to recall. Although education was a 'regional', not a 'district' subject, a city councillor sat on each schools board. Miss Jean Brodie's high school (now co-ed) was at the heart of my ward, and I assumed that I should be appointed to it. Its name still carried prestige earned in the rather different days of the past, and claim was laid to its 'governing body' (not that the regional council saw the board as such) by a senior colleague (I should have understood his claim better had he been a 'former pupil'). As the new boy I was put on another, a Catholic high school, which nobody wanted, not even a Catholic. It had three primary schools feeding it, and month by month the board went the rounds of them all. One day a colleague said in the City Chambers coffee room, 'Hell, I've got my schools council to-night, I wish I had an excuse'. 'Why?' I asked. 'All they talk about is politics, lack of resources, why doesn't the government do this or that? Yours must be worse, with all that bigotry'. I countered that I enjoyed my schools council: admittedly Father McGillicuddy, or whoever he was, did sit at the end of the table to watch that nobody sinned against the Holy Ghost, but he never interfered; the teachers present, the parents, the others, even the regional councillor, never talked about anything but education and what they could do practically to support the school, pupils and staff with books, materials, advice, sports, social events. They were bright and positive, and I was happy to be there.

Back in the second year the council had had to nominate a name to the Secretary of State for possible appointment to the Lothian Health Board. The Lord Provost suggested me as son of a former MOH. I served for eight years. Like the city council, it mixed routine boredom with inconsequential interest. The 24 members included those who read through the pile of papers that arrived for each monthly meeting; those who barely pick'n'mixed; those who saw their place on the board as to speak for and on matters related to their partisan political interests; those whose narrow professional qualifications gave them an opening for an occasional intervention; those who ostentatiously attended as if of right as public figures accorded no more than their due; and those who believed that there was duty to be done, that they might be able to fulfil it because their concern was genuine, but that they might end submerged in treacle. I will not suggest the proportions, but I do recall an honourable left-winger who clearly went through every paper with a toothcomb and raised issues that few had noticed; a qualified nurse who never spoke except to press a partisan Labour point (and to whom the Scottish Office gave the longest series of reappointments, under Tory ministers); and the wife of a prominent lawyer who served on many public committees and was invaluably pertinent. The dynamic was the British tradition in public services, that the permanent staff were perceived as decent, hard-working, intelligent and incorrupt people, whose proposals had been thought through to achieve improvement and the best use of resources – if one had not read or understood the papers, rubber-stamping the agenda would rarely be a mistake.

I was appointed to the board's ethics panel; a pair of laymen offered the senior professionals public opinion on problems posed by practitioners, and the suggested answers. After some years on the main board I suggested to the chairman that, given the huge spread of institutions and services we oversaw, nobody could expect to know all about everything. It might make sense were we to split the 24 into groups, each to concentrate on a major hospital or a geographically linked group of smaller units. After getting to know them closely, when their concerns came up in the full board, there would be some members better equipped to discuss with understanding. This novel idea appealed, and I had the dubious reward of being asked to lead a trio who would 'get to know' the Royal Infirmary of Edinburgh, our prime teaching hospital of renown. My colleagues were a retired professor of geriatrics and the good wife just mentioned. We went to see the general manager (as then known), of the RIE. Would he let it be known that we would not be spies from the Kremlin, but hoped to be the staff's friends at court? He welcomed the intention, but how did we propose to set about it? I said we would welcome advice, but as a former bureaucrat wondered whether we might start by sitting in, like friendly flies on the wall, on the committees that undoubtedly met, and so hear what the staff worried about in their own discussions. 'Mr Clark, have you any idea how many committees we have?' No, tell us. 'I have no idea myself', but he found a paper that listed many, not excluding the electricians' committee (the people whose working practices forbade anyone else to change a light bulb).

So we compromised. Not all three of us, but one at a time, we would do the sitting in and observation, speaking only when spoken to after a reassuring introduction. After a month or two of nosing around as individuals, with routine chats over coffee, we compared thorough notes. Our experiences matched exactly. Most meetings had to be over within an hour, because other duties had to be started at recognized times (a committee at 8 *a.m.* might be followed by a Grand Round or a theatre opening tabled for 9). Approval of previous minutes was often prolonged by argumentative individuals unhappy with how a point had been misrecorded. Item four was so important that it should be deferred, for separate treatment at a special single item meeting, to be called weeks later, after negotiating a convenient date. By ten to nine people were leaving so as not to be late for next duty. *Never* did the chairman round off an item by saying, 'Right, you have all had your say, this is what you will do, and you, and you; those are your instructions, come to me at once if there are problems. If it all goes wrong, I carry the can. On you go.' In our evilly litigious society, where 'compensation' is the new lotto, it helps to blur 'undemocratic' chains of command, and to point to individual exculpatory excuses, leaving no identifiably personal, transparent, responsibility. It lies at the heart of what is wrong with the world's second largest employer (the first, after the demise of the armed forces of the USSR, is the Indian State Railways). An army where the superior's order is a basis for discussion will lose its war.

Not but what monetary waste is not also a basic fault. Like other British public services, 70p in every £ spent in the NHS goes straight into the pockets of the great army of employees. The 30% is still a vast amount. Hygiene rightly demands that every sterile packet carelessly opened, so that the contents fall on the floor, must be discarded and replaced. Nobody thought me serious when I suggested that every container should have printed on it, boldly and eye-catchingly, its price to the taxpayer, which might engender a little more care in handling. As for that floor, I have no problem with contracting out to cleaning specialists the work of the moppers and sweepers, but the contract *must* enshrine the right of the ward sister (or whatever neologism has inherited the minute-to-minute management of a ward) to bawl out the ineffective wielder of bucket and broom. I myself observed dust balls under my bedside table remaining untouched for over a week, when in Chapter 1. I was nonetheless sorry that after eight years, having had one reappointment, I had to make way for fresh blood, as most members did. I was less pleased when, having walked to all the Lothian Health Board meetings and had no expenses to claim, it was soon decided to reorganize everything, and my successors began to earn £5,000 a year. I did not need the money, although I could have spent it happily, and did not begrudge it to some others, but I did bridle when a former councillor colleague who had no interest in health asked a political superior if there were any little jobs going and was appointed.

I did not entirely turn my back on national politics while a city councillor. Meeting a Tory who was prominent in the Museums Association (when English councils still sent such representatives to annual conferences) led to my joining the party's advisory committee on arts and cultural matters, in Scotland's interest. We met for years in Westminster under a succession of chairmen and were addressed by a continually changing series of arts ministers or shadows. Patrick Cormack, not yet Sir, was the longest serving chairman, but the priority accorded to the subject by the hierarchy was marked by our seldom meeting the same figurehead twice. Mellor, Renton, Bottomley (Mrs), they came and went and I shall not rank them. The one who impressed me most was the only one who said honestly that he claimed no expertise or sentimental attraction to the portfolio, but he would learn and fight for it (echoing Frank Dunlop?). This appealed to me enormously, because Richard Luce's generalist enthusiasm was learnt as a district officer in Kenya. It must have underpinned his capacity later to govern Gibraltar and finally to become Lord Chamberlain. I sat on a comparable committee in Scotland, but it dissolved, while the UK body has also evaporated.

Looking for exposure to practical (if not, heaven forfend, ideological) ideas and experience, I joined the Bow Group, thinking it neither too antediluvian nor noticeably limp-wristed. A sub-group in Edinburgh held interesting meetings, but fell into desuetude. Now for the final confession. As I absorbed more and more of politics and politicians I wondered whether I might not be no worse an MP than some. Michael Ancram was misguided enough to sponsor me, and I was accepted on to the List of potential prospective parliamentary candidates. Solid citizens with Dr Johnson's 'bottom', people with creditable success behind them, now rarely offered themselves for public ignominy. There were few women or minorities, actual or token (not that reverse discrimination guarantees quality). Only two vacancies came up within my self-imposed circuit. One was Leith, thought unwinnable, but I had enjoyed being a paper candidate before. The selection committee included a fellow city councillor, but that did not help, not that anyone offered me a *post mortem*: the chosen one did not win. The other was East Lothian, where I had a game plan of forcefeeding myself with fast-food tastings of the farming community and its organizations, which I thought I might understand and certainly sympathize with – but how was I to make an impression on the tired former mining towns? The local association would advise. I was not chosen, nor did the elect win; but the agent told me at the Blackpool Conservative conference that I should try again – wherever I was already known. I never did, and like Lamont *je ne regrette rien*. I should not have rejected fame, but its spur was not spiky enough.

Looking back, it is curious that when I pass a former fellow councillor in the street, we exchange perfunctory nods – except when it is an Old Labour survivor. They stop and have a crack, and we part with smiles. Whether this is a reflection on parties or personalities is for others to guess. The only close friends we retain are a (civilized) Scot Nat and his wife who became Lord and

Lady Provost in the year after I demitted office to concentrate on writing and museums. Leaving the city chambers was a relief. Nationally, I may still claim friendship with Michael Ancram, the party's deputy leader and shadow foreign secretary, and David McLetchie, now leader in Scotland. I have unburdened myself of critical thoughts to party officials, local and national, several times, with unsurprisingly scant acknowledgment. But I had that book to write, and have cooled my porridge.

CHAPTER 12

Images Move, into – Not Such a Dusty Life?

Excuse my dust
[Dorothy Parker's own Epitaph]

LOCAL GOVERNMENT gave me the *entrée* into the museum and gallery world. I also represented the city on Edinburgh Filmhouse, our non-profitable charitable art cinema. Only in such palaces has one access to the heritage of the moving picture, before inflammable cellulose nitrate and plastic celluloid finally surrender to digital electrons. Arthouse cinemas are the nearest that most British people have to museums of the moving image. I mentioned in Chapter 1 that I owed it to the cinema that I wore spectacles. Because I couldn't read the words (*Came the Dawn* or *Be Mine Forever* and all that) I approached the screen to see better, and saw the oculist next day.

The last film I saw in Glasgow was *Lives of a Bengal Lancer*. In those days, after queuing (even in the rain) for admission once earlier customers' seats had emptied, one had four hours of the Big Picture, the 'B' film, GB or Movietone News, a cartoon, Pathé Pictorial or other magazine, the trailers *and* some live variety or music hall entertainment, as well as an interval for cigarettes, ice cream, chocolates, even tea on a tray in afternoons. Performance was continuous. The Big Picture started around mid-day, with a last showing before eleven o'clock, followed by the National Anthem (which many sneaked out of, to avoid standing still and silent for a couple of minutes before rushing to get the tram home). Nobody arrived for a timed start, and there were always people getting up to leave because 'This is where we came in', a phrase transferred to history repeating itself.

There was the organ, the mighty Wurlitzer or Compton. Preservationists organized the retention of the Edinburgh Playhouse organ when that original Gospel Hall was being converted from a cinema into a theatre. Gerald Shaw, the organist at Glasgow's New Cinema, wore a dazzling sky blue velvet doublet with his kilt, taking care how he lifted his legs when he swung round from the console to accept applause. Edinburgh's Regal (later ABC) was built with provision for an organ, but economies were shrinking, and none was ever installed: programme-fillers were also shrinking. At the Regal my musical awareness began to expand, when for the first time I came out of a film humming the incidental music, and began to notice and listen to the soundtracks. This was Erich Wolfgang Korngold's support for Flynn, Rathbone & Fontaine in *The Adventures of Robin Hood*.

I have lost count of the great movies (and actors and cameramen's work) I have seen, but I owe much to the Oxford Film Society which brought French films shot in real, shabby and mouldering buildings or streets, not in studio sets; and much to Hong Kong, where we saw wonderful Japanese films before they became a justified cult in the West. Personal involvement began when the city council nominated me (against little competition) to the Filmhouse board when it was growing out of the Edinburgh Film Guild. We joined the director of the time in a pilgrimage to the Cannes festival, shouting with the fans 'Catherine!' when Deneuve appeared on the Croiset. When I did not seek a third term as councillor, the Scottish Film Council's director nominated me to rejoin Filmhouse in my own right. I remained until 2002, contributing little of value, except an awareness of how much public presentation of film has changed over the years, and an increasing nervous uncertainty of where it would go next.

Unless one is at an extravaganza, some would-be-dazzling première or a major festival, the day of the 2,000 strong audience is over. The question remains whether the multiplex formula of 30-seaters or even 200-seaters, provides the same buzz. I never forget the day when I left Filmhouse and noticed that Woody Allen was on at the neighbouring ABC in his b/w of *Zelig*. It was very funny, but there were only six or seven other members of the public scattered across the No 1 auditorium. There was a chilly lack of laughter or communal reaction. For the real 'good night out' mass experience one has to find a 'product package' that will get the crowds out again, to see film in a place packed with atmosphere. I cannot picture what in the mid and long runs is going to replicate the appeal of the tv-less Thirties. We are on the point of all surviving film being digitally available in databanks which one will log on to on demand in our living rooms. This worry left me ambivalent about rebuilding Filmhouse, unless some Paul Getty III gave us many millions outright without strings, and guaranteed more for revenue endowment and against the overruns of all contemporary capital projects. I loved the *idea* which had been quietly floated of a subterranean multiplex under Festival Square, but was terrified of a burden of unrepayable debt. I should have been happier to make do with a refurbishment and updating of the facilities and technology of our present home. No longer my concern. To our muttons.

When I was small, my parents spent many weekend afternoons at Glasgow's Kelvingrove museum and art gallery: they went upstairs to look at Rembrandt's man in armour, which meant nothing to me – I was occupied with pressing the

Hilary looks up at me talking down to Lord (Dickie) Attenborough at a Filmhouse opening.

buttons that turned the wheels and moved the pistons of the model engines, with mirrors reflecting the parts beneath, on the ground floor: this was akin to the Meccano which was then my principal joy in life. Later Edinburgh's Royal Scottish Museum broadened my awareness, while schoolmasters of classics, English and history were having their way with material or invisible pointers to the less obvious fascinations of life. Travel, to London and even an Antwerp Exhibition, meant more opening of eyes and provocation of thought in mind-enhancing institutions. Later in adulthood came familiarity with some of the lesser treasure houses in Jos and Ife, Angkor Wat and Delhi, Khatmandu and Texila, and everywhere else that boasted collections during our travels; I had also found myself responsible for professional curators and their holdings in Hong Kong and Honiara.

Looking back, the most lasting impressions had been from the truly great collections abroad: the Prado in Madrid, where every gallery made one want to see every single picture on every one of its walls (O, the Goyas, and the man that was then new to me, Ribera); and not just the *Night Watch* in Holland or the *Mona Lisa* in the Louvre, as it were; but the Smithsonian in Washington, with the space machinery and planes of war; the Kunsthistoriches in Vienna, with the Breughels; the Royal Ontario Museum, where for the first time I saw Chinese art interpreted in all-embracing chronological order; and above all, the Hermitage, with unending wonder upon wonder. Then there have been expansive views in Berlin, Brisbane, Budapest, Copenhagen, Dresden, Florence, Kyoto, Lucerne, Milan, Moscow, Munich, Ottawa, Peking, Prague, Stockholm, Sydney, Turin. Not but what our home museums didn't cram the corners of memory: Bloomsbury and South Ken were wonders too. The great introduction to flat art came in an Edinburgh festival retrospective in the 1950s, when for the first time I saw the bulk of the work of a still living artist, shown in order of creation, and not in reproduction, and could try to judge what had brought about each change of style (this was Braque, whom like Mondrian for a similar reason I can love much more than Picasso); and I came to realize that the Scottish National Gallery, yards away from my ultimate home, was the greatest small gallery in the world, holding my two favourite paintings of all time, not that I can begin to analyse why that should be – 19-year-old Velasquez's *bodegón*, *Old Woman Cooking Eggs* and Chardin's vase of flowers (which only when I saw it loaned to a RA retrospective did I realize was not in his usual repertoire). Still, my engineering grandfather and Meccano prevailing over my water-colourist grandfather and my parents' Japanese *ukiyo-e* prints, if I had to choose, I would always go to a museum of objects before a gallery of art.

The moment of truth came at the first group 'Recreation' meeting of the Scottish Conservative and Unionist members elected to the new City of Edinburgh (District) Council in May 1980. At last representation on the Council for Museums & Galleries in Scotland remained unallocated: the what? Silence. The newest boy shyly raised his hand and suggested that if nobody else was interested, he might be. 'Thank goodness', said the leader. A week or two later I drove on a filthy day to Stirling's Tolbooth, where CMGS was then housed. The turn-out was limited. On the agenda was the appointment to the board of someone to represent Scotland's four cities. No nominations had been received. A board member (the director of the Scottish National Galleries) asked the congregation whether there were an elected member from Aberdeen or Dundee, Glasgow or Edinburgh, present. A shy hand admitted that he had been fingered by his Edinburgh council. 'Well, if Councillor whatever-his-name-is is willing to stand, since nobody else seems to be interested and he has taken the trouble to come, I'll nominate him'. *Nem con*. The sitting chairman was an academic in the theological world, and a gentleman. One year later I was asked if I would stand for election as CMGS's chairman myself, and was elected for three years unopposed. Apart from councillor's surgery and some doorstep canvassing, this concatenation of chances led to almost the only true pleasure that involvement in politics gave me. It has been well worth it.

Three years is a short time to figurehead any organization of worth: a year to learn the ropes, a year to start initiating things, and then a year beginning to seem a lame duck to the staff. Our director had been into computers in early career, but had run a fine small museum in Inverness before coming to CMGS. The idea of not being in either the capital or Glasgow had seemed good PR for the rest of the country, but despite being at the link between main roads and rails, and equidistant from the Highlands and Borders, Stirling was inconvenient for day-to-day management of a membership body. Its purposes were to be a mouthpiece for all Scotland's museums and galleries (unlike the other UK area museum councils, Scotland's National Museums and Galleries sat on our board, by co-option); to advise and co-ordinate; to provide grants and skilled staff in conservation and other professional skills (on repayment) where small institutions could not afford their own or lengthy contract support; and generally give leadership and generate public awareness. We moved into Edinburgh, without distress, and adopted the simpler title of Scottish Museums Council (SMC). My main contribution, shared with the director, was to organize two voluntary forums (or *fora*), in which we encouraged groups of adjacent museums and galleries to meet and discuss how they could scratch each others' backs; this was often an unfelt need between local authority and independent bodies, who occasionally turned into rivals rather than seeking complementary rôles. Once the Fife, and then the Borders, Forums were up and running, we withdrew, only to speak when they wanted us, a good initiative.

In 1983 I accepted appointment to a Museums Advisory Board, with the remit to propose how the Secretary of State for Scotland should best combine the Royal Scottish Museum in Chambers Street and the National Museum of Antiquities of Scotland in York Place (Queens Street) under an arms-length NGO board of trustees, and no longer as subsidiary to the Scottish Education Department. The NMAS, sharing a splendid building with the Scottish National Portrait Gallery, had a long association with the Society of Antiquaries of Scotland who were principal among the governing body, and whose basic collection and library were integral with it. There were antique feathers to avoid ruffling. The MAB chairman was an inspired choice, the Marquess of Bute (John), a Catholic who had never taken his seat in the Lords; he was a great chairman, with a filial interest in the heritage, and a track record in raising and insuring the success of creative crafts bodies. The board members were a mixture of people with differing past successes in business, academe and public service to their credit, and after a lifetime of sitting on groups with problems to solve I may say with hand on heart that I never knew a happier body. The chairman listened with courtesy and patience to what all had to say, summed up gently and then just told us what would happen. Nobody quibbled for one moment.

My main contribution was to marshal the arguments for where the development should take place, and the decision confirmed was to clear the site already demolished since 1971, next to the RSM at the west end of Chambers Street, rather than elsewhere in Edinburgh or Scotland. John Bute was determined to see a new building 'of remark and excellence', worthy of the collections, and a modern balance to Captain Francis Fowke's great structure next door from the hi-tech period of the Crystal Palace. I failed in one regard: I introduced into discussion a phrase already in use, 'to show Scotland to the world, and the world to Scotland'. The two collections should be generically integrated, but every object with a Scottish connexion, whether indigenous, historical, found or created by a Scot or involving Scots abroad, would have the attribute clearly labelled and emphasized. We had contributed disproportionately to empire and 'globalization', and had learnt and acquired much from others. I regretted ghettoization and chauvinistic 'Wha's like us'-isms, and feared a new museum being used as a political tool. Very few museums in the world were confined to celebrating one nation or a distinct country. We would come better out of displays that showed our relative importance and achievements in international and generic contexts. Politics and naïve nationalism won. In 1981 the principal of Glasgow University had presided over a committee recommending the creation of a Museum of Scotland based on the NMAS collections. Some members, cheered on by outsiders, had never given up. The National Heritage (Scotland) Act 1985 coincided with our MAB recommendation that the two museums be integrated in Chambers Street, but with the extension solely devoted to a Museum of Scotland: our report still envisaged a single entry to the complex through the existing front door to the Main Hall, so that visitors could not ignore the all-embracing collection of what is Britain's largest general museum (Bloomsbury and South Ken are split into specialities). Sadly the architects insisted on a separate entry through the tower that embellished the other end of the new building, level with pavement and free from the stairway (daunting only to the dauntable) of the main Royal Museum's front.

As trustee I became familiar with the Museum of Flight at East Fortune, the Agricultural Museum at Ingliston (later moved as Museum of Scottish Country Life to Kittochside), the Museum of Costume at Shambellie, the Scottish United Services Museum (now National War Museum of Scotland) in

HM reopening Scottish United Services Museum with Director's son (note Hilary's hat behind the boy).

Edinburgh Castle, and the Biggar Gasworks. I was not reappointed to the National Museums board after my first period of service, although both John Bute and the director Robert Anderson made a face-to-face representation to the under-secretary concerned for my retention. Bute gave me the consolation prize of becoming a member of the new National Museums of Scotland Charitable Trust. I remained a friend of most of the curatorial staff, strengthened when later I became one of the earliest volunteer guides in the Royal Museum, and in the Museum of Scotland when it opened – such fun, after years of mission statements, business plans, budgets, arguing about 'resources' and even discipline, to talk to real live people about actual objects in collections, knowing that some of the smallest, apparently boring, things in the cases had amazing stories and intriguing backgrounds.

After my three years with SMC, and proposing my (more hands-on) successor, I was co-opted to stay on the board, and after his time was up I was asked to stand again for the chair, a vote of confidence of which I am hardly ashamed. Two matters pleased me, contributing to chaos theory (the fluttering butterfly wing causing a hurricane across the globe). I had become irritated by the meetings of the Committee of Area Museums Councils. They were pleasant occasions but never actually did anything beyond exchange hapless views on what worried us. I discussed with my first director how we might become creative. He suggested an overall look at training for the museums profession: there was a plethora of courses and qualifications of a sort, some respectable, some dubious, some of university or Museums Association level. He essayed a draft, which I edited and titivated, and put on the agenda for the next CAMC, where it was approved and sent to the Museums & Galleries Commission. Before long it was announced that a commissioner would produce a report on training. The ultimate consequence was the setting up of the Museums Training Institute, most recently known as the Cultural Heritage National Training Organization, and still subject to the evolution of (un)natural selection. About that the least said here, the better, but I should like to know the colouring of my invisible gossamer wings.

Membership of the Museums Association Council led to membership of its Public Affairs Committee and Ethics Panel; and to representation of the MA on the Advisory Council to the Committee on Export of Works of Art: this latter was more impressive in title than efficacy – the Committee sat on high, literally, and the advisory council humbly sat below, literally, to speak when spoken to, but it was of interest, not least in interpretation of the 'Waverley rules' on importance of items to our truly national heritage. When I reached 70 I conferred with the next MA President on whether in view of ageism I should stand for re-election as a rep of independent museums, by then my status; her advice was equivocal, so I didn't. However by then I was a member of the Institutional Consultative Committee; it consisted of people who represented municipal, national, independent and other institutions as such, rather than as semi- or full professional individuals. Here my wing flapped again, for much the same reason: we commented on what MA was doing, but did not initiate anything. Something had troubled me for years: too many elected local government councillors accepted appointment as full trustees of outside bodies, but saw their remit as to support the policy of their political party and nominating agency, without regard to the interests of the institution. As I saw it, such members must leave all that partisan baggage outside the door, should declare any interest or conflict, but were in duty bound to vote and act in the sole interest of the body they were now governing. The ethics panel had been revising the code of conduct of professionals in museums, so I drafted a parallel code of conduct for non-professional members of governing bodies. ICC liked

Secretary of State for Scotland Ian Lang and Scottish Museums Council chairman at opening of Royal College of Surgeons museum.

it, and it was passed on *via* Council to the ethics committee, who eventually produced their own version: details differed, but it was adopted. Most recently the two have been conflated into a single code for all concerned with museums, and a good thing too.

When my time with SMC ended (except as an elder statesman) they nominated me, without any dropped hints, to the Almond Valley Heritage Trust as a trustee. This unique body was set up under the sponsoring wing of Livingston New Town Development Corporation. A businessman appointed to the corporation was chairman. Founded on a derelict farm with a historic millwheel, it had a splendid group of volunteer Friends who put the wheel back into full working order, conserved and brightened much agricultural machinery, and generally put life back into ruins. The tiny professional staff, led by the grandson of one of my old schoolmasters, peopled the farm with small and exotic livestock, and introduced play areas reflecting the mixed purposes of the museum: these gratifyingly embraced the West Lothian shale oil industry (Scotland's own petrol, with 'Paraffin' Young), the beginnings of a narrow-gauge railway that might one day reach far out to the Seven Sisters shale bings, and the social history of West Lothian. The museum won awards, culminating in 2002 in becoming Scottish Museum of the Year. I was perpetually amazed at how much so few could achieve, and how the visiting numbers (charged for admission) kept up, despite the constant worry of all independent museums – lack of reliable funds, not least when local authorities control grants. It was a matter of pride to be elected as vice-chairman. A generalist, I love such a mish-mash. We were badly afflicted by a media-fed scare, the fear of 'kids' fondling farm animals and picking up *E-coli*, and were worse hit by the 2001 FMD shambles – but the local council came up trumps to support our shortfalls.

SMC suggested me as trustee to Bo'ness Heritage in a listed *art nouveau* cinema building in West Lothian, which it was hoped would house not only collections of local interest, but also a large and potentially important collection of one Harry Matthews. Harry had been in the radio world, as practitioner and teacher, amassing a striking amount of material relevant to 'Communications': wireless and television sets through the century, telephonic and transmitting equipment, the heart of a TV studio, with sideroads into printing, typewriting and allied subjects. The chairman was the wife of noble Tam Dalyell (straight as a die, obsessive, unafraid, and frequently right in the face of general obduracy, not least of his own party). The prospects looked good. Unfortunately, as so often, local politics intervened: another party won the funding district council, while Bo'ness ward voted in the old party, so municipal patronage evaporated. The trust folded, but there was still the Matthews collection to conserve. At a meeting held in Edinburgh University, I expressed opinions about how to move forward. This led to the creation of a Museum of Communications Foundation, to which they credited me with the title of 'Adviser', although they had sturdier support of a professional curator as 'Consultant'. A hard core of enthusiastic and skilled volunteers conserved and documented the collection. This MoCF had a stroke of good fortune, when Scottish Telecommunications (now strangely renamed 'Thus') helped to house a well-organized display of some of Harry's collection in their offices in Edinburgh's Saltire Court.

Sadly, after a year or two a new management needed the space for their own purposes and the museum was turfed out at short notice: storage space was provided as a temporary alternative, but this became flooded and much damage was done to valuable items. I had little to do with MoCF thereafter, but did not lose interest. An old school friend, Professor David Ritchie, had been a prime mover in creating the James Clerk Maxwell Foundation, to acquire the India Street house in Edinburgh where Maxwell (an Edinburgh Academical, like ourselves, but the man who opened the waves to Einstein) had lived when young. A small collection of items was put on display within it, as well as a centre for scholars of radio-magnetism. There was a golden thread of a story to be told, following through the human chain of Clerk Maxwell, Faraday, Rutherford to Marconi and Einstein and onwards, in parallel with examples of other material record from Maxwell's work (even the first colour photography) to the wired and wireless communications that have led to the internet and whatever may come after.

To me this was something that could not but grab the present day young: sensible interpretation could make them realize that their informatics were the result of past geniuses standing on a succession of preceding shoulders, that history was not bunk, and that if we did not know where we came from and why we were here now, we had little chance of judging where we should go next – in other words do what all museums are for anyway. Letting both foundations know what I was doing, I fired off a series of letters to major institutions, inviting the interest and ultimate assistance with historical relics and resources towards the creation of a major national institution (preferably in Scotland with the Clerk Maxwell connexion and the presence of the Matthews collection) to achieve this objective. Some interest was shown by some, but nothing by way of movement. The general impression must have been that this was some unknown nutter with nothing better to do than waste their time. I do not regret trying, but it is disappointing that major bodies are not willing to share innovation with supposed rivals when the benefit is for all.

I had another failure: Ramsay Garden sits beside Edinburgh castle's esplanade and immediately below what was once the city's highest reservoir. This had long ceased to function within the modern system, but presented the appearance of a mighty gatehouse to the castle at the top of the Royal Mile. The Lothian regional council, which inherited the building from the old water authority, was under threat of dissolution. It began to unburden itself of property that no longer served a current purpose, and the thought occurred to me that this white elephant could become a worthy neighbour. My upbringing in the world of preventive medicine, my classical education in Roman achievements, and my life's work in 'developing' cultures had taught me that the one sure foundation of a healthy civilization was a pure water supply. Here was a surviving symbol of our own past such blessing. Proper imagination could create a Museum of Public Health in the widest sense, catching every passing visitor to the castle; it would offer fun and interest, creepy-crawlers for the 'kids', timely reminders for the adults, and well-camouflaged education.

I gathered together a local regional councillor, a senior community health physician, two professionals from the national museums and the area museum council, a university lecturer in preventive medicine, a former water board official and a town planner. I put the idea to them. Without exception they thought it good, and capable of development. What we lacked was anyone in the business of fund-raising, and anyone else of substance who could make such noises as would stir the media, make the public listen and force the council to respond. None of the meeting was prepared to take pole position, and while I was contemplating how I might turn myself into an effective Pied Piper of Hamelin, the blow fell. The regional council had been fully informed of what we envisaged, with ample supporting argument, but we were not an organized group with a Name and impressive headed correspondence paper. Immediate sale for cash was more important to the region than investment in a project that would simply be inherited by its successor authority, which they resented. The reservoir was sold to a commercial enterprise promising historical crafts displays, but in practice a retail outlet.

The Smith Art Gallery & Museum at Stirling was looking for new faces, and approached the Museums Association. They suggested me, while making it clear that I did not represent the MA in any way. The Smith had been through a bad time. Although independent, it relied on municipal support. There had been lack of rapport between staff and local government, but although a new director had arrived, political changes had unexpectedly hit hard. Under the regional system of government in Scotland, the Central Region had funded the Smith and had occupied appropriate seats on the board in consequence, as had Stirling District. Falkirk and Clackmannan as other districts of the region had been regarded as part of the regional catchment area. But when regions were abolished and all-purpose authorities replaced the two tiers, the other districts said, 'The Smith's in Stirling, let Stirling pay.' The constitution in force was out of date, there being no region to provide a major segment of the board. One would think it would not take the lawyers long to redraw the details to give the new Stirling council the lion's share, but the years of argument and time-wasting involved in getting a non-contentious matter submitted to the court of session for a new deed to be approved pass belief. *Jarndyce vs Jarndyce* isn't in it. My small practical contribution to the Smith was to give some demonstrations to their Friends (fund-raisers in the main) of how to guide the public round a display, at which I had become a confident practitioner.

Meanwhile I had become aware through a meeting of the Museum Association's Institutional Consultative Committee of the new British Empire & Commonwealth Museum at Bristol. I saw few names among the trustees of individuals with practical experience of imperial responsibility, and even fewer of museum involvement. For once I outbrazened brass and suggested to the director that not only was I known to a couple of the trustees and a former national trustee myself, but I would be the only one, if the chairman would consider me, with solid experience in both worlds. No echo ever returned: perhaps they feared I would claim return air fares from Edinburgh and be an extravagance, but possibly inquiries cast other doubts on my suitability. Several years later, the new chairman, formerly head of the Science Museum, said she would add me to the panel of advisers on presentation, interpretation and labelling, but again silence followed. It must be my choice of ties (especially since they went out of fashion). However, the BECM Press has published my collected edition of reminiscences of the British who served Northern Nigeria during decolonization, so I remain a founder member and friend.

A friend of a friend (herself a guide at the Bodleian), who had been a guide at the Ashmolean, came to Scotland, where she introduced a volunteer guide scheme to the NMS. They asked my wife to think of guiding, and were surprised that I wouldn't mind joining. I never regretted it. I soon had a rota of three 'highlights' of the Royal Museum on which to ring the changes, spread through every gallery. I can talk in my sleep about the Nisga'a people and their totem pole (and their quarrel with governments about land rights); about geodes and agates; about Chinese boddisatvas who protect books; about western perspective creeping into Persian wall-tiles; about a masquerade cloak from my last district in Nigeria; about Hispano-Moresque and *majolica* lustre; about wall-panelling and tapestries keeping the draught out, and only secondarily being decoration; about whether our *Wylam Dilly* is older than South Ken/York's *Puffing Billy*; and so on. When we had to do 'themes' as well, I was foxed. I didn't want to concentrate on a single subject like porcelain or timepieces, although with my supposed expertise from Hong Kong, I had boned up once on Song and Yuan, my preferred period of *chinoiserie*.

One day, under pressure and to postpone a decision, I said I would do *The Seven Ages of Man*. I had been looking at Minton tiles by Sir Henry Marks, depicting Jaques's speech in *As You Like It*. I was horrified to see it written into the programme, and was hoist by my own petard. It meant trawling the whole museum, looking desperately for seven objects that might reflect the images. This set a pattern for subsequent tours. I found an infant mewling and puking on an Umbrian plate depicting the Judgment of Solomon; a schoolboy unwillingly doing his PE in the palaistra on a Attic red figure κυλιξ (with reduced atmosphere in the kiln to explain the black on the red ground); the lover in a Roman Egyptian statue (with a nummulite fossil embedded to add colour); the soldier under a helmet worn at Poitiers, once displayed above a Garter knight's tomb in Hereford cathedral; the justice in an Egyptian pair statue found by the Scottish antiquarian Rhind; the lean and slipper'd pantaloon in a commemorative pressed glass plate dedicated to Gladstone; and a Melanesian ritual dancing mask, truly sans teeth, sans eyes, sans everything. Something curious and provoking to say about them all, and in seven different galleries. I began to look for objects that most people walked straight past because they looked small or dull, but that when 'researched' told a story. The title of the theme would just be a peg. I could brush up a single topic and blether on Bohemian glassware, cast iron or Phoebe Anna Traquair, and have done so, but that's not such fun for folk without specialized interests.

My repertoire grew into the early 90s. In the Royal Museum I added *Festival Memorances*, a quirky old Scots word, objects reminiscent of Edinburgh Festivals (a Chinese *cizhou* pillow illustrating the exact story of the final aria in Mahler's *Das Lied von der Erde*, singing which in the first 1948 festival made Kathleen Ferrier a world star overnight, despite breaking down in tears in the farewell bars; an Attic black figure vase depicting Ariadne and Bacchus, and a powder horn, both opportunities to recall Beecham stories involving Richard Strauss's opera and Dennis Brain; and mittel-European glass illustrating the *gemütlichkeit* of so much 19th century Viennese music). Before long *Seven Deadly Sins (& Six Church Vices)*, interpreted by lateral thought, *Blissful Ignorance* (objects illustrating concepts that the experts still do not have the answer to, such as Darwin's 'abominable mystery' of what happened in evolution between the gymnosperms and the angiosperms, or is this little tadpolish fossil a tiny adult of one species, or a juvenile of another?), as well as understudying a colleague's *Gods & Worship* and *Home Comforts*, guiding round temporary exhibitions, featuring Robert Louis Stevenson, *Precious Cargo* (trade between Scotland and China), Robert Burns, the Shanghai school of painting, *Behind Golden Screens* (eastern arts), and others.

When the Museum of Scotland loomed over us a pack of new guides was recruited, many of whom showed no interest in interpreting the Royal Museum, although we oldies were expected to orientate visitors round the new building from its opening. For some time we were the blind leading the blind. I developed themes, one on *Edinburgh's Old Town* (searching every case in the museum for objects with relevance) and another on *Two Empires*, in which after discussion of the collected relics of Scotland's own failed empire at Darien and the quite disproportionate part played by Scots after 1707, in making the English empire of Elizabeth, the Charleses and Williamandmary, into a British Empire, I took folk down to the basement and asked them to imagine themselves as the colonized indigenes under the Roman occupation, wondering at the technical marvels introduced by these disciplined strangers with their well-ordered ways of life, just as Africans and Pacific islanders were to gape at maxim guns, transistor radios and 'close administration' or 'indirect rule.'

There were 'outreach talks' to Rotary, Probus and similar clubs on the development of the Museum of Scotland. I usually chatted about the historical development of collections and museums and public galleries in general, before showing slides of gems of our collection. In later years I was working quietly away at my books to familiarize myself with the practical working needs of curators and conservators, and to begin to share their technical languages with a little confidence: and (as recorded in an earlier chapter on acquisition of recognized knowledge) was successful in attaining Associateship of the Museums Association, a semi-professional qualification (the first Scot to get 'AMA' by the new route). I may not have deserved it: true professionals have in the past had to submit to rigorous technical inquisitions to gain what was then known as 'the Diploma', but I am happy that they opened the gates to laymen with the time and interest to dig deeper into the wider museums world from their base as trustees and volunteers.

As a boy I collected cigarette cards, which I still have in thousands and cherish. A grown man, I collected and cannot bear to part with thousands of books and records (not many 78s left, but countless LPs, cassettes and CDs, with a token start on DVD). In the far east I began to collect Japanese *netsuke*, pushing three figures. Some of our rugs are nice. A visiting Nigerian journalist described our flat as 'an arts gallery', which exaggerated more than a bit, but our walls are largely covered, with *ukiyo-e* from both our families and a few Scottish artists (McTaggart and Mactaggart, Eardley, Michie, Redpath and Houston, and a Blackadder, plus Frink prints and many etchings). It's nice to have nice things around one. As Francis Bacon wrote in 1594, the 'compleat learned gentleman should compile a goodly, huge cabinet, wherein whatsoever the hand of man by exquisite art or engine has made rare in stuff, form or motion; whatsoever singularity, chance and the shuffle of things hath produced; whatsoever Nature has wrought in things that want life and may be kept; shall be sorted and included'. One does one's best.

Looking back on two decades in museums, I have come to conclusions that to-day's generation may think the prejudices of a stick-in-the-mud. Any discussion that does not relate to research and scholarship, however remotely, is primarily only interested in entertainment or the bottom line. Any museum, however limited its collecting policy, even a general historical art collection, should leave the visitor better aware of the shoulders on which to-day's achievements have slowly and painfully (and through human inspiration) been successively built, more conscious of the wonders of to-day that are taken for granted, and thinking laterally about what unforeseeable things are yet to come in their tracks. You may bring a horse to the water, but cannot force him to drink: wild attempts to attract refuseniks do bring about 'dumbing-down', and are acts of false pretences. There must be the strongest of links with professional educators, and exchanges on how collections may illuminate curricula, but it should not be supposed that the two callings are identical. Similarly, the tidy-minded bureaucrat who sees that museums, libraries and archives are all 'collections' must not be permitted to suppose that the ethos and motives are the same and that their practitioners may be jumbled together in the same bean-bag. It is no myth that municipal museums have suffered when subordinate to 'the librarian from Hell' (There are of course a few devils within the museums world). New techniques of design and interpretation should be introduced when they clarify and excite, but not just to be *à la mode*. As in theatre and opera, the producer must serve the art and its creators, not impose ephemeral concepts. 'Interactive' monitors rarely encourage creative thought, and if regarded by the young as 'play stations' are a wasted resource. As in a health service where there are more non-medical staff than hospital beds, every saving or amalgamation of curatorial expertise that makes way for more paper-consuming management is ultimately mortal (and I have been an administrator all my life). Reliance on digital records should never ignore the permanence of acid-free paper compared with electronics that crash and back-ups that use technology no longer in production.

Are there too many museums? There might be a limit to creating general museums in major centres of population but, *always provided that they are proven viable*, we might do well to have more small, local but specialized museums, if sited with calculated awareness of access from a wider catchment. Governments, national and local, should be judged by their active interest in *enabling* the creation and maintenance of museums and galleries, but should not use them as social engineering. When they talk of 'arms' length' treatment of non-departmental public bodies or non-government organizations, they must *not* let the fingers at the ends of those arms interfere in practice or policy. When appointing trustees, the priority should be to choose persons who have already shown interest in the institution and its purpose, and only thence insure the infusion of fund-raising capacity, representation of token minorities, existing professional expertises and genderism.

There is a lasting mutual suspicion between the Museums Association and some senior officers of national institutions: this is sad, based in small part on the MA's 'diploma' or modern equivalent being prerequisite to professional support for local authority appointments to their museums, whereas traditionally nationals recruited civil servants, using differing criteria. I suspect that partisan political differences have played a part in this, and am glad to see less evidence of it to-day. I have known personally six national directors, four of them as personal friends. I believe most of them would agree with much of what I have said here. Museums represent our western civilization at its best. I am happy to have been a tiny part of them.

CHAPTER 13

Venturing into Print

The only reason people write is because they are not wonderful men
[Anthony Carson]

An author who speaks about his own books is almost as bad as a mother who talks about her own children
[Benjamin Disraeli, Glasgow, 19 November 1873]

SOMEONE SAID that a book called for pen, ink and a writing desk; to-day the rule must be that a personal computer calls for a desktop published book. When I retired, there was that thing pressing on my mind, besides what has been recounted about how I resettled at home. I was sensitive that a favourite subject for journalists and academics was the African charlatans and mountebanks, who had turned on its head the Westminster democracy that they had demanded, and by whose perversion they had won, and were determined to keep, total power. The continent's decent leaders of honour and quality were largely ignored, most of all my friend Abubakar Tafawa Balewa. The gap should be filled before it was too late. Evidently no academic and no Nigerian was going to do it. I decided to do it for them before the truth was forgotten. I contrived to gather notes and extracts of all the relevant sources in print, books and runs of newspapers and journals. This involved fruitful conversations with Lords Bottomley, Boyd, Caradon, Home, Perth and Grey, proconsuls Macpherson and Robertson, Sharwood-Smith and Bell, General Welby-Everard, the commonwealth's secretary-general Emeka Anyaoku, West Africa's leading and most knowledgeable journalist ('Matchet') David Williams, and many others who had worked in Nigeria and known Abubakar; and visits to all manner of archives.

But although they and I still had a vivid picture of the man in our memories, bald printed words, limited to what each scribe thought useful for the immediate purpose, lacked the impact Abubakar might have made on his own compatriots during the infinitely greater periods when my informants and I were not on the scene. I had to talk to his contemporaries. That meant a visit back to Nigeria to seek them out. I was blessed in having an old friend and colleague, Desmond Wilson, as our deputy high commissioner in Kaduna. His connexions with the former great and good of the North were invaluable. He was one effective referee, in an application to the Leverhulme Trust for a travelling fellowship to pursue oral research, which covered my basic expenses, and he proved a generous host and organizer for Hilary's and my first journeying. A group of mallams had asked an American sociologist, who was working in a university in the north, to write the history of Ahmadu Bello, Sardauna of Sokoto, to be produced by Hodder & Stoughton's offshoot the Hudahuda Press of Zaria. They were looking for someone to do the same for Abubakar, and I might fill the bill.

In 1981 Hilary and I made our way out for her eye-opener on to my past, and for my sparkling refreshment. Looking back over two decades, the details may become hazy, but reassurance came when, within minutes of landing at Kano, my spoken Hausa poured out, with total recall after twenty years. After long years of independence a native-speaking expatriate was a rarity, and the consequent welcomes warm and immediate. We managed to track down two dozen or more remembered Northerners with personal stories and comments that added shade and colour, and to make new acquaintances wherever we went. There was yet more pleasure in meeting once more some of the colleagues who had 'stayed on'.

The physical fascinations were, for me, to compare what had changed and what had not. On the whole what mattered was wholly recognizable, while the novelties tended, like so much of to-day, to be tawdry and quick to tarnish. Out of town all that seemed different were the strange piles of white loaves in tissue paper on roadside market stalls – that imported wheat could have become a rural staple passed belief – and that the farmers plying their hoes in the fields presented to the onlooker as they bent over, not *bante*-wearing bare bottoms but the seats of ready-made shorts imported from the orient. Oil in the south had meant that country-wide more peasants had bicycles, former cycle-owners had graduated to motorbikes, and there were far more cars for mammy wagons to drive off the hard surfaces (Zaria to Jos to Bauchi was all tarmac now, though not pothole-free). Hilary's impressions were comparable with her visits to her missionary brother in Pakistan's Punjab, and rarely surprised her. She seemed to take quickly to young and old, men and women, as I always had, but met more wives than I might.

Time passed, during which I turned the first major draft into a more considered second version. Hilary transcribed my scribbles on an electric typewriter, only for me to cover with second thought balloons, erasures, arrows and transpositions for the next assembly. Other concerns were taking priority, where I had duty to others, as a councillor. Progress was slow. In 1986 the book on the Sardauna was launched in London, twenty years after the premier's assassination: there were pages of photos of other NPC politicians, but the substance was more a sociological study of the circumstances than a life story of the individual. Embarrassingly, it was announced that I was working on a companion volume with Abubakar as the subject. This psychological pressure did not make progress easier, although what spare times I did enjoy were given to more of the reading, archive-searching and oral or epistolary interviewing already begun. Come late 1987 the prime mover in the self-appointed unofficial group of mallams, the Northern Nigeria History Committee, a successful businessman Alhaji Mamman Daura, began to press me by letter and telephone (and invitation to his St James's flat in London) to get on with it. This played the larger part in my decision not to stand for re-election to Edinburgh's city council. He undertook to arrange a second visit for me to fill any identifiable gaps and meet more informants. We were only too willing. Not quite so long ago, more of this 1988 journey is still remembered.

Nigeria Airways' logo was still the heavier-than-air flying elephant of WAAC, and we shuddered to think what it was like behind in steerage. In first class, 'one article of hand baggage' was freely interpreted as crated washing machines, bundled family-clothes-for-the-winter and suitcases, blocking aisles, overhead lockers and WC passages. The cuisine was liberally peppered, familiar enough to those used to Sunday guinea-fowl and rice stews in the club, but aggressive to the unaccustomed gut. Murtala Muhammed airport in humid Lagos was a developed descendant of Apapa wharf in the 40s, chaotic and manned by unhelpful customs officials looking for 'dash'. Relief and manners were waiting at the final barrier, with my sponsor's 'PRO' Paul Ohai and the Hudahuda Press's MD Alhaji Abdullahi Khalil, bursting with smiles and welcomes. Mamman's brother Alhaji Sani Dauda had flown down to greet us, and Abdullahi pressed a fat wad of nairas into my hand as our pocket money. Next day we recuperated, studying Mamman's itinerary planned for most of February, until Sani took us to the Lagos polo tournament.

In the morning I found an obvious Northerner at breakfast and made my mark with him, in Hausa. Two of his party came down and he introduced me ('*Ga shi, shi wani mutuminmu ne* – Look! He's "one of us"!'). Mamman's pleasant and willing Igbo driver Celestine was at our fulltime beck and call, often going hungry when our various hosts chose not to notice him outside. Visits began with Charles Lawson, Abubakar's principal private secretary, hindered by the discovery that between 10 *a.m.* and 4 *p.m.* the capital's telephones were overloaded and seldom worked. We were soon over-acquainted with traffic jams, cycle herds, windscreen-washers, touts and ambulant hawkers beyond count. Time off was well spent visiting villages round the lagoons and on Victoria beach, in wondering at the vast but underused national stadium, and in the Lagos museum, displaying not only Nok culture and Ife brasses but the bullet-riven car in which a past president had been assassinated, and the Federal Palace hotel.

Paul Ohai greeted us at Kaduna airport and took us to Mamman Daura's home, before installing us in a bungalow on Gongola Road at Kaduna south, to be supported by steward Nda (a colleague's 'small boy' from long ago) and driver Yusuf. We retraced steps to my home at 8 Sokoto Road, and to the botanic gardens beside the Kaduna river, where truly small boys still pored over homework or swam starkers, girls still carried water pots on their heads and women washed clothes, but where the old army swimming pool had seen better days. The harmattan was blowing and dust lay everywhere. There was polo practice to watch (the only white horseman was a girl), Mamman Daura's furniture factory (only one of his business interests) to visit, and in the evening a worn-out John Wayne video until the electricity failed (Later substitute videos proved to be far from soft porn, upon which discovery Paul was mortified). The shops at the Durbar hotel seemed more poorly stocked than in 1981, and the post office had run out of stamps for overseas mail. Mamman lent us whistle-blower Peter Wright's *Spycatcher*, still banned in UK.

It was as though seven months, not years, had passed to meet the educational administrator Yahaya Gusau and the first local permanent secretary (finance) Ahmed Talib again; Yahaya had retired from being a businessman, but Ahmed was still chairman of the electricity authority. There followed a visit, not as fruitful as expected, to the northern national archives, where I found some useful material but signs that there would have been more had fully professional hands and minds been at work for longer. After a week in Kaduna, including a water supply failure, temporarily solved by Nda with a leaky pail, Yusuf drove us through the savannah to Zaria, which Hilary again recognized as a real African city, after the artificiality of Lagos and Kaduna.

The road had been crammed with mammy wagons, overloaded and covered like Indian railway carriages with humanity hanging on against grim death. The mud city walls and the mud buildings, many decorated with mud mouldings, red as the laterite of the roadsides, were vernacular and naturally beautiful. The outside wall of Abdullahi Khalil's home was particularly artistic. We were taken to an elderly neighbour who was one of the five survivors of Abubakar's 30 school classmates, and again found my last steward Yak'ubu Tiraka, now head cook at the tobacco factory, his hair going grey and his excitement as palpable as seven years before (I wondered whether he still kept my picture by his bed). Back in Kaduna, the water pump had been mended, but when the electricity failed, the pump also stopped.

I made what might be hopeless inquiries among staff of the Durbar hotel about my former steward Waziri, thinking that as a former 'contractor' someone might know of him. I drew a blank, as we had done in 1981. The local ministry of information managed to produce a few relevant photographs to illustrate my book, before Yusuf had to take the car back to Zaria for emergency surgery and we were confined to quarters. Then at the end of the day a car arrived, and the driver emerged, threw himself at my feet and said (in English) 'O, my father!' I mentioned this at the end of chapter 6. Word had at last got around. On successive days Waziri brought a succession of select choices from his wives and family to see us, burdened with the traditional gifts of eggs, chickens, fruit and potatoes, not without discreet hints of a desire for keepsakes, and even for a visit to 'Ingila'. It was all quite emotional, and coincided with the water supply's recovery. S Valentine's day passed before Yusuf brought the car back, allegedly restored to roadworthiness, and we could pick up Abdullahi from his home and make our way through Jos and down from the plateau to Bauchi, where the car again forced Abdullahi to find a substitute. The Zaranda hotel was new, 'modern' and comfortable, but the provender and refreshment less welcome to Hilary's metabolism.

Next day I met Yak'ubu Wanka, NT accountant in 1954, now waziri of Bauchi and son-in-law of Abubakar Tafawa Balewa by whose daughter he had had seven of his 40 children. There followed a discussion with the Ajiya, Adamu Tafawa Balewa, who described in detail what had happened to Abubakar's body after the murder, reminding us that the victim of such a crime passed all his sins, if any, to his killer and was buried without need for further purification. He then took us to see the tomb and memorial that had been built for the martyr, an impressive structure designed by a European architect, more in keeping with an Egyptian noble on the Nile than a modest Nigerian who would be honoured by unmarked burial within his home. We then set off in the direction of Tafawa Balewa, where we hoped to find Ahmed Kari on his farm, formerly Abubakar's local factotum and now Bauchi's Garkuwa. The garrulous old guide sitting beside Yusuf suddenly put two and two together, turned and recognized with amazement, '*Musta Kilak! Di'onmu wanda ya sa takalman Filani!* (Mr Clark, our DO who wore Fulani sandals).'

Eventually we found Ahmed Kari's vast acreage of mixed farming and cleverly irrigated vegetable production, on which he had built a mosque large enough for a small town. Finding the Garkuwa himself (the title of Bauchi's defence head in olden times) was more difficult, but ultimately rewarded. Driving home in twilight on an ill-maintained 'highway' without shortcuts was covered sooner than the journey out (which had saved twelve miles by using unmaintained tracks), and we treated ourselves to superior dinner on the hotel's top floor, glancing in at the night club, hard to compare with my club record recitals over 35 years before. Next day we tracked down some of Abubakar's family, son Usman briefly, but his brother at some length. Bala was unforgiving of how the bereaved household had been ignored by all authority and fair-weather friends after the tragedy, although the headmaster of his British school had been 'wonderful' when breaking the news to him; he was now 'in business', but felt himself 'an idle revolutionary at heart'. Daughter Yalwa worked in an educational supervisory office, sweet-natured within her chador and still fond of the doll her father had given her (named 'Queen Elizabeth').

After visits to a trade fair and to Zaria, we set off for Katsina, a long drive through increasing desert, punctuated by baobabs and green neems. We shuttled back and forth between the emir's palace and the Mutawalli's home (a title of the north-west), where we found him, Alhaji Musa 'Yar'adua, at the second search. His domestic filing system was not unlike my own to-day, in sore need of a personal assistant and cabinets. He had been a schoolmate first and a fellow minister last of Abubakar, and was unconvinced that democracy had been a progressive advance on traditional ways. Depositing our formal greetings at the palace, we were on the road back to Kano. Tuesday brought an early start to Azare, where I had started my career, and where we hoped to find Madaki (master of the household) Sule Katagum, another great name from the past. The road was largely single-lane tarmac, complicated by many deep potholes, with every driver (including Yusufu) daring the oncoming competitor to make way first. Memories flooded back of my own countless encounters with flocks of sheep, goat and occasional wild warthog families. We were back in savannah, donkeys and mules as frequent as lorries, grass fodder piled high in the trees safe from wandering ruminants. Naturally when we arrived after 200 miles or so, Sule was in Lagos. As the wires were down we had not been able to confirm his presence before setting off. Back to Kano, stuck for much of the way in a regatta of overloaded mammy-wagons.

There we tracked down Dr Ahmadu Jalingo, former Edinburgh student and now dean of his faculty at Bayero university. He showed us the clearance where there had been a massacre involving 'fundamentalist' rioters and many hasty burials. Our last informant was Alhaji D'an Bappa and his European wife Betty (or 'Lola'), surrounded by peacocks (she had worked in Lagos close to Abubakar). And that was that, except that our heartfelt farewells to Alhaji Abdullahi Khalil and driver Yusufu were overshadowed by Hilary's returning desperate need for her last Immodium pills, which saw her through the infamous Kano airport WCs to the plane, Heathrow and her brother's in Peckham by February's end. All I now had to do was to finish the book, after wallowing in select memories of a country and people I had so enjoyed, then and now, and sending our thanks to Mamman Daura for all the enablement.

It took a year-and-a-half or more before I had a manuscript and collection of illustrations fit to submit to the publisher. Then came a huge technological leap forward: Mr Alan Sugar's PCW8256 word processor. Now thousands like me could afford to own a computer that would move words, phrases and paragraphs around at the pressure of a button or two, and would correct errors and allow fair copies to emerge without having to retype every character on the page. Sugar deserved a hereditary peerage, not a mere knighthood. It took time to key in the whole script again from scratch, but life became so much less of a burden, and Hilary was spared copy-typing.

The launches in 1991 of *A Right Honourable Gentleman: Abubakar from the Black Rock* went well. Lord Grey, sometime deputy governor-general, presided at the London party in the Royal Commonwealth Society. I was still able to be interviewed in Hausa for the BBC world service, and was pleased that everyone present seemed to think Abubakar to be the man and character that I knew and had tried to portray. Being by then a trustee of the National Museums of Scotland, I was spoilt by friendly curatorial staff, and a second Scottish launch was arranged in the Royal Museum, presided over by Lord Perth, sometime minister of state for the colonies, to which many people interested in the subject, besides friends of our own, came and again some bought signed copies. The museum arranged a display case of objects relevant to Northern Nigeria, including a donated item or two from myself.

So far as I can tell from the royalties accruing to the Alhaji Sir Abubakar Tafawa Balewa Memorial Trust, Hodders sold about 152 Edward Arnold hardback copies in the UK and three abroad by 1992. The unsold balance went to complement the Nigerian stock, where the royalties went to the Nigerian Society for the Blind (I have no idea of their value, but I was sent a heart-warming video of a distribution of material goods to beneficiaries at a ceremony giving full credit to the source). The Hudahuda imprint, called *A Right Honourable Gentleman: The life & times of Alhaji Sir Abubakar Tafawa Balewa*, had begun with 20,000 copies, so the term 'best-seller' may be used, for all the lack of circulation elsewhere in the world. Marketing and attention to publicity is always a matter of chance and current circumstance, but I cannot hide my disappointment. For all the encouraging words from those who actually read the book, wider coverage was minimal, and Abubakar is still an unsung hero buried under Africa's pantheon of dubious political and dictatorial characters.

I was asked with Philip Walters, the publisher's front man, to attend the launch of the Nigerian edition of the book in Lagos in 1991. A very different experience. For a change in style, this is what Hilary wrote in her diary:

'The occasion was such as Philip the editor, with all his experience of book fairs and launches, had never seen the like. We were driven by Samuel through bustling crowds and hooting vehicles, but during the build-up, roads were closed and Lagos traffic came to a standstill. At the impressive entrance we were surrounded by security men who corralled us away, and one navy-clad man more or less pushed us through a narrow gate, by which a jostling crowd was also trying to squeeze. Then we must have entered a side entrance and were led through a pitch-black passageway, full of hidden steps and holes, towards the hall. Our guide encouraged our stumbling steps, and at last I saw light at the end of the tunnel. Then suddenly we were descending the steps into the National Assembly itself. There was already a flurry of *riga*s and a sales table piled high with *A Right Honourable Gentleman*. My husband was besieged by pressmen for interviews, in English and Hausa, and asked to sign many copies of the book. Friendly Nigerians came to congratulate him (and occasionally myself) for the great tome. Mamman at one point asked me if I would wrap up the presentation books for the President and Sultan; he produced green shiny paper, beautiful silver rosettes, but no scissors, sellotape or ribbon. Thank goodness, after some struggling two girls arrived with sellotape – I hope the right book went to the right person.

'The hall was filling up, with a great hum of excitement. Chiefs of various regions embraced each other, and lesser fry stood up to welcome each leader as they arrived. At last the light-hearted and lepechraun-like master of ceremonies, Alhaji Yusuf Maitama Sule, whom we had known in Kano in 1981, started talking to keep things going, giving among other things a potted history of the author and his connexions with Abubakar, and asking him to stand up to be recognized. At about 11 the military President, General Ibrahim Babangida, entered with his immediate entourage, greeted the author with a few words, and mounted to the Speaker's chair. He is a smallish, solid and determined-looking man. He was flanked by Magajin Garin Kano Alhaji Inuwa Wada and Chief Dr Majekodunmi, former ministerial colleagues of Abubakar, for the national anthem (played on a scratchy record); below him sat the Armed Forces Ruling Council, below them the Council of Ministers, and all around the First Class Chiefs of the federation. Apart from all the expected VIPs, there was the entire diplomatic corps, with representatives of world media, BBC and Reuters in particular. Some would have looked well as a Gilbert & Sullivan chorus. Two former Presidents, Yak'ubu Gowon and Shehu Shagari, were prominent, and Abubakar's children had their own row. The programme included Prayers led by the Chief Imam and the Bishop of Lagos, and the many speeches were rightly devoted to Abubakar's simplicity, sincerity, honesty and greatness, not to the book's merit, although Professor S O Biobaku read a fulsome review of the book. All very moving. The President announced that a million of the government's naira would ensure that 10,000 copies would be placed on the library shelves of all institutions of secondary and higher learning. Then, to the added joy of Abdullahi and Philip, the pledges began of intended purchases, all vying with each other and asking for more signatures.

'There was no slot for the author in the printed programme, but the master of ceremonies inserted an unexpected item, and the author found himself delivering an *ex tempore* unscripted and unprepared harangue for ten minutes to an apparent dictator on the virtues of abandoning narrow tribalism, listening to the needs of the common man and generally following Abubakar's transparency and integrity. There followed a second unending flood of book-signings and pledges by the wealthy and others ambitious to buy competitively large numbers of the tome, more music to the publishers' ears. 7 is a lucky number: one pledge was to buy 7 copies for 7,777 naira. It was all very heady, moving stuff. That night the first twelve minutes of national television news were devoted to this launch, followed by a repeat of the interview given the previous night. The British High Commissioner was impressed enough to invite us to join a major social function. The interesting observation was that despite the presence of influential journalists, a unique celebration, involving a former junior imperial administrator in a major independent Nigerian event, received not a line in the British press. It would have been politically incorrect for media to notice a significant correction to the received belief that ex-"subjects" could not acknowledge warm affection and gratitude to former "masters".'

That should have been enough to put me off further authorship. I had been building up in desultory fashion the present effusion, with growing awareness that not only would it never be published, it was unpublishable. It was only a time-filling hobby, after all. However, it was not to be so. Those of us who had spent long years in Northern Nigeria and met annually at a well-attended reunion, began to notice the growing number of books that put on record the reminiscences, the apologies and the proud satisfactions of individuals and groups who had served in other dependencies. The imperial Indian Raj had had its fill of successful ventures into print but the colonials, late and weaker on the scene, had by and large been forced to find 'vanity publishers'. At one of our reunion lunches Tony Kirk-Greene, the collector of colonial records, wondered, 'What about us?' Agreement was soon reached that survivors should be pressed to write something to keep the truth of our lives in the decolonizing years fresh and on record, against some future time when our imperial story might be treated with honesty and dispassion. It was less clear how the material should be treated. It was noted with general relief that I had written a book with some relevance. That seemed to excuse anyone else. Our organizer Nigel Beazley invited members to deposit money in advance against publication, which placed a moral responsibility on me to produce hard copy. I let it be known that I would like pieces from the whole spectrum of 'Old Coasters', preferably third person narratives that addressed and answered a series of relevant questions, which I might knit together into a single author's coherent text combining factual history, actual attitudes and lively pictures, while fully attributing all the sources. I might have saved my breath.

Some likely contributors found reason to resile from the prospect at first sight; some unlikely pen- or keyboard-wielders responded with gems; one or two vital specialities found no willing or surviving representatives; some unexpected sources emerged – but scarcely one followed the pattern suggested. Deadlines meant nothing. Nobody offered advice on finding a publisher. I had offered for opinion a partial draft to an agent recommended by a helpful force behind the Abubakar book; she called it 'an incoherent collection'. I steeled myself to the prospect of having myself to submit a more final text to reputable publishers in succession (Hodders had politely indicated that their current priorities no longer embraced Nigeria: no doubt they had counted their UK sales of Abubakar). Both the big names and the minor specialists would probably in succession gestate their rejection for the full nine months, while we would all be dying off. This added to my gloom, although I was growing more confident that the swelling embryo would be viable in a proper midwife's hands.

There were two frustrations: I wanted a final chapter in which some of our Nigerian contemporaries who had shared our march to their freedom would comment frankly from the perspective of 'Them and Us', to keep our own 'Us and Them' in proportion. A British High Commissioner showed interest in offering to renew contacts, but his successor turned out to be only interested in trade, and never responded. Our honorary consul in Kano did make valiant efforts to induce Maitama Sule to dictate something for his wife to copy; an ex-police deputy commissioner made valiant efforts to induce former inspector-general M D Yusufu to offer thoughts; and I made my own feeble effort to persuade Mamman Daura to help, but he also could not find the time. My other hope was similarly baulked. For Abubakar I had succeeded in persuading both a British secretary of state and a Nigerian chief justice to write balancing forewords; but I failed to extract a response from the Nigerian head of state whom I asked to introduce this book, although for a British introduction I was fortunate to be able to take advantage of being married to the second cousin of a lady who was married to a well-known writer on imperial and military affairs, who allowed his arm to be twisted. *Laus Deo.*

As chapters and groups came together I sought advice on them from Tony, John and Nigel. John Smith had become involved with the British Empire & Commonwealth Museum in Bristol, where I had contacts. His position as a very generous Founder Member of the BECM led to their publishing arm accepting our book. Their retail and publishing manager, with the assistance of excellent printers next door, produced a handsome volume in September 2002. It was prominent on the museum's bookstall. Apart from regrets at what is missing, my reservation is over the illustrations: we must all have many

Looking back at the beginning (Edinburgh's Dynamic Earth exhibition).

hundreds of old photographs showing Africans and Europeans being happy together, but comparatively few came to me. It remains to be seen whether '*Was It Only Yesterday? The Last Generation of Nigeria's* Turawa' will make the tiniest puncture in the balloon of self-indulgent guilt that the mass media and supposedly scholarly histories of to-day evince over the fact that we ever had an empire at all, let alone one that left behind many foundations and gateways to betterment. There is much still to be done, but it must be done in the wider fields of popular instruction and enlightenment, and not be confined to short-run pieces of introspective research and closed-minded politics. So many of the lessons from imperial history are directly relevant to what concerns those who are now worried about the West and Islam, America and the Undeveloped World, populous Asia and shrinking Europe, globalization and environmental hazards, how to revive Iraq, not to speak of Nature's reaction to our Horacian pitchfork with AIDS, SARS and other barriers to growth. It is not about winning hearts and minds, but it is about making friends and keeping them.

I had thought of extending this already excessive, now much condensed, series of 'Not all failures but not many successes' with chapters on faith and music – and perhaps adding a supplement of '*I Once Met …,* or *We Once Went to …*' cameos. Let's leave it here. My regrets are few, my disappointments petty compared with those of many, and with only the restrictions of the years to trouble us I still share happiness with Hilary (who does so much more for me than I for her) in a pleasant home in a fine city. If the way our country is being led gives us concern, it will not be our own children who will have to find new destinations. We must cross our fingers, and pray looking forward and up.

It is enough (Misanthropist Orwell said that autobiography is only to be trusted when it reveals something disgraceful. Someone else said that everyone has a novel inside him. There is no fiction herein).